The Classical Theory of Economic Policy

This book is part of the World series in economics,
E. E. LIEBHAFSKY, *Consulting Editor.*

THE
Classical Theory
OF
Economic Policy

WARREN J. SAMUELS

With an Introduction by
HERMAN FINER

THE WORLD PUBLISHING COMPANY

Cleveland New York

Published by The World Publishing Company
2231 West 110th Street, Cleveland, Ohio 44102

Published simultaneously in Canada by Nelson,
Foster & Scott Ltd.

First Printing 1966

Library of Congress Catalog Card Number: 66-13147

Printed in the United States of America

To
George John Malanos
and
Edwin Emil Witte

In the preparation of this work I have been aided in many ways by many people. The research was facilitated by a sub-grant of a NSF institutional grant to the University of Miami and by research arrangements provided by Clark E. Myers, Eugene H. Man, James C. Vadakin, J. Everett Royer, and Edward J. Fox. More than the customary praise should be directed to the personnel of the Richter and Law Libraries of the University of Miami for their cooperation and patience. Invaluable research assistance and penetrating suggestions were provided by Jose A. Lopez, who served as my research assistant during the period in which the research and most of the writing were undertaken. My greatest debt, however, is to Grover A. J. Noetzel, who read and criticized the manuscript as it was written and whose comments, while not always followed, were always well founded. Moreover, his encouragement was equaled only by that of my wife, Sylvia: to both I am forever grateful. Finally, it should be pointed out that the substance of Chapter Two appeared in the form of a two-part article in the *Southern Economic Journal* for July and October 1964.

Several publications have appeared since the longer manuscript on the classical theory of economic policy was written— chiefly, William D. Grampp's *Economic Liberalism* (New York: Random House, 1965; two volumes). There are, between Grampp's second volume, "The Classical View," and the present study, a number of areas of both agreement and disagreement, with the latter partly a matter of emphasis. Both of Grampp's volumes are worthy of serious study, and it has been only a question of scarcity of time which has precluded consideration of Grampp's most recent contribution to the field.

For use of quoted matter in this book grateful acknowledgment is made to the following: Harper's Magazine, Inc., for an excerpt from "Schlesinger at the White House," by Henry Brandon in *Harper's* (July 1964); The American Sociological Association for material from "The Role of the Category of Ignorance in Sociological Theory: An Exploratory Statement," by Louis Schneider in the *American Sociological Review*, Vol. 27 (1962), pp. 492–508; Richard D. Irwin, Inc., for an excerpt from *Economic Policy*, First Edition, by William D. Grampp and Emanuel T. Weiler; Random House, Inc., for excerpts from *An Inquiry into the Nature and Causes of the Wealth of Nations*, by Adam Smith (New York: Modern Library, 1937), p. 724, and *The English Philosophers from Bacon to Mill*, edited by Edwin W. Burtt (New York: Modern Library, 1939), p. 1041; Alfred A. Knopf, Inc., for excerpts from *Democracy in America* by Alexis de Tocqueville (New York: Vintage Books, 1954), two volumes, Vol, 2, pp. 9, 10, 11–12; Peter Smith for material from *The English Utilitarians* (1950) by Leslie Stephen; The Macmillan Company for the use of material from *The Logic of Modern Physics* by P. W. Bridgman, "Economic Organization" by W. H. Hamilton in the *Encyclopedia of the Social Sciences*, Vol. 11, and "Economic Policy" by M. J. Bonn, Vol. 5; Basil Blackwell for material from A *Fragment on Government and an Introduction to the Principles of Morals and Legislation* (Oxford: Blackwell, 1948, pp. 4, 10), by Jeremy Bentham, Wilfrid Harrison, ed.; The Twentieth Century Fund for material from *The Economy, Liberty and the State* (1959), by Calvin B. Hoover; Columbia University Press for material from *The Autobiography of John Stuart Mill* and *The Genius of the Common Law*, by Sir Frederick Pollock; The Southern Economic Journal for material from "Free Enterprise in a Growth World," by Karl de Schweinitz, which appeared in the *Southern Economic Journal*, Vol. 29 (1962); the University of Illinois Press for material from *Problems of Economics and Sociology* (1963) by Carl Menger, edited by Louis Schneider; G. P. Putnam's Sons for material from *The Quest for Certainty*, by John Dewey, Francis J. Nock, Trans.; E. P. Dutton & Co., Inc. and J. M. Dent & Sons Ltd. for material from *The Principles of Political Economy and Taxation* by David Ricardo (Everyman's Library edition); The University of Wisconsin Press for material reprinted with permission of the copyright owners, the Regents of the University of Wisconsin, from John R. Commons, *Legal Foundations of Capitalism*, 1959; The Columbia Law Review for material from "Law and Morality in the Perspective of Legal Realism" by Harry W. Jones, reprinted from *Columbia Law Review* (Vol. 61, No. 5, May 1961) copyright by Directors of The Columbia Law Review Association, Inc.; Oxford University Press for

T. S. Ashton, *The Industrial Revolution, 1760–1830* (London: Oxford University Press, 1948); The Journal of Law & Economics for material from "The Intellectual History of Laissez Faire" by Jacob Viner and "The Problem of Social Cost" by R. H. Coase, both articles in Vol. 3 (1960) of the *Journal of Law & Economics; Economica* for use of material from "Adam Smith as an Economist" by Edwin Cannan, "The Prescriptions of the Classical Economists" by S. G. Checkland, and "Robert Torrens—1780–1864," by S. A. Meenai, the articles, in order, being from Vol. 6 (1926), n.s. Vol. 20 (1953), and n.s. Vol. 23 (1956); Stanford University Press for material from *Theories of Economic Growth and Development* by Irma Adelman; Routledge & Kegan Paul Ltd. for material from *Bentham's Theory of Fictions* by C. K. Ogden; W. Heffer & Sons Ltd. for material from *The World of Adam Smith* by C. R. Fay; Harper & Row, Publishers, Incorporated, for material from *Freedom and Reform* by Frank H. Knight, and *Comparative Economic Systems* by William N. Loucks; Henry Regnery Company, Chicago, for material from *A Humane Economy* by Wilhelm Roepke; McGraw-Hill Company for material from *Jurisprudence*, by Edgar Bodenheimer, © 1940, and *Man and His Government* by C. J. Friedrich, © 1963; Yale University Press for material from *Ricardian Economics* by Mark Blaug; Macmillan & Co. Ltd., The Macmillan Company of Canada, Ltd., and St. Martin's Press, Inc., for material from *The Theory of Economic Policy in English Classical Political Economy, Politics and Economics* and *An Essay on the Nature and Significance of Economic Science* by Lionel Robbins; Holt, Rinehart and Winston, Inc., for material from *Industrial Efficiency and Social Economy* by Nassau William Senior, copyright 1928, renewed 1955 in the name of S. Leon Levy, Editor; The Scottish Journal of Political Economy for material from "Adam Smith's Theory of Moral Sentiments," by A. L. Macfie, which appeared in the *Scottish Journal of Political Economy*, Vol. 8 (1961); Social Research for material from "Adam Smith as Sociologist," Albert Salomon, *Social Research*, Vol. 12 (1945), pp. 22–42; Harvard University Press for the following: Reprinted by permission of the publishers from William J. Baumol, *Welfare Economics and the Theory of the State*, Overton Taylor, "The Classical Liberalism, Marxism, and the Twentieth Century" and "Economics and Liberalism," F. H. Knight, "Intelligence and Democratic Action," and William D. Grampp, "On the Politics of the Classical Economists," Cambridge, Mass.: Harvard University Press, *The Quarterly Journal of Economics*, Copyright, 1952, 1960, 1955, 1960, 1948 by the President and Fellows of Harvard College; The London School of Economics and Political Science for material from "Welfare Economics and the Theory of the State," by W. J. Baumol; Constable and Company Limited for material from *The Petty Papers*, Marquis of Lansdowne, ed. (London: Constable, 1927), two vols., Vol. 1, pp. 116–17; Cambridge University Press, New York for material from *The Works and Correspondence of David*

ix

Contents

Introduction

What ethical principles permit the market economy, laissez faire, to function beneficially? What general moral principles, in law, tradition, or custom, commend and require an economic system of free competitive enterprise?

For decades I have wished that a qualified scholar would explain the general ethical assumptions about human nature in society held by the classical economists, assumptions necessary to make their principle credo, economic laissez faire, guarantee the maximum production of the wealth of nations.

Professor Warren J. Samuels has now accomplished this feat with profound scholarship and masterly skill, qualities which assure him of an important place among our teachers of economics. In achieving this, he has added to and significantly improved upon the pioneer work on the subject by Lord Lionel Robbins, *The Theory of Economic Policy*. I take pride in saying that Professor Robbins was himself a student of mine at the London School of Economics, when we were both in our youth. Professor Samuels has, in addition, made a worthy addition to the third chapter of Joseph Schumpeter's *magnum opus, The History of Economic Analysis*.

The economic element in man's behavior is concerned with the production of goods, of wealth. It concerns itself, that is to say, with decisions on their quantity and quality and kind; the organization of the means of their production; the spirit of acquisition in which these functions are undertaken and the institutions operated; and, finally, the division of the product of industry among the human partners in the productive process and the providers of the physical assets required to achieve results.

It should be clear that the economic element in man's behavior is only a part of man's behavior and aspirations in general. Man is not exclusively, as Marx is said to have taught, what he eats. Even the political scientist whose interests and scope are architectonic in society—that is, inclusive, systematically, of all interests and purposes—could be said to have a narrow point of view compared with that of the metaphysician or with universal philosophical morality. Yet the political scientist studies the polity—that is, all those actions of human beings in society involving the supreme use of authority to adjust conflicts of will, purpose, and values in the ever-changing appetites of individuals and groups. This is a much broader expanse of human concern than the economic alone. Yet the economy plays a part in the polity of tremendous importance. The polity qualifies the economy; the economy qualifies the polity; they interweave organically and, as Professor Samuels demonstrates so searchingly, changingly. He shows how the polity, the nation-state, indeed, the wider society as a whole, is the vehicle of ethical and moral values that shape the economy desirable for economic results and shape it also for general moral results—for example, individual freedoms in the grace of Western civilization.

Professor Samuels pursues his intense and luminous investigation through all the many works of Adam Smith, Ricardo, Malthus, the two Mills, McCulloch, Bentham, Senior, and Torrens.

His findings, in general, are these, though I do not include all of them:

1. In advocating the market economy—that is, laissez faire—the classical economists were imbued with the policy that the

highest value that man deserved was individual freedom. Therefore, his economic activities should be free. This freedom would also make for the maximum economic production for himself and the whole community.

2. The practice of economic freedom, of free competitive enterprise, could, however, not be anarchic. For human nature could not be expected always to be wise and virtuous. Montesquieu said, in *The Spirit of the Laws*, "virtue itself hath need of limits." Men, in pursuing the virtue of maximum economic wealth, might wreak injuries and injustices on one another and on the tranquil order of society. For the maximum economic production, even alone, social peace was essential.

3. The economists had not totally fulfilled their obligation when they had prescribed the market economy as the central dynamo and site of the nation's wealth and had merely made some exceptions in favor of public enterprise, like the building of roads and bridges and other public works of common utility for which individual entrepreneurs would not take the risk. The classical economists taught not merely a market-minus doctrine, but a market-plus framework, the framework being the general traditional and changing ethical matrix of the whole nation.

4. This general ethical matrix becomes effective in two ways (a) through laws, chiefly deliberately enacted statutes, and (b) through what Professor Samuels calls "nondeliberative" factors in society, religion, the view of the cosmos, the historical values, the time-conditioned addiction to certain principles of right and justice between man and man. A useful term, "nondeliberative," to represent the values that grow and control behavior in distinction from purpose enacted in the statutes! Another factor could have been added, even more important in contemporary circumstances than in the early nineteenth century (I know about the Napoleonic Wars and before that of the conflict with the American colonies, etc.,)

that is, as expressed in Adam Smith's *Wealth of Nations*, "Defence is much more important than opulence." Returning to the theme of ethical controls over private enterprise, Bentham said, "An absolute and unlimited right over any object of property would be the right to commit nearly every crime."

5. Thus Professor Samuels soundly demonstrates that laissez faire was no mere propaganda slogan, but a solid and considered analysis of the contribution of the economic system of a nation to its total moral and political well-being and therefore properly subservient to that well-being. In line with this, he shows how seriously the classical economists insisted on the "incremental" and "gradual" way of reform of the statutory and nondeliberative framework, and on sober consideration of each step of change by a calculus of pleasures and pains in the means and ends thereof.

6. The deservedly famous dictum of Adam Smith that "as by an invisible hand" each man by looking to his own economic benefit serves the economic benefit of the whole nation, is practicably viable if many other aspects of human behavior, some invisible, like men's consciences, some visible, like parliamentary institutions, statutes, political parties and rights and public education, are recognized as values in operation to prevent "predacious gain" and "conscious wrong-doing."

7. Professor Samuels discovers a truly formidable list of social provisos and restraints posed by the classical economists as necessary concomitants of the market economy.

8. The classical economists were statesmen. They not only passed judgment on the market economy but formulated the theory of the logic by which economic life should be organized, dynamized, and controlled, so that their methodical attitude is applicable to all societies. Thus, they pondered the role of "scientific" knowledge; the problem of change and adjustment; the conflict of social values; the necessary intervention of the statesman into economic decision, helping some decisions to

Introduction

fruition and forbidding or modifying others, on the basis of some policy of general utility, or as Bentham said, to maximize happiness and minimize pain and sacrifice and costs of production of subjective nature, and so on.

All this does not exhaust the wealth of ideas that Professor Samuel's scholarship and wisdom have uncovered and illuminated. The work is of the utmost importance not only to economists but to political scientists, sociologists, and students of jurisprudence. Of the last-named one of the geniuses was Jeremy Bentham, and he has his place in the galaxy of English thinkers presented by Warren J. Samuels in an illustrious performance of discovery and evaluation.

HERMAN FINER
Emeritus Professor of Political Science
University of Chicago
Chicago, Illinois

The Classical Theory of Economic Policy

CHAPTER ONE

The Market-Plus-Framework Interpretation

THE PROBLEM

The genius of the classical economists was to propose a system of socioeconomic organization and proceed to analyze, however imperfectly, the operation of such a system.[1] At the heart of this was a theory of economic policy, one vital to the understanding and analysis of contemporary Western society.

But the discussion by, no less than the subsequent interpretation of, the classical economists concerning their theory of economic policy focused and has continued to focus on certain facets with the consequence that other facets, as well as the system as a whole, have remained unobtrusive, unspecified, and misunderstood. It will be seen in the following pages that analysis of the classicists' writings discloses a much more sophisticated and complete classical theory of economic policy than has been hitherto generally appreciated. Thus the immediate and substantive objective of this book is to suggest the appropriateness and necessity of a more complete restatement of the classical theory of economic policy, and to suggest something of the terms of such a restatement.

The incompleteness of the classical theory of economic policy as presented in the literature is at least partly the result of continued preoccupation with the pros and cons of issues of the moment, resulting in exaggeration and distortion as well as incompleteness. It is further suggested that this incompleteness is in no small part the result of an inadequate understanding of what is involved in the concept "theory of economic policy," with respect to both the definitional scope and content of the concept and the necessity of as precise a specification of particulars as the subject will allow. Not the least reason for this is the provocative and deceptive nature of the doctrine of laissez faire, which has focused attention on the distinctive classical message to the neglect of the basic classical theory of policy, and has tended to preclude meaningful analysis by critics and advocates alike. The objective of broadest significance, then, is to suggest the necessity of more complete policy analysis and a more complete statement of what is necessarily involved in any theory of economic policy.

Restatement involves an interesting paradox, the resolution of which will have to await the concluding chapter. The paradox concerns the state of conventional interpretation of the classical theory of economic policy: it may be contended, on the one hand, that there is more to the classical theory of economic policy than is generally recognized; and, on the other, that more has been made of the classical theory of economic policy than is really or possibly there. The former contention involves the claim that fundamentals of the classical policy system have been neglected; the latter, the claim that the classical policy system has been applied to problems of policy so as to yield specific solutions to policy issues (solutions which tend to be generally considered as part of the system) to an extent beyond the system's capability. The procedure to be followed involves, first, the establishment of a more complete statement of the classical policy system; and second, a joining of the paradox through an inquiry into the meaningfulness of the classical policy system as thus restated, i.e., the limits of its applicability to specific issues.

It may be reiterated that the objective is a more complete and meaningful restatement of the classical policy system. It should be made clear from the beginning that this is no attempt to refute what already has been discounted if not discarded, at least in some quarters, namely, the laissez-faire interpretation. As Henry William Spiegel has written, "When all is said and done, one can but wonder at the persistence of a mythology which has been exploded at least once in every generation." [2] Certainly, there must be a place for the value system represented by the *doctrine* of laissez faire. There can hardly be any question that the classical economists were advocates of the market system, with a connotation of the minimization of government activity, reliance upon market forces to resolve the basic economic problems (resource allocation, income distribution, and the like), and private property and free private enterprise with private participation as buyers and sellers, consumers and investors, i.e., as private economic actors. It is, after all, just such ideas that the doctrinal slogan of laissez faire signifies. But any thorough statement of the classical theory of economic policy must go beyond doctrine into the practical realities of the way in which the classical economists dealt with the fundamental problems involved in any theory of economic policy and must specify as completely as possible the basic components to which the classical system reduces. The "solemn or sanctimonious pronouncement of doctrines in which no one could believe (as universal principles) who seriously tried to look and see and report what is palpably 'there'," [3] is neither the goal nor the object of criticism in these chapters.

The context of relevance is rather the market-plus-framework interpretation of the classical theory of economic policy, which is taken as the most meaningful analysis of the classical policy system yet formulated. The market-plus-framework interpretation, in the author's opinion, represents an advance of great analytical and interpretive significance, not only in the study of the classical policy system but also in the subject (theory of economic policy) as a whole. If further analysis is necessary, as indicated before, it is necessary in terms not of laissez faire but of the market-plus-framework approach, which constitutes the basis for such analysis.

It is the purpose of this chapter to summarize the basic reasoning of the market-plus-framework interpretation, to render a critique of that interpretation, and to indicate the general direction of the analysis to follow.

It should be pointed out that by "classical economists" are meant Adam Smith, Ricardo, Malthus, the two Mills, Mc-Culloch, Bentham, Senior, and Torrens, or substantially the same group included by Lord Robbins in the volume soon to be discussed. There is an extensive literature dealing with the respective credentials of some, if not all, of these men to be called "classicist." The author, however, finds a high degree of consonance in the views of these writers so far as the substance of his suggested restatement is concerned. (There will be some indication as to possible differentiation or qualification in a few matters.) It is one of the virtues of the proposed reinterpretation that it is possible to establish the basis in terms of which the classical theory of economic policy has meaning and of which membership in the classical school can be determined, at least with respect to policy. There is no question, however, that many problems of evidence and interpretation arise in these and other respects.

Finally, it should be pointed out that the scope of the author's problem is not classical thought as a whole but the classical theory of economic policy.

4

The Market-Plus-Framework Interpretation and Its Cosmology

Interpretation of the classical policy system was considerably improved with the publication of Lord Robbins' seminal *Theory of Economic Policy in English Classical Political Economy*.[4] Much to the credit of both Lord Robbins and his realism, the distinctive classical message remains clearly and warmly intact, though there has been gained from his restatement an understanding of the realities involved that was formerly obscured by doctrine.

In his *Theory of Economic Policy*, Lord Robbins set out to explain "what the Classical Economists were trying to do and to provide some sort of guide to what they actually said." [5] He attempted specifically to absolve the classicists from the false criticisms of having a narrow class bias, a belief in *Harmonielehre*, and an extreme laissez-faire stand on policy. Affirmatively, Lord Robbins' interpretation of the classical theory of economic policy emphasized (a) economic liberalism, or "the system of economic freedom"; (b) the createdness of whatever mutuality of interests or order exists, and a correlative reformist orientation; and (c) the importance of the framework within which private activity is undertaken, the provision of which is one of the functions ascribed to government. The general view, then, adopted by Lord Robbins is that of the "market-plus-framework" approach.

His thematic emphasis is upon the fact, operation, and significance of the framework within which individual or private economic activity and market forces operate and are constrained. According to Lord Robbins, "The invisible hand which guides men to promote ends which were no part of their intention, is not the hand of some god or some natural agency independent of human effort; it is the hand of the law-giver, the hand which withdraws from the sphere of the pursuit of self-interest those possibilities which do not harmonize with the public good." [6] The classical economists, he argues, ". . . never conceived the system of economic freedom as arising *in vacuo* or functioning in a system of law and order so simple and so minimal as to be capable of being written down on a limited table of stone (or a revolutionary handbill) and restricted to the functions of the night watchman. Nothing less than the whole complex of the Benthamite codes—Civil, Penal and Constitutional—was an adequate framework for their system." [7] This framework Lord Robbins sees as involving ". . . the provision of a set of rules which so limited and guided individual initiative, that the residue of free action undirected from the centre could be conceived to harmonize with the general objects of public interest." [8] The framework, then, is of the greatest importance: "Indeed," writes Lord Robbins, "in any logical scheme, we must regard the provision of such a framework as *prior* to the recommendation of economic freedom," and "it is to betray a total absence of acquaintance with the literature to suppose that the prior necessity of the framework would ever have been called in question." [9] To Lord Robbins, the classicists "regarded the appropriate legal framework and the system of economic freedom as two aspects of one and the same social process." [10]

The notion of a sharp separation between the political and the economic spheres, so far as the classical economists were concerned, is then, according to Lord Robbins, erroneous. If by the economic sphere is meant private economic activity, then it is composed of free action, yes, but of a "residue of free action" remaining after the withdrawal "from the sphere of the pursuit of self-interest those possibilities" which are determined through the legal process to be against the social interest. The legal process is not exogenous or superimposed; rather, it is a part of a larger process, inclusive also of private economic activity, through which the adjustment and reconciliation of interests takes place.

One of the doctrines usually associated with the classical economists is that of the harmony of interests. The idea of an underlying unity was of immense importance to the development of the social sciences, and particularly economics, for it served to assure that there was an order capable of and worthy of being studied. And not only did the idea of a preordained or providential harmony serve a methodological role; it served also to legitimize the emerging market economy, to secure it as the status quo, and to give it impetus.[11] The doctrine of *Harmonielehre* remains as a conventionally accepted classical proposition.

Yet closely related to Lord Robbins' emphasis upon the operation of the framework is a co-ordinate theme, not of the rule of harmony but of a limited harmony or mutuality of interests that was neither automatic nor inevitable. He transcends the metaphysical doctrine and inquires into the practical realities recognized by the classical theory of economic policy, and contends not only that there was no classical conviction of an automatic or natural harmony in the sense of inevitability, but also that whatever harmony would or could exist would have to be *created*.

It was then one of Lord Robbins' central objectives to refute the notion of *Harmonielehre* in the case of the classicists. His argument maintains that there was no harmony at all except under certain conditions, that "the harmony which would be established was a very limited kind of harmony," and concludes:

> In general, on any dispassionate view of the literature, it is really very hard to maintain that it gives any strong support to cosmic optimism, still less to belief in a comprehensive pre-established inevitable harmony of interests. The most that

7

can be said of the Classical Economists in this respect is that they believed that, in a world of free enterprise, certain relationships would arise which were of a mutually advantageous kind to the individuals concerned and superior to those resulting from alternative systems. . . .[12]

The whole logic of classical economics and theory of economic policy was based rather on the *createdness* of any harmonious order, upon the necessity to create such harmony as could be achieved by developing an appropriate and effective institutional system or framework. Both society and market were seen as artifacts,[13] and as artifacts that were evolving.[14] Despite occasional ex-cathedra allegations about an automatic harmony and notwithstanding a preoccupation with the facts and problems of economic adjustment,[15] the classical economists did not take the institutional system for granted.[16] To the classicists' discussions of the magnificent workings of the automatic market place, there must be juxtaposed their theory of social control, the institutions of which were to channel individual interests into amenable lines and thereby *create* harmony. Lord Robbins' framework may be considered as a system of social control to create that harmony, or alternately, to create the conditions of order: "If [the classical economists] assumed anywhere a harmony, it was never a harmony arising in a vacuum but always very definitely within a framework of law." [17] Within the constraints of the market-plus-framework interpretation as specified by Lord Robbins, the transformation or conversion of private interest into social interest was accomplished not only through the medium of the competitive market place but also through the legal process, which become "two aspects of one and the same social process," namely, the total economic decision-making process.

The same conclusion is reached by Taylor in his effort to restate the central logic of the classical policy system and its meaning for the liberal tradition: "With the legal order closing to all alike all doors to private gains through injuries to others, the liberal economy can open to all alike all doors to private gains through services to others, and the two together can thus largely create an effective harmony of or among the interests of all." [18] The notion of the framework considered as a system of social control and the correlative createdness of harmony through the framework constitute the fundamental cosmological premise of the classical theory of economic policy.

THE MEANING OF "THEORY OF ECONOMIC POLICY"

The important if not crucial question arises whether there was in fact a classical theory of economic policy, and if there was, by what criterion or in what sense. According to Lord Robbins, there was a classical theory of economic policy, "in the sense of a body of precepts for action," for, "by the theory of economic policy I mean the general body of principles of governmental action or inaction—the *agenda* or *non-agenda* of the state as Bentham called them—in regard to economic activity." [19] Yet Mark Blaug concludes that, "There was no such thing as a Ricardian theory of economic policy." [20] And Frank H. Knight maintains that the classical economists ". . . never developed either a clear and defensible program of action or a 'theory' of economic policy." [21]

In his review of Lord Robbins' *Theory of Economic Policy*, S. G. Checkland is critical of the dualism in the market-plus-framework interpretation as representing a construction based on merely "a series of *ad hoc* policy measures which common sense and common humanity told them could hardly be

9

avoided." He suggests that the classical theory of policy is rather to be focused on a "recognized emphasis," or what "the English classical economists gave as their message to their time." [22] According to Checkland, then, a theory of economic policy has to do with the doctrine or ideal comprising the valuational *differentia specifica* of the relevant body of thought. On the other hand, Knight, although concluding that there is no classical theory of economic policy, and also recognizing the importance of the propaganda element, approaches the definitional problem differently. According to Knight,

> . . . the central issue of economic policy *is* the distribution of power between individuals (families and other actual units or organizations) and between these and the "community", ultimately the sovereign state. . . . And the main question about the "theory of policy of the English Classical Economists" would be that of how far they dealt with this issue.

He then proceeds to conclude, "My own answer would be, not very far or effectively, indeed, hardly at all, though J. S. Mill discoursed about it at length." [23]

The question whether there is a classical theory of economic policy, as well as the substantive answer to the question of what it is, turns on the definition assigned to the concept "theory of economic policy." This in turn may be said to involve two subsidiary matters; the first is of primary relevance at this point, and the second will be discussed in the concluding chapter: first, by what criterion or criteria is the concept to be defined; and, second, what is its level of meaningfulness in the sense of applicability to policy issues? Before considering the problems in terms of which the concept "theory of economic policy" may be defined, the issue of the place of doctrine (or valuational premise) must be examined.

According to Checkland, a theory of economic policy has to do with "a system of ideas . . . to guide policy," [24] a notion not dissimilar to that of Robbins' "body of precepts for action." But if the system of ideas *is* to guide policy, Checkland maintains, "it must have a recognized emphasis, however many minor concessions may be necessary, in order that conscientious men may know which way to push." [25] Acknowledging Robbins' identification of the role of the framework as administering "a most useful corrective," he nevertheless proceeds to acclaim the "older view, taken by Halevy," in which the classical message of individualism is identified as *the* classical theory of economic policy.[26] "If too much is made of artifice through law," he argues, "surely the characteristic virtues of the market must fade." [27] So far as the definition of the concept "theory of economic policy" is concerned, the criterion in question would appear to be that of *valuational doctrine:* the definitional focus of a theory of economic policy would be upon the valuational premise which establishes the ideological or doctrinal presumption characteristic of the system constructed upon it.

There must be a place in any theory of economic policy for the valuational system, or message, or premise, distinctive to it. But, it may be queried, what is it that the valuational system of a theory of economic policy has to do with? Is there not something more to a theory of economic policy than its doctrinal expression, however distinctive and appealing? Certainly, if individualism is important, it is so because that which it has to do with is important. A theory of policy must be viewed for the valuational premise it upholds and from which it derives its distinctive character, but it must also be searched for something logically prior and in a sense more relevant, both ultimately and immediately. It must be expressed in terms of a set of social problems to which the valuational system claims to provide in some sense a distinctive solution. Moreover, if these problems are problems in any real or ultimate sense— involving the reconciliation of apparently contradictory social

11

demands or needs—then any doctrinal expression must (because it focuses on that which is distinctive) do injustice to the way in which the theory of policy under study resolves those basic social problems. A theory of policy involves—and must be viewed in terms of—certain problems to the resolution of which the theory of policy must ultimately be addressed. Doctrine is important in respect to influence; but complete analysis is necessary for understanding, just as complete or effective provision for the resolution of those basic problems is a condition of any substantial efficacy for the theory of policy in question. (It would appear that any theory of economic policy which failed somehow to provide *some* mode of resolution would connote the epitome of unrealism so far as the problems necessary of resolution are ultimate and real problems. Such an unreal theory of policy, however, would not thereby necessarily be deprived of influence.)

The approach of Lord Robbins—"the general body of principles of governmental action or inaction"—would seem to be more to the point, for if individualism (to use the classicists as example) connotes the minimization of government, there still needs to be a clear statement of the "principles" involved. Actually, however, the approach of Lord Robbins may be subsumed under that of Knight, in terms of which the concept "theory of economic policy" has to do with the total division of power in society, encompassing both the distribution of power within the nominally private or individual sphere and between that and the rest of "the 'community,' ultimately the sovereign state." Knight's view appears to center on the heart of what is involved in any theory of economic policy.

Given the conventional understanding of the phrase "basic economic problems," the economy may be seen as a decision-making process through which those basic economic problems are continuously resolved. A theory of economic policy thus ultimately has to do with the structure of the economic decision-making process, i.e., the distribution of decision-making participation, or what Knight refers to as "power." Its central problem is the manner in which the economy is to be organized and controlled, and comprises a theory of the structure and operation of a particular economic decision-making process.

A theory of economic policy thus is involved with the problem of order, i.e., the continuing resolution of the dual basic social problems of freedom and control, and continuity and change. That is to say, it has to do with the resolution of what Spengler has called the combination and reconciliation of autonomy, cooperation, continuity, and change.[28] Any theory of economic policy, in the sense in which the concept is here proposed to be understood, must comprise both a theory of social control and a theory of social change.

If this is the case, a theory of economic policy must also encompass a theory of knowledge in relation to social policy. Meaning by knowledge, knowledge of values and of the world (reality), then a theory of economic policy involves a theory of the organization of knowledge in society and necessitates something of both a theory of the *determination* and the *role* of knowledge in respect to social policy.

The analysis of any theory of economic policy, to be meaningful and complete, would have to specify the scope and structure of the economic decision-making process contemplated therein, and treat, *inter alia*: (a) the area of policy encompassed in the particular theory of economic policy under study, i.e., the scope of recognized effective choice; (b) the participants in the economic decision-making process described or postulated therein; and (c) the respective roles of each participant. No doubt the doctrinal message would remain distinctive for the particular theory, but more meaningful analysis would be possible than hitherto, when analysis has been generally limited to the metaphysics of doctrine. It has been this very preoccupation with doctrine that has hindered complete analysis, and it is the genius of Lord Robbins'

Theory of Economic Policy to have moved in the direction of substituting careful analysis for metaphysical exercises.

Knight would conclude, however, that so far as that is concerned, the classical economists had "hardly at all" a theory of economic policy. (Indeed, with respect to the matter of doctrine, Knight finds that the classicists "did not clearly state" even "the basis of a propaganda for economic freedom. . . ." [29]) It may be suggested, however, that quite the opposite is true: that, as Lord Robbins has shown at least in part and as the present author will endeavor to show further, the classical economists did in fact have a theory of economic policy in accordance with the definitional criteria established above. By Knight's own specification there will be seen to be a classical theory of policy.

While this remains, of course, to be demonstrated, analysis may proceed upon the understanding that the study of a theory of economic policy has to do not just with its doctrinal expression but with the identification of how it would substantively resolve the basic problems generic to any theory of economic policy. This understanding is fundamental to the positivist approach to be followed here, no less than in the case of Lord Robbins, whose realistic approach is at one with that of the present study.

THE MARKET-PLUS-FRAMEWORK APPROACH

The market-plus-framework interpretation of the classical theory of economic policy, particularly as elucidated by Lord Robbins, has the great virtue of specifying more completely what the classical theory of policy was all about than had been indicated by the ambiguous but doctrinally useful laissez-faire

14

or laissez-faire-plus-exceptions views. It has replaced a caricature with a more complete analysis. The most significant particular contributions *in re* the classical policy system include:
(a) calling attention to the importance of the institutional
organization of society and economy as a mode additional to
market forces or private participation for the resolution of the
basic economic problems; (b) establishing the createdness of
order and of the resolution of the problems of freedom and
control, and continuity and change, thereby directing attention to a more accurate understanding of the complexities of
establishing mutuality of interests and to the role of the system
of social control; and (c) suggesting the subtleties involved
in reconciling freedom and order (as will be seen in greater
detail below). The market-plus-framework interpretation indicates that the classical economists were more sophisticated
than the doctrinally oriented approaches would allow. Lord
Robbins clearly shows that much of the debate over the classicists' views on policy has been misdirected and naive. There
are, however, a number of serious difficulties with the market-
plus-framework approach, relating both to the dualism of
market and framework and to the particular interpretation
given to the approach by Lord Robbins.

One problem concerns the meaningfulness of the notion of
"framework." The idea of a framework essentially involves a
truism: a truistic relation between that which is and that which
is not in the category of "framework," between framework
and nonframework; or the truism that everything within which
individual or private market activity takes place is the "framework" thereof. In a very direct sense, *all* other activity constitutes the more or less proximate framework of any particular
act or set of actions. The notion of a framework does indicate
the recognizedly important operation of social control. Yet, as
Checkland points out, "the phenomenon taking place within
the frame may well operate upon the frame—the dichotomy

15

may break down by variations in the rules brought about by the distribution of the winnings. This of course occurs—the market is not merely the creation of the frame, but the reverse also is true." [30] A meaningful analysis of the decision-making process advocated by the classical economists must encompass the phenomenon of interaction between the participants. The recognition of interaction, however, only complicates an already difficult problem, namely, that of meaningful differentiation between framework and nonframework. Most important, the danger for analysis exists that the notion of a framework will be allowed or used to rigidify artificially part of the economic decision-making process and preclude adequate cognizance not only of interaction per se but also of the resolution of the problem of continuity and change.

The market-plus-framework interpretation posits not only a differentiation between framework and market (or nonframework), but also a differentiation between two types of government activity. It requires a distinction between actions of government to provide or fill the framework and other nonframework-filling interventions. But much liberalist criticism of the latter can also be levied against the former, so far as specific government activities are concerned. In addition, not only may the actions of the first group be *seen* by the participants at the time as being in the second group (which is quite likely), but can differentiation be made between the two? Can specific content be unequivocally adduced to each of the two types of government activity? The problem, like that of the differentiation between framework and nonframework, is made further complicated by the operation of government, at the very minimum, to change the substance of the legal framework. Again, the danger of artificial rigidity arises, warranting closer examination of the classical resolution of the problem of continuity and change.

At least three problems are involved, one of which has to

do with the meaningfulness of the classical policy system—namely, its capacity to resolve particular issues of policy—and which therefore need not be discussed *in extenso* until the concluding chapter. The other two problems relate to the classical resolution of the problem of continuity and change: first, the role of the notion of "framework"; and second, the staticity of either whatever content is adduced to the framework or the framework itself. Both the latter problems will be examined in Chapters Four and Five. Yet both constitute one facet of the major general defect of the Robbinsian view of the classical policy system as a whole.

It is suggested that the interpretation rendered in the *Theory of Economic Policy* considerably understates the scope, complexity, and sophistication of the classical theory of economic policy when examined in the context of the dual basic problems of freedom and control, and continuity and change. Particularly, it will be seen that the market-plus-framework interpretation as specified by Lord Robbins (a) neglects the nonlegal forces of social control; (b) fails to specify what is involved in the framework-providing function of government, at the very minimum and regardless of whatever else may be said of the framework concept; and (c) inadequately characterizes the classical view of the role of law as an instrument or mode of change. Chapters Two through Four contain examinations of the classical literature with a view to correcting these deficiencies. It will be upon the affirmative insight provided by the market-plus-framework approach of Lord Robbins, together with the proposed corrective analyses of those chapters, that the suggested reinterpretation of the classical theory of economic policy will be undertaken in Chapter Five. This reinterpretation should avoid the formalism of the market-framework dualism, minimize the danger of artificial rigidity, and more accurately, it is to be hoped, represent the classical theory of the economic decision-making process in respect to the problems of freedom and control, and continuity and change.

In partial summary, an attempt will be made in this work to restate more completely the classical theory of economic policy. The study is ultimately concerned with what the classical policy system reduces to in resolution of the basic problems of any theory of policy, with adequate perspective given to the classical message, and with an attempt at faithful consideration of the evidence in the classical literature. The frame of reference is the market-plus-framework interpretation, which has rendered the affirmative contributions sketched above, but the proposed restatement will attempt a still more complete understanding of the classical theory of policy. The definitional meaning of the concept of "theory of economic policy" and the general approach of both Lord Robbins and the present study have both been indicated. What remains is to specify more completely the classical theory of economic policy and the character of its meaningfulness so far as its applicability to problems and issues of policy is concerned.

NOTES: CHAPTER ONE

1. Cf. Overton H. Taylor, *The Classical Liberalism, Marxism, and the Twentieth Century* (Cambridge: Harvard University Press, 1960), p. 26; and Joseph J. Spengler and William R. Allen, eds., *Essays in Economic Thought* (Chicago: Rand McNally, 1960), p. 259.

2. Henry William Spiegel, Book Review, *American Economic Review*, vol. 43 (1953), p. 636.

3. Frank H. Knight, "Theory of Economic Policy and the History of Doctrine," *Ethics*, vol. 63 (1953), p. 287.

4. Lionel Robbins, *The Theory of Economic Policy in English Classical Political Economy* (hereafter cited as *Theory of Economic Policy*) (London: Macmillan, 1953).

5. *Ibid.*, p. 7.

6. *Ibid.*, p. 56.

7. *Ibid.*, p. 188.

8. *Ibid.*, p. 190.
9. *Ibid.*, p. 190.
10. *Ibid.*, p. 191.
11. The notion of harmony was, like that of the labor theory of value, "among the shibboleths of the time, a convenient weapon against mercantilist thinking." Mark Blaug, *Economic Theory in Retrospect* (Homewood, Ill.: Irwin, 1962), p. 52. The same is true of laissez faire: "To Smith the institutional variable is an important policy variable. Indeed, much of the burden of his argument in favor of free trade and *laissez faire* is designed to show how the institutional environment might best be altered in order to maximize the economy's rate of growth." Irma Adelman, *Theories of Economic Growth and Development* (Stanford: Stanford University Press, 1961), p. 28. But the "idea that individuals, each following his own interest, created laws as impersonal, or at least as anonymous, as those of the natural sciences was arresting. And the belief that these must be socially beneficial quickened the spirit of optimism that was a feature of the revolution in industry." T. S. Ashton, *The Industrial Revolution, 1760–1830* (London: Oxford University Press, 1948), p. 139. The crucial question for policy analysis is of course "harmony of interests" by what criteria, on what terms, and in the context of what system of social control (or decision-making process). The problem may also require the definition of the "true interests of all the different members of society." Taylor, *op. cit.*, p. 96. Moreover, the ideas of an invisible hand or of a pre-existent and pre-eminent order or of harmony itself, were epistemologically either mere assertion or hypothesis. The history of subsequent economic thought may be viewed as efforts aiming at the specification of the conditions of mutuality or harmony of interests.
12. Robbins, *op. cit.*, pp. 25, 26, 28–29. *In re* the notion of mutual advantage, cf. Knight, *op. cit.*, pp. 279, 284.
13. Robbins, *op cit.*, pp. 55, 57. Cf. S. G. Checkland, "The Prescriptions of the Classical Economists," *Economica*, n.s., vol. 20 (1953), p. 71.
14. The sophistication of the classicists concerning social control was at least equaled by their sophistication concerning the dynamics of social change. See below, particularly Chapters Two, Four, and Five.
15. See A. P. Usher, in *Explorations in Economics: Notes and Essays Contributed in Honor of F. W. Taussig* (New York: McGraw-Hill, 1936), p. 407.
16. Cf., for example, the views of Edwin Cannan and Karl de Schweinitz, Jr. Wrote Cannan: "Throughout history society has been fashioning and modifying its institutions so as to make it the interest

of its members to do the right thing . . . the very fact which Smith ignored, namely, that such harmony as is found between the pursuit of self-interest and the general good is dependent on the existence of suitable human institutions." ". . . [Smith] failed to see that self-interest had been put in the shafts and harnessed by law and order, products of collective wisdom . . ." "Adam Smith as an Economist," *Economica*, vol. 6 (1926), pp. 132–33, 134. But compare de Schweinitz: "Unlike neo-classical economics, classical economics never was far removed from the social and political institutions which formed the framework of economic activity . . . the classical economists could not take the institutional framework of the economy for granted, simply because it too was being transformed. Especially could they not take for granted the maintenance of social order, so severe were the strains imposed on the community by the industrial revolution. The classical economists, therefore, were very much aware of the coercive relationships of economic and social organization and not inclined to apply freedom to the former indiscriminately. Adam Smith, for example, was not so far convinced of the harmony of interests in society that he lost sight of the coercive role of the state." "Free Enterprise in a Growth World," *Southern Economic Journal*, vol. 29 (1962), p. 105. See also, Chapter Two, notes 5 and 7.

17. Robbins, *op. cit.*, p. 191.

18. Taylor, *op. cit.*, p. 97; cf. pp. 26, 27, 96. For a similar interpretation of the central classical cosmological position, see Friedrich A. Hayek, *Individualism and Economic Order* (Chicago: University of Chicago Press, 1948), pp. 12–13, 19–20. See also Chapter Two and the references cited there in notes 5 and 7.

19. Robbins, *op. cit.*, pp. 177, 2.

20. Mark Blaug, *Ricardian Economics* (New Haven: Yale University Press, 1958), p. 194.

21. Knight, *op. cit.*, p. 279.

22. Checkland, *op. cit.*, pp. 71–72.

23. Knight, *op. cit.*, p. 282.

24. Checkland, *op. cit.*, p. 71.

25. *Ibid., loc. cit.* See also Anonymous, Book Review, *Edinburgh Review*, vol. 52 (1831): "The true church in political economy is still a church militant; and every teacher must act the part of a controversialist." (P. 339.)

26. Checkland, *op. cit.*, p. 72.

27. *Ibid.*, p. 71.

28. Spengler and Allen, *op. cit.*, pp. 9–10.

29. Knight, *op. cit.*, p. 279.

30. Checkland, *op. cit.*, p. 71.

CHAPTER TWO

The Nonlegal Forces of Social Control

Man is a Religious Animall, and onely men hope that their Earthly Soveraines will deale very justly, when such soveraines beleive there is a most just God above them.

Men, either for the Love of God or the feare of Hell, will forbeare doing such mischief to their Neighbor as the Law cannot reach.

Men, after prayer to God, proceede more cheerfully on their businesses when they believe that such prayers shall procure them successe.

Men beare paines & wrongs more patiently, when they hope that God will ballance all in the next life.

—Sir William Petty*

THE PROBLEM

The objective of broadest significance of this chapter is to suggest the necessity of considering a definition of wider scope for the concept of "theory of economic policy." The immediate and substantive objective is to consider the appropriateness

21

and necessity of such a broader definition in the case of the classical theory of economic policy.

It has already been pointed out in the *Theory of Economic Policy*, that the concept of "theory of economic policy" was defined as "the general body of principles of governmental action or inaction . . . in regard to economic activity." [1] This definition, it is suggested, is incomplete for it does not adequately (if at all) acknowledge or reflect the fact that the state is but one reciprocally interacting part of larger parallelograms of power, the total system of social control and the total economic decision-making process. As a consequence, any theory of economic policy which fails to recognize all relevant subsystems or participants in social control (and in the economic decision-making process), and their interaction, is inadequate, however much need there is for careful study of the subsystems themselves. [2]

The market-plus-framework interpretation, taken as the most meaningful analysis of the classical system yet formulated, nevertheless understates the significance and content of the forces of social control considered as the framework. Indeed, the literature on classical economic policy, as a whole, generally understates the significance of the social control system. Such understatement is serious in the case of the classical economists, for the resolution of the problem of social control was a conspicuous facet of the classical theory of economic policy.

In particular, the nonlegal, or nondeliberative, forces of social control, operating as morals, religion, custom, and education, were included as necessary and significant participants in the policy process. [3] This concept is true, notwithstanding the general and distinctive classical aim for reasoned, and therefore deliberate, policy and policy analysis. Such deliberate policy-making as would or could take place had to operate under conditions of order and the existence of socialized individuals, both of which were to a substantial extent the result of the working of the nondeliberative forces of social control. The operation of the nonlegal forces was a facet of the classical theory of social control, all the institutions of which were to channel individual interests and create harmony. These forces were among the institutions "within which action is so limited and co-ordinated as to create the good society," withdrawing "from the sphere of the pursuit of self-interest those possibilities which do not harmonize with the public good." [4] It will be seen now in detail that to the classical economists an order is harmonious largely to the extent to which the system of social control, and largely the nondeliberative forces thereof, perform their functions well.[5] Ricardo expressed it in this way:

> To keep men good you must as much as possible withdraw from them all temptations to be otherwise. The sanctions of religion, of public opinion, and of law, all proceed on this principle, and that State is most perfect in which all these sanctions concur to make it the interest of all men to be virtuous, which is the same thing as to say, to use their best endeavour to promote the general happiness.[6]

In this way not only did the classicists recognize the created character of the social order, indeed its continual creation, but also they were cognizant of the roles of both the legal and nonlegal or nondeliberative forces of social control in the process of creation. Moreover, and this fact is of great importance, the classicists' case for the relative de-emphasis of the legal forces, i.e., the role of government in the economy, was in effect premised on the effective operation of the nondeliberative forces of social control.[7] Unfortunately, however, the operation of the nondeliberative forces is seriously neglected by the literature on the classical theory of economic policy; an occasional terse reference to "morals" utterly fails to do the subject justice. This chapter inquires into the drama of the forces of morals, religion, custom, and education as the non-legal forces of social control in the classical theory of economic policy.

Preliminarily, it is instructive to note that Hayek acknowledges the relevance of the nondeliberative forces in respect to the classicists, yet concludes that they are truly important only in the case of Adam Smith; whereas "the classical economists of the nineteenth century, or at least the Benthamites or philosophical radicals among them," had much less and perhaps progressively less of a place for them, coming increasingly to emphasize deliberateness and conscious design.[8] So far as the Hayekian conclusion is concerned, however, it will be seen below that there is a much greater degree of consonance among the classicists with regard to reliance upon the nondeliberative forces than he recognized: *less* relative reliance in the case of Smith and *more* in the case of the others. The problem ultimately is one of the relative proportion between deliberate and nondeliberate (i.e., between legal and non-legal) forces. This proportion, however, is a facet of the larger problem of the degree of specificity and the meaningfulness of the classical policy system, which is examined, to reiterate, in the concluding chapter. Another problem concerns what may be significant variations among the classicists as to the role afforded to organized religion as a nondeliberative force of social control.

It may be pointed out that Taylor also specifies the market-plus-framework interpretation to include the correlative operation of both the legal and nonlegal forces, at least in general terms. Therefore he writes of "the limits of free choice allowed by the society's effective ethics and legal system," such that "the public, ethical, political, and legal task is to so develop the society's institutions and effective moral code and the structure of its economic system that the natural working of that system's economic laws or processes will result in economic justice among all and the greatest welfare of all severally and collectively." [9]

In brief summary, so far as the idea of a framework is itself at all meaningful, it is argued that (1) the framework is more significant than has as yet been made clear in the literature on classical policy; (2) this significance is in part the result of the classical emphasis on the nonlegal forces of social control; and (3) the failure to recognize such significance is in no small part the result of an inadequate definition of the scope of the concept of the "theory of economic policy." The objective of this chapter, then, is to demonstrate the appropriateness and necessity of considering the nonlegal forces of social control as a facet of the classical theory of economic policy, and, further, to specify the functional roles thereof as a participant in the classical decision-making process.

This chapter will examine Morals and Religion, Custom, and Education, in that sequence, in each case examining, first, Smith, in some detail, and then showing the consonance of Smith's views with those of the later classicists. Included in the section on Morals and Religion are discussions developing the nondeliberative character of all the nonlegal forces of social control.

MORALS AND RELIGION: THE PRINCIPLES OF IGNORANCE AND INDIRECTION

It is appropriate to turn first to Smith's *Theory of Moral Sentiments*, for not only was this remarkable essay a treatise on "natural theology" and a great work in social analysis, but it was held in high repute by the English classicists at least down through Stuart Mill.[10] Its basic ideas on morals and reli-

13—928—Economic Policy ——11 - 13 Electra —(2)—
gion as control forces, it will be seen, were largely adhered to
by the later classicists. Smith was primarily concerned with the
operation and, perforce, the immediate or observable source
of the moral sentiments. Reflecting the ambivalent character
of his age and possibly the influence of Hume, Smith's analysis
finds the origin of the *content* of morals in experience, so as
to be perhaps ultimately indistinguishable from revered custom.[11] Through the working of sympathy and the principles
of approbation and disapprobation of the conduct of one's
self and of others, operating through the guidance of the "im-
partial spectator" (". . . reason, principle, conscience, the in-
habitant of the breast, the man within, the great judge and
arbiter of our conduct. . . ."),[12] Smith charts the incremental
development of standards of conduct which, more or less internalized in the socialized behavioral patterns of all men,
evolve and emerge as general rules of conduct.

> Our continual observations upon the conduct of others,
> insensibly lead us to form to ourselves certain general rules
> concerning what is fit and proper either to be done or to be
> avoided.
> The general rule . . . is formed, by finding from experience,
> that all actions of a certain kind, or circumstanced in a certain
> manner, are approved or disapproved of.
> . . . The general rules which determine what actions are,
> and what are not, the objects of each of those sentiments, can
> be formed no other way than by observing what actions
> actually and in fact excite them.
> When these general rules, indeed, have been formed, when
> they are universally acknowledged and established, by the con-
> curring sentiments of mankind, we frequently appeal to them
> as to the standards of judgment. . . .[13]

These general rules not only vary, however, in respect to
time and place,[14] but were seen as imprecise and ambiguous,[15]

except for those of justice. Yet this very ambiguity is derived from, and tends to promote the pervasive functioning of the rules to provide both flexibility and individual spheres of autonomy (however ambiguous, situational, and transitory) within the requirements and restraints of order. The ambiguity, that is, provides the flexibility necessary to attain workable adjustments between freedom and order.

So it is that the needs of *order* are a central preoccupation of Smith in the *Moral Sentiments*, to the provision of which it is the task of morals and religion alike to contribute. Indeed, the *Moral Sentiments* places great weight on *order*, which is perhaps to be expected in a work on the role of morals as an instrument of social control.

> Man, it has been said, has a natural love for society and desires that the union of mankind should be preserved for its own sake, and though he himself was to derive no benefit from it. The orderly and flourishing state of society is agreeable to him, and he takes delight in contemplating it. Its disorder and confusion, on the contrary, is the object of his aversion, and he is chagrined at whatever tends to produce it. He is sensible too that his own interest is connected with the prosperity of society, and that the happiness, perhaps the preservation of his existence, depends upon its preservation. Upon every account, therefore, he has an abhorrence at whatever can tend to destroy society, and is willing to make use of every means, which can hinder so hated and so dreadful an event.[16]

Justice is important because of its contribution to order, which is consequently the higher value. "Beneficence," wrote Smith, "is less essential to the existence of society than justice. . . . Justice, on the contrary, is the main pillar that upholds the whole edifice. If it is removed, the great, the immense fabric of human society . . . must in a moment crumble into atoms. . . . Society may subsist, though not in the most comfortable state, without beneficence; but the prevalence of injustice must utterly destroy it." [17] Indeed, "The peace and order of society, is of more importance than even the relief of the miserable." [18]

Smith demonstrates, then, that morals, manifest through the general rules of conduct, conduce to social order, serving as an instrument of control in the process. Says Smith:

> The regard to those general rules of conduct, is what is properly called a sense of duty, a principle of the greatest consequence in human life, and the only principle by which the bulk of mankind are capable of directing their actions.[19]

> The coarse clay of which the bulk of mankind are formed, cannot be wrought up to such perfection. There is scarce any man, however, who by discipline, education, and example, may not be so impressed with a regard to general rules, as to act upon almost every occasion with tolerable decency, and through the whole of his life to avoid any considerable degree of blame.

> Without this sacred regard to general rules, there is no man whose conduct can be much depended upon. . . . But upon the tolerable observance of these duties depends the very existence of human society, which would crumble into nothing if mankind were not generally impressed with a reverence for those important rules of conduct.

> Upon whatever we suppose that moral faculties are founded, . . . they were given us for the direction of our conduct in this life. They . . . were set up within us to be the supreme arbiters of all our actions, to superintend all our senses, passions, and appetites, and to judge how each of them was either to be indulged or restrained.

> All general rules . . . have a much greater resemblance to what are properly called laws, those general rules which the sovereign lays down to direct the conduct of his subjects. Like them they are rules to direct the free actions of men: . . .[20]

Morality serves, according to Smith, as a social cement through its role as an instrument of social control. Whatever the theological status of the general rules of conduct, Smith acknowledged the operation, nondeliberatively, of control through social interaction.

> The all-wise Author of Nature has, in this manner, taught man to respect the sentiments and judgments of his brethren; to be more or less pleased when they approve of his conduct, and to be more or less hurt when they disapprove of it. He has made man, if I may say so, the immediate judge of mankind; and has, in this respect, as in many others, created him after his own image, and appointed him his vicegerent upon earth, to superintend the behaviour of his brethren.[21]

Wrote Morrow: "The individual's moral consciousness with its judgments of approval and disapproval is a reflection, or a derivative of the social consciousness; it grows through experience in society, and represents the demands of his fellow-men upon the individual." [22]

The promulgation of morals is a concern of religion, though it is clear that Smith and the other classicists considered morals as having sources other than from religious offices. Religion was, however, a participant in the development of morals, and had to do, at the minimum, with the "impulse to reverence," the "sense of duty," or of "being good."

With respect to religion, or organized religion, the classicists as a group generally: (a) advocated religious liberty with toleration and without persecution; (b) were critical of totalitarian religious institutions; (c) were critical of what Bentham referred to as the "mischief" of religion; and (d) generally were, or at least tended to be, humanistic. But most important for present purposes, the classicists (e) acknowledged the role of religion as a restraint, or source of restraint, upon behavior. In this respect the classicists often analyzed organized religion as another social institution. In so doing, they some-

29

what ambiguously acknowledged or developed the customary character of the content of religious or other moral codes. But they clearly envisioned religion as a force at least tending to operate as an effective instrument of social control. Religion itself might not be sufficient to produce moral behavior, nor was belief in the existence of a Supreme Being necessarily sufficient (compare Smith and Stuart Mill, *infra*), but even in a humanist regime (Stuart Mill acknowledged) such belief would be efficacious. Religion was seen as inculcating a compulsion or feeling of necessity to be good (Smith's "sense of duty"), whatever the moral system, thereby serving to enforce the extant moral system—and, of course, as participating in defining the content of the moral system. Religion also was seen as serving to induce a feeling of consolation or resignation, which was understood as a derivative of the necessity for order but also as the basis of meaningful social improvement.

There is some question as to how far several of the classical economists would have relied upon organized religion as part of the institutionalized ethical system. The preceding paragraph is generally correct, though there is ambivalence. Thus Smith, whose religiosity is ambiguous, none the less evidences a greater willingness to rely upon religion than Stuart Mill— but the difference may reflect the passage of three quarters of a century in time, manners, sentiments, and openness of speech.

Smith was lucid in his discussion of the role of religion as an instrument of control. After stressing that "upon the tolerable observance of these duties depends the very existence of human society, which would crumble into nothing if mankind were not generally impressed with a reverence for those important rules of society," he declares that,

> This reverence is still further enhanced by an opinion, which is first impressed by nature, and afterwards confirmed by reasoning and philosophy, that those important rules of

30

morality are the commands and laws of the Deity, who will finally reward the obedient and punish the transgressors of their duty.

These natural hopes, and fears, and suspicions, were propagated by sympathy, and confirmed by education; and the gods were universally represented and believed to be the rewarders of humanity and mercy, and the avengers of perfidy and injustice. And thus religion, even in its rudest form, gave a sanction to the rules of morality, long before the age of artificial reasoning and philosophy. That the terrors of religion should thus enforce the natural sense of duty, was of too much importance to the happiness of mankind, for nature to leave it dependent upon the slowness and uncertainty of philosophical researches.

Since these, therefore, were plainly intended to be the governing principles of human nature, the rules which they prescribe are to be regarded as the commands and laws of the Deity, promulgated by those vicegerents which he has thus set up within us.

When the general rules which determine the merit and demerit of actions, come thus to be regarded as the laws of an all-powerful Being . . . ; they necessarily acquire a new sacredness from this consideration. That our regard to the will of the Deity ought to be the supreme rule of our conduct, can be doubted of by nobody who believes his existence. The very thought of disobedience appears to involve in it the most shocking impropriety. . . . The idea that, however we may escape the observation of man, or be placed above the reach of human punishment, yet we are always acting under the eye, and exposed to the punishment of God, the great avenger of injustice, is a motive capable of restraining the most headstrong passions, with those at least who, by constant reflection, have rendered it familiar to them.

It is in this manner that religion enforces the natural sense of duty: and hence it is, that mankind are generally disposed to place great confidence in the probity of those who seem deeply impressed with religious sentiments. Such persons, they imagine, act under an additional tie, besides those which regulate the conduct of other men.[23]

None the less, Smith is rather sophisticated about the role of religion so far as the content of morality is concerned. Though he cautions that there can be "no solid happiness to any man who is not thoroughly convinced that all the inhabitants of the universe, the meanest as well as the greatest, are under the immediate care and protection of that great, benevolent, and all-wise Being," [24] and that religion is the source of "magnanimous resignation," [25] he stresses an activism with respect to man and acknowledges ambiguity in the obligations enforced by religion. With respect to the former, Smith's division of responsibility has a place for both God and man: "The administration of the great system of the universe, . . . the care of the universal happiness of all rational and sensible beings, is the business of God and not of man. To man is allotted a much humbler department. . . ; the care of his own happiness, of that of his family, his friends, his country: . . . The most sublime speculation of the contemplative philosopher can scarce compensate the neglect of the smallest active duty." [26]

On the ambiguity of obligation, Smith recognizes that "Religion affords such strong motives to the practice of virtue, and guards us by such powerful restraints from the temptations of vice, that many have been led to suppose, that religious principles were the sole laudable motives of action." They are not, and, what is more: "That the sense of duty should be the sole principle of our conduct, is no where the precept of Christianity; but that it should be the ruling and the governing one, as philosophy, and as, indeed, common sense directs. It may be a question, however, in what cases our actions ought to arise chiefly or entirely from a sense of duty, or from a regard to general rules; and in what cases some other sentiment or affection ought to concur, and have a principal influence on our conduct." It "will depend upon the natural agreeableness or deformity of the affection itself, how far our actions ought to arise from it, or entirely proceed from a regard to the general rule," and "it will depend partly upon the precision and exactness, or the looseness and inaccuracy of the general rules themselves, how far our conduct ought to proceed entirely from a regard to them." [27] Religion, then, serves to promote morality but is no unequivocal answer to the problem of the content of moral rules: "The general rules of almost all the virtues, . . . are in many respects loose and inaccurate, admit of many exceptions, and require so many modifications, that it is scarce possible to regulate our conduct entirely by a regard to them." Although the rules of justice are "precise, accurate, and indispensable," the rules of the other virtues "are loose, vague, and indeterminate, and present us rather with a general idea of the perfection we ought to aim at, than afford us any certain and infallible directions for acquiring it." [28] Like the general cosmology of the time (discussed in the following paragraphs), the general moral system, while unable to unequivocally resolve all the particulars of moral content, gains in strength as an instrument of social control what it otherwise loses in precision, for its *general* attractiveness is most important as a force of social control.

Moreover, analyzing religion as merely another social institution, Smith finds that its operation is not always unobjectionable. "False notions of religion are almost the only causes which can occasion any very gross perversion of our natural sentiments in this way; and that principle which gives the greatest authority to the rules of duty, is alone capable of distorting our ideas of them in any considerable degree." Notwithstanding the foregoing statement, Smith again subsumes equity and justice to order: "That to obey the will of the Deity, is the first rule of duty, all men are agreed. But concerning the particular commandments which that will may impose

33

upon us, they differ widely from one another. In this, therefore, the greatest mutual forbearance and toleration is due; and though the defence of society requires that crimes should be punished, from whatever motives they proceed, yet a good man will always punish them with reluctance, when they evidently proceed from false notions of religious duty." [29]

It is no accident, then, that Smith, even in the *Wealth of Nations*, applauded "the uniformity of faith, the fervour of devotion, the spirit of order, regularity, and austere morals in the great body of the people...." [30] To Smith, says Bittermann, "Religion is a natural response to human needs for ethical sanctions." [31] Religion co-ordinate with the pressures generic to any moral system, served, in the eyes of Smith, as a force of social control. It restricted and channeled behavior, always in terms of the more or less ambiguous content of the extant moral system, and thereby governed the ostensibly "spontaneous" activities of men as economic and noneconomic actors and, consequently, also governed the resolution of the basic economic problems. Yet it was stressed previously that such control is itself but a facet of any system of freedom and control only in terms of which both freedom and control acquire substantive meaning. As Commons would have put it, morals and religion-sanctioning-morals are nondeliberative collective action in control of, but also in enhancement and liberation of, individual action.

Certain facets of the nondeliberative forces are of such profound import as to render the term "nondeliberative" a meaningful synonym for "nonlegal." This underscores the importance of these forces for the classical theory of economic policy. Smith and other classicists acknowledged and demonstrated the significance of morals and religion, and the nondeliberative forces in general, by subscribing (albeit often reluctantly, as with Bentham and Stuart Mill) to the at least partial necessity of what has come to be known as the operation of *ignorance* (or deception) and *indirection*. That is to say, the classicists had a place for the practice and force of *ignorance* and *indirection*. The basic idea of the concept and role of *ignorance* is the functional necessity of "social actions and arrangements intended by no one and *unknown* to some (unspecified) proportion of actors," [32] such that greater long-run benefits are to be accrued from not confronting (or not publicizing the confrontation) directly and openly the resolution of some social problem or goal. Therefore *indirection* has to do with the achievement of ends through the nondeliberative institutions and forces, the benefits accruing through focusing attention and activity on "intermediate" attractions or goals conducive to securing the "intended" goal (or goals). The underlying reasoning is complex, but two points may be noted: first, that order to some extent at least may be held to require that there not be much (open) questioning of received arrangements; and, second, that the effectiveness of goal achievement may be adversely affected if the participants are directly knowledgeable of what is at stake. The operation of religion, and the sanctions of religion, has long been recognized as a prime example." [33]

Adam Smith, as Schneider recognizes, is a "prime text" in these matters:

> . . . we may take Adam Smith's famous and familiar observation that the individual "neither intends to promote the public interest, *nor knows* (italics supplied) how much he promotes it" when he pursues his own gain, but that, nevertheless, "by pursuing his own interests he frequently promotes that of the society more effectually then when he really intends to promote it." This significantly represents the individual as ignorant of the circumstance that he promotes public interest, indicates that the pursuit of the individual's interest leads indirectly to public interest, and asserts that this combination of ignorance and indirection is "more effec-

tual" than would be an alternative combination of knowledge of one's objects and effort to attain them. The locus of wisdom, one may say, is neither in the individual nor in any combination of individuals deliberately seeking to attain some large social end such as public welfare; it is in a set of arrangements, well-worn and traditional paths of action, that older organic theorists were inclined to regard as providentially given.[34]

The strength of Smith's adherence to these ideas, fundamental to the operation of the nondeliberative forces, is evidenced throughout his writing.[35] With respect to religion in passages already quoted, Smith maintains that reverence for the general rules of morality is "still further enhanced *by an opinion* . . . that those important rules of morality are the commands and laws of the Deity . . . ," that the prescribed rules "are *to be regarded as* the commands and laws of the Deity," that the general rules have "come thus *to be regarded as* the laws of an all-powerful Being," and that requires that man be "*thoroughly convinced* that all . . . are under the immediate care and protection of that great, benevolent, and all-wise Being. . . ."[36] (Italics added.) Throughout the *Moral Sentiments* it is clear that the process of moralization, through the internalization of the moral sentiments, is a process involving the attention on intermediate ends rather than upon ultimate confrontations; in this way, for example, partiality to one's own interests is a check upon the "spirit of innovation": "It tends to preserve whatever is the established balance among the different orders and societies into which the state is divided; and while it sometimes appears to obstruct some alterations of government which may be fashionable and popular at the time, it contributes in reality to the stability and permanency of the whole system."[37]

And on the dangers of tinkering, of failing to abide by the principles of ignorance and indirection, Smith is no less explicit.[38] With respect to the role of religion as a sanction operating upon these principles, Smith is clear that the obligation "not to hurt or disturb in any respect the happiness of our neighbour, even in those cases where no law can properly protect him" is or should be a matter of a "sacred and religious regard." [39] Since Smith held, with Hume, that the value and esteem of the "artificial" virtues derived from their role intermediately promotive of the higher or natural virtues, including in the former "all the virtues connected with Property," [40] it is no surprise that he refers to property as "sacred and inviolable." [41]

It is especially noteworthy that Smith explicitly utilizes the idea of deception itself in connection with economic activity. "The pleasures of wealth and greatness," he tells us, ". . . strike the imagination as something grand and beautiful and noble, of which the attainment is well worth all the toil and anxiety which we are so apt to bestow upon it. . . . And it is well that nature imposes upon us in this manner. It is this deception which rouses and keeps in continual motion the industry of mankind." [42] As Bonar notes, "It is, too, 'the (world's) bustle and business' that have trained 'the man of real constancy and firmness,' who keeps his self-control and is always mindful of his inward monitor." [43] Moreover, these " 'deceptive pleasures' find their justification or utility in the beauty of the system," [44] i.e., in order. In this and in the other respects noted, the profound significance of the nondeliberative forces is clear: Smith's doctrine is precisely, within the scope of applicability of the nondeliberative forces, "an effort to think of the social order as a genuine organic unity, with principles of structure and functioning which maintain themselves independently of the wills of individuals." [45]

One specific significance of this, and another facet of the operation of the nondeliberative forces, concerns the disciplining of those very "wills of individuals." The operation of any system of social control, by its very nature, "disciplines" the individuals involved by governing the range and content of private choice; by disciplining is then meant the effective defining of opportunities—here economic opportunities—and consciousness, including the acceptability of one's limited range of opportunities. It has to do with, first, fitting the individual into the economy as a satisfactorily performing and satisfied economic actor; and, second, fitting the individual into the thoughtways of the time, the success of the latter being important for the success of the former. It has already been pointed out that Smith understood industry to serve as a controlling force over behavior and traits (text at note 43, *supra*), but Smith also saw that the individual would have to be disciplined *into* that same system of industry. So he contends that "Our admiration of success is founded upon the same principle with our respect for wealth and greatness, and is equally necessary for establishing the distinction of ranks and the order of society." Moreover, "By this admiration of success we are taught to submit more easily to those superiors, whom the course of human affairs may assign to us; to regard with reverence, and sometimes even with a sort of respectful affection, that fortunate violence which we are no longer capable of resisting; . . ." [46] The absolute importance of this reasoning, of the need for discipline not only in industry but also in the industrial system, cannot be discounted. The role of discipline extends to satisfy the requirements of an industrial labor market and wage system, and of the market economy itself. This is related to the need for some group in society to have an interest in, and power to seek and attain, greater material abundance. As de Schweinitz has indicated, ". . . growth during the classical period of the industrial revolution required not so much free choice for all individuals regardless of their position in society as opportunities for the capitalists at the expense of the workers and landlords. . . . The industrial labor force had been formed and was committed to the disciplinary requirements of the economic order. . . ." Thus future economic development "requires that a minority imbued with a growth perspective take it in hand, and regardless of individual preferences, create the institutions favorable to growth. . . . Saving must be forced out of society. . . ." [47] Among other things, then, the moral sentiments, and their sanctions, discipline the economic actors in the process of ordering and integrating them.

Returning to the matter of primary concern, the status of morals and religion as nonlegal forces of social control, the classical economists other than Smith evidence much the same position. Ricardo (note 6, *supra*) acknowledged the "sanctions of religion" as one of the forces directing behavior to those "virtues" promotive of the "general happiness." Ricardo did not write much on morals and religion, but he liked to walk and ride with James Mill and discuss moral philosophy, as well as politics and political economy.[48] In Parliament, seconding a motion (of Joseph Hume) for free discussion of religious opinions, Ricardo acknowledged "the moral interests of society" and the fact and need for the "control of moral impressions." With respect to religion, while it was not the only obligation, "It was, in fact, one which was superadded to the general force of moral impressions—it were a libel upon human nature to say otherwise." [49] In the discussion, Ricardo was primarily interested in showing that "the obligation of religion was not alone considered as the influential test of moral truth, and that a man might be very sceptical upon doctrinal points, and yet very positive in the control of moral impressions distinct from religious faith." He quoted John Tillotson, former Archbishop of Canterbury, to the effect, in part, of recognizing the role of religion in inculcating the obligation to duty and as a source of restraint upon behavior.[50] It is not surprising, therefore, to find in the essay, "On Christianity as An Organ of Political Movement," by Ricardo's disciple de Quincey, a clear recognition of both the moral element in economic issues and of Christianity as part of the total system of social control and social change.[51] Nor is it surprising to find McCulloch concerned over the ties of sympathy and the content of what amounts to the moral sentiments.[52]

We have recently been told that Robert Torrens "expressed great satisfaction at . . . efforts to revive public interest in religious matters." In a letter to the editor of the *Edinburgh Review*, Torrens applauded the "symptoms of a reviving taste" for what he called "the science of mind" and looked forward to "the national intellect . . . (engaging) in profound enquiries and . . . metaphysical studies again prevalent among our educated classes." [53]

But the most extensive attention, next to Smith's, given to morals and religion by classical economists was rendered by Jeremy Bentham and John Stuart Mill (who reflected the views of his father). In the writings of both of these men, the necessity of a system of morals, and perhaps of some "religion" as a sanctioning force, was clearly acknowledged. It is unfortunate that important but essentially tangential or marginal differences between them and other writers on these subjects have obscured the great sophistication they clearly possessed. Although they were critics of the established churches and not sympathetic to components of the extant moral code considered out-of-date,[54] it remains ambiguous as to how much place they would allow to organized religion, a sacerdotal class, theological creeds, and belief in a Supreme Being. Both were, after all, exponents of rational or humanist religion. In any event, it remains true that in the their respective total systems the nonlegal forces have an important place,[55] and that they appreciated that freedom was freedom only within the context of the larger pattern of freedom and control.

It is necessary to understand that Bentham's felicific calculus, the pleasure-pain principle, considered only in respect to morals or ethics, was not a complete system. Its significance lies not as a self-contained ethical system but rather as a manifestation of an underlying quest for reasoned knowledge as the basis of action, both private and public, with the calculations of pleasure and pain, as he put it, serving to force reasoned analysis of alternatives, i.e., reasoned choice. The felicific calculus is thus a manifestation of the transition from nondeliberative to deliberative collective and private decision-making.[56] The significant point for present purposes is the place nevertheless left for the nondeliberative forces. To Bentham, the *content* of pleasure and pain would be given or conditioned by, among other things, the operation of the system of morals and, perhaps, religion. Social interaction, and perforce internalized controls (i.e., customary morals), is the relevant force, not the autonomous individual, however relevant the latter is in other respects and for other problems.

In the third chapter of his *Introduction to the Principles of Morals and Legislation*,[57] having discussed in the preceding chapters "the principle of utility" and "principles adverse to that of utility," Bentham examines "the four sanctions or sources of pain and pleasure," namely, the physical, political, moral and religious, which are the "sources from which pleasure and pain are in use to flow." [58] Considering the origin of the word "sanction," Bentham relates that "Sanctio, in Latin was used to signify the act of binding, and, by a common grammatical transition, any thing which serves to bind a man: to wit, to the observance of such or such a mode of conduct," (italics deleted) and that "among the Romans, with a view to inculcate into the people a persuasion that such or such a mode of conduct would be rendered obligatory upon a man by the force of what I call the religious sanction. . . ." [59] "A Sanction then," says Bentham, "is a source of obligatory powers or *motives:* That is, of *pains* and *pleasures;* which according as they are connected with such or such modes of conduct, operate, and are indeed the only things which can operate, as *motives.*" [60] All of the four sanctions "can be experienced in the present life," and "from each of these sources may flow all the pleasures or pains of which, in the course of the present life, human nature is susceptible. With regard to . . . any one of those sanctions, (they) differ not ultimately in kind from those which belong to any one of the other three: the only difference there is among them lies in the circumstances that accompany their production." [61] Thus the sanctions (for present purposes, the nonlegal vis-a-vis the legal) have a common basis in their functioning as forces of social control notwithstanding the different "circumstances that accompany their production," i.e., their genesis. Bentham has a place for morals, then, as well as the other sanctions,[62] and it is particularly instructive in this regard that he defines *ethics* in terms generic to social control analysis: "Ethics at large may be defined, the art of directing men's actions to the production of the greatest possible quantity of happiness, on the part of those whose interest is in view." [63]

Bentham's utilitarianism, placed in proper perspective, must have an appropriate place for morals as an instrument of social control. Davidson quite correctly holds that, "Bentham insists that, in a civilized community, conduct is moulded for us in large measure by convention and society, and that social rules are generated and laws enacted embodying results of actions as they have been crystallized by centuries of experience, so that individual deliberate calculation is rather the exception than the rule." [64] Clearly, this statement applies equally to Smith as to Bentham. And further note Leslie Stephen, with respect to Bentham's utilitarianism: " 'The dictates of utility,' as he (Bentham) observes, are simply the 'dictates of the most extensive and enlightened (that is, *well advised*) benevolence.' " [65]

Bentham's moral sanction, although his language is ambiguous,[66] appears to be essentially that of Smith's moral sentiments, that is, through social interaction, or experience. Whereas his specific definition of the religious sanction is ambiguous with respect to the theology involved,[67] the role of religion as a sanction, i.e., as an instrument of social control, is clear. Asked Bentham, ". . . what place is left for *religion?*" and his answer was that religion could serve for social-control purposes in a manner beyond the power of the state:

> But whether or no a man has done the act which renders him an object meet for punishment or reward, the eyes of those, whosoever they be, to whom the management of these engines is entrusted cannot always see, nor, where it is punishment that is to be administered, can their hands be always sure to reach him. To supply these deficiencies in point of power, it is thought necessary, or at least *useful* (without which the *truth* of the doctrine would be nothing to the purpose), to inculcate into the minds of the people the belief of the existence of a power applicable to the same purposes, and not liable to the same deficiencies: the power of a supreme invisible being, to whom a disposition of contributing to the same ends to which the several institutions already mentioned are calculated to contribute, must for this purpose be ascribed. It is of course expected that this power will, at one time or other, be employed in the promoting of those ends: and to keep up and strengthen this expectation among men, is spoken of as being the employment of a kind of allegorical personage, feigned, as before, for convenience of discourse, and styled *religion*. To diminish, then, or misapply the influence of religion, is *pro tanto* to diminish or misapply what power the state has of combating with effect any of the before-enumerated kinds of offences: that is, all kinds of offences whatsoever. Acts that appear to have this tendency may be styled *offences against religion.*[68]

Indeed, Bentham considered "the ministers of religion . . . as charged with the maintenance of one of the sanctions of morality (the religious sanction). . . . They are a body of inspectors and teachers of morals, who form, so to speak, the advanced guard of the law; who possess no power over crime, but who combat with the vices out of which crimes spring; and who render the exercise of authority more rare, by maintaining good conduct and subordination." [69] Bentham has at least a clear place for "moralists" and moral leaders.[70]

In an important chapter of the *Morals and Legislation* (chapter 6, "Of Circumstances Influencing Sensibility"), which strongly shows his position affirming the circumstantial or social character of the content of the moral sentiments,[71] Bentham directly discusses the effect of varying religious beliefs (i.e., of varying operation of the religious sanction) upon the resolution of the basic economic problems:

> The ways in which a religion may lessen a man's means, or augment his wants, are various. Sometimes it will prevent him from making a profit of his money: sometimes from setting his hand to labour. Sometimes it will oblige him to buy dearer food instead of cheaper: sometimes to purchase useless labour: sometimes to pay men for not labouring: sometimes to purchase trinkets, on which imagination alone has set a value: sometimes to purchase exemptions from punishment, or titles to felicity in the world to come.[72]

Moreover, Stark has disclosed an instance in which Bentham was even prescriptive in regard to the content of religious preaching to be utilized for purposes of economic policy.[73]

The position of Bentham, however, is made ambiguous by consideration of his antireligious works, even allowing for their polemic character. In these writings, taken together, Bentham was severely critical of organized religion, its theological creed and sacerdotal class. The polemic nature of these works, consequent to Bentham's emotional involvement in the issues of the day, is important, however much it renders interpretation difficult. It is instructive, none the less, that

Bentham does temper his often outspoken criticism with a recognition of religion as a promulgating and sanctioning instrument of social control.

In his *Church-of-Englandism*,[74] Bentham directs his odium against the catechism of the church [75] and the exclusionary system of education.[76] Transcending that, however, is criticism directed against a particular church and its practices in a particular time and place: against an absolutist theological system whose catechism was personally unpalatable and dehumanizing, and which was intentionally employed (however unobtrusively) to create humble docility, and to prostrate the understanding and will of the great mass of men.[77] In this respect, his position is in general that of the Cartesian rationalist and the individualist anti-authoritarian.[78] In addition, Bentham is preoccupied with criticism of the closed, highly structured, Establishment-oriented sociopolitical system of his day.[79] There is thus criticism of the aristocratism of the ruling few, and the accompanying denigration of the social and intellectual status of the masses, notably the poor. There is also criticism of philosophical absolutism facilitated by Caesaropapist tendencies and of the reign of theological domination of the quest for knowledge.[80] Bentham takes his position against a temporal-power oriented Church of England, which he sees as corrupt and corrupting, engaged in the sanctification of corruption,[81] a part of the Establishment preoccupied with the maintenance of its own power position.

On the other hand, Bentham tempers his analysis, such as it is, by occasional recognition of the social control function of religion in connection with criticism directed not against such function but against absolutist and totalitarian misuse thereof, and the Church view of the needs of order and continuity,[82] and by applause directed to the Church of Scotland, which he considers a more effective instrument of social control because it is more liberal.[83]

Bentham's *Influence of Natural Religion* [84] has as its object,

" . . . to ascertain, whether the belief of posthumous pains and pleasures, then to be administered by an omnipotent Being, is useful to mankind—that is, productive of happiness or misery in the present life." [85] His conclusions are recapitulated by Bentham as follows:

> 1. That in the absence of any authorised directive rule, the class of actions which our best founded inference would suggest as entitling the performer to post-obituary reward, is one not merely useless, but strikingly detrimental, to mankind in the present life; while the class conceived as meriting future punishment, is one always innocuous, often beneficial, to our fellow creatures on earth. 2. That from the character and properties of posthumous inducements, they infallibly become impotent for the purpose of resisting any temptation whatever, and efficient only in the production of needless and unprofitable misery. 3. That the influence exercised by these inducements is, in most cases, really derived from the popular sanction, which they are enabled to bias and enlist in their favour.

"If these conclusions are correct," he goes on, "I think it cannot be denied, that the influence possessed by natural religion over human conduct is, with reference to the present life, injurious to an extent incalculably greater than it is beneficial." Although there may be what amounts to "casual and peculiar" benefits produced in "the minds of some few believers," they "form an exception to the larger body"; rather, "the inquiry has demonstrated that the agency of superhuman motives must in the larger aggregate of instances, produce effects decidedly pernicious to earthly happiness." [86]

This work is preoccupied with the theological creed as such, with the efficacy of belief in a Supreme Being, and with the perverse effect of certain moral rules in this world.[87] On the other hand, the analysis, more systematic than in the preceding work, also acknowledges the role of religion as the promulgator and sanctioner of moral rules. Bentham recognizes the necessity of moral rules and the role of the moral sentiments.[88] Indeed, his analysis with respect to the moral sentiments is once again the same as that of Smith. Bentham emphasizes experience as the basis of moral rules, and the operation of approbation and disapprobation (or enjoyment and discomfort) as the mode of their development.[89] More significant is an analysis in which Bentham discusses the context in which religion has a perverse effect and, further, indicates the substance of its "only legitimate and valuable function." According to Bentham, every community must "ensure on the part of every individual a preference of actions favourable to the happiness of the community," [90]—a postulate consonant with the interpretation followed by Robbins, Taylor, and the present author with respect to the forces of social control serving to create harmony or happy mutuality of interests. The problem, of course, is to determine that which benefits vis-a-vis that which injures. In any event, one of the injuries is hate, and Bentham believed that, in the work, "religion has been shown to create a number of factitious antipathies," with the alleged consequence that, "Religion, therefore, attaches the hatred of mankind to actions not really injurious to them, and thus seduces it from its only legitimate and valuable function, that of deterring individuals from injurious conduct." [91] So far as religion serving as an instrument of social control is concerned, then, the primary issue would appear to be the *substance* of what religion was to sanction, prescribe and proscribe. It is clear that religion would serve as one of the forces of social control to channel, direct, and withdraw behavior.

Much the same position is developed in Bentham's *Not Paul, But Jesus*,[92] the general theme of which is that Paul was not an apostle, and that Paul's theological doctrines run counter to those of Jesus.[93] It would appear that Bentham's criticism is directed against Paulist churches and theological doctrine as then practiced. He finds, however, that the opposition to the religion of Jesus is the result of Paul's doctrines,[94] and is critical of the dissensions caused thereby and of the mischiefs produced by those dissensions.[95] None the less, Bentham differentiates between theological doctrines and the "benevolent system of morals," whose "additional extent," he argues, may be promoted by clearing the religion of Jesus of the incumbrance of Paul's doctrines.[96]

Like Smith, then, Bentham acknowledged the usefulness and operation of religion as an instrument of social control, however ambiguous the place of religion in his ideal system. As Viner has put it, "Bentham did not completely bridge the gulf between private interests and the general interest, but neither did he deny the existence of such a gulf, and he did propose two ways, education and government, by which the gulf could be somewhat narrowed—with religion, though grudgingly, accepted as a useful part of education in so far as it educates for virtue." [97] Coupled with this place given (however reluctantly) to the religious sanction, was denigration of institutionalized religion, the sacerdotal class, theological creed and belief in a Supreme Being; an opposition to totalitarian religion; [98] an acknowledgement of the "mischief" of religion; [99] and criticism based on the fallacy of appeal to authority; [100] but also criticism of governmental interference with religion.[101] Morals and religion had their place, but, as with classicism as a whole, that place was in an essentially pluralist society.

John Stuart Mill provides the most extensive analysis of the functioning of religion in society of all of the classicists, many facets and ramifications of which are beyond the scope of this study. Mill's various writings demonstrate a profound appreciation of the subtleties of balancing freedom and control, and his liberalist antagonism to concentrated power, as in the form

of organized religion, does not detract therefrom: his individualism and liberalism did not obscure from him the necessities of
social control. This, it is suggested, is true, whatever one thinks
of his personal (and inherited) liberal humanism as a partial
solution to the problems of social control. One may disagree
with his solution, but he *knew* the problem and what was
involved. Critical analysis of his writings (as, for example,
The Spirit of the Age) clearly evidences that the younger
Mill's idealism was coupled with a realism far more sophisticated than possessed by realists of lesser stature.

Mill's essay, "On Liberty," is perhaps the most moving and
eloquent plea ever composed promotive of meaningful human
and individual freedom. Yet his presentation of the grand
theme of liberty is not naïve, for he carefully indicates that
the liberty that he is endeavoring to promote is not only
liberty *versus* the state but liberty *within* the state (and liberty
versus yet within society including the nonlegal forces of social
control). Thus Mill declares:

> Protection, therefore, against the tyranny of the magistrate
> is not enough: there needs protection also against the tyranny
> of the prevailing opinion and feeling; against the tendency
> of society to impose, by other means than civil penalties,
> its own idea and practices as rules of conduct on those who
> dissent from them; to fetter the development, and, if possible
> prevent the formation, of any individuality not in harmony
> with its ways, and compels all characters to fashion them-
> selves upon the model of its own. There is a limit to the legiti-
> mate interference of collective opinion with individual inde-
> pendence; and to find that limit, and maintain it against
> encroachment, is as indispensable to a good condition of
> human affairs, as protection against political despotism.
>
> But though this proposition is not likely to be contested
> in general terms, the practical question, where to place the
> limit—how to make the fitting adjustment between individual
> independence and social control—is a subject on which nearly

everything remains to be done. All that makes existence valuable to anyone, depends on the enforcement of restraints upon the actions of other people. Some rules of conduct, therefore, must be imposed, by law in the first place, and by opinion on many things which are not fit subjects for the operation of law. What these rules should be is the principal question in human affairs. . . . [102]

Stuart Mill was an avowed critic of nonrational supernatural religion; but he was also cognizant of the necessity of moral controls. While he discounts the role of religion in connection therewith [103] and is critical of the dehumanizing and tyrannical tendencies of orthodox religion, his humanist religion (advocated as a more humane and progressive mode of control) is a sanctioning instrument none the less. Throughout his writings on the subject, Mill is in favor of extensive liberty for the cultivated minds or "best informed," [104] within some social control of course, but is opposed to debilitating and oppressive controls over the rest of mankind precluding their individual development. His position on this is correlated with his defense of power-diffused pluralistic capitalism or "competition" against the Socialists' "declamations against competition." [105]

On the necessity and operation of morals as an instrument of social control Mill writes in the "Utility of Religion":

> Undoubtedly mankind would be in a deplorable state if no principles or precepts of justice, veracity, beneficence, were taught publicly or privately, and if these virtues were not encouraged, and the opposite vices repressed, by the praise and blame, the favourable and unfavourable sentiments, of mankind. . . . the influence in human affairs which belongs to any generally accepted system of rules for the guidance and government of human life. [106]

Over the immense majority of human beings, the general concurrence of mankind, in any matter of opinion, is all

powerful. Whatever is thus certified to them, they believe
with a fulness of assurance which they do not accord even to
the evidence of their senses when the general opinion of mankind stands in opposition to it. When, therefore, any rule
of life and duty, whether grounded or not on religion, has
conspicuously received the general assent, it obtains a hold
on the belief of every individual, stronger than it would have
even if he had arrived at it by the inherent force of his own
understanding.[107]

  . . . it is reasonable to think that any system of social
duty which mankind might adopt, even though divorced from
religion, would have the same advantage of being inculcated
from childhood, and would have it hereafter much more perfectly than any doctrine has it at present, society being far
more disposed than formerly to take pains for the moral tui-
tion of those numerous classes whose education it has hitherto
left very much to chance. Now it is especially characteristic
of the impressions of early education, that they possess what
it is so much more difficult for later convictions to obtain—
command over the feelings. . . . [and] which operate[s]
through men's involuntary beliefs, feelings and desires. . . .[108]

The inculcation of morals as a constraint upon behavior is
thus clearly acknowledged.

With respect to religion as one source of such inculcation,
Mill would prefer a nonsupernatural religion, but the sanctioning also clearly needs to be performed, and there are other
roles as well. Despite the fact that there is much historical
truth supporting "these nobler spirits [who] generally assert
the necessity of religion, as a teacher, if not as an enforcer, of
social morality . . . that religion alone can teach us what morality is; . . . that, only when a morality is understood to come
from the Gods, do men in general adopt it, rally round it, and
lend their human sanctions for its enforcement," [109] Mill
contends that moral truths are "strong enough in their own
evidence," [110] and that: "The essence of religion is the strong

51

and earnest direction of the emotions and desires towards an ideal object, recognized as of the highest excellence, and as rightfully paramount over all selfish objects of desire. This condition is fulfilled by the Religion of Humanity in as eminent a degree, and in as high a sense, as by the supernatural religions even in their best manifestations, and far more so than in any of their others." [111]

It is significant, then, that the "direction" has to be done, whatever the character of the religion or ethical system serving the role. Mill would have the "moral influences" "cultivate the unselfish feelings," [112] and "The deeply rooted conception which every individual even now has of himself as a social being, [which] tends to make him feel it one of his natural wants that there should be harmony between his feelings and aims and those of his fellow creatures. . . . This conviction is the ultimate sanction of the greatest happiness morality." [113] Indeed, Mill's defense of utilitarianism acknowledges the necessity of a moral system and the operation of utilitarianism as a moral system.[114]

It would be misleading, however, not to note that Mill was not so absolute about the role of supernaturalism as he sometimes seems: the realist does win out over the idealist, so far as the theory of social control is concerned. Wrote Mill: "So long as human life is insufficient to satisfy human aspirations, so long there will be a craving for higher things, which finds its most obvious satisfaction in religion. So long as earthly life is full of sufferings, so long there will be need of consolations, which the hope of heaven affords to the selfish, the love of God to the tender and grateful." [115] Writing of Mill's Religion of Humanity, Stephen maintains, "That religion, 'with or without supernatural sanctions,' will be the religion of the future; but it will be strengthened by the feeling that we are 'helping God' and supplying 'co-operation' which 'he, not being omnipotent, really needs.' " [116] The ideas of John Stuart

Mill were basically consonant with the other classicists concerning the role of *order* in human affairs (to the sophistication of his ideas on this *The Spirit of the Age* is ample testimony) and the role of morals, and, at the very least, a liberal humanist religion as a social cement and controlling and socializing instrument. And his personal and intellectual antipathy to deception did not preclude a place for it in his theory of social control.

In the same manner the later classicists exhibited a position equivalent to that of Smith as to the operation of ignorance and indirection, as well as discipline. Thus Ricardo, who adhered to the necessity of the "sanctions of religion," also contended that it was "essential . . . to the cause of good government, that the rights of property should be held sacred. . . ." [117] And the same Ricardo who shared Dr. Tillotson's concern over the passive and nondeliberate but necessary operation of the restraints of religion also most certainly sympathized (in principle at least) with his friend Trower, against the background of London riots opposing a proposed Corn Law, who, (wrote Trower), " . . . if I were to consider this question with the eye of a *moralist*, rather than that of a *statesman*, I should strenuously recommend that employment of the public industry which leads to the peaceful pursuits of agriculture, in which

> With silent course that *no loud storms* annoy
> Glides the smooth current of domestic joy." [118]

Nor was Ricardo alone among the post-Smithian classicists who so held: Malthus thus wrote that: ". . . it is so absolutely necessary for the general interests of society to consider private property as sacred. . . ." [119] and Bentham, that, ". . . a state can never become rich but by an inviolable respect for property." [120]

One of the most interesting aspects of the classical approach to nonlegal control relates to what amounts to their partial substitution of ideas-in-general (cosmology or ideology) for what Smith included in the moral sentiments. The role as nondeliberative constraint remains the same, and reflects the operation of the principles of ignorance and indirection through the pervasive influence of an Hayekian collective wisdom. In this the classicists certainly concurred with de Tocqueville, who wrote that:

> . . . men will never cease to entertain some opinions on trust and without discussion. . . .
>
> But obviously without such common belief no society can prosper; say, rather, no society can exist; for without ideas held in common there is no common action, and without common action there may still be men, but there is no social body. In order that society should exist, and, *a fortiori*, that a society should prosper, it is necessary that the minds of all the citizens should be rallied and held together by certain predominant ideas; and this cannot be the case unless each of them sometimes draws his opinions from the common source and consents to accept certain matters of belief already formed.
>
> . . . he is reduced to take on trust a host of facts and opinions which he has not had either the time or the power to verify for himself, but which men of greater ability have found out, or which the crowd adopts. . . .
>
> A principle of authority must then always occur, under all circumstances, in some part or other of the moral and intellectual world. Its place is variable, but a place it necessarily has. The independence of individual minds may be greater or it may be less; it cannot be unbounded. Thus the question is, not to know whether any intellectual authority exists in an age of democracy, but simply where it resides and by what standard it is to be measured. [121]

The classicists' reliance upon the nondeliberative forces indicates their general adherence to these ideas; as Hume put it, "Though men be much governed by interest, yet even interest itself, and all human affairs, are entirely governed by *opinion.*" [122] S. G. Checkland thus wrote, "As Malthus himself knew, it is often more important and more productive of lasting effects to condition minds than to instil in them particular ideas." [123] But the most extensive analysis of this subject by a classical economist is to be found in Stuart Mill's *The Spirit of the Age*, wherein he substantively concurs with de Tocqueville. The importance of the essay for present purposes and for understanding Mill warrants quotation at length. The "spirit of an age," says Mill,

> . . . is deeply important: for, whatever we may think or affect to think of the present age, we cannot get out of it; we must suffer with its sufferings, and enjoy with its enjoyments; we must share in its lot, and, to be either useful or at ease, we must even partake of its character. . . . the multitude (by which I mean the majority of all ranks) have the ideas of their own age, and no others. . . .
>
> . . . The proofs of these truths may be brought down to the level of even the uninformed multitude, with the most complete success. But, when all is done, there still remains something which they must always and inevitably take upon trust: and this is, that the arguments really *are* as conclusive as they appear; that there exist no considerations relevant to the subject which have been kept back from them; that every objection which can suggest itself has been duly examined by competent judges, and found immaterial.
>
> In these circumstances the people, although they may at times be unhappy and consequently discontented, habitually acquiesce in the laws and institutions which they live under, and seek for relief through those institutions and not in defiance of them. Individual ambition struggles to ascend by no other paths than those which the law [and, we should add, institutions, particularly of the nondeliberative sort] recognizes and allows.
>
> In endeavouring to give an intelligible notion of what I

have termed the *natural* state of society, in respect of moral influence—namely, that state in which the opinions and feelings of the people are, with their voluntary acquiescence, formed *for* them, by the most cultivated minds which the intelligence and morality of the times call into existence. . . .

. . . howsoever defective the morality which (the early church) taught, they had at least a mission for curbing the unruly passions of mankind, and teaching them to set a value upon a distant end, paramount to immediate temptations, and to prize gratification consisting of mental feelings above bodily sensation. . . .[124]

Mill's analysis of the *natural* and *transitional* states of society remains a most brilliant analysis in the theory of social change, in effect a theory of the conditions of *order* or continuity, (vis-a-vis change) and the role of the nondeliberative forces in connection therewith, relying upon the principles of ignorance and indirection through the operation of "the spirit of the age." And, as was seen above in connection with "On Liberty," Mill is demonstrating that the conditions of *order* also specify the character and conditions of the *freedom* that exists co-ordinately. As with de Tocqueville, to whom "salutary restraint" necessarily complemented a free society,[125] Stuart Mill argued that continuity and order required that the multitude adhere to the cosmology of the time as an indirect instrument of social control,[126] but that within its constraints free minds could pursue with a meaningful measure of independence. Although "It is, therefore, one of the necessary conditions of humanity, that the majority must either have wrong opinions, or no fixed opinions, or must place the degree of reliance warranted by reason, in the authority of those who have made moral and social philosophy their peculiar study," still, "It is right that every man should attempt to understand his interest and his duty. It is right that he should follow his reason as far as his reason will carry him, and cultivate the faculty as highly as possible." [127]

On the operation of discipline the views of the classicists were also essentially the same as those of Smith, as suggested, for example, by the letter of Trower to Ricardo, quoted previously. Ricardo himself would have impressed "on the poor the value of independence, by teaching them that they must look not to systematic or casual charity, but to their own exertions for support, that prudence and forethought are neither unnecessary nor unprofitable virtues. . . ." [128] McCulloch also favored inculcating "the spirit of emulation, industry, and invention," and argued that discipline was necessary to induce acquiescence in the industrial order, and to assure progress within the constraints of scarcity and the given industrial order. Wrote McCulloch, appreciative of the need to make the manufacturing population "in general orderly, and disposed to respect and support the right of property and the established institutions of the country,"

> Something, perhaps, may be done to strengthen the existing institutions of the country, by improving the education of the poor, and showing them how closely their interests are identified with those of their employers, and with the preservation of tranquillity and good order.
>
> By raising the intelligence of the poor, and enabling them the better to appreciate the worthlessness of the nostrums on which they are so often called to depend, and to estimate the more remote, as well as the immediate consequences of their actions, it could hardly fail to contribute materially to their advantage.

And he quotes Bentham:

> "To enjoy immediately—to enjoy without labour, is the natural inclination of every man. This inclination must be restrained; for its obvious tendency is to arm all those who have nothing against those who have something. The law which restrains this inclination, and which secures to the humblest individual the quiet enjoyment of the fruits of his

industry, is the most splendid achievement of legislative wisdom—the noblest triumph of which humanity has to boast." [129]

Indeed, so far as the classicists were concerned, the poor-law
controversy turned on the interference thereby with the disciplining forces of the market through poverty and industrial
competition.[130] Bentham's criticism precisely turned on the
matter of the disciplining forces of the market:

> The law which offers to poverty an assistance independent
> of industry, is, so to speak, a law against industry itself; or at
> least, against frugality. The motive to labour and economy is
> the pressure of present, and the fear of future, want: the law
> which takes away this pressure, and this fear, must be an
> encouragement to idleness and dissipation. This is the re-
> proach which is reasonably brought against the greater num-
> ber of establishments created for the poor.[131]

Bentham considered idleness and prodigality to be "offenses
against the national wealth," and would have relied upon the
discipline of market forces, or as he called it, "the gentle
motive of reward," to promote material well-being.[132] So also
with Stuart Mill, who wrote in his "Chapters on Socialism,"
that

> In the case of most men the only inducement which has
> been found sufficiently constant and unflagging to overcome
> the everpresent influence of indolence and love of ease, and
> induce men to apply themselves unrelaxingly to work for the
> most part in itself dull and unexciting, is the prospect of
> bettering their own economic condition and that of their
> family; and the closer the connection of every increase of
> exertion with a corresponding increase of its fruits, the more
> powerful is this motive. To suppose the contrary would be to
> imply that with men as they now are, duty and honour are
> more powerful principles of action than personal interest, not
> solely as to special acts and forbearances respecting which
> those sentiments have been exceptionally cultivated, but in

the regulation of their whole lives; which no one, I suppose, will affirm.[133]

Indeed, "Education, habit, and the cultivation of the sentiments, will make a common man dig or weave for his country, as readily as fight for his country." [134] The operation of discipline, which de Schweinitz has stressed as perhaps a *sine qua non* of economic development, was thus recognized by the classical economists as a group, and constituted one facet of the operation of the nondeliberative forces functioning as part of the system of social control conditioning the grand pattern of freedom and control.

Custom

The classicists differentiated between morals and custom. They generally referred to "morals" in the context of discussions of social control, wherein individuals were seen as bound together, integrated and channeled; and "custom" in contexts having to do with the import and impact of the nondeliberative forces (e.g., Smith's general rules) on particular usages affecting market forces of demand and supply. Custom would govern the structure of economic organization, and condition the substance of the resolution of the basic economic problems through structuring the economic decision-making process and through influencing or conditioning the content of behavior. In particular, customs operated on tastes, expectations, and capacities to participate as an economic actor. In their formal analysis such factors were ruled out by utilizing the logic of *ceteris paribus*. In his well-known chapter, "Of Competition and Custom," Stuart Mill indicated the importance of this consideration when he wrote that "only through the principle of competition has political economy any pretension to the character of a science." [135] The methodology of the Ricardian economic analysis has been erroneously criticized as if Ricardo, *et al*, were not aware of broader considerations, and other determining causes, than were included in the model.

In *The Theory of Moral Sentiments* Smith devoted a short but lucid discussion to the influence of custom and fashion (which is "a particular species" [136] of custom). In the first of two chapters comprising Part V, Smith shows the influence of custom and fashion upon the sense of what he calls "beauty and deformity" and therefore upon what present-day economists would call *taste*. It is thus of the greatest significance for the present study that Smith considers the operation of custom as extending to the field of consumption, or demand: his examples include dress, furniture, and decoration. It is clear from these pages that Smith's analysis therein may be reduced to considering custom as a governing influence upon relative demand schedules. (The scarcity of diamonds exists, after all, because of their *customary* status whatever their value-in-use.) [137]

In the second chapter of Part V of *Moral Sentiments*, Smith discusses the influence of custom and fashion upon the moral sentiments as they relate to conduct. Smith's analysis here is not entirely clear (largely due to the ambiguity of his differentiation between morals and custom), but there is no question that custom governs the usages that are so much the stuff of life. Wrote Smith:

> But though the influence of custom and fashion upon moral sentiments, is not altogether so great, it is however perfectly similar to what it is every where else. When custom and fashion coincide with the natural principles of right and wrong, they heighten the delicacy of our sentiments, and in-

crease our abhorrence for every thing which approaches to evil.

All these effects of custom and fashion, however, upon the moral sentiments of mankind, are inconsiderable, in comparison of those which they give occasion to in some other cases; and it is not concerning the general style of character and behaviour, that those principles produce the greatest perversion or judgment, but concerning the propriety or impropriety of particular usages.

It is not therefore in the general style of conduct or behaviour that custom authorises the widest departure from what is the natural propriety of action. With regard to particular usages, its influence is often much more destructive of good morals, and it is capable of establishing, as lawful and blameless, particular actions, which shock the very plainest principles of right and wrong.[138]

Indeed, what people ". . . have been familiarized with . . . from their infancy, custom has rendered . . . habitual to them, and they are very apt to regard it as, what is called, the way of the world . . ." [139] (In another context, Smith argues that, "It is absurd to preserve in people a regard for their old customs, when the causes of them are removed.")[140] Looked at another way, it is not surprising for Smith to have discussed "the Influence of Commerce on Manners," [141] or, given the relativity of custom acknowledged in the *Moral Sentiments*, for him to write: "The difference between the most dissimilar characters, between a philosopher and a common street porter, for example, seems to arise not so much from nature, as from habit, custom, and education." [142]

In Ricardo's *The Principles of Political Economy and Taxation*, the chapter on rent is a model of brilliant theorizing, as is the work as a whole, with scarce reference to institutional and other data. But despite the theoretical character of the *Principles*, its author is not really justifiably open to the charge that *he* neglected institutional data. His chosen task in the *Principles* was simply different from that of, say, Richard Jones in his well-known complementary work. Elsewhere Ricardo gives ample evidence in his written works to support the claim that he was a master realist, whatever the structure and compass of his theory.

Thus Ricardo, in a letter to Trower, acknowledges that the pricing of the rent of land and the distribution of the proceeds is, in part, to be attributed to the particular institutions of time and place.[143] But perhaps the general principle applicable to Ricardo that is relevant here was in the form of a question by Wesley Mitchell: "And whenever there is occasion to go back of prices, are not wants standardized and made dependable for business purposes by 'habits and custom'?"[144] That there is such a role for custom and habit in the Ricardian (and classical) theory of economic policy is further supported by the recognition that the level of wages in the Ricardian system depended on several factors, one of which clearly was custom and habit. Indeed, Ricardo states in his *Principles* that, "It is not to be understood that the natural price of labour, . . . is absolutely fixed and constant. It varies at different times in the same country, and very materially differs in different countries. It essentially depends on the habits and customs of the people."[145]

Irma Adelman concludes that, "Ricardo's natural wage rate is therefore a function of the socio-cultural environment and of the marginal productivity of land. In fact, the variations of customs and agricultural productivity with time are responsible for the time-dependent behavior of the natural wage rate." Discussing further the "influence of the socio-cultural environment" in the Ricardian system, she writes: "By affecting the economy's subjective minimal standards of living, changes in outlook and in institutions can modify the rates of growth of the labor force, of investment, and therefore of output, and the nature of the stationary state of the economy."[146]

Moreover, Ricardo's awareness of the role of custom as a factor in the economic decision-making process is well illustrated by the following excerpt from another letter to Trower: "Great evils however result from the idea which the Poor Laws inculcate that the poor have a *right* to relief." [147] And in a letter to McCulloch, Ricardo demonstrated the realism with which he interpreted or applied his own basic theory: "You think otherwise because you are of opinion that capital will be constantly drawn away from this country whilst the corn laws are in force. I acknowledge the tendency of capital to flow from us, but I think you very much overrate it. I have always said that the desire to stay in our own country is a great obstacle to be overcome." [148]

There can be no question that custom and habit (or differential institutions) had a place and an important place in the Ricardian theory of economic policy: custom and habit dictated much of the substance of resource allocation and income distribution, i.e., governed the operation of market forces, and thus comprised part of the structure of the economic decision-making process.

The foregoing interpretation is further supported by reference to Malthus and McCulloch. Both acknowledge the circumstantial character of the determination and distribution of rent,[149] and both consider that wages depend in part upon custom and habit. McCulloch, after quoting Smith to the same effect, contends that the "natural or necessary rate of wages" depends "essentially on the physical circumstances under which every people is placed, and on custom and habit." [150] It is also relevant to note that it is largely through the reconstruction of custom (i.e., the preventive checks) that the possible adverse consequences of the Malthusian law of population are to be overcome. It can be said that the classicists would all have concurred in the statement that beneficial changes in customs, together with improvement of the "moral and intellectual condition of mankind," [151] would have operated to improve the economic and social conditions of both higher and lower orders of humanity.

Passing to Bentham, it is clear that just as the operation of the greatest happiness principle was conditioned on at least the moral and perhaps also the religious sanctions, so also was the content of the solutions to the problems of man achieved by using the felicific calculus also dependent upon custom and its role in providing continuity. Bentham was aware of the mantle of custom and the fixity of authority bestowed by habit, just as he recognized that the accumulation of property required the appropriate customs (and laws) to produce security.[152] Moreover, his emphasis on gradual change (characteristic of all the classicists, including Stuart Mill) related in part to his cognizance of the importance of custom.[153] As a matter of general principle, Bentham and the other classicists emphasized that the structure of the decision-making process that was the market economy required reliance upon custom, as Mitchell stated in the case of Ricardo. Writing of the principle of utility, Lord Robbins has contended:

> It was perfectly consistent with this principle to attach, as indeed there was attached, the greatest value to stable institutions and general rules of conduct. The greatest happiness was not the greatest happiness at the moment, but the greatest happiness over time; and, on the basis of this principle, the most powerful arguments could be deployed in favour of security of expectation and consistency in behaviour, which in turn afforded strong grounds for more or less settled codes of law and morals. On the utilitarian outlook, social arrangements were not provisional in the sense that they were liable to day-to-day change and upset; they were provisional only in the sense that they were all liable to the ultimate test of their ability to promote human happiness.[154]

Perhaps the most intense sentiment on the role of custom was held by John Stuart Mill. First, Mill is at one with the other classicists in holding that custom is important in determining the structure of property rights, and thereby the structure of private participation in the economy.[155] Second, Mill contended that, unlike the production of wealth, the distribution of wealth is a matter of institutions. In his chapter on property, Mill wrote: "The distribution of wealth, therefore, depends on the laws and customs of society. The rules by which it is determined are what the opinions and feelings of the ruling portion of the community make them, and are very different in different ages and countries; and might be still more different, if mankind so chose." [156]

This position is reflected in his consideration of rent, which he held to be regulated by custom.[157] Third, and most general, for his analysis extends in effect to both income distribution and resource allocation, Mill contends that custom is coordinate with competition (by which he meant the operation of market forces) in governing the resolution of the basic economic problems. In his chapter "Of Competition and Custom," Mill accepts the practice by political economists of assuming competition as the field of their concern: "The political economist justly deems this his proper business: and as an abstract or hypothetical science, political economy cannot be required to do, and indeed cannot do, anything more." "But," he goes on to say, "it would be a great misconception of the actual course of human affairs, to suppose that competition exercises in fact this unlimited sway." This is because there are cases "in which the result is not determined by competition, but by custom or usage." In these cases, competition "rather acts, when it acts at all, as an occasional disturbing influence; the habitual regulator is custom, modified from time to time by notions existing in the minds of purchasers and sellers of some kind of equity or justice." Thus, "Where competition, though free to exist, does not exist, or where it exists, but has its natural consequences overruled by any other agency, the conclusions will fail more or less of being applicable," [158] unless the operation of custom and other influences is brought into account. The matter of methodology is, as indicated above, not presently important. What is decisive is the recognition, for purposes of the classical theory of economic policy, that custom is one of the forces comprising the decision-making structure of the market economy and governing the play of market forces.

EDUCATION

To the classical economists, the provision of education was one of the crucial functions of society, whether instruction be handled privately or institutionally. As a matter of fact, the classicists' understanding of the importance of education was responsible for their unanimous holding that the provision of instruction be a pre-eminent function of the state. Seen against the context of the preceding pages, the provision of education, which is so inextricably bound up with the role of knowledge in society, reflects the profoundly complex problems of freedom and control, and continuity and change. Thus the classicists acknowledged that education was a social-control force operating through the inculcation of individuals in the prevailing moral code, training individuals for a place in the *status quo*, and impressing upon individuals the existent cosmology within the constraints of which private thought takes place. Yet this understanding of the role of education as an instrument of social control was coupled with the fervent desire for pluralism shown, for example, in Stuart Mill's "On

Liberty," and with a vision that education could provide *the* means whereby future if not present generations of the common man could improve their intellectual, social, political and material status.[159] Not many of the other classicists shared Stuart Mill's hopes for co-operativism, but they all shared the view that progress for the common man required his education, and perhaps all were aware that education, by redistributing opportunity, was a means of social transformation. Here, however, the concern is mainly with one facet of this complex area, the role of education as nondeliberative social control.

In the *Moral Sentiments*, the promulgation and dissemination of the general rules of morality are essentially an educative process such that the foregoing discussion of Smith's notions of the social-control function of morals is, in effect, appropriate here. Both the logic and the importance of Smith's ideas thereon are well underscored by the following terse but seminal line from the *Moral Sentiments*: "The great secret of education is to direct vanity to proper objects." [160] Perhaps no other single sentence from any work by a classicist so well illustrates and specifies the role of the nonlegal forces of social control in the market system: freedom to choose is freedom only within the pattern and range of choice allowed or inculcated by the society within which the choosing individual lives.

In both the *Lectures* and *The Wealth of Nations* Smith strongly called for the utilization of education as a remedy for some of the disadvantages of an industrial civilization.[161] It is in the concluding paragraph of the relevant section of *The Wealth of Nations* that Smith expresses most clearly the social-control role of education in a society that is "free" only in the context of the constraints of that control:

> The same thing may be said of the gross ignorance and stupidity which, in a civilized society, seem so frequently to

benumb the understandings of all the inferior ranks of people. A man without the proper use of the intellectual faculties of a man, is, if possible, more contemptible than even a coward, and seems to be mutilated and deformed in a still more essential part of the character of human nature. Though the state was to derive no advantage from the instruction of the inferior ranks of people, it would still deserve its attention that they should not be altogether uninstructed. The state, however, derives no inconsiderable advantage from their instruction. The more they are instructed, the less liable they are to the delusions of enthusiasm and superstition, which, among ignorant nations, frequently occasion the most dreadful disorders. An instructed and intelligent people besides, are always more decent and orderly than an ignorant and stupid one. They feel themselves, each individually more respectable, and more likely to obtain the respect of their lawful superiors, and they are therefore more disposed to respect those superiors. They are more disposed to examine, and more capable of seeing through, the interested complaints of faction and sedition, and they are, upon that account, less apt to be misled into any wanton or unnecessary opposition to the measures of government. In free countries, where the safety of government depends very much upon the favourable judgment which the people may form of its conduct, it must surely be of the highest importance that they should not be disposed to judge rashly or capriciously concerning it.[162]

It is a manifestation of this view of the social-control role of education that Ricardo wrote to McCulloch, "I have long been convinced that our security for good government must rest on the institutions themselves, and the influence under which those who govern us act, and not on the more or less virtue in the character of our governors. The conduct of two different sets of men educated nearly in the same manner, acting under the same checks, and with the same objects in view, as far as their own personal interest is concerned, cannot be materially different." [163]

Malthus also saw education as necessary to raise the "standard of wretchedness" and also to "chasten" individuals by inculcating individuals in the ways of the time; indeed, Bonar would have Malthus hold that "education will not do its perfect work if it has not included the particular doctrines which it has fallen to me more than any man to bring home to the public mind." [164] The Reverend Malthus must have been quite sophisticated in these matters.

McCulloch, who sincerely desired the improvement in the conditions of the working classes that they themselves variously sought, was afraid of the disorders accompanying this quest by the workers, and, in his *Principles*, indicated the danger to order from education itself reducing the sentiments of resignation and generating discontent, radicalism, and in particular Chartism. He says:

> Education is valuable, and in various ways; but it is by no means clear that it is at all calculated to reconcile the labouring classes to their lot. A stupid or an ignorant individual most commonly regards the privations incident to his situation as the effect of circumstances beyond human control, and submits to them as to the dispensations of Providence, without reflection or murmur; but he who is instructed, who is acquainted with the constitution of society, and with the privileges and advantages enjoyed by other classes, will not be so apathetic, nor, probably, so resigned to his fate. We are not, we confess, of the number of those who can contemplate the condition and prospects of the labourers in our great manufacturing towns without serious apprehensions. . . . workmen have less chance than formerly of advancing themselves. . . . But, under these circumstances, can anything be more natural, than that instructed workmen, who are thus condemned as it were to perpetual helotism, to continued poverty and hard labour, should become discontented?

It is a few lines after this that McCulloch writes, "Something, perhaps, may be done to strengthen the existing institutions of the country, by improving the education of the poor, and showing them how closely their interests are identified with those of their employers, and with the preservation of tranquillity and good order. But, after all, we incline to think that but little stress can be safely laid on education. A man must have a lively and grateful sense of the advantages he derives from established institutions before any species of training will make him anxious for their preservation."

These passages are from his chapter dealing with the different employments of capital and labor; in a chapter on the education of the poor in the same work, McCulloch relates how he would counter the foregoing tendency, and it is not by having the poor remain uninstructed:

> . . . it is most for the interest of the poor, as well as of the other classes, that they should be well informed. To render education productive of all the utility that may be derived from it, the poor should, in addition to the elementary instruction now alluded to, be made acquainted with the duties enjoined by religion and morality, and with the circumstances which occasion that gradation of ranks and inequality of fortunes that usually exist; and they should be impressed, from their earliest years, with a conviction of the important truth, that they are, in a great measure, the arbiters of their own fortune; that what others can do for them is but little compared with what they may do for themselves; and that the most tolerant and liberal Government, and the best institutions, cannot shield them from poverty and degradation, without the exercise of a reasonable degree of forethought, frugality, and good conduct, on their part.

(This view is clearly consonant with that interpretation of the Malthusian doctrine on population which has it not a statement of inevitable adversity and thereby pessimism but which sees in it a statement of the conditions [or some of them] necessary for the improvement of the life of the masses.) But, says McCulloch,

It would be unreasonable, indeed, to expect that it should produce any very immediate effect on their habits; and we are not of the number of those who expect that any system of education will ever ensure tranquillity in periods of distress, or that it will obviate the vicissitudes and disorders inherent in the manufacturing system. But, . . . the harvest of sound instruction . . . [by] raising the intelligence of the poor, and enabling them the better to appreciate the worthlessness of the nostrums on which they are so often called to depend, and to estimate the more remote, as well as the immediate consequences of their actions, . . . could hardly fail to contribute materially to their advantage.[165]

The danger to order is thus not averted, but education, argues McCulloch, can contribute to both order and progress in a compatible manner; what is instructive here is the role of education as social control instrumental in securing both order and progress.

Jeremy Bentham was also cognizant of the possible ill effects of education,[166] but he also supported governmental education as control promotive of morality yet within the constraints of a free society.[167] His understanding of the role of education as the inculcator of the cosmology of the time and place has been well put by Mitchell: "Since whatever is amiss in the opinions or conduct of mankind is due to 'intellectual weakness, indigenous or adoptive,' education must be the one great agency of reform. And since the understanding is made up of associations among ideas, the forming and strengthening of proper associations must be the one great aim of education." [168] James Mill, of course, was instrumental in the development of associationism.

John Stuart Mill, his idealism notwithstanding, is basically at one with his predecessor and contemporary classicists on the role of education as an instrument of social control. In his posthumously published "Chapters on Socialism" Mill applauded the gradual improvement in the intellectual character

71

of man through education to transcend the necessities of market inducements to effort; [169] and in his *Autobiography* he seconds his father's views on the matter:

> In psychology, his fundamental doctrine was the formation of all human character by circumstances, through the universal Principle of Association, and the consequent unlimited possibility of improving the moral and intellectual condition of mankind by education. Of all his doctrines none was more important than this, or needs more to be insisted on: unfortunately there is none which is more contradictory to the prevailing tendencies of speculation, both in his time and since.[170]

But, as has been seen before in other respects, Mill coupled his optimism with realism, and his quest for meaningful freedom with an understanding of the operation of the social-control system. Thus, in the "Utility of Religion," the main theme of which has already been stated, Mill asks,

> . . . consider next how tremendous is the power of education; how unspeakable is the effect of bringing people up from infancy in a belief, and in habits founded on it.
> . . . what vast efficacy belongs naturally to any doctrine received with tolerable unanimity as true, and impressed on the mind from the earliest childhood as duty.[171]
> The power of education is almost boundless: there is not one natural inclination which it is not strong enough to coerce, and, if needful, to destroy by disuse.[172]

CONCLUSION

This chapter has had a relatively limited objective, and, underscoring Schneider, ". . . it would be a gross misinterpretation of the paper to take it as a paean in praise of ignorance;" [173] rather, with Lord Robbins, the aim has been "to describe and to analyse rather than to judge." [174]

Classical economics was an attempt to provide a meaningful understanding of the market economy, perhaps of economic life in general, that would comprise a body of knowledge capable of serving as the basis of policy. In this the concern of the classicists was with the role of the deliberative action or inaction of the state, and that it be appropriate given the classical body of knowledge of the economy. Clearly, then, the classicists were preoccupied with the governmental or legal facet of their theory of economic policy.

But it has been the limited objective of this chapter to demonstrate the classical acknowledgement of the nonlegal forces of social control, and the important roles attributed thereto. These forces have been definitely identified as at least morals, custom, and education, and the generalized nondeliberative operation of indirection, ignorance, cosmology, and discipline. It is also possible that religion may be included, for the not infrequently expressed antireligion attitude on the part of at least some classicists must be juxtaposed to their general acknowledgement of religion as a restraint or sanction, if not also a promulgator of moral rules. Assessment turns on such matters as the composition of idealism and realism, and the differentiation between religion as church, sacerdotal class, theological creed, belief in a Supreme Being, and institutionalized promulgating and sanctioning of moral rules. Certainly, religion in one or more of these senses was a part of the nonlegal forces of social control in the minds of most if not all classicists. The author is therefore inclined to argue a place for religion as a sanctioning and promulgating instrument of social control in the classical theory of economic policy with the two caveats, first, that evidence and interpretation to the contrary makes unequivocal assertion unwarranted, and, second, that any religion would have to operate under the con-

73

straints of a pluralist society. This latter point, together with the problem of varying composition among the classicists, will be further discussed in Chapter Five. The general objective, however, has been accomplished, in establishing the relevance and necessity to consider the nonlegal forces of social control as such, whatever their specific composition.

This objective requires the extension or broadening of the definitional scope of "theory of economic policy" in the case of the classicists at least, to include the nonlegal forces. The classicists were aware, or their analysis may be reduced to the proposition, that the economy *in toto* is a decision-making process in which both private, legal and nonlegal participating forces interact and together resolve the basic economic problems within the constraints of the dual problems of "freedom and control" and "continuity and change." By "theory of economic policy" must be meant, then, the principles of the respective roles of all the participants in the economic decision-making process.[175]

The economy of the classical economists was a market system with primarily individual participation. Critics of classicism have long objected (among other things) to a supposed tendency to anarchism, or failure to appreciate the claims and problems of order. If the classicists had merely premised some natural beneficent harmony of interests or of results, the criticism would have merit. But *Harmonielehre* has no central place in the classical theory of economic policy. Rather, the foregoing paragraphs indicate that whatever the role of government in the economy attributed to the classicists, and even aside from "competition," there would not be chaos; and, further, that competition (by which the classicists meant the market system) itself depends for its orderly process and the content of its decisions upon the functioning of the nonlegal forces. So far as the market-plus-framework interpretation is meaningful, the nonlegal component of the framework is clearly of co-ordinate importance with any other facet, e.g., the market considered independently of the role of government, or government per se. Knight's criticism [176] of institutionalists for ostensibly having ignored the historically developed and largely nondeliberative institutions (however appropriate a criticism of the institutionalists) should be translated into praise for the classicists for their appreciation of such institutions. This is required notwithstanding the Ricardian methodology.

It has been seen that the nondeliberative forces were, in the consensus of the classicists, in part at least, responsible for the maintenance of order, for the achievement of social control constraining individual behavior. Moreover, the nonlegal forces and their promulgating and sanctioning complements, with which they are often indistinguishable, are in many respects responsible for the specific content of the market resolution of the basic economic problems. To the extent that government is passive and the forces of demand and supply operate, relatively wide scope, however unobtrusive, is given to the nonlegal forces, no less in the modern than in the medieval age, though the genesis of the nonlegal forces are at present more diffused. The nonlegal forces also may be said to comprise and shape not only the content of resource allocation but also the structure of the decision-making process operating to resolve the basic economic problems and, thereby, both directly and indirectly influence the resolution of those problems.

In partial summary, then, in the classical theory of economic policy the nonlegal forces of social control (1) comprised part of the economic decision-making process; (2) helped structure that process; (3) helped govern the content of the effective decisions made and conduct in general; (4) were important in regard to the maintenance of order, and thereby the resolution of the dual basic social problems of freedom and control, and continuity and change; and (5) helped govern the process of the determination and role of knowledge as a basis for policy both deliberative and non-deliberative.[177]

NOTES: CHAPTER TWO

* Marquis of Lansdowne, ed., *The Petty Papers* (London: Constable, 1927), two volumes, vol. I, pp. 116–17.

1. Lionel Robbins, *Theory of Economic Policy* (London: Macmillan, 1953), p. 2.

2. Joseph J. Spengler and William R. Allen, eds., *Essays in Economic Thought* (Chicago: Rand McNally, 1960), pp. 7–9.

3. It is no accident that two outstanding contemporary advocates of the classical tradition of economic liberalism, Frank H. Knight and F. A. Hayek, both stress the unobtrusive workings of the nondeliberative forces. Also cf. O. H. Taylor, *The Classical Liberalism, Marxism, and the Twentieth Century* (Cambridge: Harvard University Press, 1960), pp. 96 ff. and 106 ff. *In re* Wilhelm Roepke, see notes 5 and 7, *infra*.

4. Robbins, *op. cit.*, pp. 41–42, 56. Thus, according to Morrow, to Adam Smith the individual "is social through and through. It is because he is the product of society that his acts conform to the social welfare. His very interests are those which have been instilled into him by his social environment, and hence in pursuing his own interests he is also pursuing those of his society." Morrow also points out that "The *Moral Sentiments* shows the inner organic relation which exists between all the individuals of a society and the social unity," and acknowledges the coexistence of elements of "reflective consciousness" and "unconscious unity." These facets will be discussed extensively below. Glenn R. Morrow, *The Ethical and Economic Theories of Adam Smith* (New York: Cornell University Studies in Philosophy; Longmans, Green, and Co., 1923), p. 84.

5. Writing of *The Theory of Moral Sentiments*, Glenn R. Morrow concludes that "It is because the individual is in his very nature socialized, a product of the social environment, that he can in general be left without external interference to act in accordance with the demands of his individual nature." *Adam Smith, 1776–1926* (Chi-

cago: University of Chicago Press, 1928), p. 178. And Wilhelm Roepke: "The market is only one section of society. It is a very important section, it is true, but still one whose existence is justifiable and possible only because it is part of a larger whole which concerns not economics but philosophy, history, and theology. . . . Adam Smith, whose fame rests not only on his *Wealth of Nations* but also on his *Theory of Moral Sentiments*, would have known better." *A Humane Economy: The Social Framework of the Free Market* (Chicago: Regnery Co., 1960), p. 92. For similar interpretations of the *Theory of Moral Sentiments* and of Smith in general, see Henry J. Bittermann, "Adam Smith's Empiricism and the Law of Nature," *Journal of Political Economy*, vol. 48 (1940), pp. 487–520, 703–34; Albert Salomon, "Adam Smith as Sociologist," *Social Research*, vol. 12 (1945), pp. 22–42; J. Bonar, " 'The Theory of Moral Sentiments,' by Adam Smith, 1759," *Journal of Philosophical Studies* (now *Philosophy*), vol. 1 (1926), pp. 333–53; A. L. Macfie, "Adam Smith's *Moral Sentiments* as Foundation for his *Wealth of Nations*," *Oxford Economic Papers*, n.s., vol. 11 (1959), pp. 209–28; Nathan Rosenberg, "Some Institutional Aspects of the *Wealth of Nations*," *Journal of Political Economy*, vol. 68 (1960), pp. 557–70; and K. W. Kapp, *The Social Costs of Private Enterprise* (Cambridge: Harvard University Press, 1950), pp. 28–29. See also Jacob Viner, "Bentham and J. S. Mill: The Utilitarian Background," *American Economic Review*, vol. 39 (1949), pp. 365, 367; William D. Grampp, "On the Politics of the Classical Economists," *Quarterly Journal of Economics*, vol. 62 (1948), pp. 730–31, 741–42; Overton H. Taylor, *Economics and Liberalism* (Cambridge: Harvard University Press, 1955), chaps. 2 and 3, and *The Classical Liberalism, Marxism, and the Twentieth Century* (Cambridge: Harvard University Press, 1960), pp. 26, 27, 96, 97; and William L. Davidson, *Political Thought in England* (New York: Holt, n.d.), p. 17. The appropriateness of a social vis-a-vis an abstract individualist approach to the *Moral Sentiments* and to Smith in general is discussed, *inter alia*, in Glenn R. Morrow, *The Ethical and Economic Theories of Adam Smith*; H. J. Davenport and Glenn R. Morrow, "Discussion: The Ethics of the *Wealth of Nations*," *Philosophical Review*, vol. 34 (1925), pp. 599–611; A. L. Macfie, "Adam Smith's Theory of Moral Sentiments," *Scottish Journal of Political Economy*, vol. 8 (1961), pp. 12–27, particularly pp. 23 ff. "But the belief, so popularly accepted in the economic world, that Smith was primarily an individualist, is the very reverse of the truth. For him as for Hume, the interests of society were the end. By all means let the individual be encouraged to chase 'trinkets,' so long as this conduced to that end." (P. 23.) See also Friedrich A. Hayek, *Individualism and*

Economic Order (Chicago: University of Chicago Press, 1948), and notes 7 and 22, *infra*.

6. J. R. McCulloch, ed., *The Works of David Ricardo* (London: John Murray, 1881), p. 554. See also W. Stark, *Jeremy Bentham's Economic Writings* (New York: Burt Franklin, 1954), vol. 3, p. 311; and James Mill, "An Essay on Government," in Edwin A. Burtt, ed., *The English Philosophers from Bacon to Mill* (New York: Modern Library, 1939), p. 858.

7. Thus Roepke quotes Burke: "Society cannot exist unless a controlling power upon will and appetite be placed somewhere, and the less of it there is within, the more there must be without." (*Op. cit.*, p. xiii.) In the *Moral Sentiments* Smith wrote: "What institution of government could tend so much to promote the happiness of mankind as the general prevalence of wisdom and virtue? All government is but an imperfect remedy for the deficiency of these." Adam Smith, *Essays Philosophical and Literary* (hereafter cited as *Essays*) (London: Ward, Lock, & Co., 1880), p. 165. A number of writers compare Smith's "natural" identicity of interests with Bentham's "artificial" identicity of interests. J. Bartlet Brebner, "Laissez Faire and State Intervention in Nineteenth-Century Britain," *Journal of Economic History*, vol. 8, Supplement (1948), pp. 61–63; Elie Halevy, *The Growth of Philosophic Radicalism* (Boston: Beacon Press, 1955), pp. 88–120; Wesley C. Mitchell, *The Backward Art of Spending Money* (New York: Kelley, 1950), pp. 195–96. See also Robbins, *op. cit.*, pp. 188–92; Viner, *op. cit.*, pp. 368–70; and Overton H. Taylor, *A History of Economic Thought* (New York: McGraw-Hill, 1960), pp. 131, 133. All of the classical economists contemplated the use of both the deliberative and nondeliberative forces of social control, but with relatively greater emphasis on the latter. The idea of "natural," defined as inevitable is simply wrong or question-begging. See John Stuart Mill, "Utilitarianism," in Burtt, *op. cit.*, pp. 919–20; Leslie Stephen, *The English Utilitarians* (New York: Peter Smith, 1950), vol. III, pp. 436–37; William Ashley, "A Retrospect of Free-Trade Doctrine," *Economic Journal*, vol. 34 (1924), pp. 502, 513; and Taylor, *Economics and Liberalism*, chaps 2, 3; conceived as independent of legal controls, logically allows for the role of the nondeliberative forces but fails to specify their existence—a frequent and misleading practice. With respect to Bentham, it will be seen below that he had no unimportant place for religion, morals, custom, and education: see, for example, G. W. Keeton and G. Schwarzenberger, eds., *Jeremy Bentham and the Law: A Symposium* (London: Stevens, 1948), essay by A. J. Ayer, at p. 253, and see text at note 69, *infra*; and with respect to Smith, Rosenberg has contended that "Smith's search [was] for an

institutional scheme which will establish and enforce an identity of interests between the public and private spheres . . . ," and that "Far from assuming a 'spontaneous' identity of interests (in the mere absence of government restrictions) . . . Smith was obsessed with the urge to go beyond the ordinary market-structure definition of competition and to evaluate the effectiveness of different institutional forms in *enforcing* this identity." Rosenberg, *op. cit.*, pp. 559, 567; cf. Taylor, *Economics and Liberalism*, pp. 92–95. See also Adelman, *op. cit.*, p. 28; and V. B. Singh, "Adam Smith's Theory of Economic Development," *Science and Society*, vol. 23 (1959), pp. 108–9, 113. Also see below. If there is any meaning to the differentiation between Smith and Bentham, it is not that of an automatic vis-a-vis artificial harmony, for both adhered to the *createdness* and *ergo* "artificiality" of harmony, but on the basis of Bentham's greater reliance upon law; but note Smith's emphasis upon the dependence of private property on law. See Karl de Schweinitz, Jr., "Free Enterprise in a Growth World," *Southern Economic Journal*, vol. 29 (1962), pp. 105–6; and William D. Grampp, "Adam Smith and the Economic Man," *Journal of Political Economy*, vol. 56 (1948), pp. 326–27. See also Chapters Three to Five, *infra*. With respect to Smith and the Utilitarians as a group, see the important note by W. H. Hutt in *Economists and the Public* (London: Cape, 1936), p. 137, also referred to in Robbins, *op. cit.*, p. 191. Also see Alfred F. Chalk, "Natural Law and the Rise of Economic Individualism in England," *Journal of Political Economy*, vol. 59 (1951), pp. 332–47.

8. Hayek, *op. cit.*, p. 4; cf. pp. 11, 26, 28–29. See also L. M. Haney, "The Ricardo Centenary—Discussion," *American Economic Association Bulletin* (hereafter cited as *AEA Bulletin*), Fourth Series, vol. 1 (1911), Supplement, pp. 100–101.

9. Taylor, *The Classical Liberalism, Marxism, and the Twentieth Century*, p. 26.

10. Mill's *Three Essays on Religion* (3rd ed., London: Longmans, Green & Co., 1885), particularly the essay, "Utility of Religion," his *The Spirit of the Age* with Introductory Essay by F. A. Hayek (Chicago: University of Chicago Press, 1942), and "Utilitarianism" (Burtt, *op. cit.*, pp. 895 ff.), were in a sense sequels to the *Moral Sentiments*, for Mill shared Smith's humanism, his ambivalent recognition of the role of religion as an instrument of social control, and his sophistication regarding social change. The same may be said of his *Autobiography. Autobiography of John Stuart Mill* (New York: Columbia University Press, 1924).

11. In *The Wealth of Nations*, Smith wrote: "In every age and country of the world men must have attended to the characters, de-

signs, and actions of one another, and many reputable rules and maxims for the conduct of human life must have been laid down and approved by common consent." Adam Smith, *An Inquiry into the Nature and causes of the Wealth of Nations,* hereafter cited as *Wealth of Nations.* (New York: Modern Library, 1937), p. 724. Smith differentiated between the moral sentiments and custom, as is being done in this study, though he says: "But though the influence of custom and fashion upon moral sentiments, is not altogether so great, it is however perfectly similar to what it is every where else." Smith, *Essays,* p. 177; see also pp. 185–87.

12. *Ibid.,* p. 120. See Glenn R. Morrow, "The Significance of the Doctrine of Sympathy in Hume and Adam Smith," *Philosophical Review,* vol. 32 (1923), pp. 60–78.

13. Smith, *Essays,* pp. 139–40.

14. "The different situations of different ages and countries are apt, in the same manner, to give different characters to the generality of those who live in them, and their sentiments concerning the particular degree of each quality, that is either blamable or praise-worthy, vary according to that degree which is usual in their own country, and in their own times. . . . And as this varies, according as their different circumstances render different qualities more or less habitual to them, their sentiments concerning the exact propriety of character and behaviour vary accordingly." *Ibid.,* p. 181.

15. Thus Smith states that ". . . situations may occur, in which it is doubtful, whether the highest propriety of conduct consists in observing or in receding from what, in ordinary cases, are the rules of our duty." *Ibid.,* p. 303; see also pp. 150–58, 203, 290–91; and see Bittermann, *op. cit.,* p. 513.

16. Smith, *Essays,* pp. 80–81.

17. *Ibid.,* p. 79.

18. *Ibid.,* p. 200. Thus, "Our respect for the great, accordingly, is most apt to offend by its excess; our fellow-feeling for the miserable, by its defect," with a resulting corruption of our moral sentiments. But, "The distinction of ranks, the peace and order of society, are in a great measure, founded upon the respect which we naturally conceive for the former. . . . Nature has wisely judged that the distinction of ranks, the peace and order of society, would rest more securely upon the plain and palpable difference of birth and fortune, than upon the invisible and often uncertain difference of wisdom and virtue." (P. 200; cf. pp. 224–25.)

19. "Many men behave very decently, and through the whole of their lives avoid any considerable degree of blame, who yet, perhaps, never felt the sentiment upon the propriety of which we found our

approbation of their conduct, but acted merely from a regard to what they saw were the established rules of behaviour . . . if the regard to the general rules of conduct has been very strongly impressed upon them. . . ." *Ibid.*, pp. 142–43.

20. *Ibid.*, pp. 143–46. See also Macfie, "Adam Smith's Theory of Moral Sentiments," *op cit.*, p. 22.

21. Smith, *Essays*, p. 114.

22. Morrow, in *Adam Smith, 1776–1926*, p. 177. "This theory, therefore, looks upon the individual not as an absolute and irreducible entity existing prior to social experience, but as a product of his social environment." (P. 177.) "The concrete social environment must also be taken into consideration in explaining the nature of the individual man, and Adam Smith is one of the very few thinkers of his time who had any realization of this complementary point of view." "This concrete social point of view is best expressed, not in the *Wealth of Nations*, but in the *Theory of Moral Sentiments*." (P. 172.) "In short, unregulated self-interest is no more advocated in the *Wealth of Nations* than it is in the *Moral Sentiments*, whereas in the latter work the moral value of the inferior virtues, when properly regulated, is fully recognized." (P. 167). Both the *Moral Sentiments* and the *Wealth of Nations* were part of a larger sociology and cosmology, with the former comprising essentially the analysis of the nondeliberative forces of social control within which the autonomous (or almost autonomous, save for the further control through law and competition) individual "spontaneously" acted.

23. Smith, *Essays*, pp. 144, 145, 149–50.

24. *Ibid.*, p. 208.

25. *Ibid.*, p. 209; cf. pp. 210, 243-45.

26. *Ibid.*, p. 210.

27. *Ibid.*, pp. 150–51, 153.

28. *Ibid.*, pp. 153–54, 155.

29. *Ibid.*, p. 156.

30. Smith, *Wealth of Nations*, p. 765. Having quoted Petty at the head of this essay, it is appropriate to note that one of his twelve criteria for promoting "the most convenient, commodious, and comfortable livings" is "for peace and uniformity in religion." He criticized the proliferation of parishes and thereby of sermons, such that ". . . it were a miracle, if a million of sermons composed by so many men, and of so many minds and methods, should produce uniformity upon the discomposed understandings of about 8,000,000 of hearers." He would rather have "an uniformity of common prayer, [and] in preaching also." Sir William Petty, *Essays on Mankind and Political Arithmetic* (London: Cassell, 1888), pp. 42, 43, 46.

31. Bittermann, *op. cit.*, p. 716. "Smith's argument, then, is that the sanctions for morals are to be found directly in human nature. . . . Religion provided an external sanction, at least in men's thought, but religion itself was in accord with basic passions of human nature." (*Loc. cit.*) On the psychological role of religion, to Smith, see pp. 710–17.

32. Louis Schneider, "The Role of the Category of Ignorance in Sociological Theory: An Exploratory Statement," *American Sociological Review*, vol. 27 (1962), p. 493.

33. "Durkheim's analysis has repeatedly raised the question of how effectively religion would function, or how nearly it would still have the consequences he claims for it, if the 'veil' were penetrated by the ordinary participants in religious exercises. By penetration of the veil is meant the acquisition by the participants in the exercises of the knowledge that feelings of awe and of the presence of the transcendent are simply occasioned by the attributes and constraints of society and that actions initially addressed in good faith to subjectively significant religious objects merely lead to outcomes like group solidarity. . . . But more than this: Durkheim's view was that the solidarity, cohesiveness, integration of the individual with the group, and the like, that religion brought about, were brought about indirectly. *Indirection* is the first in a set of terms bearing on ignorance that will be specified here. Social solidarity is not achieved in the religious context through a deliberate fixing of solidarity as an end to be achieved. It is achieved, in Durkheim's theory, through actions subjectively addressed to other ends, and 'ends' such as solidarity are achieved in ignorance *and* indirectly." (*Ibid.*, pp. 495–96.) Schneider subsequently proceeds to an analysis of Hayek as a theorist who "is partial to the general notion that historically evolved institutions, as they stand at any particular time, are likely to incorporate considerable 'wisdom' based on past experience and reflection. This wisdom is not necessarily present to the minds of those who act in the terms of the institutions; it is indeed more likely to be unknown to them, but that does not preclude its having 'beneficent' effects. From Edmund Burke to Friedrich Hayek, law, polity, language, religion, the market and other phenomena have been lauded . . . for their supposed incorporation of a wisdom that was never direct and deliberate but, rather, indirect and inadvertent. The organic, spontaneously developed institutions are opposed to deliberate, rationally constructed social arrangements . . . [and the] claim for the superiority of the organically evolved is associated with an insistence that the organically evolved institutions attain their efficacy precisely *because* they involve indirection and ignorance." (Pp. 497–98.)

34. *Ibid.*, p. 498; cf. p. 500. See also Salomon, *op. cit.*, p. 36; Macfie, "Adam Smith's *Moral Sentiments* as Foundation for his *Wealth of Nations*," pp. 210–11, 224–25; *Adam Smith, 1776–1926*, pp. 171–72; and Ashley, *op. cit.*, pp. 508–9.

35. Including his interest in the formation of language: see Smith, *Essays*, pp. 305–25. Bentham also, for example, had an interest in language. John Bowring, ed., *The Works of Jeremy Bentham* (New York: Russell & Russell, 1962), vol. 8, pp. 295–338. In both Smith's essay, "Considerations Concerning the Formation of Language," and Bentham's "Essay on Language," particularly the latter, one can perceive strains of language serving as a nondeliberative force shaping the cosmology of the users. See also C. K. Ogden, *Bentham's Theory of Fictions* (London: Kegan Paul, 1932), pp. ix ff. and 7 ff. James F. Becker's "Adam Smith's Theory of Social Science," *Southern Economic Journal*, vol. 38 (1961), pp. 13–21, also develops the importance of language *in re* Smith, particularly as a force of social control (see, e.g., pp. 17, 19, 20, 21). *In re* John Stuart Mill, see his *A System of Logic* (London: Longmans, Green, and Co., 1879), two volumes, vol. 1, book 1.

36. Smith, *Essays*, pp. 144, 145, 149, and 208. Italics added.

37. *Ibid.*, p. 205; see also pp. 136, 163–64, 196–97. Note also, for example, the interesting reasoning of Stuart Mill, who "earnestly hoped that Owenite, St. Simonian, and all other anti-property doctrines might spread widely among the poorer classes; not that I thought those doctrines true, or desired that they should be acted on, but in order that the higher classes might be made to see that they had more to fear from the poor when uneducated, than when educated." *Autobiography*, p. 121; quoted also in Hayek's introductory essay to *The Spirit of the Age*, pp. xxxi–xxxii.

38. "The man of system . . . seems to imagine that he can arrange the different members of a great society with as much ease as the hand arranges the different pieces upon a chess-board. He does not consider that the pieces upon the chess-board have no other principle of motion besides that which the hand impresses upon them; but that, in the great chess-board of human society, every single piece has a principle of motion of its own, altogether different from that which the legislature might choose to impress upon it. If those two principles coincide and act in the same direction, the game of human society will go on easily and harmoniously, and is very likely to be happy and successful. If they are opposite or different, the game will go on miserably, and the society must be at all times in the highest degree of disorder." (Smith, *Essays*, p. 207. See also Alexander Gray, *Adam Smith* (London: The Historical Association, 1948), p. 24.

39. *Ibid.*, p. 193.

40. Bonar, *op. cit.*, p. 347.

41. Smith, *Wealth of Nations*, pp. 121–22. See also C. R. Fay, "Adam Smith and the Dynamic State," *Economic Journal*, vol. 40 (1930), pp. 32–33: "Liberty goes with justice, and both rest on the bosom of natural right, as in the frequent phrase, 'evident violation of natural liberty and justice.' "

42. Smith, *Essays*, p. 162. See also Bittermann, *op. cit.*, p. 721; Singh, *op. cit.*, p. 128; and George J. Stigler, *Five Lectures on Economic Problems* (London: Longmans, Green and Co., 1949), p. 4. See also Macfie, "Adam Smith's Theory of Moral Sentiments," pp. 22 ff.

43. Bonar, *op. cit.*, p. 342. Cf. Smith, *Essays*, p. 48, and *Lectures on Justice, Police, Revenue and Arms* (hereafter cited as *Lectures*). (New York: Kelley & Millman, 1956), pp. 253–55; and Edwin Cannan, "Adam Smith as an Economist," *Economica*, vol. 6 (1926), p. 130.

44. Macfie, "Adam Smith's *Moral Sentiments* as Foundation for his *Wealth of Nations*," p. 211; cf. Smith, *Essays*, pp. 163–64. See also Gray, *op. cit.*, p. 18: "This reverential regard for the wealthy and the great, our desire for 'place' that we may gain the consideration they enjoy, has on the one hand inspired the labours of mankind, and made progress possible; on the other hand it is a guarantee of stability of government."

45. Morrow, in *Adam Smith, 1776–1926*, pp. 171–72. Cf. Taylor, *Economics and Liberalism*, pp. 89–91. This discipline, it should be clear, is a manifestation of an underlying or more general process. As Morrow interprets Smith, "The individual moral consciousness is the result of social intercourse, the individual moral judgments are the expression of the general sentiments of the society to which the individual belongs." "The Significance of the Doctrine of Sympathy in Hume and Adam Smith," p. 70. The operation of "cosmology" in respect to the other classicists is discussed below.

46. Smith, *Essays*, pp. 224–25; cf. p. 74.

47. De Schweinitz, *op. cit.*, pp. 106, 107, 108, 109. "The price system, as Smith saw it, was an intensely coercive mechanism." Rosenberg, *op. cit.*, p. 560. See also Francis A. Walker, "Recent Progress of Political Economy in the United States," *American Economic Association, Publications*, First Series, vol. 4 (1889), p. 39; and Edwin Cannan, *A Review of Economic Theory* (London: King, 1929), p. 433.

48. Piero Sraffa, ed., *The Works and Correspondence of David Ricardo* (Cambridge: Cambridge University Press, 1952), vol. 9, p. 377.

49. *Ibid.*, vol. 5, pp. 325–326, 327, 328.

50. *Ibid.*, p. 328. The quote from Tillotson reads as follows: "As for most of those restraints which Christianity lays upon us, they are so much both for our private and public advantage, that, setting aside all considerations of religion, and of the rewards and punishments of another life, they are really good for us; and if God had not laid them upon us, we ought in reason, in order to our temporal benefit and advantage to have laid them upon ourselves. If there were no religion, I know men would not have such strong and forcible obligations to these duties; but yet, I say, though there were no religion, it were good for men, in order to temporal ends, to their health and quiet, and reputation, and safety, and, in a word, to the private and public prosperity of mankind, that men should be temperate, and chaste, and just, and peaceable, and charitable, and kind, and obliging to one another, rather than the contrary. So that religion does not create those restraints arbitrarily, but requires those things of us, which our reason, and a regard to our advantage, which the necessity and conveniency of the things themselves, without any consideration of religion, would in most cases urge us to." (P. 327.) On Tillotson, see Louis G. Locke, *Tillotson* (Copenhagen: Rosenkilde and Bagger, 1954; *Anglistica*, Vol. IV), e.g., p. 88.

51. Thomas de Quincey, *Theological Essays* (Boston: Ticknor, Reed, and Fields; 1854), two volumes, vol. 1.

52. J. R. McCulloch, *The Principles of Political Economy* (Edinburgh: Tait, 1843), pp. 187, 265; cf. 432.

53. S. A. Meenai, "Robert Torrens—1780–1864," *Economica*, n.s., vol. 23 (1956), p. 55.

54. Cf., e.g., Bowring, *op. cit.*, vol. 1, p. 192.

55. See note 7, *supra.*

56. Thus, wrote Alfred Marshall some years later, "It is deliberateness, and not selfishness, that is the characteristic of the modern age." *Principles of Economics* (8th ed., New York: Macmillan, 1920), p. 6.

57. Jeremy Bentham, *An Introduction to the Principles of Morals and Legislation,* hereafter cited as *Morals and Legislation.* (London: Oxford University Press, 1907); also in Bowring, *op. cit.*, vol. 1. The juxtaposition of morals *and* legislation is very suggestive, particularly since Bentham is considered to be the father of the science of legislation.

58. Bentham, *op. cit.*, p. 24.

59. *Ibid.*, pp. 24–25.

60. *Ibid.*, p. 25.

61. *Ibid.*, p. 26.

62. The following, from Bentham's "Constitutional Code," is instructive: "Thus, on taking, on the one hand, a view of the deleterious influence of the temptation presented by arrangements which,

in the first instance, may have presented themselves in no other character than that of arrangements of civil or distributive law, operating on no other than the passive faculty, care should be taken, on the other hand, not to suffer to pass unheeded, the moral forces by which, in the character of tutelary sanctions, the force of the temptation may be, and, in the ordinary state of things, is, effectually resisted." Bowring, *op. cit.*, vol. 9, pp. 20–21.

63. Bentham, *op. cit.*, p. 310.

64. Davidson, *op. cit.*, p. 67; cf., *inter alia*, p. 60. See also Macfie, "Adam Smith's Theory of Moral Sentiments," pp. 15–17.

65. Stephen, *op. cit.*, vol. 1, p. 257.

66. Bentham, *op. cit.*, p. 25.

67. *Ibid., loc. cit.*

68. *Ibid.*, pp. 219–20. In his "View of a Complete Code of Laws," Bentham puts it essentially the same way: "The distribution of rewards and punishments is often opposed or misdirected, or rendered useless, because the state has neither eyes which can see everything, nor hands which can attend to everything. Religion is calculated to supply this deficiency of human power, by inculcating upon the minds of men the belief that there is a power engaged in supporting the same ends, which is not subject to the same imperfections. It represents the Supreme Invisible Being as disposed to maintain the laws of society, and to reward and punish according to infallible rules, those actions which man has not the means of rewarding and punishing. Everything which serves to preserve and strengthen in the minds of men this fear of the Supreme Judge, may be comprehended under the general name of Religion; and for the purpose of clearness of discourse, we may often speak of religion as if it were a distinct being, an allegorical personage, to whom certain functions are attributed. Hence, to diminish or pervert the influence of Religion, is to diminish or pervert, in the same proportion, the services which the state might derive from it, for the repression of crime or the encouragement of virtue. Everything which tends to weaken or mislead the operations of this power, is an offence against Religion." Bowring, *op. cit.*, vol. 3, p. 170. See also Nassau W. Senior, *Industrial Efficiency and Social Economy*, S. Leon Levy, ed. (New York: Holt, 1928), two volumes, vol. 1, pp. 194–95.

69. Bowring, *op. cit.*, vol. 1, p. 316.

70. On this see Viner, *op. cit.*, pp. 364, 365, 367; Stephen, *op. cit.*, vol. 1, p. 312; and Elmer Louis Kayser, *The Grand Social Enterprise* (New York: Columbia University Press, 1932), who concludes his chapter on "Public Opinion and the Moral Sanction," in respect to Bentham, "In good government, that 'harmony established between legislation and enlightened opinion,' the work of the legislator would become lighter and lighter and many of his functions would be assumed by the moralist." (P. 64.)

71. Like Smith, Bentham acknowledges the ambiguity of content: "The dictates of religion are, under the infinite diversity of religions, so extremely variable, that it is difficult to know what general account to give of them, or in what rank to place the motive they belong to." Bentham, *op. cit.*, p. 124. See the text at the following note. Cf. "Of the Influence of Time and Place in Matters of Legislation," in Bowring, *op. cit.*, vol. 1, pp. 171 ff.

72. Bentham, *op. cit.*, p. 64. Also see Senior, *op. cit.*, vol. 2, pp. 305–6, 353, 362–63.

73. "That a homily to be read in churches be composed by the authority and under the direction of the persons by whom forms of prayer for particular occasions are composed, recommending to the labouring classes the acquisition of Annuity Notes by shewing the advantages that may be derived from this species of property as well in a moral as in an economical point of view by industrious persons to themselves and their families, by laying up a provision against sickness, accidents and old age, to the encouragement of sobriety and frugality, and the proportionable discouragement of drunkenness and every other species of dissipation and extravagance." Stark, *op. cit.*, vol. 3, p. 480.

74. Jeremy Bentham, *Church-of-Englandism and Its Catechism Examined* (hereafter cited as *Church-of-Englandism*) (London: Wilson, 1818). The volume contains two sequences of Roman-numeral pagination, the first for the "Preface on Publication," and the second for the "Preface." All references will be to the latter. The volume also contains two sequences of Arabic-numeral pagination. References to the first sequence will be prefixed by "I"; and to the second, by "II."

75. *Ibid.*, I, pp. 1–51; and II, pp. 1–86.

76. *Ibid.*, I, pp. 52–236; and II, pp. 180–92.

77. *In re* the practice of hypocrisy and falsehood, cf. *ibid.*, pp. xv, xxi ff., xxxii–xxxiii, and pages there indicated; and II, pp. 83–84, 87 ff., 143, 185, 187. *In re* the creation of intellectual depravity, mendicity and docility, cf. pp. xxxi–xxxii and pages there indicated, xlii–xliii; and I, pp. 174–75, 246; and II, pp. 87 ff. and 145. See also note 99, *infra*.

78. See note 80, *infra*.

79. *Ibid.*, I, pp. 23, 168, 169, 171; and II, pp. 86, 99 ff., 294.

80. *In re* sole reliance upon the sacerdotal class for knowledge, cf. I, pp. 173–75; and II, pp. 90, 148, 298. *In re* appeal to authority, cf. p. xx; and II, p. 369. *In re* philosophical-intellectual absolutism and the transition to political absolutism, cf. p. liv; I, pp. 44, 170–71, 246; and II, pp. 85, 90, 397.

81. *Ibid.*, I, p. 246; and II, pp. 99 ff., 124–26, 128–29, 143.

82. *Ibid.*, I, pp. 65, 247; and II, pp. 123, 185, 191: *In re* the Church view of order and continuity, cf. I, pp. 236–37; and II, p. 145. Bentham's view is much the same as that of Stuart Mill (see text at note

127, *infra*), to the effect that although minds are made they should be free to develop within the constraints imposed. Cf. II, pp. 88–89.

83. *Ibid.*, I, p. 60; and II, pp. 130–31. *Per contra*, cf. II, pp. 378–79. It is also relevant that the Church of Scotland was, vis-a-vis the Church of England, more liberal and also more social-reform oriented. See also John Stuart Mill, *Auguste Comte and Positivism* (Ann Arbor: University of Michigan Press, 1961), pp. 112–13.

84. (Philip Beauchamp,) *Analysis of the Influence of Natural Religion on the Temporal Happiness of Mankind* (hereafter cited as *Influence of Natural Religion*) (London: Carlile, 1822).

85. *Ibid.*, p. 3.

86. *Ibid.*, pp. 65–66. On the role of the "popular sanction," see pp. 54 ff., 58 ff., and notes 103 and 107, *infra*.

87. *Ibid.*, pp. 84, 86; see also pp. 130–31, 133–35, and 138.

88. *Ibid.*, pp. 57, 70, 86, 88–89.

89. *Ibid.*, pp. 12, 20 ff., 54 ff., 60, 93 ff. *In re* ambiguity and variety, cf. p. 38; also pp. 10 ff., 59, 129.

90. *Ibid.*, p. 84.

91. *Ibid.*, pp. 84, 84–85. For criticism of religion as an adjunct to law, cf. pp. 43–46; *per contra*, see note 68, *supra*.

92. (Gamaliel Smith,) *Not Paul, But Jesus* (London: Hunt, 1823).

93. *Ibid.*, pp. vi. vii, xiv-xv, xvi, 371–73.

94. *Ibid.*, p. vi.

95. *Ibid.*, p. v. Criticism of the divisiveness of the church may also be found, *inter alia*, in (Smith,) *Church-of-Englandism*, I, pp. 85, 119.

96. (Gamaliel Smith,) *Not Paul, But Jesus*, p. vi.

97. Viner, *op. cit.*, p. 371.

98. See, e.g., Bowring, *op. cit.*, vol. 8, pp. 546 ff.; vol. 9, p. 35; vol. 10, p. 70.

99. See, e.g., *ibid.*, vol. 1, pp. 75–76, 412, 566; vol. 5, pp. 457–58; vol. 6, p. 117 (note); vol. 8, p. 547; and vol. 10, p. 70. Also see (Smith,) *Church-of-Englandism*, I, pp. 30 ff., and II, pp. 82 ff., 369 ff.; and (Beauchamp,) *Influence of Natural Religion*, pp. 116 ff. for Petty's enumeration of the "disadvantages to the world" of "Worshipping, honoring, & glorifying God," cf. Marquis of Lansdowne, ed., *op. cit.*, vol. 1, pp. 117–18.

100. See, e.g., Bowring, *op. cit.*, vol. 2, p. 393; and Harold A. Larrabee, ed., *Bentham's "Handbook of Political Fallacies"* (Baltimore: Johns Hopkins Press, 1952), pp. 17–82.

101. See e.g., Bowring, *op. cit.*, vol. 1, p. 147.

102. Burtt, *op. cit.*, p. 952. "The rules which obtain . . . appear . . . self-evident and self-justifying. This all but universal illusion is one of the examples of the magical influence of custom, which is not only, as the proverb says, a second nature, but is continually mistaken for the first. The effect of custom, in preventing any misgiving respecting the

rules of conduct which mankind impose on one another, is all the more complete because the subject is one on which it is not generally considered necessary that reasons should be given, either by one person to others or by each to himself." (P. 952. On the latter point, see Mill's *The Spirit of the Age*, and *infra*.)

103. The theme of his essay on the "Utility of Religion" concerns the ostensible effect of supernatural religion, which he attributes not to the supernatural character of the religion but rather to the opportunity for organized religion to educate and inculcate morality. Mill, *Three Essays on Religion*, pp. 72, 74, 78–79, 83, 87, 100. See note 171, *infra*.

104. Mill, *The Spirit of the Age*, pp. 17, 25, 29, 30–32, 75, 86.

105. John Stuart Mill, *Principles of Political Economy* (New York: Kelley, 1961), p. 792.

106. Mill, *Three Essays on Religion*, pp. 77–78.

107. *Ibid.*, pp. 78–79.

108. *Ibid.*, pp. 81, 84.

109. *Ibid.*, p. 96.

110. *Ibid.*, p. 97.

111. *Ibid.*, p. 109.

112. *Ibid.*, p. 111. "What is called morality in these times is a regulated sensuality; in the same manner exactly as the love of gain is regulated by the establishment of a law of property." Hugh S. R. Elliot, ed., *The Letters of John Stuart Mill* (London: Longmans, Green and Co., 1910), vol. 2, p. 376. Diary entry for March 4, 1854.

113. Burtt, *op. cit.*, p. 922.

114. *Ibid.*, pp. 918–19.

115. Mill, *Three Essays on Religion*, p. 104.

116. Stephen, *op. cit.*, vol. 3, p. 449. Cf. Mill, *Three Essays on Religion*, pp. 256–57. For further discussion by Mill on the role of religion as an instrument of social control, see the concluding section of *The Spirit of the Age*, e.g., pp. 61 ff., 76–77, 79, 83.

117. Such that ". . . I would agree to deprive those of the elective franchise against whom it could justly be alleged that they considered it their interest to invade them." McCulloch, *The Works of David Ricardo*, pp. 554–55. For an example of Ricardo's use of the sacredness of private property as an argument against a legislative proposal, see Sraffa, *op. cit.*, vol. 5, p. 69. With respect to the role of private property being sacred as an intermediate, see Jacob H. Hollander, "The Work and Influence of Ricardo," *AEA Bulletin*, Fourth Series, vol. 1 (1911), Supplement, p. 80: "Yet withal Ricardo was an outright individualist, with profound respect for property rights and vested interests not as things desirable in themselves but as the essential bulwark of social stability."

118. Sraffa, *op. cit.*, vol. 6, p. 184. (Trower is quoting Goldsmith's

Traveller, ll. 432–33.) Wrote Ricardo to Malthus on the same rioting: "I am too much a friend to good order to wish to succeed through such means, besides that I am persuaded that they hurt rather than promote the object which they and I have in view." *Ibid.*, p. 180. See, however, Sraffa, vol. 5, pp. 28–29, and vol. 8, p. 80. Note also Sraffa, vol. 8, p. 102.

119. T. R. Malthus, *The Principles of Political Economy* (The London School of Economics and Political Science, Series of Reprints of Scarce Works on Political Economy, no. 3; 1936), p. 410.

120. "The more the principle of property is respected, the more is it strengthened in the minds of the people. Small attacks upon this principle prepare for greater." Bowring, *op. cit.*, vol. 1, pp. 310, 321. In other instances, where Bentham was an advocate of a more conscious deliberative approach, he was critical of what amounts to the operation of indirection and ignorance; see Bentham, *Morals and Legislation*, p. 125, 220; Bowring, *op. cit.*, vol. 3, pp. 310, 484; Ogden, *op. cit.*, pp. xvii, 121; (Smith,) *Church-of-Englandism*, pp. xxxviii, l–li, I, pp. 246–47 and II, pp. 87 ff, 370–71; and (Beauchamp,) *Influence of Natural Religion*, p. 123.

121. "In the United States the majority undertakes to supply a multitude of ready-made opinions for the use of individuals, who are thus relieved from the necessity of forming opinions of their own. Everybody there adopts great numbers of theories, on philosophy, morals, and politics, without inquiry, upon public trust; and if we examine it very closely, it will be perceived that religion itself holds sway there much less as a doctrine of revelation than as a commonly received opinion." Alexis de Tocqueville, *Democracy in America* (New York: Vintage Books, 1954), two volumes, vol. 2, pp. 9, 10, 11–12.

122. Quoted by Brebner, *op. cit.*, p. 60. See James Bonar, *Philosophy and Political Economy* (New York: Macmillan, 1893), pp. 128, 318.

123. S. G. Checkland, "The Propagation of Ricardian Economics in England," *Economica*, n.s., vol. 16 (1949), p. 51.

124. Mill, *The Spirit of the Age*, pp. 4, 16, 28, 36, 75–76, 79. On the subject of religion, or, rather, the practice of religion, de Tocqueville was more orthodox than Stuart Mill, but it is crucial that both men acknowledged the role of ignorance and indirection. (Stuart Mill's first review of *Democracy in America* deeply gratified de Tocqueville. See de Tocqueville, *op. cit.*, vol. 2, pp. 412–13.) Perhaps the difference lies in de Tocqueville's greater affection or adherence to the idea of religious orthodoxy (e.g., de Tocqueville, *op. cit.*, vol. 2, pp. 21–23). Wrote Mill: ". . . I think that few men of my father's intellect and public spirit, holding with such intensity of moral conviction as he did, unpopular opinions on religion, or on any other of the great subjects of thought, would now either practise or inculcate the witholding of

them from the world, unless in the cases, becoming fewer every day, in which frankness on these subjects would either risk the loss of means of subsistence, or would amount to exclusion from some sphere of usefulness peculiarly suitable to the capacities of the individual. . . . Such an avowal would put an end, at once and for ever, to the vulgar prejudice, that what is called, very improperly, unbelief, is connected with any bad qualities either of mind or heart." Then Mill acknowledges the practice of deception, or ignorance, and indirection: "The world would be astonished if it knew how great a proportion of its brightest ornaments—of those most distinguished even in popular estimation for wisdom and virtue—are complete sceptics in religion; many of them refraining from avowal, less from personal considerations, than from a conscientious, though now in my opinion a most mistaken apprehension, lest by speaking out what would tend to weaken existing beliefs, and by consequence (as they suppose) existing restraints, they should do harm instead of good." Mill, *Autobiography*, pp. 31, 32. Mill was clearly torn between a sense of the necessity of indirection, et cetera, with respect to social control and a feeling of intellectual disapprobation toward deception. See also Stephen, *op. cit.*, vol. 2, pp. 109–19; and J. S. Mill, *Auguste Comte and Positivism*, pp. 75–76, 97–98, 123, 171, 176, 198.

125. De Tocqueville, *op. cit.*, vol. 2, pp. 22–23.

126. But Mill's sympathies were clearly not with what General Francis A. Walker later called "the aristocratic economics of the early part of the century." Wrote Walker: "I don't think that I exaggerate when I say that, among those who deemed themselves the guardians of the true faith, it was considered far better that a man should know nothing about economic literature, and have no interest whatever in the subject, than that, with any amount of learning and any degree of honest purpose, he should have adopted views varying from the standard that was set up." Walker, *op. cit.*, pp. 26, 33. See also Ronald L. Meek, "The Decline of Ricardian Economics in England," *Economica*, n.s., vol. 17 (1950), for excerpts from the writings of Longfield, Scrope, Read, and Cooper, of whom Meek concludes, "Their fundamental approach, in other words, was determined by a belief that what was socially dangerous could not possibly be true." (P. 61.)

127. "But reason itself will teach most men that they must, in the last resort, fall back upon the authority of still more cultivated minds, as the ultimate sanction of the convictions of their reason itself." Mill, *The Spirit of the Age*, p. 31. In "Utilitarianism" Mill wrote: "Any condition, therefore, which is essential to a state of society, becomes more and more an inseparable part of every person's conception of the state of things which he is born into, and which is the destiny of a human being." Burtt, *op. cit.*, p. 920.

128. David Ricardo, *The Principles of Political Economy and Taxation* (New York: Dutton, 1911), p. 62.

129. McCulloch, *Principles of Political Economy*, pp. 88–89, 181, 182, 265, 432.

130. See James Bonar, *Malthus and His Work* (New York: Harper, 1885), pp. 176 ff.

131. Bowring, *op. cit.*, vol. 1, p. 314.

132. *Ibid.*, vol. 1, p. 312, and vol. 3, p. 170.

133. John Stuart Mill, "Chapters on Socialism," *Fortnightly Review*, vol. 31 (1879), p. 516.

134. Mill, *Autobiography*, p. 163. In *The Spirit of the Age*, Mill notes the difficulty of securing discipline in an age of transition: "Who can hope to sway the minds of the public by the old maxims of law, or commerce, or foreign policy, or ecclesiastical policy? . . . Nay, what landlord could call forth his tenants, or what manufacturer his men?" *Op. cit.*, pp. 7, 8. On the "influence of sound religion" as a source of the motive to voluntary exertion and capital accumulation, see Senior, *op. cit.*, vol. 1, p. 99; and the following: "As a general rule, it may be laid down that in proportion to the diffusion in a community of habits of reflection and self-control—to the wish to provide for the happiness of others, and to the weakness of the solicitations of sense and of vanity—in short, in proportion to its moral improvement will be the force of the principle of accumulation, and consequently, the increase of capital." Senior, vol. 1, p. 196, italics deleted.

135. Mill, *Principles of Political Economy*, p. 242. See also Viner, *op. cit.*, pp. 379–80. See note 144, *infra*.

136. Smith, *Essays*, p. 172.

137. Smith, *Wealth of Nations*, p. 28; *Lectures*, p. 253.

138. Smith, *Essays*, pp. 177, 185, 185–86.

139. *Ibid.*, p. 177.

140. Smith, *Lectures*, p. 235.

141. *Ibid.*, pp. 253 ff.

142. Smith, *Wealth of Nations*, p. 15. See also p. 734: "But the understandings of the greater part of men are necessarily formed by their ordinary employments." Cf. Stigler, *op. cit.*, p. 4.

143. Sraffa, *op. cit.*, vol. 7, p. 297; and cf. vol. 9, p. 314. See also Mitchell, *op. cit.*, p. 215; and H. C. Taylor, "The Ricardo Centenary—Discussion," *AEA Bulletin*, Fourth Series, vol. 1 (1911), Supplement, p. 109.

144. Mitchell, *op. cit.*, p. 220. David Hume had stressed that the principle of continuity underlying scientific analysis rested upon custom and habit. See O. H. Taylor, *Economics and Liberalism*, p. 47–48.

145. Ricardo, *op. cit.*, pp. 54–55. In the note commencing at p. 54, Ricardo quotes Torrens' *Essay on the External Corn Trade* to the same effect.

146. Irma Adelman, *Theories of Economic Growth and Development* (Stanford: Stanford University Press, 1961) pp. 49, 59; cf. p. 141. See also Mark Blaug, *Economic Theory in Retrospect*, (Homewood, Ill.: Irwin, 1962), p. 68; *Ricardian Economics*, (New Haven: Yale University Press, 1958), p. 22; and Cecil Clare North, "The Sociological Implications of Ricardo's Economics," *American Journal of Sociology*, vol. 20 (1915), p. 812. On the social relativity of custom, law, and religion, see Sraffa, *op. cit.*, vol. 7, pp. 227–28. According to Senior, "the amount of wealth which a people can acquire and preserve depends principally upon their habits and their institutions." Senior, *op. cit.*, vol. 1, p. 12. See also Haney, *op. cit.*, pp. 99–100.

147. Sraffa, *op. cit.*, vol. 7, p. 248.

148. *Ibid.*, vol. 8, p. 357. See also Ricardo, *op. cit.*, p. 83; and James Bonar, "Where Ricardo Succeeded and Where He Failed," *AEA Bulletin*, Fourth Series, vol. 1 (1911), Supplement, pp. 88–89.

149. See McCulloch, *Principles of Political Economy*, pp. 263–66, and *A Treatise on the Succession to Property Vacant by Death* (London: Longmans, Brown, Green, and Longmans; 1848); and Malthus, *op. cit.*, pp. 372 ff.

150. McCulloch, *Principles of Political Economy*, pp. 390–91. See also Malthus, *op. cit.*, pp. 223 ff.

151. John Stuart Mill, *Autobiography*, p. 75. Wrote McCulloch: "It is, therefore, to the principle of moral restraint, or the exercise of the prudential virtues, that we should exclusively trust for the regulation of the increase of population." *Principles of Political Economy*, p. 235.

152. See, e.g., Stark, *op. cit.*, vol. 3, pp. 411, 482; and Bowring, *op. cit.*, vol. 6, p. 7.

153. See, e.g., Bowring, *op. cit.*, vol. 1, p. 181 (really the entire work "Of the Influence of Time and Place in Matters of Legislation").

154. Robbins, *op. cit.*, pp. 178–79. Stephen's interpretation of Bentham is too narrow when he criticizes Bentham for allegedly failing to consider custom as the basis of law. Stephen, *op. cit.*, vol. 1, p. 304.

155. Mill, "Chapters on Socialism," *op. cit.*, pp. 527, 530; and "The Claims of Labor," in *Dissertations and Discussions* (New York: Holt, 1882), vol. 2, pp. 260 ff. All of the classicists recognized custom as one of the foundations or sources of the particular rules of the institution of private property. On Hume, for example, see Robbins, *op. cit.*, p. 54, and Bernard Wand, "Hume's Non-utilitarianism," *Ethics*, vol. 72 (1962), p. 193 (cf. p. 196).

156. Mill, *Principles of Political Economy*, p. 200. In his "Preliminary Remarks," Mill wrote that the laws of distribution "are partly of human institution: since the manner in which wealth is distributed in any given society, depends on the statutes or usages therein obtaining" (p. 21), but in the chapter on property he wrote that the distribution

of wealth "is a matter of human institution solely. The things once there, mankind, individually or collectively, can do with them as they like." (P. 200.)

157. See Alexander Bain, *John Stuart Mill: A Criticism* (London: Longmans, Green, and Co., 1882), pp. 200–201. See also, e.g., Mill, *Dissertations and Discussions*, vol. 5, pp. 225 ff., particularly, but not only, pp. 279 ff.

158. Mill, *Principles of Political Economy*, pp. 242, 242–43, 246–47, 247. Among other interesting passages, note the following: "In many trades the terms on which business is done are a matter of positive arrangement among the trade, who use the means they always possess of making the situation of any member of the body, who departs from its fixed customs, inconvenient and disagreeable." (P. 247.) This is undoubtedly one of the earliest references to what has come to be called standardized contracts, or contracts of adhesion. See also Bain, *op. cit.*, pp. 200–201; and Richard T. Ely, "The Past and the Present of Political Economy," *Johns Hopkins University Studies in Historical and Political Science*, vol. 2 (1884), p. 39.

159. With respect to the vision of improvement through education, Frank H. Knight has written: "Education provides no formula by which a society can lift itself culturally by its bootstraps, and the faith in education now appears as one of the most pathetic items in the entire creed of liberalism." "Organized education, democratically controlled, is, on its face, as regards fundamental ideals, an agency for promoting continuity, or even for accentuating accepted values, not a means by which 'society' can lift itself by its own bootstraps into a different spiritual world." *Freedom and Reform* (New York: Harper, 1947), pp. 32, 40.

160. Smith, *Essays*, p. 230. See note 172, *infra*.

161. Smith, *Lectures*, p. 259; *Wealth of Nations*, pp. 734–38.

162. *Ibid.*, pp. 739–40. Thus wrote Grampp: "As long as freedom was in danger of being abused, authority had necessarily to be great. As the danger lessened, authority would be diminished, and the maintenance of government by law would rest in ever growing measure on the self-responsibility of individuals. For such a condition to come about, it was essential to increase the political intelligence of the masses —to make it possible for them to acquire an interest in peace." "This condition, the economists believed, depended on the material welfare of the people." "On the Politics of the Classical Economists," p. 747. It is the very next paragraph, commencing the section "Of the Expence of the Institutions for the Instruction of People of all Ages," that Smith begins, "The institutions for the instruction of people of all ages are chiefly those for religious instruction." (P. 740.) In the *Lectures*, Smith is reported to have said, "We may observe an utility in this con-

stitution of our nature that children have so long a dependence upon their parents, to bring down their passions to theirs, and thus be trained up at length to become useful members of society. Every child gets this piece of education, even under the most worthless parent." *Op cit.*, p. 74; cf. p. 160.

163. Sraffa, *op. cit.*, vol. 8, p. 317; cf. Ricardo, *op. cit.*, pp. 61–62.

164. Bonar, *Malthus and His Work*, pp. 194–95, 199.

165. McCulloch, *Principles of Political Economy*, pp. 181–82, 431–32. McCulloch then quotes from Sumner's "Records of the Creation," including the following: "As fast as the standard of intelligence is raised, the poor become more and more able to cooperate in any plan proposed for their advantage, more likely to listen to any reasonable suggestion, more able to understand, and therefore more willing to pursue it. Hence it follows, that when gross ignorance is once removed, and right principles are introduced, a great advantage has been already gained against squalid poverty." (P. 432.) On the role of government promotive of morals, see also p. 294; also see Bowring, *op. cit.*, vol. 1, p. 568, and vol. 4, p. 493; John Stuart Mill, *The Spirit of the Age*, p. xx, and *Principles of Political Economy*, pp. 887–88. *Per contra*, see, e.g., Bowring, *op. cit.*, vol. 1, p. 147; and (Nassau Senior,) Book Review, *Edinburgh Review*, vol. 88 (1848), p. 331.

166. Bowring, *op. cit.*, vol. 1, p. 318.

167. *Ibid.*, vol. 1, pp. 568–69; Bentham, *Morals and Legislation*, pp. 311–12.

168. Mitchell, *op. cit.*, p. 194.

169. Mill, "Chapters on Socialism," *op. cit.*, p. 516.

170. Mill, *Autobiography*, pp. 75–76.

171. Mill, *Three Essays on Religion*, pp. 78, 80. "A little reflection will, I think, lead us to the conclusion that it is this which is the great moral power in human affairs, and that religion only seems so powerful because this mighty power has been under its command." (P. 78.)

172. *Ibid.*, p. 82. See also the passage from p. 81, quoted *supra*, text at note 93. Thus wrote Stephen: "Now Mill, believing even to excess in the power of education, included in education the whole discipline of life due to the relations of the individual to his social environment; and it is his essential principle that this force should be directed to enforcing a sense of 'responsibility' in the widest acceptation of the word." *Op. cit.*, vol. 3, p. 273. See also J. S. Mill, *Auguste Comte and Positivism*, pp. 138–39, 141, 143, 146. In the view of Senior, education would help to discipline the labor force and serve as a basis of wealth accumulation. Senior, *Industrial Efficiency and Social Economy*, vol. 2, pp. 328–31. "In its widest sense," wrote Senior, "the word *education* comprehends all the external influences by which the disposition implanted by nature in any animal is subsequently modified. In its nar-

rower sense, it is confined to the influences which one person intentionally exercises over another by precept or by example. . . . These influences are of two kinds: first, the imparting knowledge, which may be called *teaching;* secondly, the creation of habits, which may be called *training.* . . . As between teaching and training, there can be no doubt that training is by far the more important. It is the more important even for the purposes of knowledge; knowledge may be forgotten, and requires some trouble to keep it up. Habits once thoroughly acquired cannot be discontinued without pain; they are therefore permanent. And even the knowledge which has been forgotten, if it be worth recovering, will generally by recovered by a man of good intellectual habits. . . . Moral training is, obviously, still more important than intellectual training; . . . Training, therefore, or the formation of habits, rather than teaching, or the imparting knowledge, is the great business of education." (Pp. 329–31.)

173. Schneider, *op. cit.*, p. 494.

174. Robbins, *op. cit.*, p. 6.

175. The theory of economic policy thus defined has to do with the structuring of the economic decision-making process as a whole and thereby with the way in which society organizes for, and controls, economic development. It is not surprising, then, nor inappropriate to note, that economists increasingly concerned over problems of economic development have returned to the classical view of the economic problem which, according to Myint, was how to increase the material well-being of nations. Spengler and Allen, *op. cit.*, pp. 442–53. Students of economic development theory and policy have learned anew the lessons of Weber and Tawney that were known to the classicists: that economic development requires recourse to the nondeliberative forces of social control and social change. See, e.g., Clark Kerr *et al, Industrialism and Industrial Man* (Cambridge: Harvard University Press, 1960), and Everett E. Hagen, *On the Theory of Social Change* (Homewood, Ill.: Dorsey Press, 1962). Finally, it is a tribute to the genius of the institutionalists, primarily of the Commons-Witte variety, that they were preoccupied with the problems of institution building that are at the heart of promoting economic development; what Usher says of the classicists is equally applicable to the institutionalists whatever one thinks of the content of their respective contributions, for both groups "made substantial contributions to state policy designed to develop or modify private institutions essential to economic activity." A. P. Usher, *Explorations in Economics: Notes and Essays Contributed in Honor of F. W. Taussig* (New York: McGraw-Hill, 1936), p. 407.

176. Frank H. Knight, *On the History and Method of Economies* (Chicago: University of Chicago Press, 1956), p. 18.

177. It should be clear that to establish the nondeliberative forces

of social control as correlative (in the classical theory of economic policy) with the legal or deliberative is also to establish the coexistence of rational and emotive elements in policy. That such is the case with Smith, vis-a-vis Hayek, is excellently developed by Macfie, "Adam Smith's Theory of Moral Sentiments," pp. 19 ff. This is further discussed in Chapter Five, *infra*.

CHAPTER THREE

The Economic Role of the State (I)

THE PROBLEM

In the market-plus-framework interpretation of the classical theory of economic policy, the operation of the framework is essential to the creation of harmony in the sense of order, or mutuality of interests, or the resolution of the problems of freedom and control, and continuity and change. The provision of the framework, identified by Lord Robbins as legal in character, is thus one of the basic components of what he calls the "broad conception" [1] of the classicists as to desirable government activity. The market-plus-framework interpretation, so construed, thus indicates that *laissez faire* (*in the sense identified in Chapter One*, namely, reliance upon market forces, private property and private enterprise, i.e., "the market") *requires not precludes* government participation, and makes it clear that the state *is* an instrument of control and *is* a participant in the economic decision-making process, at least in the view of the classical economists.

It has been seen in Chapter Two that there is more to the significance and scope of the concept "framework," and "theory of economic policy," than is indicated by the Robbinsian specification thereof as being legal in character. Abstracting from that, and abstracting also from the question of the meaningfulness of the concept of "framework" per se, the framework-provision function of government remains of central importance to the market-plus-framework interpretation.

The question arises, however, as to what it is that government does when it provides the framework. That is to say, what is the set of activities and results, or, alternately, what are the roles or facets of government participation, comprised in such framework-provision? The objective of this chapter is to specify the classical theory of the economic role of the state so far as the components of government participation in the provision of the "framework" is concerned, at the same time indicating something of the scope of policy in the classical theory of economic policy. Whatever is resolved as to the meaningfulness of the concept of "framework," what is specified concerning the relevant facets of government participation will be fundamental to any restatement of the classical policy system and further, will be of great importance for the theory of economic policy of the market system itself. At the very minimum, the chapter will provide a further specification of the Robbinsian framework-provision function of government.

The task of this chapter is therefore relatively simpler than that of the preceding one, since the framework-provision role of law has already been established. Yet it may be argued that the conventional and unspecified understanding of the content of that function itself considerably understates the significance of what is involved. Indeed, it will be seen that the classical theory of economic policy unmistakably had a serious and extensive place for the ordinarily unobtrusive and subtle, yet none the less fundamental presence of government in the economic process, and in the pattern of freedom and control.

The analysis of this chapter will focus upon the two fundamental facets or roles of the framework-provision function of
government: first, the role of law in the division of public and
private decision-making participation; and, second, the role of
law in the structuring (or division) of private decision-making
participation. As indicated, the analysis abstracts from the
operation of the nonlegal forces of social control, such that
the concept "public" will refer to legal social control or participation; and the concept "private," to nominally private
participation, however otherwise governed by the nondeliberative forces.

Law and the Division of Public and Private Decision-Making Participation

Law and Order: The classical economists, as they should have
been in an epoch called by Stuart Mill an "age of transition," [2] were profoundly aware of the dual problems of freedom and control, and continuity and change. Moreover, they
were of the belief, as Lord Robbins and the preceding chapter
have shown, that the resolution of these problems was not
something that could be taken entirely for granted. In their
view, the social process was to a large extent involved with
the need for a continuous resolution of these problems. The
conditions of order, or harmony, or mutuality of interests,
however it is expressed, were things that had to be created
and continuously re-created. The classicists recognized that
fundamental to the creation of such harmony as could be
created were the forces of social control, whose general task,
to reiterate, was to channel behavior, and to integrate individuals into the ways of society. The preceding chapter has

shown the importance of order, and the operation of the non-legal or nondeliberative forces of social control with respect to order, and to the economic decision-making process as a whole, in the classical theory of economic policy. It is elementary but nevertheless significant that law, or the state, was also seen as a necessary participating force in the creation and maintenance of order.

The classicists acknowledged the state as an instrument of social control and gave it, correlative to the nonlegal forces of social control, a pre-eminent place in the creation of order. Although the efficacy of the state in that role generally was seen as dependent upon the operation of the other forces of control, the force of organized society in the form of the state was neither secondary nor peripheral, but correlative. Among other things, this reflects the transition from nondeliberative to deliberative forces in the general pattern of social control (see Chapter Five, *infra*), but it is to be remembered that this role of politically organized society antedates that transition. Law was instrumental with respect to order, harmony, and the security that was seen as a condition of economic progress.[3]

Thus, for example, the classicists recognized the inevitable and innumerable conflicts of interests, claims, and values that develop in any society, and are most obtrusive in a pluralist or free society. They acknowledged the role of the nondeliberative forces in muting these conflicts; in like manner they recognized the role of government in settling disputes, and serving as a mode of conflict resolution in general.[4] In no small way this was the role of the common law and the system of courts—an important, however usually unobtrusive, facet of the role of government. Thus wrote Ricardo to Trower: "Nothing can be more useful to the public than that enlightened men, with no motives for the misapplication of the powers entrusted to them should take upon themselves the duties of magistrates. I am convinced that you are performing very essential services to the community about you by settling the disputes,—preserving the peace, and affording securities for the protection of property within the circle of your influence." [5]

Adam Smith, who lectured on jurisprudence; Jeremy Bentham, student of William Blackstone, teacher of John Austin, and eminent legal thinker in his own right; James Mill, author of "Jurisprudence" and "Government"; and John Stuart Mill, student of Bentham and Austin in jurisprudence—these men knew that the state was an integral component of organized society in the post-medieval world. The economic liberalism of the classical theory of economic policy has to be related to this fundamental role of law and government, whose criminal, or penal-law sanctions, are, of course, of importance far beyond the field of economic policy.

Law and the Order: But the classical theory of economic policy, given the idea of a framework-provision function of government, involves more than the usual relationship between *law and order,* however significant that may be. In addition to the idea of law *and* order, the classical policy system has as one of its basic facets the relation between law and *the* order: for the classical economists understood that the economic order was itself in part a product of legal choice. The classicists recognized that the legal system, by virtue of making law, together with the other nonlegal forces of social control and otherwise nominally private forces, participated in, and was fundamentally involved in, the division of public and private decision-making participation. The economic decision-making process was seen as comprising private, legal, and nonlegal participants, and it was through the interaction between these three components, and their subcomponents, that the respective spheres were to be continually determined and redetermined, however unobtrusive the subcomponents and their interaction may be. Indeed, it is one of

102

the central themes of these chapters that the classical policy system involves the interaction between these components in the development of perhaps every facet of economic policy.

What is important at this point is that the structure of the economic decision-making process was not taken as something given; rather, it was a function of the operation of society, and law was one of the central component forces. The private sector was what it was in part through the process of its inter- action with the other forces, including law. Thus, for example, it is clear in James Mill's "Jurisprudence" that the scope of the private sector is not autonomous, but reflects the other forces in society including law. The state must exercise choice in determining its participation in structuring the process, doing this by considering the respective benefits accruing from al- ternative allocations of decision-making participation.[6] So, also, does Bentham differentiate between "special interfer- ence" by government, and state participation in the allocation of power, as it were, among *agenda, sponte acta,* and *non- agenda,* i.e., "the distribution made and maintained, and the protection afforded, by the civil and penal branches of the law." [7] Given this recognition by the classicists of the role of law in the division of power in society, it is not surprising for McCulloch to have quoted Burke on "one of the finest problems in legislation, namely, to determine what the state ought to take upon itself to direct by the public wisdom, and what it ought to leave, with as little interference as possible, to individual exertion." [8] The problem of the scope of the role of government is clearly a facet of the division of power in society, and it is equally clear that legislation was one of the sources or modes establishing that division. One might even say that it was the *de jure* source. Legislation (via court and parliament) was a mode of determining the scope of legisla- tion and the role of government, and thereby, also, the over- all division of power.[9] It therefore follows that whatever

103

theory of the end of law is possessed by those who are in a position to decide the scope and content of legal participation, that theory governs, *pro tanto*, the division of public and private decision-making power.[10] Participation in the interplay comprising the division of power in society was one of the crucial roles of government in the classical policy system, and one taken for granted in every discussion of the subject.

Law and the Market System: The classical economists thus were aware that the structure of the economic decision-making process, i.e., the system of economic organization, was a partial function of law; that law served to establish, adjust and maintain the desired economic system; and that the theory of economic policy operative through the state to that extent governed the organization of the economy. This facet is one of the two major ones necessarily involved in the further specification of the framework-provision function of government: the role of law in the division of power (decision-making participation) in society.

For the classical economists, this meant the *market system:* in every discussion by a classicist on the role of the state in economic life, it is the regime of competition, or the market economy, that law must secure, strengthen, and maintain. The market system, or the system of economic freedom, is the distinctive classical policy postulate. This is not merely to say that the classicists were in favor of the market system, which, of course, they were. Rather, it is to establish that *the* order, or *the* decision-making process, whose institutionalization law was to help secure, was that of the market economy. As Lord Robbins points out, the market is an artifact,[11] and it is one of the created objects of law. As with the Physiocrats,[12] law was an instrument for the attainment of economic objectives, and economy was an object of legal control; and for the classicists this included the institutionalization of the system itself. The choice and development of the market system was a principal facet and criterion of the classical policy system as a whole, and a basic facet and criterion of their theory of the economic role of the state. In this respect, if in no other, the framework-provision function of government is logically prior to the system of economic freedom.

But law was not only to promote the market system *writ large*. In view of the classicists, the task of law was also to participate in the development and promotion of the institutions of the market economy, which were, perforce, at least partially legal in character. Law was to help promulgate the basic institutions that make the market system what it is: forms of business organization, negotiable instruments, money, contractual and other relations, and, of course, private property.[13]

Moreover, in so doing, the state would be promoting economic development within or under the aegis of the market economy. Whether or not the classical view of the economic problem was, as Myint suggests, that of economic development, the classicists were institutionalist in their preoccupation with the problems of institution-building that are at the heart of promoting economic development.[14] For the classicists this generally meant legal promotion of institutions conducive to economic development through the free market, given the conditions of time and place;[15] legal encouragement to saving and investment, or capital formation;[16] facilitating individual or private initiative in general;[17] and the supplying of social capital, or public works.[18] As the material in the citations will indicate, these were implementational criteria of state policy in the classical system, and often became manifest in particular recommendations. It is unquestionably true that, vis-a-vis mercantilism and Physiocracy, this program was in part one of governmental retrenchment. But it is nevertheless also true, and a facet of the classical theory of economic policy, that the state was to promote the market system, the particular institutions comprising the "framework" of private sector activity, and economic development within and through the system.

To the classicists, moreover, a correlative of using the legal process to create a market economy out of the landlord-dominated, semi-feudal, and mercantilist *status quo*,[19] was, in the language of Auerbach,[20] to prevent the consolidation of social life antagonistic to the advent of industrialization and the market system per se. Although, for example, both Malthus and McCulloch had some misgivings about industrialization, both were advocates of the market economy in principle, and, with the other classicists, were not unwilling to use government to prevent and remove obstacles (as they conceived them) to the operation of the market system. Included among the obstacles were rival theories of economic policy (or at least implementations different from and rival to their own); thus government was to protect the enterprise-oriented from machinations (or some, or many, of them) deemed anathema to the viable operation of the system, and the industrialization it involved.[21]

LAW AND THE STRUCTURE OF PRIVATE DECISION-MAKING PARTICIPATION

In the preceding paragraphs the idea has been stressed that the classical theory of economic policy (and the Robbinsian idea of the framework-provision function of government) may be interpreted to include as a central facet the participation of the state in the process of ordering the economic system, interacting with nominally private and nonlegal forces in society. This was seen to include state participation in the establishment of the market system and the institutions comprising it, the facilitating of economic development through private enterprise, and the prevention of antagonistic consolidations of social life—through the participation of the state in the provision of the fundamental ordering of society, however unobtrusively taken for granted.

This complex of legal operations, relating to the role of law in the *division of public and private decision-making power*, is but one of two presently relevant facets of a broader process. This larger process is the structuring of the economic decision-making process as a whole, the basic problem of which is the allocation of participation in the exercise of choice in the resolution of the basic economic problems, the structure of which at any point in time is the result of the interaction of all the participants. As indicated before, it is contended that the classical policy system acknowledged the role of the state as but one interacting participant, together with the nonlegal forces of social control and the spheres of private participation, the forces of the private sector. Law thus participated in the determination of its own scope, and in the scope and role of private enterprise *writ large*. The second facet has to do with the structure of these very same forces of the private sector, and for present purposes relates to the role of law in the *structuring of private decision-making participation*. The classical economists, who had such a significant place for the spontaneous forces of the free market, nevertheless also acknowledged the role of law (in addition to the nonlegal forces of social control) as a force governing the structure and decisions made by the nominally private sector and, thereby, underlying the operation of market forces. This acknowledgment is of crucial significance for the classical theory of economic policy, for, given state support of the market system per se, it involves the more or less unobtrusive state founding of the ostensibly free forces of the market place. The resolution of the basic

107

economic problems so far as they are resolved through the private or market sector, in part therefore also reflects the operation of law as an instrument of social control, functioning to structure the nominally nonlegal sector. While this role of the state was often taken for granted in the classicists' discussions of particular policy questions, there is considerable evidence that it was an important facet of their theory of the economic role of the state and a facet of which they were quite aware, manifested in important discussions on the relation of law to rights in general, and to property rights in particular.[22] What is involved throughout is the exercise of legal choice in the determination of the conditions and structure of private participation.

Law and Private Rights: In the classical theory of economic policy, private participation in the economic decision-making process was nominally expressed through the notion—or fiction, as Bentham called it [23]—of "rights." Rights, following James Mill, are powers, and are ultimately indicators of loci, or conditions of participation, as economic actors.[24] Alternately, rights connoted liberties reciprocally related to one's exposures to the liberties (or rights, or powers) of others, considered individually or collectively.

Perhaps nothing is more "natural" in a society characterized by private participation than the notion of "natural rights" as a mode for expression of the claim for private rights in general and for specific rights in particular.[25] The pattern of private participation was generally seen in terms of the developing pattern of rights, in terms of which it was discussed and argued.[26] Moreover, nothing is more linguistically "natural," in the same society, for the role of government to be expressed in the proposition of "protecting rights." [27] The idea that government should protect rights reduces to the proposition that government should protect *existing* rights, or, since the rights of one are reciprocally related to the rights of others, protect

108

the existing *pattern* of rights. The protection of existing rights, or the existing pattern of rights, is a facet of the need or desire for continuity, which is itself a facet of the basic problem of continuity and change. Reasonable security of expectations is a fundamental legal postulate in the market system: "Without law there is no security; consequently no abundance, nor even certain subsistence." [28] Therefore, "The object and end of the science . . . of jurisprudence" was, to James Mill, "the protection of rights. . . . What we desire to accomplish is the protection of rights; . . . That men are susceptible of happiness only in proportion as rights are protected, is a proposition which, taken generally, it is unnecessary to prove." [29] The notions, then, of natural rights and rights' protection, like that of the sacredness of rights, are *intermediates* (in the sense developed in Chapter Two), functioning to secure continuity, i.e., continuity of the existing pattern or structure of private decision-making participation.

But the basic question relevant to the theory of economic policy has to do with the *determination* of such rights as are or are to be legally enforceable, i.e., actual or proposed specific loci of participation. Although these rights are also nonlegal (i.e., customary or *de facto*) in character and while, further, there is interaction between the legal and nonlegal sources, the crucial facet pertinent here concerns the nature and content of such rights as are enforceable at law. The notions of "natural rights" and "protection of rights" are clearly relevant so far as the problem and rhetoric of continuity are concerned. But this does not exhaust the content of the classical theory of economic policy on the relation of law and private rights. Although individual rights were at times defined "in such a way that only a very limited amount of state activity appeared to be necessary," [30] the classicists, on the contrary, postulated a much more fundamental relationship between law and private rights. Far more important to the classical analysis was the understanding that the rights involved in questions of economic policy, so far as the economic role of the state is concerned, were rights already at least partially *legal* in status, which were relative, first, to the limitations imposed by law, and, second, to the participation of others.[31]

The classical economists, it has already been suggested, included in the role of law the institutionalization of private property as a basic economic institution, giving substance to the market system. Indeed, the classical economists attributed the most intimate of connections between the institutions of government and private property. "Property and civil government," Smith is said to have lectured, "very much depend on one another." [32] Property, wrote Bentham, "is entirely the creature of law." "Property and law are born and must die together. Before the laws, there was no property: take away the laws, all property ceases." [33] Moreover, the classicists were clearly aware of the relation of the fact of a law of property to the structure of the private decision-making sector. "Till there be property," lectured Smith, "there can be no government, the very end of which is to secure wealth, and to defend the rich from the poor." [34] In the *Wealth of Nations*, the parallel sentence is qualified, but the basic relationship is yet asserted.[35] It is of the greatest importance that the relation is not merely one way: the notion that private property was the institutional creature of law did not preclude an understanding that both the fact of, and the law of, private property were responsive to private power.[36] The institution of the state was thus seen as crucial to the institution of private property, or, rather, both were seen as crucial to each other; in any event, the security of private property rested upon the law.[37]

But the legal institutionalization of private property has to do with the fact of private property *writ large*. What of the specific rights of private property as such? In the classical theory of economic policy the law was to protect private property or the rights of private property, but the law also was seen as a source of those very same rights. If every man, in other words, was to be protected with respect to what is his very own, that which is his "very own" was what is so protected and secured by law.[38] Before there can be "offences against property," "legislation must first determine what things are to be regarded as each man's property." [39] Even though "property rights" as such were often taken for granted, the classical economists did acknowledge the legal basis of such rights as did exist.[40]

What was true of property rights was true of rights in general: according to the classical economists the operation of the state encompassed its participation in the process of defining the rights, and, conversely, the exposures to the rights of others, which lie at the foundation of the private sector, i.e., which structure participation in that sector and, thereby, underlie market forces. If rights connote loci or conditions of participation in the private sector, i.e., if "rights are powers," [41] then in the classical policy system one of the sources of such loci or conditions was law: rights were a partial function of law. The rights that the law was said, in other contexts, to protect were themselves partially *de jure*, which is to include law in the logically antecedent determination (recognition and enforcement) of the substantive content of rights denoting the conditions of participation. As James Mill put it, "The grand object of the civil code is the definition of rights." [42] According to Bentham, since "The care of providing for his enjoyments ought to be left almost entirely to each individual," the role of government in this connection was that of "creating rights which it confers upon individuals. . . ." [43] Although for some purposes it was appropriate to consider the existing pattern of rights as given (and to be protected), these rights, the classicists recognized, were what they were in part through the operation of the legal system.

If the distinction is drawn between rights as interest-claims, and rights as interest-recognition-and-enforcement, then to the extent that law is involved in the resolution of competing claims, and the determination (recognition-and-enforcement) of rights as secured loci or conditions of participation, such resolution involves structuring the private decision-making process. It also follows that such loci or conditions as the law enforces are relative to the limitations imposed by law. According to James Mill, "Rights are sometimes more, sometimes less extensive . . . for the definition of rights two things are necessary." "It is necessary for the legislature . . . to fix not only what are the facts which shall give commencement to a right, but what are the facts which shall put an end to it." [44]

In the classical theory of economic policy, then, the legal process participates in the determination of the pattern of rights that connote loci and conditions of participation in the private market process, and which, perforce, structure the private sector. Recognition of this relatively unobtrusive role of law gives rise to the question of *which rights* it is to which the law is to give effect. The language of rights ultimately reduces to the juxtaposition of *interests*, and law participates in the process of choosing between competing interest-claims. As the references cited in notes 41 through 44 will confirm, the classical economists were aware of the exercise of legal (both judicial and legislative) *choice* in the process of selecting *which interests* the law would secure, i.e., translate into "rights." The state gives effect to certain claims as opposed to others and thereby participates in the structuring of the private sector by whatever criteria of choice but by choice constituting policy none the less. This role is one of the crucial co-ordinates to which the framework-provision function of government may be reduced. However much the classicists were critical of mercantilism and the "privileges" granted special interests, they were fundamentally aware that all private rights were at least partially legal in character, and that the pattern of private participation was partially what it was because of legal selection of some interests over others.[45]

As with rights in general, the classicists acknowledged the role of government in *choosing* between relative property rights' claimants, and thereby defining the particular rights of property (the content of the bundle of rights) that make private property what it is and, in the aggregate, determining the loci and conditions of private participation so far as this is done through the institutionalization of property rights. Property rights, as with other rights, were what they were because in part of the law of property, and the loci of participation that they connoted were relative both to the limitations imposed by law and to each other, in each case resting upon the exercise of legal choice.[46]

So also with contract law: it represents a class of objects with respect to which "however disinclined, [government] cannot help interfering, in an infinite variety of ways, and for an infinite variety of purposes." [47] If private property is the locus and condition of private participation in the economy, then contract is a mode of transacting such participation, and the role of government is essentially the same. Through the law of property and contract, government will structure such participation; among other things, government will "decide as to the species of contracts to which it will lend its sanction" and "give a legal effect." [48] McCulloch thus indicates that contract law structures and channels private participation through the establishment of legal choice and, perforce, of legal policy, ultimately transcending the autonomy of contract: "It may be laid down in general, that every government is bound to assist in enforcing all contracts fairly entered into between individuals, unless they are made in opposition to some existing law, or are clearly such as cannot fail of being prejudicial to the public interests." [49]

The same conclusion is reached by John Stuart Mill:

Is it no part of the duty of government to enforce contracts? Here the doctrine of non-intervention would no doubt be stretched a little, and it would be said that enforcing contracts is not regulating the affairs of individuals at the pleasure of government, but giving effect to their own expressed desire. . . . But governments do not limit their concern with contracts to a simple enforcement. They take upon themselves to determine what contracts are fit to be enforced. . . . But when once it is admitted that there are any engagements which for reasons of expediency the law ought not to enforce, the same question is necessarily opened with respect to all engagements. . . . Every question which can possibly arise as to the policy of contracts, and of the relations which they establish among human beings, is a question for the legislator; and one which he cannot escape from considering, and in some way or other deciding.[50]

The law of contracts, as does the law of property, structures the private decision-making process by giving effect to some claims and not to others, between which the legal process must somehow choose, by "reinforcing" the private economic power of certain participants and not that of others, and by determining the substance of "the public interests" and of "public policy." The framework-provision function of government, then, necessarily involves questions of choice and of policy, questions of the "relations" which the law establishes among human beings, each "a question for the legislator, . . . and one which he cannot escape from considering, and in some way or other deciding," with the inevitable consequence of governing the division of private decision-making power.

Finally, it should be pointed out that the process of selection between competing rights' claimants being one process of making legal policy, this process involved the exercise of legal choice in terms of what the classicists understood to be the "current needs of the community." [51] This meant that the adjudication of relative rights' claims would be undertaken

114

in the context of the felt needs of industrialization and the
market system. That is to say, the legal process was to be
essentially utilitarian and materialist in choosing those interests whose fruition would promote industrial and economic
development under the market system. As both Spengler and
de Schweinitz, among others, have stressed, the classical system involved the elevation of the strategic middle class, and
the social ordering of differential opportunities conducive to
economic development.[52] Once again, that this ordering was
unobtrusive to many, if not most, participants in the economic
process did not vitiate its importance. The practice of indirection and ignorance was not limited to the nondeliberative
forces.

CONCLUSION

This chapter has attempted further to identify what has been
generally unobtrusive and ambiguous in the framework-
provision function of government. It has attempted to specify
the facets of the logically prior and pre-eminent existence of
government, however much in the context of the market system. These facets have been identified as (a) the role of law
in the division of public and private decision-making participation, and (b) the role of law in the structuring or division
of private decision-making participation.

In the case of the former, it was seen that government
participates in the ultimate establishment of the market system as *the* institutionalized economic decision-making process
which, thereby, necessarily includes government participation
by its very genesis and character. In the case of the latter, the
rights that connote loci and conditions of private participa-

tion, expressed as property rights or otherwise, are themselves also partially legal in character, and represent the exercise of social choice through the legal process; and in the aggregate they serve to structure the private sector, however otherwise viable it may be, and whatever scope remains for the spontaneous activities of private economic actors. The law then functions as an unobtrusive structuring force, exercising control over the conditions of spontaneous activity in general, and the conditions of individual participation.

In the case of both facets of legal participation, as with the nonlegal forces of social control, not only does the framework-provision function of government mean that government is part of the total economic decision-making process, serving to structure that process, but also it signifies that the legal process helps govern the content of the effective decisions made, as well as economic activity in general. This is accomplished both by governing the conditions of private participation, and by direct legal participation comprising the public sector as such; the latter will be further examined in the next chapter.

The fact that the law in many respects serves to legitimize that which has its origin elsewhere (e.g., the results of the pressures of competing private economic actors) does not vitiate these conclusions; rather, it reflects the aforementioned process of interaction between all the participants in the total economic decision-making process, notably the influence of private forces and custom upon the law.

That the classical theory of the economic role of the state, and, perforce, the classical theory of economic policy acknowledged both of the indicated facets of government participation is beyond question. If the framework-provision function of government does not reduce to these two components, it reduces to nothing. It is therefore further testimony to the sophistication of the classicists that they did acknowledge these functions of government, so conventionally taken for granted or ignored, however much they themselves also tended to take them for granted in discussions of particular issues of policy. The conventional laissez faire interpretation (which differs from that given in Chapter One, *supra*) and emphasis upon the market as the distinctive classical message have obscured these facets of classical thought. The brilliant and penetrating analyses of such writers as Commons and others,[53] as surprising as it may seem, have the parallel ideas of the classical theory of economic policy as a distinguished precursor.

NOTES: CHAPTER THREE

1. Lionel Robbins, *Theory of Economic Policy* (London: Macmillan, 1953), p. 188.

2. John Stuart Mill, *The Spirit of the Age* (Chicago: University of Chicago Press, 1942).

3. See, for example, Adam Smith, *Essays* (London: Ward, Lock & Co., 1880), pp. 145–46, 205; Nassau William Senior, *An Outline of the Science of Political Economy* (New York: Kelley, 1951), pp. 74–76, 87, 182–84; John Stuart Mill, *Dissertations and Discussions* (New York: Holt, 1882), vol. 4, pp. 157–226; John Bowring, ed., *The Works of Jeremy Bentham* (New York: Russell & Russell, 1962), vol. 1, p. 307; W. Stark, *Jeremy Bentham's Economic Writings* (New York: Burt Franklin, 1954), vol. 3, p. 311. See also William D. Grampp, "On the Politics of the Classical Economists," *Quarterly Journal of Economics*, vol. 62 (1948); William Clyde Dunn, "Adam Smith and Edmund Burke: Complementary Contemporaries," *Southern Economic Journal*, vol. 7 (1941), e.g., p. 342; Henry J. Bittermann, "Adam Smith's Empiricism and the Law of Nature," *Journal of Political Economy*, vol. 48 (1940), e.g., p. 519; Karl de Schweinitz, Jr., "Free Enterprise in a Growth World," *Southern Economic Journal*, vol. 29 (1962), pp. 105–7; C. A. Cooke, "Adam Smith and Jurisprudence," *Law Quarterly Review*, vol. 51 (1935), pp. 326–32; C. F. Bastable, "Adam Smith's Lectures on 'Jurisprudence,'" *Hermathena*, vol. 10

(1889), pp. 210–11; Glenn R. Morrow, in *Adam Smith, 1776–1926* (Chicago: University of Chicago Press, 1928), p. 141; D. H. Macgregor, *Economic Thought and Policy* (London: Oxford University Press, 1949), pp. 71 ff.; and O. H. Taylor, *Economics and Liberalism* (Cambridge: Harvard University Press, 1955) e.g., pp. 92, 95.

4. J. R. McCulloch, *The Principles of Political Economy* (Edinburgh: Tait, 1843), pp. 258, 268 ff.; Smith, *Essays*, e.g., p. 303. See also Bittermann, *op. cit.*, pp. 728–29; and A. L. Macfie, "Adam Smith's *Moral Sentiments* as Foundation for his *Wealth of Nations*," *Oxford Economic Papers*, n.s., vol. 11 (1959), p. 224.

5. Piero Sraffa, ed., *The Works and Correspondence of David Ricardo* (Cambridge: Cambridge University Press, 1952), vol. 8, pp. 131–32. According to Adam Smith, "The civil magistrate is entrusted with the power not only of preserving the public peace by restraining injustice, but of promoting the prosperity of the commonwealth, by establishing good discipline, and by discouraging every sort of vice and impropriety; he may prescribe rules, therefore, which not only prohibit mutual injuries among fellow-citizens, but command mutual good offices to a certain degree." Smith, *Essays*, p. 74.

6. Philip Wheelwright, ed., *Selected Writings of Jeremy Bentham, James Mill and John Stuart Mill* (Garden City, N. Y.: Doubleday, Doran & Co., 1935), pp. 213–24. See also Leslie Stephen, *The English Utilitarians* (New York: Peter Smith, 1950), vol. 3, pp. 269–70; and *infra*. O. H. Taylor's statement that "'the system of natural liberty' was Smith's ideal legal system," really means that what Robbins calls the "system of economic freedom" was what it was in part because law determined (again, in part) its own scope and thereby the scope of the private sector. Taylor, *op. cit.*, p. 92.

7. Stark, *op. cit.*, vol. 3, p. 323.

8. McCulloch, *op. cit.*, p. 257.

9. It should not need reiteration that the content of law, and therefore the scope of the role of government in the economy, was itself responsive to and influenced by the forces of the private sector as well as the nonlegal forces.

10. See Roscoe Pound, *Jurisprudence* (St. Paul: West Publishing Co., 1959), five volumes, vol. 1, pp. 506–7; and D. Hughes Parry, "Economic Theories in English Case Law," *Law Quarterly Review*, vol. 47 (1931), pp. 195 ff.

11. See Chapter One, note 13, *supra*.

12. Warren J. Samuels, "The Physiocratic Theory of Economic Policy," *Quarterly Journal of Economics*, vol. 76 (1962), p. 162; cf. p. 150.

13. McCulloch, *op. cit.*, pp. 256, 258, 287; and *A Treatise on the*

Succession to Property Vacant by Death (London: Longmans, Brown, Green, and Longmans, 1848), pp. 171–72; John Stuart Mill, *Principles of Political Economy* (New York: Kelley, 1961), pp. 795 ff. Also see A. P. Usher, in *Explorations in Economics: Notes and Essays in Honor of F. W. Taussig* (New York: McGraw-Hill, 1936), p. 407.

14. See Chapter Two, note 175, *supra*.

15. James Bonar and J. H. Hollander, eds., *Letters of David Ricardo to Hutches Trower* (Oxford: Oxford University Press, 1899), p. 105; Stark, *op. cit.*, vol. 1, pp. 260 ff.; and vol. 3, pp. 338–39; McCulloch, *Principles*, pp. 268–91; Bowring, *op. cit.*, vol. 1, p. 317. See also Irma Adelman, *Theories of Economic Growth and Development* (Stanford: Stanford University Press, 1961), p. 140; Nathan Rosenberg, "Some Institutional Aspects of the *Wealth of Nations*," *Journal of Political Economy*, vol. 68 (1960), e.g., pp. 561–62; R. D. Collison Black, "The Classical Economists and the Irish Problem," *Oxford Economic Papers*, vol. 5 (1953), pp. 30–31; de Schweinitz, *op. cit.*, pp. 106 ff.; Morrow, in *Adam Smith, 1776–1926*, pp. 150 ff.; Kurt Singer, Book Review, *The Economic Record*, vol. 29 (1953), p. 269.

16. David Ricardo, *Principles of Political Economy and Taxation* (New York: Dutton, 1911), p. 96; Stark, *op. cit.*, vol. 3, pp. 482-83; McCulloch, *Principles*, p. 287. See also Adelman, *op. cit.*, p. 41; T. W. Hutchison, "Bentham as an Economist," *Economic Journal*, vol. 66 (1956), p. 303, reprinted in Joseph J. Spengler and William R. Allen, *Essays in Economic Thought* (Chicago: Rand McNally, 1960), p. 343.

17. Edwin A. Burtt, ed., *The English Philosophers from Bacon to Mill* (New York: Modern Library, 1939), p. 1041; McCulloch, *Principles*, p. 257.

18. McCulloch, *Principles*, pp. 285 ff.; Bonar and Hollander, *op. cit.*, *loc. cit.*; Smith, *Wealth of Nations* (New York: Modern Library, 1937), p. 651. See also Singer, *op. cit.*, *loc. cit.*; Jacob Viner, "Bentham and J. S. Mill: The Utilitarian Background," *American Economic Review*, vol. 39 (1949), p. 371; Edmund Whittaker, *Schools and Streams of Economic Thought* (Chicago: Rand McNally, 1960), p. 169; and R. H. Inglis Palgrave, *Dictionary of Political Economy* (London: Macmillan, 1894–1899), three volumes, vol. 2, p. 535.

19. Dudley Dillard, "Ricardo in Retrospect," *Journal of Economic History*, vol. 13 (1953), pp. 95, 100.

20. Carl A. Auerbach, "Law and Social Change in the United States," *UCLA Law Review*, vol. 6 (1959), p. 521; reprinted in Auerbach *et al*, *The Legal Process* (San Francisco: Chandler, 1961), p. 650.

21. McCulloch, *Principles*, pp. 257, 260, 263–64, 266–67, 282, and

A Treatise on the Succession of Property . . .; Sraffa, *op. cit.*, vol. 5, pp. xxvi, 293; Ricardo, *op. cit.*, pp. 61–62. See also Robbins, *op. cit.*, pp. 11, 19.

22. The same themes are manifest in discussions developing the relation of law to freedom, discussed in Chapter Five, *infra*.

23. C. K. Ogden, *Bentham's Theory of Fictions* (London: Kegan Paul, 1932), p. 118.

24. Wheelwright, *op. cit.*, pp. 214, 221, 224. Cf. Smith, *Lectures* (New York: Kelley and Millman, 1956), pp. 5–8.

25. Ogden, *op. cit.*, p. 121. Cf. Jeremy Bentham, *The Limits of Jurisprudence Defined*, C. W. Everett, ed. (New York: Columbia University Press, 1945), pp. 35 ff. In the *Fictions*, after maintaining that "This imaginary natural right is a sort of thread" that the rights' claimant "clings by," Bentham defends his position in a manner evidencing the transition from nondeliberative (and reliance upon indirection and ignorance) to deliberative forces: "It may, however, be said to deny the existence of these rights which you call imaginary, is to give a *carte blanche* to the most outrageous tyranny. The rights of a man anterior to all government, and superior as to their authority to every act of government—these are the rampart, and the only rampart, against the tyrannical enterprises of government. Not at all—the shadow of a rampart is not a rampart; a fiction proves nothing; from that which is false you can only go on to that which is false. When the governed have no right, the government has no more. The rights of the governed and the rights of the government spring up together;—the same cause which creates the one creates the other." Ogden, *op. cit.*, p. 121. See also Robbins, *op. cit.*, pp. 46 ff.; and Chapter Two, note 7, *supra*.

26. See, e.g., Smith, *Lectures*, pp. 35 ff. and 107 ff.; Bentham, *op. cit.*; Harold A. Larrabee, ed., *Bentham's "Handbook of Political Fallacies"* (Baltimore: Johns Hopkins Press, 1952); Ogden, *op. cit.*, pp. 118–21; John Stuart Mill, "Chapters on Socialism," *Fortnightly Review*, vol. 31 (1879), pp. 526–30; Wheelwright, *op. cit.*, pp. 211 ff.

27. Ricardo, e.g., opposed a merchant vessels apprenticeship bill (subsequently passed over his lone dissenting vote) because it interfered "with the private rights of the individuals connected with that trade." Also, in his view, the measure imposed "injurious restrictions on a particular trade." But the "rights" argument was clearly "only" argument, reducible to a position maintaining the existent pattern of rights. Thus Ricardo argued the maxim "that no person ought to be controlled in his own arrangements, unless such control was rendered necessary by paramount political circumstances." Proponents of the bill were "bound to show, that there were some circumstances in this particular trade which ought to take it out of the general rule." And

Ricardo's position was that, "Now, no such necessity could be shown in support of this bill." Sraffa, *op. cit.*, vol. 5, pp. 276, 282.

Now Ricardo's position on this particular measure was of course (and with no connotation of denigration intended) subjective. But neither his particular personal conclusion nor the subjective character of his judgment vitiates the two immediately relevant basic points: (a) that Ricardo's position was, or was reducible to, that of maintaining the continuity of the existent pattern of rights as between apprentices and owners or operators, and (b) that Ricardo's approach clearly encompassed the *possibility* of altering the existing pattern of rights as between apprentices and operators or owners, should the advisability of such alteration be convincingly (and subjectively) shown. For an example of a contrary position by Ricardo, see Chapter Four, *infra.* The main relevant implication, however, is to be developed in the text.

28. Bowring, *op. cit.*, vol. 1, p. 307. Cf. O. H. Taylor, *A History of Economic Thought* (New York: McGraw-Hill, 1960), p. 139.

29. Wheelwright, *op. cit.*, p. 211. Thus Smith argues that partiality to one's interests (i.e., the equivalent of a rights' claim) checks innovation and "contributes in reality to the stability and permanency of the whole system." Smith, *Essays*, p. 205. See also Chapter Two, note 37, *supra.*

30. Taylor, *Economics and Liberalism*, p. 98. See also Davidson, *Political Thought in England* (New York: Holt, n.d.), p. 73; Robbins, *op. cit.*, pp. 40–41, 46–48, 179, 188; Bentham, *op. cit.*, pp. 35–36; Ogden, *op. cit.*, pp. 119–20; Bowring, *op. cit.*, vol. 2, pp. 501, 503; and Stephen, *op. cit.* vol. 1, p. 292. On Smith's distinction between beneficence and justice, see *Essays*, pp. 70 ff., with implications relating to (a) the scope of the "administration of justice" called for in the *Wealth of Nations* (p. 651), and (b) what Robbins calls the sphere of indiscriminate benefits (*Theory of Economic Policy*, pp. 188–89). The question of "injury," involved in the distinction between beneficence and justice, is discussed in Chapter Five, *infra.*

31. On the latter point, see, e.g., Bowring, *op. cit.*, vol. 3, p. 181; and Chapter Five, *infra.*

32. Smith, *Lectures*, p. 8.

33. Bowring, *op. cit.*, vol. 1, pp. 308, 309.

34. Smith, *Lectures*, p. 15; cf. p. 160.

35. According to Smith, "Civil government supposed a certain subordination. But as the necessity of civil government gradually grows up with the acquisition of valuable property, so the principal causes which naturally introduce subordination gradually grow up with the growth of that valuable property." He then examines "The causes or circumstances which naturally introduce subordination, or which naturally, and antecedent to any civil institution, give some men some superiority

over the greater part of their brethren. . . ." The inequality of fortune, he contends, "introduces among men a degree of authority and subordination which could not possibly exist before. It thereby introduces some degree of that civil government which is indispensably necessary for its own preservation: and it seems to do this naturally, and even independent of the consideration of that necessity. The consideration of that necessity comes no doubt afterwards to contribute very much to maintain and secure that authority and subordination. The rich, in particular, are necessarily interested to support that order of things, which can alone secure them in the possession of their own advantages. Men of inferior wealth combine to defend those of superior wealth in the possession of their property, in order that men of superior wealth may combine to defend them in the possession of theirs. All the inferior shepherds and herdsmen feel that the security of their own herds and flocks depends upon the security of those of the great shepherd or herdsman; that the maintenance of their lesser authority depends upon that of his greater authority, and that upon their subordination to him depends his power of keeping their inferiors in subordination to them. They constitute a sort of little nobility, who feel themselves interested to defend the property and to support the authortiy of their own little sovereign, in order that he may be able to defend their property and to support their authority. Civil government, so far as it is instituted for the security of property, is in reality instituted for the defence of the rich against the poor, or of those who have some property against those who have none at all." Smith, *Wealth of Nations*, pp. 670, 674; cf. de Schweinitz, *op. cit.*, pp. 105–6. On the close relation between law and private property, see also John Stuart Mill, *Principles of Political Economy*, p. 201; McCulloch, *Principles of Political Economy*, pp. 77, 80; Stark, *op. cit.*, vol. 3, p. 310; Bowring, *op. cit.*, vol. 1, pp. 307, 309; and (Nassau W. Senior,) Book Review, *Edinburgh Review*, vol. 88 (1848), pp. 74–76.

36. In addition to the discussion by Smith quoted in the preceding note, see also John Stuart Mill: "That government is always either in the hands, or passing into the hands, of whatever is the strongest power in society, and that what this power is, does not depend on institutions, but institutions on it . . ." (*Autobiography*, p. 114), and the more elaborate and sophisticated analysis in *The Spirit of the Age*. Cf. J. Bartlet Brebner, "Laissez Faire and State Intervention in Nineteenth-Century Britain," *Journal of Economic History*, vol. 8, Supplement (1948), p. 69.

37. Bowring, *op. cit.*, vol. 1, pp. 307, 309. "Law alone has accomplished what all the natural feelings were not able to do: Law alone, has been able to create a fixed and durable possession which deserves the name of Property. The law alone could accustom men to submit

to the yoke of foresight, at first painful to be borne, but afterwards agreeable and mild: it alone could encourage them in labour—superfluous at present, and which they are not to enjoy till the future." (P. 307; but see p. 303.)

38. Cf. J. Bonar, *Malthus and His Work* (New York: Harper, 1885), p. 201, and Stephen, *op. cit.*, vol. 3, p. 270.

39. Jeremy Bentham, *Morals and Legislation* (London: Oxford University Press, 1907), p. 322.

40. "It has been common since Adam Smith's day to take for granted *in economics* the role of the state with reference to the protection of legal property rights and the enforcement of contracts, leaving it to juristic inquiry to explore the problems of theory and of practice in this field. Such was also the procedure of Bentham, and in his juristic writings he keeps very much in mind that 'passion . . . from the excesses of which, by reason of its strength, constancy, and universality, society has most to apprehend; I mean that which corresponds to the motive of pecuniary interest.' Here he deals with the problem of 'repression' of harmful economic activity by means of civil and penal law. If Bentham believed that there was a natural harmony of private and public interests in the economic field, it was one, therefore, which would prevail only after the magistrate and the constable had performed their duties." Viner, *op. cit.*, p. 369. See also Grampp, "On the Politics of the Classical Economists," *op cit.*, pp. 722–23.

41. Cf. note 24, *supra*.

42. Wheelwright, *op. cit.*, p. 220. On the idea that the relevant rights are a function of law, see also: John Stuart Mill, *Dissertations and Discussions*, vol. 4, pp. 157–226, and *Principles of Political Economy*, pp. 797 ff., 884 ff., 889–915; Burtt, *op. cit.*, p. 1030; McCulloch, *Principles*, pp. 256, 259, 268–79, 287; Bowring, *op. cit.*, vol. 1, p. 307. See also Mortimer J. Adler, *The Idea of Freedom* (Garden City, N. Y.: Doubleday, 1958), pp. 234–35.

43. Bowring, *op. cit.*, vol. 1, p. 301. ". . . When a man is said to have a right (mentioning it), the existence of a certain matter of fact is asserted; namely, of a disposition, on the part of those by whom the powers of government are exercised, to cause him to possess, and so far as depends upon them to have the faculty of enjoying, the benefit to which he has a right." Ogden, *op. cit.*, p. 119. Cf. Bentham, *The Limits of Jurisprudence Defined*, chaps. 2, 8.

44. Wheelwright, *op. cit.*, pp. 220, 225. See also Bowring, *op. cit.*, vol. 3, pp. 181–85, and vol. 6, pp. 7–8; and the references cited in note 42, *supra*.

45. With respect to the legislation discussed in note 27, *supra*, Ricardo's position as a Member of Parliament (was his judgment "better" than that of any other Member, or of Parliament, or Commons,

collectively?) is illustrative of the operation of the state as itself a decision-making participant, making judgments as to rights' claimants and other facets of indiscriminate benefits.

On the Benthamite "vision of a self-equilibrating system of interest pressures operating on and through the government," see Taylor, *A History of Economic Thought*, p. 125 *et seq.*; and Grampp, "On the Politics of the Classical Economists," *op. cit.*, p. 741.

"Not until Parliament was called upon to determine whether legislative policy should be shaped, first, in the matter of the Bank, in the interest of debtor or of creditor; second, in the matter of corn laws, in the interest of agriculturalist, rather than of manufacturer; third, with respect to taxation and funding, in the interest of consumer instead of property owner—not until then was it that the economic thinker, deriving his philosophical creed from the new utilitarianism, felt impelled to inquire what will be the natural shares of these several classes, destined to be effected in one way or another by this contemplated legislation." J. H. Hollander, "The Work and Influence of Ricardo." *AEA Bulletin*, Fourth Series, vol. 1 (1911), Supplement, p. 74.

46. See. e.g., John Stuart Mill, *Principles of Political Economy*, *op. cit.*, pp. 199–237, 787, 885; McCulloch, *Principles of Political Economy*, pp. 79, 263–64, 275; and Bowring, *op. cit.*, vol. 1, pp. 308, 313–14.

47. McCulloch, *op. cit.*, p. 256.

48. *Ibid.*, pp. 256, 258.

49. *Ibid.*, p. 259.

50. John Stuart Mill, *Principles of Political Economy*, pp. 798–99.

51. Parry, *op. cit.*, p. 192. Cf. McCulloch, *Principles*, p. 281; John Stuart Mill, *Principles*, pp. 797 ff. As an important corollary, the classicists used the essentially collectivist criterion of public interest, or, alternately, of avoiding injury to others, as an injunction enabling consideration of limitations upon otherwise unencumbered rights. Cf., e.g., McCulloch, *Principles*, pp. 256, 281, 289; and Bowring, *op. cit.*, vol. 1, pp. 313–14, and vol. 3, p. 182. See also Taylor, *A History of Economic Thought*, pp. 139–40; cf. pp. 125, 131. The subject of injury is discussed in Chapter Five, *infra*.

52. Joseph J. Spengler, "Adam Smith's Theory of Economic Growth," Part II, *Southern Economic Journal*, vol. 26 (1959), p. 11; and de Schweinitz, *op. cit.*, pp. 106, 108–9. This is not to say that the classicists were never critical of what they subjectively considered the misuse of law in the process of ordering differential opportunities: in addition to the general critique of mercantilism, the anti-combination laws are a case in point, as is Smith's criticism that the law tended

to operate on the side of the masters. Smith, *Wealth of Nations*, pp. 66–67.

53. The approach taken in this chapter not only reflects (and reflects upon) the work of John R. Commons (see Chapter Five, *infra*, text at note 82), but also the analysis presented in Auerbach (*op. cit.*). At an advanced stage in the research, the Auerbach analysis was used as an hypothesis to check the author's own analysis.

CHAPTER FOUR

The Economic Role of the State (II)

THE PROBLEM

The central problem of a theory of economic policy being the way in which the economy is to be organized and controlled, the genius of the market-plus-framework interpretation is that it establishes the fundamental participation by the state in the multifaceted division of power in the classical policy analysis. Lord Robbins' statement that the classicists "regarded the appropriate legal framework and the system of economic freedom as two aspects of one and the same social process," [1] clearly expressed the classical view of the underlying operation of law in the decision-making process. The preceding chapter has attempted to specify the major components of this underlying operation of the legal process, so far as the classical theory of economic policy is concerned.

Given the framework-provision function of government, as further specified or *in toto*, the question arises as to the role of the state with respect to the problem of continuity and change. It has already been shown that the classicists acknowledged and gave considerable weight to the needs of order and of continuity. But what of the problem of change? Specifically, what was the role of law as an instrument of socioeconomic change? Perspective on this latter question is the main objective of this chapter, which will attempt to indicate the dimensions of the economic role of the state with respect to change in the classical theory of economic policy.

Consideration of any theory of economic policy with respect to change necessarily involves a number of important questions, all of which, among their other facets of significance, bear upon the scope of policy comprehended in the particular theory of policy under examination. This is markedly true in the case of the classical economists, and is reflected in the interpretive literature. Several questions emerge couched in terms of change, which, since change is the quintessence of policy, also have import for the classical view of the scope of policy: How malleable is the socioeconomic order or facets of it? Through what process is that order, or facets of it, to be changed, if at all? Moreover, and this is important given the market-plus-framework interpretation, is it meaningful to differentiate between (legal) changes of the legal framework, and other particular (change-bringing) legal interventions? This latter question involves the further question of the meaningfulness of the differentiation between framework-filling operations of government and particular, nonliberalist, interventions; and ultimately involves the framework-nonframework dichotomy itself. Finally, there is the question of the meaningfulness of differentiating between the provision of general or formal rules, and specific interventions. Facets of these questions relating to change will be examined in this chapter; facets relating to the scope of policy, and to the interpretation of the classical theory of economic policy as a whole, will be examined in the concluding chapter.

Discussion may commence with reference to Checkland's comments on the question of law as a mode of change. Checkland poses the question, "Was the framework to be instituted once and for all, and then work towards its own liquidation, or were fairly frequent adjustments called for? Clearly," he responds, "the more often the need to alter the frame, the greater the element of 'interference.' " He then points out that the limitation of knowledge which is so important an impediment to "direct intervention," is just as important, if not more so, in the case of filling the framework, particularly "if we are to be frame-setters on the scale Professor Robbins believes the classics thought appropriate. . . ." He concludes the immediately relevant discussion with two questions: "In short, is not the classical view, as Professor Robbins presents it, as vulnerable to delusion as that taken by those who disdain the fiction of the frame and operate more directly? In this matter of acting upon the market mechanism, is the distinction really so significant, between those who meddle from without and those who tinker from within?" [2]

It is significant that Checkland questions the meaningfulness of the several differentiations involved. It is also interesting that his discussion is founded upon making the classicists' message the criterion of analysis. Is not, however, the appropriate question, so far as the interpretation of the classical theory of economic policy is concerned, rather, what *was* the theory of the classical economists, with respect to the role of law as an instrument or mode of socioeconomic change? There must be a place for doctrine, as there must be a role for what Knight calls "a propaganda for economic freedom," [3] but there must also be a place for the classicists' effective resolution of the problem of continuity and change.

Checkland's critique of Lord Robbins is especially interesting because in the *Theory of Economic Policy*, Lord Robbins' specification of the malleability of the framework through the artifice of law involved legal provision of general, formal rules, with a minimization not so much of government per se but certainly of the exercise of governmental *discretion*, and there-

128

fore of change secured through government. "Thus," he maintains, "if we dig right down to the foundations, what distinguishes the Classical outlook from the authoritarian systems is not a denial of the necessity for state action on the one side and an affirmation on the other, but rather a different view of what kind of action is desirable." The difference is precisely this: "To the one is assigned the task of establishing formal rules, to the other responsibility for the substance of specific action." Robbins contends that "For the Classical liberal, the characteristic function of the state in this connexion is the establishment and the enforcement of law. . . . So far as the general organization of production is concerned, his essential conception of the role of the state is the conception of the law-giver. For the authoritarian, on the other hand, the characteristic function of the state is, not the law, but the quantitative plan." "The contrast," he cautions, "must not be pressed too far; the authoritarian submits to some laws, the Classical liberal conceives of some public discretion. But, in the main, it holds: the System of Economic Freedom, so far as the organization of production was concerned, was a system of rules which was supposed to make individual freedom conducive to social advantage." [4]

This position of Lord Robbins, which involves no serious qualification of the fundamental participation of government established above, would interpret the classical view of the role of the state with respect to social change in terms of a conservative interpretation of the concept, "rule of law." This is also the approach of Hayek:

> To Adam Smith and his immediate successors the enforcement of the ordinary rules of common law would certainly not have appeared as government interference; nor would they ordinarily have applied this term to an alteration of these rules or the passing of a new rule by the legislature so long as it was intended to apply equally to all people for an indefinite

period of time. Though they perhaps never explicitly said so, interference meant to them the exercise of the coercive power of government which was not regular enforcement of the general law and which was designed to achieve some specific purpose. The important criterion was not the aim pursued, however, but the method employed. There is perhaps no aim which they would not have regarded as legitimate if it was clear that the people wanted it; but they excluded as generally inadmissible in a free society the method of specific orders and prohibitions. Only indirectly, by depriving government of some means by which alone it might be able to attain certain ends, may this principle deprive government of the power to pursue those ends.[5]

It may be contended, however, that the distinction between formal rules and specific interventions, and also that between legal change of the legal framework and other legal interventions, however ideologically pregnant, is substantively ambiguous and may utterly lack any meaning at all. All general or formal rules have specific impact, or, rather, differential specific impact, inasmuch as (at the very least): (a) if, as is usually the case, people are differently situated, rules, "equally applicable" to all will have differential impact, and (b) the object of most legislation (judicial as well as parliamentary) is to deal with specifics in at least some critical respects. There is also the question of the requirement of the law to be definitive, and the relevance of limitation of knowledge.[6] Moreover, are there not formal rules whose operation could conceivably be anathema to the classical vision of the market system; and may not some rules be unpalatable or anathema, however equally applicable to all they may be? The distinction would seem sterile for purposes of analysis, as would the difference between legal change of the legal framework, and other legal interventions. Not only would alteration of the so-called rules, or otherwise labeled parts of the frame, appear to objectors thereto as

130

indistinguishable from other legal interventions but also, since *all* government operations constitute the framework (or part of the framework) of any residual and nominally private activity, no operational difference can be made. "Formal rules" of property law, for example, have their specific impact, however unobtrusive they may be vis-a-vis more obtrusive "interventions." There is no meaningful basis to the distinction between "discrimination" and "reasonable classification," and all law ultimately involves specific prohibitions or impositions.[7] To say merely that "the conception of the role of the state is the conception of the law-giver" is to beg the question of change and the substance of change, as well as to make obscure the ultimate element of specificity involved in any law. Similarly, to consider the framework as given is to rigidify what may not have a given substance, that is, to make static that which may be a matter of dynamic evolution. Finally, it is certainly largely irrelevant to invoke comparison with the quantitative plan, for the question is not over a comprehensive plan governing all the particulars of economic life, but rather, as Hayek calls it, legislation "designed to achieve some specific purpose," or, in Robbins' terms, legal responsibility "for the substance of specific action." Just as taking the framework as given begs the very question of change that is at issue, so this false comparison obscures the question of the most likely type of change: some specific action for some specific purpose.

All this notwithstanding, the fundamental question remains as to what the *classical theory* was of the economic role of the state with respect to socioeconomic change. It is not a matter of logical coherence and substantive adequacy; it is rather a matter of what the classical economists' position actually reduces to. It is suggested that in the classical policy system there was no substantively meaningful distinction between framework-filling operations of government and other non-acceptable (because not framework-filling) legal interventions, nor between formal rules applicable equally to all, and specific interventions directed at particular purposes. These distinctions are not so much forced and artificial as they are quite beside the point, so far as the classical theory of legal change is concerned.

It is suggested, rather, that in the classical policy system law was acknowledged to be an instrument or mode of change, however much it was anathema to the ideology concerned, and that such change did involve attention to particular purposes. Specifically, it will be seen: (a) that law served as a mode of restructuring private decision-making participation; and (b) that with respect to the scope of the public or legal sector as such, law functioned as a mode of altering what would otherwise have been the consequences of private participation or market forces, and so involved direct legal participation in the resolution of the basic economic problems. In other words, the classical conception of a created harmony involved the law as a creative force (yes, artifice through law), including legal change of the specifics involved therein. It is suggested, then, that the interpretation herein suggested with respect to law as a mode of change, and in Chapter Five with respect to the reconciliation of the problem of continuity and change as a facet of the classical theory of economic policy, is much more accurately reflective of what the classical theory of economic policy is all about than the foregoing approaches of Checkland and Robbins-Hayek involving artificial and inaccurate distinctions. The task of this chapter is relatively simple compared with the pretensions of these other approaches to the classical view of legal change. The author intends to show the only things that can be shown, namely: (a) the existence of legal activism as a mode of change and the two primary components to which it may be reduced (as indicated at the beginning of this paragraph); and (b) the irrelevance of the general or formal rules approach, as demonstrated by the particular or specific character of the changes wrought, and by the specific character of the purposes sought.

Neglect of the role of the legal process, as a mode of socio-economic change, in the classical theory of economic policy is remarkable, not solely because it presumes an utterly unrealistic classical solution to the problem of continuity and change but also because of the perhaps equally universal recognition of the classical economists—and not just the Benthamites among them—as reformers. Indeed, as Lord Robbins proclaims, ". . . the Classical Economists were reformers and . . . the theory of economic policy in English Classical political economy was a theory of economic and social reform. . . . The English Classical School . . . must be regarded in its attitude to policy as a school of economic and social reform."[8] Karl Marx's dictum that the liberal theory of economic policy would overthrow "all forms of government interference in the activities of bourgeois society," and that "it allowed the State to live on only in the pores of this society, as Epicurus placed his Gods in the pores of the world!"[9] is no more accurate in the case of the English classicists than it was of the Physiocrats against whom Marx's invective was specifically directed.[10]

Neglect of the inevitable effect of governmental change upon the particulars of economic policy is perhaps equally remarkable. It is, for example, widely recognized that the classicists themselves acknowledged that the substance of the *agenda* of the state was variable—yet it is difficult to envision how change of the details of the *agenda* can take place without being themselves specific, or directed toward specific or particular purposes, or having their differential effect. Moreover, emphasis upon the nonspecific character of whatever legal change is recognized, appears inconsistent with the notion often encountered that the classical general rule was in favor of legal abstention from intervention *except for* special or particular purposes. If, according to Bentham, the general rule is to be that "nothing ought to be done or attempted by government for the purpose of causing an augmentation to take place in the national mass of wealth, with a view to encrease of the means of either subsistence or enjoyment, without some *special reason*" [11] then it is hard to see how legal change can avoid the exercise of legal discretion over, and influence upon, the particulars of economic life in the Hayekian sense: legal action for "some special reason" must involve action "designed to achieve some specific purpose." [12]

Some of this is brought into focus by O. H. Taylor, though even his position is made ambiguous by inclusion and juxtaposition of general laws which are general, but which also have exact and detailed effect. According to Taylor,

> The main or principal proper function of the democratic political process is to shape *and reshape*, in adaptation to the changing circumstances, needs, and desires of the people and all groups among them, all the general laws which together make up the order or system of legal justice—which in the relevant aspects, in relation to the economy, is the framework of legal limits around all areas of free, private, economic choices and activities, . . . The shaping *and reshaping* of this framework, or system of general laws which all must obey, of course, necessarily and properly affects or modifies, from time to time, the exact limits and areas of all private, economic freedoms and the detailed structure and working of the economy.[13]

Translated into terms consistent with the language used in the preceding chapters, Taylor clearly recognizes that law is a mode of change *reshaping* the structure and results of the economic decision-making process. This recognition of legal activism, however restricted such activism may be in the classical policy system, is, as will be seen in the paragraphs to follow, laudable for its accuracy in that regard. Yet it will also be seen that the notion of general laws equally applicable to all is inconsistent with the very character of such reshaping: if legal change is to involve change of the "*exact* limits and areas of all private, economic freedoms," and also "the *detailed* structure and working of the economy," then they can hardly be general and equally applicable, nor can they avoid having differential or specific effects, and effective specific purposes.

Law as a Mode of Change

Restructuring Private Participation: Both the fact and scope of legal activism or legal participation as a mode of change, and the specific character of the changes thus wrought, or the purposes sought, are manifest in the classicists' position toward the role of law, restructuring private participation in the economic decision-making process. What is involved is legal change of private rights, affecting both the composition of the private decisional structure as a whole, and specific rights, and legal impact, through the changed decisional structure, upon the resolution of the basic economic problems. Legal alteration of the pattern of rights includes, among other things: (a) enhancing already existing loci of participation; (b) checking the participation of private power-holders, thereby effectuating change of structure negatively, as it were; and (c) restructuring through the creation of new loci tending both to broaden participation, and limit existing loci of participation. Such restructuring, or reshaping, of private participation must be considered as one facet of the economic role of the state, with respect to change, in the classical theory of economic policy.

McCulloch, for example, recognized that the laws of bankruptcy, as with the laws governing all private rights, are subject to change, for they "differ exceedingly in different countries and stages of society. . . ," [14] such that the very decisions to change necessarily involve legal discretion as to the fact, direction, and substance of change or variation. Perhaps the clearest statement of the general classical position is that contained in John Stuart Mill's posthumously published "Chapters on Socialism." After contending in his introductory remarks that "The future of mankind will be gravely imperilled, if great questions are left to be fought over between ignorant change and ignorant opposition to change," [15] his concluding paragraph establishes the necessary fact, and basic issue of law, as a mode of restructuring private participation through the alteration of relative rights.

We thus see that the right of property is differently interpreted, and held to be of different extent, in different times and places; that the conception entertained of it is a varying conception, has been frequently revised, and may admit of still further revision. It is also to be noticed that the revisions which it has hitherto undergone in the progress of society have generally been improvements. When, therefore, it is maintained, rightly or wrongly, that some change or modification in the powers exercised over things by the persons legally recognised as their proprietors would be beneficial to the public and conducive to the general improvement, it is no good answer to this merely to say that the proposed change conflicts with the idea of property. The idea of property is not some one thing, identical throughout history and incapable of alteration, but is variable like all other creations of the human mind; at any given time it is a brief expression denoting the rights over things conferred by the law or custom of some given society at that time; but neither on this point nor on any other has the law and custom of a given time and place a claim to be stereotyped for ever. A proposed reform in laws or customs is not necessarily objectionable because its adoption would imply, not the adaptation of all human affairs

136

to the existing idea of property, but the adaptation of existing ideas of property to the growth and improvement of human affairs.[16]

So, also, with Bentham. Although "the legislator owes the greatest respect to these expectations to which he has given birth," [17] "... an important distinction is to be made between the ideal perfection of security, and that perfection which is practicable. The first requires that nothing should be taken from anyone; the second is attained if no more is taken than is necessary for the preservation of the rest." [18] This choice, the choice necessarily involved in each particular instance, is at least partially a function of law. The law, moreover, can influence the course of expectations.[19] While "Innovations in the laws should be made with great caution," [20] security being the work of the legislator, still there is need for change in the substance of what is under "the controul and guidance of the legislator." [21] What is true of all law is true of the laws that govern private rights: after all,

> When, reckoning from the day on which a measure has received the force of law, a certain period of time has elapsed, custom covers it with its mantle; and, regarding it as an unauthorized act of daring to look into the nature of the measure, men inquire no further than into the existence of the law; habit gives it a fixed authority: and thus it is that, in every country, worship is bestowed on laws and institutions vying in absurdity with any scheme of extravagance which the imagination of man could produce.[22]

No wonder that in his critique of Blackstone, Bentham argues that the particular "capital blemish" of Blackstone's *Commentaries* is its "antipathy to reformation":

> Thus much is certain; that a system that is never to be censured, will never be improved: that if nothing is ever to be found fault with, nothing will ever be mended: and that a

resolution to justify every thing at any rate, and to disapprove of nothing, is a resolution which, pursued in future, must stand as an effectual bar to all the *additional* happiness we can ever hope for; pursued hitherto would have robbed us of that share of happiness which we enjoy already.[23]

It is no surprise, then, to find in the writings of all the classicists evidence of the restructuring of private participation through law: *inter alia,* Smith, Bentham, McCulloch, and both Mills on the reform of the law of property as such; [24] Malthus, Bentham, and Stuart Mill on land tenure reform; [25] Smith and Stuart Mill on the legal alteration of the purposes of foundations and endowments, as well as perpetual entails; [26] Senior and Stuart Mill on legislation to give effect to, or enable the fruition of, the collective interests of groups of the population unable by themselves to effectuate their felt interests; [27] and Bentham and McCulloch on the need for restructuring the relative rights of debtors and creditors, including the law of bankruptcy and insolvency.[28] There is, in addition, the position taken by several of the classicists, perhaps most of them at various times, on the desirability of what has since come to be called protective labor legislation; [29] and the general classical position toward reform of the conspiracy laws governing the legal status and therefore conditions of participation or relative rights of unions and union members.[30] Finally, there may be noted instances in which classical economists (Smith, Bentham, McCulloch, and both Mills) would have government serve as a check on private concentrations of power.[31]

Interesting and important also in this regard is the active participation by several of the classicists in the movement for Parliamentary reform. In no small part, the force of these reforms was directed at the influence of existing private concentrations of power upon the decisions reached through the legal process itself. Ricardo, Bentham, and both Mills recognized that, since change of the structure of a decision-making process results in a changed pattern of decisions reached by that process, Parliamentary reform would mean a change in the substance of legal participation, including change in the structure of private participation, so far as it is governed by law. Thus in Bentham's *Plan of Parliamentary Reform*, it is clear that Bentham understood that reform of the power-conferring rules defining the structure of government would have consequences for the pattern of interests to which the law would give effect, in structuring the private sector.[32] What the reformers wanted was of course, a more democratic suffrage as one key to a government responsive to the people as a whole—the principle on which "all real reformers are agreed," wrote Ricardo to Trower, is this: "they want a house of commons which shall speak the sentiments of the people, and are willing to agree to any details which shall not interfere with that important principle." [33] That this would affect the existing property-foundation of the private sector, and its influence upon legal policy, was both clear and the obvious objective. Writing of the Peers, Great Landholders, and Country Gentlemen, Bentham commented sarcastically, "In those men is the chief *property* of the country, and with it—(for in the language of the Aristocratic School, *property* and *virtue* are synonymous terms)—the *virtue* of the country." [34] No wonder, then, at Bentham's comments in respect to Wedderburn (Lord Loughborough):

> So long as the form of Government continues to be what it is, . . . must the condition of the people be . . . the sacrifice of the interest of the many to the interest, joint or several, of the one or of the few. . . . Opposite to the interest of the greatest number—opposite through the whole field of Government—is that same ruling interest. That which this interest requires, is—that the quantity of power, wealth, and factitious dignity, in the possession and at the disposal of the ruling few, should be at all times as great as possible.[35] . . . But

Loughborough was too well acquainted with the state of government in this country (not to speak of other countries,) not to know that it is the greatest happiness of the ruling few, and not that of the greatest number, that is the end pursued on each occasion by the ruling few. . . . But the interest of the ruling few is, on the greatest part of the field of government, in a state of continued opposition to that of the greatest number: accordingly, a principle which, in case of competition, and to the extent of the competition, called for sacrifices to be made of the interests of the class to which he belonged, and which alone was the object of his solicitude, could not but in his eyes be a dangerous one.[36]

To advocate Parliamentary reform was in effect to attack the pattern of existing rights, and specific existing rights, themselves. Indeed, it was seen by opponents of reform that to attack the rights in question was "simply confiscation of private property," [37] for, among other things that might be said, they were after all objects of purchase and sale. It has been said that the law of private property has been the Constitution of England: be that as it may, to the extent that the structure of government was, or was considered in terms of, private property, reform would necessarily mean alteration of the structure of private rights. Such was the case with the classicists.

It should be clear that alteration of the legal structure of private participation would necessarily result in alterations in the resolution of the basic economic problems, and further, that such alterations would necessarily involve the particulars of economic life in such matters as income distribution, resource allocation, and cost and risk distribution. Consider, for example, Smith's comment that the civil magistrate was on the side of the masters in the case of conflict between them and the workmen; [38] Senior's inclusion "among the evils of poverty the carelessness with which the individual interests of the poor are dealt with by the legislature . . .";[39] and Bentham's willingness to operate upon the principle of equality, albeit tempered by that of security: "the principle of equality requires that so far as may be, without taking away the inducement to productive industry and frugality, the opulent few should be prevented from doing injury to the indigent many, by means of the power necessarily and proportionably attached to opulence: and that so often as this can be done, without the production of the sensation of loss, opportunity should be taken of breaking down large masses into smaller ones."[40] Cases in point include protective labor legislation, and limitations upon inheritance: Stuart Mill's recommendation in the latter (which he thought would be received as radical, but was not) is described by Lord Robbins "as an example of the extent to which a Classical Economist was willing to alter the framework provided he believed that the market and incentive system was not seriously affected."[41]

Perhaps the most revealing example, however, involves Ricardo's support of a proposed particular legislative change, which would have intentionally altered the distribution of risk, and the cost of risk. The petition had to do with the law of principal and factor, and the reporting committee (the Committee on Law Merchant, of which Ricardo was a member) had as its main recommendation, "That a person possessing a bill of lading, or other apparent symbol of property, not importing that such property belongs to others, shall be considered as the true owner, so far as respects any person who may deal with him, in relation to such property, under an ignorance of his real character."[42] According to the *Morning Chronicle*, whose report is somewhat fuller than that of *Hansard*,

> Mr. Ricardo said he would suppose a case. Suppose a foreign merchant, who knew nothing of him, were to consign goods to him as an agent, and suppose for a moment that he

(Mr. Ricardo) were a dishonest man [a laugh], and, having without authority from his principal deposited those goods as a security for an advance from a banker, were to disappear,— according to the existing law the banker would lose his money. Now, in point of justice, which of the parties ought first to suffer—the banker who had the precaution to take the goods as a security, or the foreign merchant who had trusted him (Mr. Ricardo) as his agent without proper precaution? It was certainly unjust that either party should suffer; but, if either, surely it ought to be the man who had not used proper precaution. It had been said that the person who lent the money ought to ask the person to whom he lent it whether he was an agent, or the principal? A very good observation, if the truth could be got; but who did not know the difficulty of obtaining it.[43]

To much the same effect also is Ricardo's plan for a capital levy to pay off the national debt in such a manner that, as Cannan remarks, "makes it clear that it involved repudiation of a large proportion of the debt." [44] As reported in *Hansard*, Ricardo "did not mean that it should be redeemed at par; the public creditor possessed no such claim—were he paid at the market price, the public faith would be fulfilled." [45]

Change through Direct Participation: Governmental participation in the restructuring of private participation is but one of two conceptual facets of law as a mode of change. The other involves governmental activity comprising the substance of the public sector, or public participation itself, generally, but not always, distinct from those operations of government structuring private participation. These presently relevant activities of government may be considered as evidence of the fact, and possible scope of, direct legal participation in the resolution of the basic economic problems in the classical theory of economic policy. Even more obtrusive than in the case of restructuring private participation, here is legal activism directly participating in the resolution of such problems

142

as resource allocation and income distribution. Inasmuch as these activities ultimately involve the legal imposition of change from what otherwise would have been the consequences of nominally private market forces, such activities may be said to constitute the second facet of law as a mode of change.

As was indicated earlier, Lord Robbins considers the "broad conception" of the classical theory of the economic role of the state to have "postulated a whole complex of necessary functions of government," quite in addition to the transcendental framework-provision function.[46] These additional functions of government, according to Lord Robbins, are two in number. The first is said to have "embraced the whole sphere of activities affording indiscriminate benefit." [47] According to the classicists, "by consumption is meant not only the consumption of private individuals, the benefit of which is limited to themselves, but also the consumption of government services such as defence, the benefit of which is indiscriminate." [48] Further, although market determination reflecting individual private judgments is to be the general rule, "it is not argued that the exercise of consumers' choice in the market is the best possible mechanism for bringing into being goods and services affording indiscriminate benefit." [49] The provision of such indiscriminate benefits, or of the goods and services affording them, is thus one of the functions of government. "Not, of course, that it implied that each and every possible kind of indiscriminate benefit should actually be provided; that was a matter for weighing in some rough-and-ready manner the benefits thus obtained against the benefits which would be withdrawn from the discriminate benefit sector if scarce resources were used for this purpose. But the formal principle," contends Lord Robbins, "was assumed. . . ." [50] There is, then, in the classical theory of economic policy, direct governmental participation in resource allocation and income distribution, and to an extent, according to Lord Robbins, "much more *etatiste* than the *status quo*." [51] There is, as a consequence, the exercise of legal choice over which "kind of indiscriminate benefit should actually be provided," which choice comprises the essence of policy participation, and necessarily involves governmental alteration of the processes of resource allocation and income distribution from the directions they otherwise would have followed. It should be clear that this means *pro tanto* legal determination of the division between the indiscriminate and discriminate benefit sectors, and ultimately involves legal participation in the determination of the specifics of what will be indiscriminately and discriminately provided (provided or not provided, at least so far as *agenda* and *nonagenda* are concerned).

The second additional function of government, according to Lord Robbins, has to do with "that wide range of activities which may be grouped under the headings of the educative and the eleemosynary functions." [52] These activities are largely discussed in the lecture constituting the third chapter of his work, "The Condition of the People," and include health and education, the poor laws, contract and factory legislation, and wages and combinations. According to Lord Robbins, "The functions of the state as a supplement to the family find extensive recognition in the Classical theory of policy." [53] As in the case of indiscriminate vis-a-vis discriminate benefits, the main point is not only the fact of existence of government activity of an educative and eleemosynary variety, but also the fact of legal determination of the content thereof to be governmentally provided—there was no closed category of educational and eleemosynary activities any more than there was with respect to the provision of indiscriminate benefits. Finally, it again follows that such activities directly change the allocation of resources and the distribution of income from the channels they otherwise would have taken, and moreover, that any such activities will necessarily be specific in substance and purpose.

The division of public and private decision-making power contemplated in the classical theory of economic policy therefore involves no small scope for possible direct legal participation in the resolution of the basic economic problems, involving change with respect to both (a) changing content of legal participation, and (b) changing what would otherwise have been determined by private participation through market forces, or relative private power. It must be understood, however, that Lord Robbins' classification of (a) the provision of (some) indiscriminate benefits, and (b) the provision of educative and eleemosynary activities, does not exhaust the relevant scope of the classical theory of the economic role of the state with respect to direct participation or, alternately, as a mode of change. Lord Robbins' framework-provision function of government also encompasses substantive governmental activity serving to transmute private into social interest—for example, operations generally regulatory in character are included in the general concept of the public sector, as discussed in part in Chapter Three. In the remaining paragraphs of this section, there is presented further indication of the scope of the role of government involved, inclusive of what Lord Robbins has identified, but attempting different and additional specification.[54]

Several comments, however, are appropriate at this point. First, so far as the substance of what is being discussed may be referred to as the *agenda* of government, such *agenda* is essentially open-ended, and, further, "the *agenda* differ according to historical circumstances."[55] As was the case with the restructuring of private rights, the substance of legal change was variable. "Among these several classes, *agenda*, *sponte acta*, and *nonagenda*," wrote Bentham, "the distribution of the imaginable stock of institutions will differ in a very considerable degree according to the different circumstances of the several political communities. . . . The greater the degree of opulence, the greater the list of *sponte acta*—the less, therefore, that of *agenda*. In England, abundance of useful things are done by individuals which in other countries are done either by government or not at all." [56] It might even be said, though it is hardly demonstrable (nor is it generic to the argument of this chapter), that there is perhaps nothing that the classicists would have individually excluded from the *agenda*, if they could have been persuaded that it was in the general interest.[57]

Second, it must be appreciated that the relevant facet of the role of government, as a mode of change, fundamentally centers on the policy-making exercise of legal choice through the determination of *which* (if any) specific change is to be effectuated through the adoption (or change) of this or that item of *agenda*. As with the case of Lord Robbins' indiscriminate benefits, if the scope of *agenda* is not to be all-inclusive, choice has to be made, and extends to the selection of the *specific* changes the legal process would attempt to secure. The fact that the *agenda* are a function of circumstances does not make them predetermined, nor should it obscure the specificity involved in the decisional process, particularly (but not only) with respect to the revocability of legal decisions to effectuate, or not to effectuate, particular changes.

Third, it should be recognized that the specific content of legal change, or alternately, of direct legal participation in the resolution of the basic economic problems, would be a matter of sensibilities, as was the case of Ricardo, and the regulation of apprenticeship, discussed in the preceding chapter. It is to be expected that there would be, as indeed there was, considerable variation between the classicists as to their particular recommendations, just as each classicist himself evidences some change over time (as in the cases of poor-law reform and factory legislation). These matters, however, relate to what will be discussed in Chapter Five as the problem of specific content, as part of the broad problem of assessing the meaningfulness of the classical theory of economic policy. That being the case, only three points need be made here: (a) that the examples noted are evidence of the themes in respect to which they are raised; (b) that the examples are evidence further of the breadth of scope of what were by various classicists, and at various times, included among the *agenda*; and (c) that these examples are neither exhaustive nor addible in such a way as to provide an accurate list of anything like a "classical *agenda*."

Finally, the distinction between legal change through restructuring private participation and legal change through direct participation imposed upon what otherwise would have been determined by nominally private forces, while conceptually clear, does not enable unequivocal classification of particular legal actions. Some governmental activities could be classified either way as they would have both types of effects: cases in point are protective labor legislation, and legal control of private economic power concentrations. Indeed, perhaps all direct legal participation to effectuate change could be translated into restructuring actual or potential private participation. As a practical matter, however, the distinction is not as forced as these remarks might suggest. In any event, the basic argument establishing law as a viable mode of change in the classical theory of economic policy is not disturbed.

Returning to the main discussion, it is suggested that the fact, activism, and breadth of scope of law as a mode of change, with respect to direct legal participation to change what otherwise would have been consequent to nominally private market forces may be more thoroughly appreciated by analysis additional to, and somewhat different from, that of Lord Robbins. Such analysis involves recognition of functions of gov-

147

ernment: (a) remedial with respect to resource allocation; (b) remedial with respect to income distribution; and (c) remedial through substitution of legal for market or private determination, and other regulation of market conditions. (The use of the word "remedial" is in no way crucial, as a useful synonym would be "promotional," for the one is largely the converse of the other. What is intended is the notion that legal change would logically involve the remedying or changing of what, otherwise, would be considered deficient or undesirable. However it is spelled out, the central idea is legal change so directed "that the residue of free action undirected from the centre could be conceived to harmonize with the general objects of public interest.") [58]

The classical economists would have utilized the state as a mode of changing the allocation of resources, with or without accompanying alterations in the structure (as distinct from the results) of private participation. This is further indicated by recommendations that the state directly promote, or undertake the provision of social capital (roads, harbors, canals and the like, including the postal service); [59] help alleviate natural accidents or disasters; [60] engage in agricultural protection, including the use of the tariff, and undertake other exceptions to the free trade principle; [61] provide often extensive hospital and health care; [62] and secure public education on a national basis (itself a considerable revolution vis-a-vis the exclusionary system), and varied governmental research activities. Closely related are legal allocations of risk and the cost of risk, a basic facet of resource allocation: in debtor-creditor relationships; [63] in the case of bank-note issues;[64] the socialization of the costs of social capital; [65] technological unemployment; [66] and, as discussed before, the risk of fraud as between principal, agent, and third parties.

A similar position by the classical economists existed in respect to governmental alteration of income and wealth distribution, within the constraints already noted. Income distribution, Stuart Mill has been seen to have held, is a partial function of law, and is therefore changeable by law, as a general rule.[67] This principle is manifest not only in unemployment relief,[68] but also in poor relief in general,[69] aid to large families,[70] limitation upon inheritance,[71] and the socialization of land rent,[72] among other instances. It is also relevant to note that the classicists were aware of the redistributionist implications of universal education.

It should be stressed again that these examples are not addible, but are merely adduced to demonstrate the scope of *agenda*, and the specific character of the changes and purposes sought, in terms of the basic economic problems. Moreover, it should be clear that what is intended is neither a complete catalogue of *agenda* nor a detailed analysis of each item—neither is necessary for the purpose at hand, namely, further specification of law as a mode of changing the resolution of the basic economic problems through direct participation.

Law as a mode of change in the classical theory of economic policy further extended to the regulation of the conditions and results of private economic activity, tending (in part through the superimposition of legislation upon common-law-determined property rights) to affect the structure, as well as the consequences of, private decision-making, thereby substituting legal for market determination. Among the variety of examples found in the classical literature are: the regulation of consumer frauds, quality and purity in production, and the competency of physicians;[73] regulation of the price of bread in the hands of a monopoly;[74] public utility regulation generally, and in many, if not all, aspects thereof (as well as legal determination of whether a particular business, or type of business, was subject to such intensive regulation);[75] regulation of interest rates;[76] regulation of the supply of money, the conditions of its issuance, and commercial bank operations generally, including the nationalization of money creation; [77] protective labor legislation, as well as social insurance; [78] prevention of overspeculation in security markets; [79] the promulgation and enforcement of building codes; [80] regulation, if not prohibition of, the truck system; [81] regulation of the conditions of sale of poisons; [82] taxation for regulatory purposes; [83] regulation of land utilization in new colonies; [84] and compensatory fiscal policy (as well as monetary policy).[85] The fact that not all of the classicists would have agreed upon these proposals, jointly and severally, and the fact that many of these schemes do not begin to approach what has since become established public policy in either (or both) the United Kingdom and the United States (though some in fact do go substantially further), does not vitiate the testimony of these and other examples as evidence of the activism of law as a mode of change or reform. These examples, and the general role of law of which they are evidence, are all the more interesting when juxtaposed to the fact that opposition to programs of a similar or identical nature was subsequently expressed in the name of the classical economists.[86]

CONCLUSION

The basic point of departure, or frame of reference, in the examination of the classical theory of the role of the state as a mode of change must be the classicists' cosmology and, perforce, their effective concept of a created harmony. Preliminary to their general position concerning the resolution or balancing of continuity and change, which is discussed in

Chapter Five, the classical economists not only did not consider harmony, or mutuality of interests, as automatic, but
also they did not consider that any particular division of
public and private decision-making power, or any particular
division of private decision-making power, was final. In their
view, one of the functions of the state as a social-control force
was to effectuate such change as was determined through
the legal process to be warranted for the creation and re-
creation of harmony. Whatever agreement or disagreement
there was concerning the specific content of the *agenda* of
legal change, it is clear that the conditions of harmony were
something that had to be created, and continually re-created,
and that law was a mode of such re-creation or change. The
role of law as a mode of change therefore is clear with respect
both to the redivision of public and private decision-making
power, and the redivision of private participation.

Moreover, the selective and purposeful character of change
through the exercise of governmental discretion—vis-a-vis always allowing ignorance to make existing rights so sacrosanct
as to be untouchable—indicates the inappropriateness of the
general or formal-laws approach. Re-creating the conditions
of mutuality of interests through legal change meant changing the participation of law with respect to specific details
both as to particular rights and particular changes through
direct participation. The classical theory of economic policy
incorporated no grandiose or utopian scheme for (re-)creating
harmony once and for all; rather it was manifest in an *ad hoc*
pattern of expedient (according to the sensibilities), yet presumably reasoned, alterations in response to changing conditions, changing ideas and values, and changing felt needs, as
well as in response to the dynamics of a changing decisional
process. These changes are meaningful, not in terms of a
priori injunctions or declamations, but in particularized contexts, with changing details—changing specific details—where,

151

through the determination by the legal process, it was deemed necessary or desirable. No other explanation fits the data: there is ample evidence that in the classical theory of economic policy, law was a mode of change, and such change involved seeking specific objectives for specific reasons through specific means, whether it be in revision of the law of principal and agent, revision of debtor-creditor rights, factory legislation, intensive regulation of business, or the use of the tariff. The debate was not in terms of some notion of "rule of law"; rather, legal discretion there indeed had to be, and was, and the determination of specifics, including when classification was reasonable, was if anything a contextual matter, and not precluded by artificial injunction.[87]

What, then, may be said of "noninterventionism"? It should be clear that whatever else may be said about the concept of "nonintervention" and its role (see Chapter Five), the notion could not preclude recognition of the fundamental and pervasive operation of government, as indicated in the framework-provision function, and as further specified in Chapter Three. This means that "intervention" could *not* constitute, in the classical policy system, the introduction of government into a situation in which government was previously absent, for government was recognized as a fundamental force in the determination of the existent sphere of private participation and its structure. It could not mean the introduction of the state into such situations *de novo*, for the state was already present, however unobtrusive or taken for granted. "Intervention" could mean, rather, a change in the substance of what government is in any event already doing, that is, a change in the pattern of relative rights, or a change in the division of public and private decision-making power (i.e., direct participation), the existing pattern of both of which is a partial function of law. "Nonintervention" thus could mean, not abstention on the part of government but rather maintenance of the *status quo* with respect both to what government was literally and substantively doing and what private participation was doing by virtue of what (say) the law of property enabled it to do: allowing private participation to maintain the same sphere, with the same structure of participation, as presently existent.

If "nonintervention," then, is taken to mean the nonexistence of the state (or existence in some remote, unimportant, and minimal way), it is simply inappropriate and inapplicable to the classical policy system. Moreover, if "nonintervention" is taken to mean the abstinence by the state from bringing about change, *then by this definition also it is inapplicable* to the classical theory of economic policy, for in this chapter it has been seen that the classical theory of the economic role of the state clearly encompassed change through law.

NOTES: CHAPTER FOUR

1. Lionel Robbins, *Theory of Economic Policy* (London: Macmillan, 1953), p. 191.

2. S. G. Checkland, "The Prescriptions of the Classical Economists," *Economica*, n.s. vol. 20 (1953), p. 70. For Checkland's comments on the character of choice involved, see Chapter Five.

3. Frank H. Knight, "Theory of Economic Policy and the History of Doctrine," *Ethics*, vol. 63 (1953), p. 279.

4. Robbins, *op. cit.*, pp. 192–94.

5. F. A. Hayek, *The Constitution of Liberty* (Chicago: University of Chicago Press, 1959), p. 221.

6. The point is essentially the same as that made by Checkland (text, at note 2, *supra*.) In another context: "The issue is partly what rules to lay down but is largely one of degree, as to how definite the rules can be." Frank H. Knight, *Intelligence and Democratic Action*

(Cambridge: Harvard University Press, 1960), p. 105. And see Edward H. Levi: "It is important that the mechanism of legal reasoning should not be concealed by its pretense. The pretense is that the law is a system of known rules applied by a judge; the pretense has long been under attack. In an important sense legal rules are never clear, and, if a rule had to be clear before it could be imposed, society would be impossible. The mechanism accepts the differences of view and ambiguities of words. It provides for the participation of the community in resolving the ambiguity by providing a forum for the discussion of policy in the gap of ambiguity. On serious controversial questions, it makes it possible to take the first step in the direction of what otherwise would be forbidden ends. The mechanism is indispensable to peace in a community. . . . Yet this change in the rules is the indispensable dynamic quality of law. It occurs because the scope of a rule of law, and therefore its meaning, depends upon a determination of what facts will be considered similar to those present when the rule was first announced. The finding of similarity or difference is the key step in the legal process . . . the kind of reasoning involved in the legal process is one in which the classification changes as the classification is made. The rules change as the rules are applied. . . . Not only do new situations arise, but in addition peoples' wants change." *An Introduction to Legal Reasoning* (Chicago: University of Chicago Press, 1948), pp. 1, 2, 3–4.

7. See Chapter Five. Lord Robbins' *Theory of Economic Policy* is replete with examples of specific action attributed to government by classical economists. Any distinction between law as details of action and law as general framework is begging the question. Lord Robbins himself points out the classicists' "complete willingness to apply special rules and regulations where, for technical reasons, competition was not possible," a position the analysis of this chapter will substantively broaden. Robbins, *op. cit.*, p. 191.

8. Robbins, *op. cit.*, pp. 169–70, 170–71.

9. Karl Marx, *Theories of Surplus Value* (New York: International Publishers, 1952), p. 55.

10. Warren J. Samuels, "The Physiocratic Theory of Economic Policy," *Quarterly Journal of Economics*, vol. 76 (1962).

11. W. Stark, *Jeremy Bentham's Economic Writings* (New York: Burt Franklin, 1954), vol. 3, p. 333. Italics added.

12. Hayek, *op. cit.*, p. 221.

13. Taylor, *The Classical Liberalism, Marxism, and the Twentieth Century* (Cambridge: Harvard University Press, 1960), pp. 109–10. Italics added.

14. J. R. McCulloch, *Principles of Political Economy* (Edinburgh: Tait, 1843), p. 270.

15. *Fortnightly Review*, vol. 31 (1879), p. 220.

16. *Ibid.*, pp. 529–30. He goes on to point out that subject to the condition of compensation, which itself has limits, "society is fully entitled to abrogate or alter any particular right of property which on sufficient consideration it judges to stand in the way of the public good." (P. 530.)

17. John Bowring, ed., *Works of Jeremy Bentham* (New York: Russell & Russell, 1962), vol. 1, p. 309.

18. *Ibid.*, vol. 1, p. 313.

19. *Ibid.*, vol. 1, pp. 322–23.

20. *Ibid.*, vol. 1, p. 326.

21. Stark, *op. cit.*, vol. 3, p. 311.

22. *Ibid.*, vol. 3, p. 411.

23. Jeremy Bentham, *A Fragment on Government and An Introduction to the Principles of Morals and Legislation*, Wilfrid Harrison, ed., hereafter cited as *A Fragment on Government* (Oxford: Blackwell, 1948), pp. 4, 10.

24. Examples noted but not otherwise examined in this chapter are intended to be suggestive and illustrative and not exhaustive; so also the appended references are informational and are not exhaustive. On property law reform, see, *inter alia*, McCulloch, *A Treatise on the Succession of Property* . . . (London: Longmans, 1848), p. vi; Glenn Morrow, in *Adam Smith, 1776–1926* (Chicago: University of Chicago Press, 1928), p. 134; Leslie Stephen, *The English Utilitarians* (New York: Peter Smith, 1950), vol. 1, p. 308 and vol. 2, pp. 48–49.

25. John Stuart Mill, *Dissertations and Discussions* (New York: Holt, 1882), vol. 5, pp. 225–94; Stark, *op. cit.*, vol. 3, pp. 338–39; D. H. Macgregor, *Economic Thought and Policy* (London: Oxford University Press, 1955), p. 84.

26. Smith, *Lectures* (New York: Kelley & Millman, 1956), pp. xxiii, 124; John Stuart Mill, *op. cit.*, vol. 1, pp. 28–67.

27. Nassau W. Senior, *Industrial Efficiency and Social Economy*, S. Leon Levy, ed. (New York: Holt, 1928), vol. 2, pp. 362–63; Stephen, *op. cit.*, vol. 3, p. 229.

28. Bowring, *op. cit.*, vol. 1, pp. 77, 546; vol. 3, p. 428; vol. 5, p. 533; vol. 6, pp. 135, 176, 180; vol. 7, p. 381. Also see McCulloch, *Principles of Political Economy*, pp. 270–79.

29. Robbins, *op. cit.*, pp. 100 ff.; Kenneth O. Walker, "The Classical Economists and the Factory Acts," *Journal of Economic History*, vol. 1 (1941), pp. 168–77; Clem Linnenberg, Jr., "The Laissez-Faire State in Relation to the National Economy," *Southwestern Social Science Quarterly*, vol. 24 (1943), pp. 101–17, 230–48; Lloyd R. Sorenson, "Some Classical Economists, Laissez Faire, and the Factory Acts," *Journal of Economic History*, vol. 12 (1952), pp. 247–62; and Mark

Blaug, "The Classical Economists and the Factory Acts—A Re-examination," *Quarterly Journal of Economics*, vol. 72 (1958), pp. 211–26.

30. Robbins, *op. cit.*, pp. 103 ff.; and Stephen, *op. cit.*, vol. 2, p. 57.

31. Robbins, *op. cit.*, pp. 31, 38, 58; Edwin A. Burtt, ed., *The English Philosophers From Bacon to Mill* (New York: Modern Library, 1939), p. 1032; McCulloch, *Principles*, p. 286; Bowring, *op. cit.*, vol. 9, p. 34; Abram L. Harris, "J. S. Mill on Monopoly and Socialism: A Note," *Journal of Political Economy*, vol. 67 (1959), pp. 606 ff.

32. Jeremy Bentham, *Plan of Parliamentary Reform* (London, 1817). Cf. Bentham, *A Fragment on Government*, p. lxii. Wrote Smith to La Rochefoucauld: "I expect all the bad consequences from the Chambers of Commerce and Manufacture, establishing in different parts of this country, which Your Grace seems to foresee. In a country where clamour always intimidates and faction often oppresses the Government, the regulations of commerce are commonly dictated by those who are most interested to deceive and impose upon the public." Quoted in C. R. Fay, *The World of Adam Smith* (Cambridge: Heffer, 1960), p. 36. See also Henry J. Bittermann, "Adam Smith's Empiricism and the Law of Nature," *Journal of Political Economy*, vol. 48 (1940), pp. 729, 730; Smith, *Wealth of Nations*, p. 250; and T. R. Malthus, *Principles of Political Economy* (The London School of Economics, 1936), p. 381.

33. P. Sraffa, ed., *The Works and Correspondence of David Ricardo* (Cambridge: Cambridge University Press, 1952), vol. 9, pp. 267–68.

34. Bentham, *Plan of Parliamentary Reform*, p. xix.

35. Bowring, *op. cit.*, vol. 1, p. 245.

36. *Ibid.*, vol. 2, p. 463.

37. Stephen, *op. cit.*, vol. 2, p. 63.

38. Smith, *Wealth of Nations*, p. 67; and V. B. Singh, "Adam Smith's Theory of Economic Development," *Science and Society*, vol. 23 (1959), p. 110.

39. Senior, *op. cit.*, vol. 2, p. 311.

40. One example that Bentham gives is that of foundations: "Foundation is another name for legislation," a clear anticipation of the more recent concept of "private government." Bowring, *op. cit.*, vol 9, pp. 34–35.

41. Robbins, *op. cit.*, p. 65. See also Alexander Bain, *John Stuart Mill: A Criticism* (London: Longmans, 1882), p. 89.

42. Sraffa, *op. cit.*, vol. 5, p. xxvi.

43. *Ibid.*, vol. 5, p. 293.

44. Edwin Cannan, "Ricardo in Parliament," *Economic Journal*, vol. 4 (1894), p. 421.

45. Sraffa, *op cit.*, vol. 5, p. 34. Also remarks Cannan: "No one seems to have thought it worth while to protest against this astonishing

view of the nature of the contract between the nation and the fund-holder." "Ricardo in Parliament," *op. cit.*, p. 421. Cannan also goes on to say (p. 423), "Whether it was justifiable to demand that the fund-holders should contribute their proportion to the tax necessary to pay them off is more doubtful. McCulloch, in 1816, it may be remembered, wrote an essay . . . recommending a compulsory reduction of the interest on the debt." See also R. O. Roberts, "Ricardo's Theory of Public Debts," *Economica*, n.s. vol. 9 (1942), pp. 257–66. Compare the following from a letter of Ricardo to McCulloch: ". . . laws are made for the benefit of the whole community and not for the benefit of any particular class—they may therefore be enacted or repealed as expediency may require. A parental Government however will never be unmindful of the consequences of their acts to a large class of individuals. But on the question of the sinking fund they have no choice— I consider it as a positive bargain between the nation and the stock-holder, which cannot be infringed by one of the contracting parties." Sraffa, *op. cit.*, vol. 7, p. 106.

46. Robbins, *op. cit.*, p. 188.

47. *Ibid., loc. cit.*

48. *Ibid.*, p. 9.

49. *Ibid.*, p. 13.

50. *Ibid.*, pp. 188–89.

51. ". . . it was the Classical Economists who were among the leaders of the movement for making private monopolies public property in this respect. There was no use for private armies, private police, private highways in their system; in this respect they were far less *laissez-faire* than the Mercantilists." *Ibid.*, p. 189.

52. *Ibid., loc. cit.*

53. *Ibid., loc. cit.*

54. See also the important articles by Viner: "Adam Smith and Laissez Faire," *Journal of Political Economy*, vol. 35 (1927), pp. 198–232; also in Morrow, in *Adam Smith, 1776–1926*, pp. 116–55; and reprinted in Joseph Spengler and William R. Allen, *Essays in Economic Thought* (Chicago: Rand McNally, 1960), pp. 305–29, notably the section entitled "The Functions of Government"; and Jacob Viner, "Bentham and J. S. Mill: the Utilitarian Background," *American Economic Review*, vol. 39 (1949).

55. Robbins, *op. cit.*, p. 39.

56. Stark, *op. cit.*, vol. 3, p. 322; cf. pp. 338 ff. See also Bowring, *op. cit.*, vol. 1, pp. 171–94 ("Of the Influence of Time and Place in Matters of Legislation"); Robbins, *op. cit.*, pp. 39–40; and Karl de Schweinitz, Jr., "Free Enterprise in a Growth World," *Southern Economic Journal*, vol. 29 (1962).

57. ". . . although there is an explicit presumption that, over a wide

field, interference is inadvisable, there is no suggestion that it is ruled out *a priori* by some system of natural rights. . . . According to the principle of utility, as distinct from the *Naturrecht*, the expediency of any act of government must be judged solely by its consequences and not regarded as ruled out in advance by some metaphysical system of rights." Robbins, *op. cit.*, pp. 40–41, Cf. O. H. Taylor, *Economics and Liberalism* (Cambridge: Harvard University Press, 1955), p. 99.

58. Robbins, *op. cit.*, p. 190.

59. See Chapter Three, note 18.

60. McCulloch, *Principles*, pp. 257–58, 290 ff.; Robbins, *op. cit.*, p. 41; and Viner, "Bentham and J. S. Mill: the Utilitarian Background," *op. cit.*, p. 371.

61. The classicists' qualified advocacy of free trade is extensively discussed in William D. Grampp, *The Manchester School of Economics* (Stanford: Stanford University Press, 1960), pp. 16–38, 46, 98, 107. See also Charles F. Dunbar, "The Reaction in Political Economy," *Quarterly Journal of Economics*, vol. 1 (1886), pp. 21–22; J. A. R. Marriott, "Adam Smith and Some Problems of To-day," *Fortnightly Review*, vol. 82 (1902), pp. 976–81; Morrow, in *Adam Smith, 1776–1926*, pp. 150–53; Grampp, "On the Politics of the Classical Economists," *Quarterly Journal of Economics*, vol. 62 (1948), pp. 737–39; Joseph J. Spengler, "Malthus the Malthusian vs. Malthus the Economist," *Southern Economic Journal*, vol. 24 (1957), pp. 8–11; Robbins, *op. cit.*, p. 59; William D. Grampp, Book Review, *American Economic Review*, vol. 52 (1962), p. 230. With respect to Ricardo's proposal for a countervailing duty, see Sraffa, *op. cit.*, vol. 5, pp. 81–91, and vol. 8, pp. 351–60, 364–66; and see Edwin Cannan, "Ricardo in Parliament," *Economic Journal*, vol. 4 (1894), p. 258; and William Ashley, "A Retrospect of Free-Trade Doctrine," *Economic Journal*, vol. 34 (1924), p. 501.

62. Robbins, *op. cit.*, pp. 89 ff.; Viner, "Bentham and J. S. Mill: The Utilitarian Background," *op. cit.*, pp. 362, 371; D. H. Macgregor, *Economic Thought and Policy* (London: Oxford University Press, 1949), pp. 85–86; and R. H. Inglis Palgrave, *Dictionary of Political Economy* (London: Macmillan, 1894–1899), three volumes, vol. 2, p. 535.

63. McCulloch, *Principles*, pp. 272–73, 275.

64. *Ibid.*, pp. 280–81.

65. *Ibid.*, p. 291.

66. Lionel Robbins, *Robert Torrens and the Evolution of Classical Economics* (London: Macmillan, 1958), p. 250.

67. J. S. Mill, *Principles of Political Economy* (New York: Kelley, 1961), pp. 21, 200; Adam Smith, *Essays* (London: Ward, Lock, & Co., 1880), p. 149.

68. McCulloch, *Principles,* p. 185.

69. Robbins, *Theory of Economic Policy,* pp. 93 ff.; Blaug, *Ricardian Economics* (New Haven: Yale University Press, 1958), pp. 196 ff.; Bowring, *op. cit.,* vol. 1, p. 316; Spengler and Allen, *op. cit.,* pp. 342–44.

70. Macgregor, *op. cit.,* p. 46.

71. Robbins, *Theory of Economic Policy,* p. 65.

72. Abram L. Harris, "J. S. Mill on Monopoly and Socialism: A Note," *op. cit.,* p. 611.

73. McCulloch, *Principles,* pp. 275 ff., 282; Robbins, *Theory of Economic Policy,* pp. 13, 38; Bowring, *op. cit.,* vol. 1, p. 568; Morrow, in *Adam Smith, 1776–1926,* p. 145; J. R. McCulloch, ed., *The Works of David Ricardo* (London: John Murray, 1881), p. 408; Viner, "Bentham and J. S. Mill: The Utilitarian Background," *op. cit.,* p. 362.

74. Robbins, *Theory of Economic Policy,* p. 48.

75. McCulloch, *Principles of Political Economy,* pp. 287–88, 293; J. S. Mill, *op. cit.,* pp. 962–63; Robbins, *Theory,* p. 58.

76. Smith, *Wealth of Nations* (New York: Modern Library, 1937), pp. 339–40.

77. Robbins, *Theory of Economic Policy,* p. 31; McCulloch, *Principles,* p. 279 ff.; Stark, *op. cit.,* vol. 3, pp. 175 ff.; Bowring, *op. cit.,* vol. 2, pp. 599–600; B. A. Corry, *Money, Saving and Investment in English Economics, 1800–1850* (New York: St. Martin's Press, 1962), p. 71; Sraffa, *op. cit.,* vol. 5, p. 193, vol. 6, p. 268, vol. 7, p. 103; R. S. Sayers, "Ricardo's Views on Monetary Questions," *Quarterly Journal of Economics,* vol. 67 (1953), pp. 43, 49; and Meenai, "Robert Torrens—1780–1864," *Economica,* n.s., vol. 23 (1956), p. 60.

78. See note 29, *supra,* and Mitchell, *The Backward Art of Spending Money* (New York: Kelley, 1950), pp. 109–10; H. M. Robertson, *The Adam Smith Tradition* (London: Oxford University Press, 1950), p. 19; Smith, *Wealth of Nations,* pp. 734–35, and *Lectures,* pp. 256–57; Macgregor, *op. cit.,* pp. 84 ff.; Robbins, *Theory,* pp. 100 ff.; J. Bonar, *Malthus and His Work* (New York: Harper, 1885), p. 196; Robbins, *Robert Torrens and the Evolution of Classical Economics,* p. 250.

79. Robbins, *Theory of Economic Policy,* p. 41.

80. McCulloch, *Principles,* p. 291; Dunbar, *op. cit.,* pp. 21–22; Edmund Whittaker, *Schools and Streams of Economic Thought* (Chicago: Rand McNally, 1960), p. 169.

81. McCulloch, *op. cit.,* pp. 284–85.

82. *Ibid.,* p. 293.

83. Burtt, *op. cit.,* p. 1023; Nathan Rosenberg, "Some Institutional Aspects of the *Wealth of Nations,*" *Journal of Political Economy,* vol.

68 (1960), p. 561; Smith, *Wealth of Nations*, p. 784; Morrow, in *Adam Smith, 1776–1926*, pp. 152–53.

84. Robbins, *Theory of Economic Policy*, p. 38.

85. Spengler and Allen, *op. cit.*, pp. 335 ff.; T. W. Hutchison, "Robert Torrens and Classical Economics," *Economic History Review*, vol. 11 (1958), pp. 318, 319; Corry, *op. cit.*, chaps. 4, 9; Robert G. Link, *English Theories of Economic Fluctuations, 1815–1848* (New York: Columbia University Press, 1959), e. g., pp. 67–70; Grampp, Book Review, *op. cit.*, p. 229; Morton Paglin, *Malthus and Lauderdale, the Anti-Ricardian Tradition* (New York: Kelley, 1961).

86. See Grampp, "On the Politics of the Classical Economists," *op. cit.*, p. 716; Walton H. Hamilton and Douglass Adair, *The Power to Govern* (New York: Norton, 1937), pp. 95, 218; John Neville Keynes, *The Scope and Method of Political Economy* (New York: Kelley & Millman, Fourth Edition, 1955), p. 73; and John Rae, *Contemporary Socialism* (2nd ed., New York: Scribner's, 1891), pp. 351 ff.

87. On automatism, see Robbins, *Theory*, pp. 29–33, 192–94, and *Robert Torrens and the Evolution of Classical Economics*, pp. 117 ff., 251 ff., 340.

The Classical Theory of
Economic Policy

The preceding chapters have been both critical and constructive. Criticism has been directed at various facets of both the conventional laissez faire (or laissez faire-plus-exceptions) interpretation and that of Lord Robbins, as well as at doctrinally oriented approaches to interpretation. Through constructive analysis relying in no small part upon the foundations provided by Lord Robbins, the author has attempted to demonstrate, in general terms, (a) the relevance and importance of the nondeliberative or nonlegal forces of social control; (b) the co-ordinates of the fundamental participation by the state through what Lord Robbins identifies as the framework-provision function of the state; and (c) the activism by the state as a mode of change through both restructuring private participation and direct participation, with an overlapping of effects. In addition, the analysis tends to confirm the idea of a created harmony as the cosmological foundation of the classical theory of economic policy, and the role of the forces of social control in connection with the createdness of harmony. The goal throughout has been to identify and specify the components and grounds of a meaningful restatement of the classical theory of economic policy, one that would have a place for valuational premise, but which would also be confirmable by reference to the materials involved, and which would accurately reflect that material, and one which would specify the classical theory of policy in terms of the basic problems of any theory of economic policy.

The objective of this chapter is to restate the classical theory of economic policy in terms both reflective of, and consistent with, the findings of the preceding chapters. Accordingly the first major section of this chapter presents a suggested reinterpretation of the substance of the classical policy system as a theory of economic policy, and the second major section attempts to ascertain the meaningfulness of the classical policy system so far as it is applicable to specific problems of policy. Except with respect to several matters where further analysis is conducted, the objective in the first major section is to draw together the strands of reasoning that will be retrospectively apparent in the preceding chapters.

THE CLASSICAL THEORY OF ECONOMIC POLICY

It certainly must be clear that the classical theory of economic policy encompasses more than the economic role of the state, that the role of government (however *it* be specified) is but part of a larger system of policy. The classical theory of economic policy rather must be interpreted as a theory of the way in which economic life should be organized and controlled, in providing for the continuing resolution of the basic economic problems common to all societies. As such, it is a theory of the economic decision-making process, and of that process as a whole, and ultimately involves both

162

theories of (a) the resolution of what has been called the pervasive and basic social problems of freedom and control, and continuity and change; and (b) the determination and role of knowledge in the decision-making process. Among other things that might be said in this connection, the underlying realism of the classical theory of economic policy involves its direct confrontation with these matters, such that its essentially and necessarily normative or idealist character[1] is tempered by appreciation of the problems and necessities involved. For example, the error of the noninterventionist or laissez faire interpretation (not as defined in Chapter One) lies in its utter incompleteness or unrealism derived from the importance of the questions that the interpretation begs. It is in the nature of propaganda for such questions to be begged— and the propaganda or legitimation role of the conventional interpretation has already been acknowledged,[2] but as scientific and objective analysis or description the interpretation is grossly inadequate.

The procedure of this section will be as follows. A restatement of the classical theory of economic policy will commence with an interpretation of the resolution of the problem of freedom and control. This will be followed by discussion and statement of the character of the decision-making process actually contemplated or proposed in the classical policy system, at which time (a) the participants, (b) their respective roles, and (c) the scope of effective policy will be specified along with (d) something of the classical theory of the determination and role of knowledge in respect to social policy (which will also be discussed in the following major section). The analysis will conclude with an interpretation of the classical theory of the resolution of the problem of continuity and change.

Freedom and Control: It is one of the fundamental attributes of the classical economists that they did not take "freedom" for granted, in the sense of leaving unanalyzed the process by which freedom is determined in society as they knew it. However much their formal economic analysis started with the premise of free men and a free society and did not deal with this directly, and however much their writings were or were not used as propaganda for the free market, the resolution of the problem of social control was a recognized and conspicuous co-ordinate of their theory of economic policy. The classicists were more sophisticated in matters of social control than has been generally recognized, and their theory of policy was more than a propaganda.

There can be no question that classical economic liberalism had as its distinctive characteristic resounding pleas for human freedom, for the importance of human development, for individual independence of thought and action, and for freedom from arbitrary control.[3] The classical economists from Smith to Stuart Mill shared the historic theme of liberalism—meaningful human freedom as a value—and the cognate importance, as will soon be seen, of an open and pluralist society. Individuals were to be free in pursuit of their economic objectives, and resource allocation and income distribution were to emerge as the result of the interaction of market forces, in a resolution of the basic economic problems reflecting the interplay of ostensibly spontaneous individual private demanders and suppliers.

But correlative to this desideratum of human freedom was a recognition of the fact and necessity of the system of social control, extending to both the nonlegal and legal forces thereof. The classicists acknowledged the dualism of freedom and control, the desire for meaningful freedom vis-a-vis the necessity of control. Moreover, they also acknowledged the necessity of, and the complexity of, choice governing the pattern of freedom and control.

The system of control, as a whole, greatly conditioned and

integrated individual behavior patterns by channeling the exercise of individual choice, the range of which in any given circumstance was more or less flexible, depending upon the pattern of historical accretion of control, and the exigencies of time and place. More important in a way, the pattern of social control related to, and perhaps provided more or less specifically, the institutional conditions of life and behavior patterns. One's freedom was freedom only within the pattern of freedom reigning at the time and place: this was the classicists' understanding of the meaning of freedom. Freedom, then, was largely circumstantial.[4] This reflected, first, the more encompassing notion that the character of man was in part social and situational[5] (though man may be examined either as an abstract individual, or in terms of his social character); [6] and, second, the idea that the crucial element in the situation, given the pattern of latent passions of human nature, was the system of social control, particularly but not exclusively the nonlegal forces ranging from the moral code, and ideology or cosmology, to education, all performing, among other things, the role of legitimation. Freedom was therefore essentially relative and historical, and with it also, the pattern of rights in terms of which the developing pattern of freedom was crystallized, discussed, and argued. But notwithstanding the circumstantial nature of freedom and the situational character of man, the role of social control was crucial in establishing and securing order, as a condition of life and progress. The exercise of social control was, then, in some respects, to discipline man in the interests of order and the manifestations of order, e.g., discipline in effect directed at inducing the orderly practice of economic pursuits.

Individual freedom of choice was an important desideratum, both as propaganda and as part of the larger theory of policy. As Robbins cautions in a parallel discussion,[7] this should not be obscured or eclipsed because it has been necessary to concentrate on the positive operation of social controls both legal and nonlegal. Yet, notwithstanding this caveat, the classicists acknowledged that individual behavior and choice were channeled by the forces of morals, religion, custom, and education as nondeliberative constraints, and by law. The economy, considered as a decision-making process in the resolution of the basic economic problems, was also seen governed by the nondeliberative and deliberative forces, which were important with respect both to the *structure* of that process and the *content* of the decisions made and hence with the pattern of freedom as the system channeled the exercise of choice.

The substance of this, with respect to the nonlegal forces of social control, has been examined in Chapter Two. In the remaining paragraphs of this subsection the legal forces will be analyzed, going beyond the relevant discussions in Chapters Three and Four. The underlying theme is the partial dependence of freedom upon law, the importance of which warrants examination of the several facets from which the classicists approached the subject although some redundancy results.

It was seen in Chapter Three that, in the classical theory of economic policy, the idea of "rights" connoted loci and conditions of private participation in the economic decision-making process. One's rights were relative to the participation of other private participants and to the forces of social control in terms of which the pattern of private rights was meaningful and through which private rights were in part determined. Law, as a force of social control, was specifically seen as itself a participant in determining the rights and consequently the structure of private participation. This being the case, rights were, *pro tanto*, a function of law.

Rights, however, are intermediates, both in the adjudication of conflicting claims in the process of determining

166

spheres of participation or, to say the same thing, spheres of freedom, and in the resolution of the problem of continuity and change with respect to such spheres. Freedom in the classical policy system was relative in the sense that one's freedom was meaningful only in the context of the pattern of freedom actually existing; that is to say, one's freedom was relative to (a) the freedom of others, and the limitations imposed by both (b) the nonlegal and (c) the legal forces of social control. Freedom was freedom in the context of the economic decision-making process as a whole, and its relative, situational, circumstantial and historical character derives both from its inherent relativity in the sense of spheres of freedom limiting each other, and from the process of change, in which, as was seen in Chapter Four, the legal forces were not inactive.

The theory of freedom in the classical policy system was manifest in several ways, each indicating the partial dependence of the pattern of freedom and specific spheres of freedom upon the state. This understanding of the meaning of freedom was approached in the classical literature through the analysis of rights as such, and involved what was considered to be a required juxtaposition of rights and obligations. "Correspondent to rights," says Bentham, "are obligations. Without the idea expressed by the word obligation, no clear or correct idea can be annexed to the word right." [8] All rights are powers, according to James Mill, but rights "always import obligations. . . . If a right is conferred . . . , an obligation is laid upon other men. . . . It thus appears that it is wholly impossible to create a right without at the same time creating an obligation." [9] ". . . It is by imposing obligations, or by abstaining from imposing them, that rights are established or granted. All rights rest therefore upon the idea of obligation as their necessary foundation." [10] Freedom, then, if it is to be interpreted in the language of rights, must be considered, according to the classicists, in the context of rights *and* obligations, such as they substantively may be, and however unobtrusively determined. Alternately the classicists approached the meaning of freedom directly. If there is "no right without a correspondent obligation," it is also true that "as against the coercion applicable by individual to individual, no liberty can be given to one man but in proportion as it is taken from another." [11] The concept of coercion in relation to freedom will be discussed in a moment, but with respect to these two approaches to freedom, in both cases freedom was seen to be mutual and reciprocal: the essence of freedom in the context of the economic decision-making process reduced to unencumbered participation, but plural private participation meant mutual limitation or encumbrance. Freedom, to the classicists, was not the hypothetical freedom of a Crusoe, but rather "that of men living together in society." [12]

Whichever approach is taken, the reliance or dependence of freedom upon law is clearly evidenced in the classicists' writings, although the terms of its specification enabled conflict of emphasis. It was thus argued that law is prima facie the opposite of liberty, for law is destructive of liberty, by its very nature. The coerciveness of law is "a property which is of the very essence of all law. . . ." [13] But it was also argued that the liberty which law destroys is the liberty that, *pro tanto*, the law itself had helped to create. The state, say, that regulated and thereby destroyed liberty was only changing the pattern of freedom that the previously existing law (e.g., of property) had allowed. Inasmuch as it is true that "in the same proportion as it creates obligations, the law curtails liberty," then "these curtailments of liberty are inevitable." The law that had created the existing liberty itself has destroyed liberty. "It is impossible to create rights, to impose obligations, to protect the person, life, reputation, property, subsistence, or liberty itself, but at the expense of liberty." [14] ". . . To say that a law is contrary to natural liberty, is simply to say that it is a law; for every law is established at the expense of liberty—the liberty of Peter at the expense of the liberty of Paul." [15] In the classical theory of economic policy, law is per se an infringement upon liberty, but it is also per se a source of liberty. The relation is reciprocal, and although one part may be stressed over the other, from context to context, "the law cannot create rights," and therefore cannot create spheres of freedom, "without creating the corresponding obligations," [16] which is to say, without limiting freedom: ". . . all laws creative of liberty, are, as far as they go, abrogative of liberty." [17] The question then is whose liberty shall be sacrificed as the price of someone else's liberty.

Liberty in the classical policy system, then, was relative to the liberty of others, and moreover, law was a mode through which such relative liberty, i.e., the pattern of liberty and of exposure to the liberties of others, is determined. Legal limitation upon liberty is a co-ordinate following from legal determination of liberty. According to Adler, the classicists were generally adherents to the circumstantial self-realization theory of freedom, such that freedom was, *inter alia*, meaningful only in terms of the circumstances of each situation, and included therein were the legal forces of social control. The classicists, as he puts it, held that "law restricts freedom," but, as he points out, "they also acknowledge the necessity of some legal restrictions on human behavior." While the classicists never "repudiate the proposition that laws *always* take away liberty,"

> They point out that the individual is unfree under two sets of circumstances: (1) when he is coerced or intimidated by law or government, and (2) when he is coerced or intimidated by the force or pressure his fellow men exert when they are not restrained by law or government from trying to impose their will on him. Consequently, though law always takes away

169

some liberty, it may also create some; and it is even possible for the balance to be in favor of freedom when laws are made with this end in view.[18]

Freedom was, again, freedom only in the context of the pattern of freedom: since "rights" is the language of freedom, the analysis, in Chapter Three, of rights, interpreted in terms of freedom, implies that freedom is freedom to participate in the economic process and freedom from other participants. Further, as was suggested in Chapter Four, law served as a check on private loci of power, both directly and through the creation of new loci of participation or power. Freedom in the classical system was not an abstract thing; it involved private participation in the decisional process, and the division or structure of such participation and therefore of freedom was in part a function of law.

It was noted before that the classical economists also approached the problem of the meaning of freedom from the facet of coercion. In this respect, the classicists generally conceived the meaning of coercion as the impact of other private participants, as well as the impact of the forces of social control, as is clear, for example, in the quotation from Adler at note 18. In this way if relative rights, and therefore relative freedom, is a function of legal determination (or legal reinforcement of private claims), among other things, it follows that, to that extent, the unrestrained or allowed private participation, or pressure, or coercion exerted through market forces is itself a partial product of law. In other words, the private sector was a coercive process—a pattern of private coercion—in the sense indicated above, and this pattern of coercion which, in a sense, is the converse of the pattern of private freedom was a partial function of the operation of law. This pattern of private coercion was clearly recognized by the classicists. That "every right is a benefit: a command to a certain extent over the objects of desire," i.e., "means

170

for the obtaining of services," [19] connoted freedom for the right-holder, but coercion or exposure for others. Although McCulloch contends that "the right of property gives no advantage to one over another," [20] James Mill recognized that "every man has the means of acquiring authority over others in proportion" to his property rights, [21] and Bentham described "the power necessarily and proportionably attached to opulence. . . ." [22] The meaning of this is clear and of the utmost importance. If we follow Adler, and accept a classical presumption against law [23] ("the general reason against every law," [24] namely its coerciveness); concur that that liberty should be allowed which incurs no injury or damage to the community; [25] and further concur that, according to the classical view, "legal coercion is justified only if, by preventing extra-legal forms of coercion, it tends to increase rather than reduce the total amount of individual freedom," [26] it follows that the resultant pattern of freedom and coercion is a partial function of law, and not pre-existent to, or independent of, law.

Whether specified in terms of rights, or freedom, or coercion, (a) the structure of private decision-making, i.e., the division of private participation, is a partial function of law; (b) such structuring becomes a facet of the classical theory of the economic role of the state; and (c) the state is a fundamental participant in the resolution of freedom and control. The classicists were far from defining freedom as the absence of the state; they rather considered that one's freedom was a partial function of law. In this respect as in others, the fundamental ideas of modern analysts—notably Commons—may readily be found in the writings of the classicists.[27]

But Adler's juxtaposition of "legal coercion" and "extra-legal forms of coercion," like the expression of allowing liberty so long as it incurs no injury or damage, raises the question of content: what coercion, or what private freedom, will

171

be legal and what extralegal? Thus, to the extent that the pattern of freedom and coercion is a partial function of law, it also follows that it is a partial function of social choice exercised through law. As Grampp has pointed out, in the classical view the system of legal restraints "should merely negate all illegitimate expressions of interest while opening the way for those which were desirable and permissible." [28] As put by Bentham, ". . . when most of us speak of liberty, what we mean is security—and security is the work of law, coercing those who would interfere with or injure those whom it means to favor." [29] To speak of "injury" is not sufficient and is question-begging besides: it is a matter of choice as to who will be allowed the freedom to "coerce" or "injure" whom. It is a matter of choice as to which interests are desirable and permissible, and those that are not to be. What this really means is that the law is choosing, or being used to choose, those interests whose claims it will reinforce, as was seen in Chapter Three, or in other words, choosing those coercions and those injuries it will restrain, and perforce those freedoms and those exposures to the freedoms of others it will allow—all of which is to say that law gives effect to one pattern of private freedom and exposure or coercion, as opposed to another. So far as freedom is concerned, when Lord Robbins declares, and accurately so far as he goes, that "it is the hand of the lawgiver, the hand which withdraws from the sphere of the pursuit of self-interest those possibilities which do not harmonize with the public good," [30] he is really saying that there is legal determination of which freedom (viz., to pursue self-interest) the law will allow, and which the law will disallow. This exercise of legal choice is a preeminent facet of the classical theory of freedom and control. Freedom as an ideal is one thing; but for the theory of economic policy it is more than that, and it is neither abstract nor independent of law.

With respect to the general problem of freedom and control, in partial conclusion it may be said that the classical economists neither merely considered the abstract individual without examination of the contextual meaning of individual freedom, nor defined freedom as antithetical to the state, or as existent only in the absence of the other nonlegal forces of social control. Although for some problems they did take the free individual for granted without further immediate inquiry into, or specification of, the meaning thereof, in the classical theory of economic policy the individual was free only in terms of the pattern of freedom and control. This pattern was a function of both the nonlegal and legal forces of control, as well as the interplay of private participants, and the existing pattern at any time represented the exercise of effective social choice as to the structure of the decision-making process. Put another way, in the classical theory of economic policy there coexisted authority and individual utility, but this is only another way of saying that there coexisted freedom and control.

Economic Pluralism: One of the basic conclusions that emerges from this study is that the classical theory of economic policy, interpreted in terms of a minimum or minimum-necessary role of government, is demonstrably inaccurate and question-begging. Notwithstanding the value of the propaganda or legitimation role of the minimization concept or formula, the interpretation, as an interpretation, is a distortion and a caricature. Moreover, it has been seen that however sophisticated and useful Lord Robbins' interpretation may be, it is incomplete *at least* because of its neglect of the nonlegal forces.

If the analyses of the preceding chapters are correct and further, if the following discussion integrates them correctly, then the classical theory of economic policy is fundamentally a theory of the economic decision-making process, and the way that it should be organized and controlled. The distinguishing characteristic, then, of the classicists' proposed policy system is not the negative one of some "minimization" of the role of government but, rather, the affirmative espousal of a theory of a *pluralist* socioeconomic order. By *pluralist* is meant a wide diffusion of power or, to say the same thing in other words, a wide diffusion of participation in the decision-making process functioning toward the resolution of the basic economic problems. The classical theory of economic policy was thus a theory of widespread and meaningful private participation, a theory that was the ultimate foundation of their theory of competition. Theirs was the system of the liberal idea, conceived as a system of economic organization to achieve freedom through progress, and progress through freedom, with freedom defined ultimately in terms, not just of individual freedom of choice, but also of the wide diffusion of power. Both the limited role of government and individual choice are derived from and reflective of, rather than central to, the postulated underlying pluralism, and are not desiderata in themselves: freedom was, after all, freedom only within the pattern of freedom and control, and the fundamental classical policy postulate was that that pattern be pluralist.

This system was one of private participation in economic affairs. The truly distinctive element of the classicists' system *is* private participation. Both private property, and the free market, are themselves not ends, but are means instrumental to the enabling of such private participation. It should be noted that it is the *institution* of private property that is important, and not any particular rights or loci a priori. Private property is essentially institutionalized private participation in the decision-making process; that is to say, the institution of private property was the mode through which private decision-making participation was effectuated, and the law of private property a formal means of structuring that participation. It is this role of private property as the mode of institutionalized private participation which is important, as distinct from any particular rights or rights' claims.

It should be clear that this private participation was meaningful, or that it conformed to the classicists' requirement of pluralism, only so far as it involved a system in which the resolution of the basic economic problems was substantially accomplished through nominally private market forces *upon a foundation of diffused and widespread private participation.* In other words, freedom to the classicists was meaningful and desirable only in a pluralist society. With respect to economic policy, as Lord Robbins has urged, "the conception of a decentralized organization of production resting on private property and the market was central to their whole position." [31]

But the classical theory of economic policy, as the theory of a pluralist regime of economic decision-making, involves more than the postulate of a competitive private decisional process. Rather, the pluralist structure of private participation is but one facet of a (generally) thoroughly pluralist system. The point is that the economic decision-making process of the classical theory of economic policy was not only pluralist in the structure of the private or market sector, but also it was pluralist in that it encompassed, or postulated, the co-ordinate participation of the legal and nonlegal forces. As has been brought out throughout the foregoing analyses, the decisional structure of the classical policy system as a whole involves both private, legal, and nonlegal participants and is, for that reason also, pluralist.

Various aspects of all this will be developed in paragraphs to come. Suffice it to say, at this point, that the classicists' decision-making process encompassed more than the private or market forces, that it was pluralist in including the non-

175

legal and legal forces of social control; moreover, it was pluralist with respect to the structure of each of the private, legal and nonlegal components. This latter point is particularly important, and goes beyond what has already been brought out.

The minimum or minimum-necessary role of government interpretation thus does not get to the heart of the classical theory of policy. Although it is a manifestation of the fact that the state, in that system, is but one of several participating forces in a generally pluralist decision-making system, the interpretation not only neglects this larger system, but also understates the importance of legal participation (for which it offers but a truism as a substitute) and neglects the nonlegal forces, at least substantively (if not logically), in which respect it is also incomplete. Preoccupation with the minimum-necessary role of government interpretation derives from both the propaganda use thereof, and from definition of "theory of economic policy," limiting its scope to the doctrinal "message."

It is simply not true, aside from propaganda in the Knightian sense, that the classical system is essentially a theory of the minimum or minimum-necessary role of government in the economy. It is a theory of a pluralist economic decision-making process, utilizing the institution of private property to enable private participation as the distinguishing element, and utilizing also the institution of the market and market forces as one regulatory system, through which not only were the basic economic problems *pro tanto* resolved, but which also "provided a rough pointer and a rough discipline whereby the tumultuous forces of self-interest were guided and held in check." [32] Furthermore, it is of the greatest importance that government participation was seen as vital to such operation, as one of the forces giving effect to the system, and as one of the forces transforming private interest into social interest. As such an instrument of transformation, the state is an important supplement to the market, or to Smith's invisible hand of competition, and the nonlegal forces of social control.

The classical message then is not so much the combination of the injunction "let individualism operate," [33] plus the doctrine of the minimum-necessary role of government, but is rather something more basic, of which these formulas are but manifestations. The classical message is rather this: meaningful human freedom as a value, the cognate importance of an open and pluralist society, and an economy encompassing meaningful private participation through a viable private sector. In a word, *pluralism,* or widespread diffusion of participation. It is missing the point in the classical policy system to conclude that it is merely or mainly a declamation against the state. Yes, the state is but part of a larger, pluralist regime, and an ideology is necessary to secure and enforce that this part will be limited, but the classical theory of policy as a whole affirms that of which the declamation against the state is but a negative manifestation, namely, a socioeconomic system in which decision-making power is widely distributed and in which, perforce, existing loci of power are held in check by other loci both legal, nonlegal and private.

It has been indicated before that it is the genius of the market-plus-framework interpretation to call attention to and emphasize the createdness of order, the role of institutional organization in the form of the legal forces of social control in the creation of harmony, and the subtleties of freedom and control. Yet it has also been seen that the Robbinsian specification thereof is incomplete through its neglect, if not formal omission, of the nondeliberative forces, and that the Hayekian view underestimates the importance of these nondeliberative forces in the case of the later classicists, and overestimates their role in the case of Smith. Moreover, it has also

177

been seen that the Robbins-Hayek approach (as identified in Chapter Four) rigidifies the framework in such a manner that, with respect to the legal forces at least, it misses the fact of legal activism with respect to the specifics of policy determination. The classical decision-making process not only incorporates legal, nonlegal, and private participation, but all these classes of participants are *fundamental* and *active* participants, however much their relative participation is inherently limited by virtue of the postulated *pluralist* regime. While it is true, and a truism, that all other activity constitutes the framework within which any act or set of actions takes place, the concept of a "framework" establishes a dichotomy quite erroneous so far as a clear understanding of direct participation and the process of change is concerned. The primary point is that of *active joint participation:* although the question of continuity and change will be examined in the following subsection, it is important at this point to emphasize that the classical policy system is not one of framework and nonframework, but rather one of the active joint participation of several forces *mutually limiting and interacting* as part of a continuing and changing economic decision-making process.

The classical theory of economic policy in this way postulates what we have called the legal, nonlegal, and private forces as the basic classes of participants in the decisional process. With respect to their respective roles, it should be clear that not only are all of these participants part of the decision-making process but also that, through their interaction, the decision-making process is itself structured. The only requirement imposed by the classical economists that need be specified at this point is that the decision-making process, as a whole and in its parts, be pluralist. Expressed differently, the basic condition is the maintenance of a viable pluralist total decisional organization, and a viable pluralist private sector.

178

Therefore, with respect to the operation of the forces of social control, the condition imposed is a constraint requiring the maintenance of a viable system of market forces, or of meaningful private participation. The fact that the constraint may take the form of a libertarian injunction does not preclude, however, the operation of social control, legal and nonlegal, channeling private activity, although such operation must proceed upon the prerequisite of the continuance of a viable system of meaningful private participation. The doctrinal or ideological injunction or propaganda may be in the form of an exhortation for "freedom"—yet there is very little of this in the classical literature—but it should be clear that the individual is a socialized individual, and the conditions of individual participation and choice are governed by the operation of the deliberative and nondeliberative forces of control. Freedom, as we have seen, is not in the classical theory of economic policy only an abstract goal but, as private participation, is freedom only within the total decision-making process. The freedom that was desired by the classicists was that derived from, and existing within, a power-diffused, yet variously controlled, economic process.

The legal and nonlegal forces of social control are operative not only in the structuring of the decision-making process as a whole, but they are also demonstrably important and operative in the governance of the content of the effective decisions made, with respect both to the resolution of the basic economic problems, and behavior in general. Both the legal and nonlegal forces are passive *and* active participants in the decisional process and directly *and* indirectly govern the substance of resource allocation and income distribution. The concept or caveat of *pro tanto* needs of course to be appended, for the legal and nonlegal forces themselves interact both together, and with the nominally private forces of the market.

179

Thus, in Chapter Two, it was concluded that in the view of the classicists, the nondeliberative forces of social control (1) comprised part of the decision-making process; (2) helped structure that process; (3) helped govern the content of the effective decisions made and conduct in general; (4) were important in regard to the maintenance of order, and thereby the resolution of the dual, basic, social problems of freedom and control, and continuity and change; and (5) helped govern the process of the determination and role of knowledge as a basis for policy, both deliberative and nondeliberative. In Chapter Three, it was likewise seen that the state was instrumental in the division of public and private decision-making participation, with respect to the maintenance of law and order, the establishment and maintenance of *the* economic regime—specifically the market system—and all that that implies; and was instrumental also in the structuring of private decision-making participation, notably through the legal promulgation of private rights, i.e., the legal determination of the loci and conditions of private participation. Finally, in Chapter Four, it was seen that state participation is activist in respect to specific alterations in the structure of private participation, effectuated both directly and indirectly consequent to direct governmental participation in the resolution of the basic economic problems for specific purposes. The fact that the activism of the state is essentially and necessarily a *limited* activism, as part of a pluralist regime, does not vitiate and should not obscure the activism as such.

But preoccupation with the forces of social control should not itself obscure the importance of private participation in the decisional process. This is, of course, true for the general reason that the classical policy system was, after all, a theory espousing such private participation as its distinctive, valuational premise. But more specifically, private participation is operative with respect to the substantive decisions as to resource allocation and income distribution so far as these problems are resolved through market forces and, further, both the legal and nonlegal forces are not abstract forces but are processes themselves responsive to the power play of the private sector. To have specified the requirement of the maintenance of a viable private market sector is the equivalent to having established the importance of private participation as an interacting force in the decisional process.

Two aspects of the classical decision-making process are of sufficient importance to warrant further emphasis and elaboration. The first is the *interaction* through which the respective and changing spheres of participation are continually determined and redetermined. The legal, nonlegal and private forces influence and check the conduct, and the conditions of conduct, of each other. It is through this interactive process that the three classes of forces, and their components, jointly participate in the resolution of the basic economic problems. There is, then, no ultimate demarcation between the political and economic spheres (meaning by "economic," in this context, the private market forces), nor between those spheres and the nonlegal or moral or customary spheres. None is independently determined; all are rather the product of the interactive process, of which they each are a part. Finally, this being the case, there can be no substantive meaning to the framework-nonframework dichotomy.

The second aspect is the *pluralism* of which such interaction is but a manifestation. It has already been stressed that the classical decision-making process as a whole is pluralist, and that the private sector therein is pluralist, and therefore competitive. Beyond this, it should be pointed out that, in the classical view, it was necessary that the legal and nonlegal forces themseves be pluralist. As a matter of fact, it is their insistence upon the interaction of the legal and nonlegal forces, together with the free market, that distinguished the

181

classicists from many of their contemporaries. Although the political process might not have been as unqualifiedly responsive to the desires of the masses as others might have deemed possible and desirable, still it was true that, to the classicists, the concept of a free government was defined in terms of a general political pluralism, including substantial political or civil rights, as well as a suffrage and a Commons consonant with the reforms in the adoption of which the Benthamites were instrumental.[34] Much the same is the import of Stuart Mill's enthusiasm for women's rights, whatever the role of Mrs. Taylor.[35] Finally, and this is of extremely great importance, it was without question the classicists' position that the nonlegal forces themselves were not to be the monopoly of an established and privileged sacerdotal class. Whatever the religiosity of the individual classicists, and whatever the attitude toward the utilization of an institutionalized religion as an instrument of social control, both the operation of the nonlegal forces and of social control in general were to be under the constraint of the requirements of pluralism—in particular, this meant religious pluralism.[36] The classical economists were fervent opponents of monism, both philosophical and political and particularly of caesaro-papism. The narrowness of the Church of England view of the needs of order, and the antipluralist practices of the established church and ruling class, were anathema to most, if not all, of the classicists. Accordingly, any general or particular principle applicable to, or descriptive of, the classical theory of social control must be understood to have the constraint of the operation of a rather thoroughgoing pluralism appended to it. In every respect meaningful freedom was considered to be, or was, reducible to a function of widespread diffusion of participation, political, private, and ecclesiastical. This is so, however much it is true that the various spheres of freedom were themselves a function of the interaction of all these forces. Indeed, although it might be said that the fact that such interaction was operative was *the* condition of freedom, ultimately even this reduces to pluralism and the wide diffusion of effective power, within and among legal, nonlegal, and private participants. The nonlegal forces, e.g., religion, would serve the social-control function, but would so operate only under pluralist conditions. There is no brief in the classical theory of economic policy, as presented here, for an unqualified and unlimited ecclesiastical regime. Although Stuart Mill's Religion of Humanity might still utilize an accompanying mythology, the practice of that nondeliberative process would have to be consonant with the underlying liberalism or pluralism of the general system.

The classical theory of economic policy has now been examined in terms of the problem of freedom and control; in terms of its distinctive specification of how the economic decision-making process should be organized and controlled; and in the identity, status, and major roles of the several participants in that process. In the following subsection, the theory of the classical economists concerning the problem of continuity and change will be examined. What remains at this point is to specify the scope of policy in the classical policy system, and to indicate as much as is necessary, for the moment, of the classical theory of the determination and role of knowledge with respect to social policy, all of which will be further examined below.

With respect to the scope of policy, it clearly emerges from the foregoing analyses that, in the classical theory of economic policy, the scope of effective choice extended to include the economic decision-making process as a whole, as well as the content of the actual resolution of the basic economic problems. That is to say, choice in economic policy was not merely limited to matters of resource allocation and income distribution, within the given system. Policy did encompass such mat-

183

ters. But the scope of policy, or effective social choice, included, also, the structure of the decision-making process itself. That structure was not taken as something given. Rather, as suggested in Chapter Three, it was a function of the interaction of all the forces that comprised it, including law, the nonlegal forces, and private centers of power. Quite aside from any presumed need to avoid discussion of artifice, what Lord Robbins calls the framework, or what has been identified here as the total decisional process, is an artifact, whether of deliberative or nondeliberative construction, but of construction and therefore of effective choice none the less. This is true, notwithstanding the occasional use of the language of naturalism. (See later discussion.) The effective view of the classicists was that the scope of effective social choice was extensive, that while the system as a whole was not, or should not be, subject to immediate and capricious choice or change, still the effective choice involved was broad. This choice in part extended, it will be recalled, to the structure of the private sector as such, and encompassed choice of the interests that law (or custom, however unobtrusively) would effectuate into "rights." As indicated before, this will be more exhaustively examined in the subsection to follow, on continuity and change.

Finally, on the classical theory of the determination and role of knowledge, it should be clear that, in the classical policy system, pluralism extended to include the coexistence of both a Hayekian wisdom, embodied in received institutions, and operating nondeliberatively through (at least) the cosmology of the time and place, and a deliberative process, in which more or less rational analysis is directed at whatever are seen as "social problems." Again, this will be discussed later in some detail, but the important point needs iteration here that the classicists' decisional process was both deliberative and nondeliberative. In other words, not only was there the necessary coexistence of authority and personal utility but there was also the necessary coexistence of emotion and reason.

Continuity and Change: The sophistication of the classical economists and, perforce, of their theory of economic policy derives not solely from their confrontation with the problem of freedom and control, but also from their coming to grips with the problem of continuity and change. Indeed, in addition to the fundamental postulate of pluralism, the truly distinctive component of the classical theory of economic policy involves the conditions, or terms, specified in their proposed resolution of this problem. It even may be argued that, at the margin, the crucial components of the classical policy system are their resolution of continuity and change and, in particular, but again at the margin, their theory of the role of the state as an instrument of socioeconomic change. Yet this, like the phenomenon of interaction, is also derivative of the underlying pluralism.

It has been seen in Chapter Four that the classicists did envision some activism, however limited, to the state as a mode of socioeconomic change. But, transcending that question for the moment, it should be clear, from the discussions in Chapters Two and Three, that the problem of order *was* an important one to the classicists, that balancing the claims of continuity and of change, respectively, *was* a basic social problem. Two points must be stressed here. First, the classicists were quite conscious of the desideratum of "social peace" [37] and were, with Ricardo, for example, ". . . much a friend to good order. . . ." [38] But, second, they were aware of the claims of *both* continuity and change, and did not exclusively support one to the prejudice of the other. As with freedom and control a dualism results, with emphasis now on one side, now, the other, so that, to some, and at some times, the classicists appeared (or were) conservative (and not too distinct from the Tories, however different their respective positions might have been); to others, and at other times, they were, or appeared to be, quite radical. The sophistication of this awareness is evident, as was suggested in Chapter Two, throughout the classical literature, but notably, in Smith's *Theory of Moral Sentiments* and Stuart Mill's *Spirit of the Age*. It is from the first work that this highly suggestive quotation is taken:

> In peaceable and quiet times, . . . (the) support of the established government seems evidently the best expedient for maintaining the safe, respectable, and happy situation of of fellow-citizens; when we see that this government actually maintains them in that situtaion. But in times of public discontent, faction, and disorder, . . . even a wise man may be disposed to think some alteration necessary in that constitution or form of government, which, in its actual condition, appears plainly unable to maintain the public tranquillity. In such cases, however, it often requires, perhaps, the highest effort of political wisdom to determine when a real patriot ought to support and endeavour to re-establish the authority of the old system, and when we ought to give way to the more daring, but often dangerous, spirit of innovation.[39]

Whatever may be said in the coming discussion concerning change, it is clear that the classicists recognized and allowed an important place for continuity. A case in point is Bentham's eagerness to establish the claims of security against those of equality (or of liberty against equality), however much opportunity he saw for egalitarianism through law.[40]

With respect to the central issue, namely, the role of the state as an instrument of change, it has been seen, in Chapter Four, that the concept of noninterventionism, in the classical theory of economic policy, cannot be defined as the nonexistence of the state (or existence in some remote unimportant or minimal way), but rather that the concept must be defined in terms of change through law. It has been seen also that the classical theory of economic policy did, in fact, encompass some activism by the state as an instrument of change.

The meaning, then, of the doctrine of noninterventionism, if it has any at all, must be defined in terms of the weight imported to continuity against change. But this definitional basis needs further specification. The notion of nonintervention involves not so much an emphasis upon continuity per se, but more a presumption favoring, allowing, or securing such change as will come about, not by legal means, but otherwise, through the nonlegal and private forces in the decision-making process. Nonintervention is not per se a presumption in favor of continuity, but would operate to leave unaltered what otherwise would come about through the operation of these other forces, which might involve continuity or change. Such passivity as would be imposed upon, and limit, change through law means not so much the preservation of the *status quo* but rather, *pro tanto*, opportunity for other participants, or power centers, to resolve the problem of continuity and change. Another facet of this indicates that noninterventionism is conservative only so far as it would leave the substance of existing legal participation unchanged. To the extent that it means this, it obviously enables the inference of the possibility for change through the nonlegal and private forces (a change the legal process may, or may not, be used later to reinforce).

Noninterventionism, laissez faire, and naturalism (natural order, natural rights) all derive their significance, in this context, from the service they perform in the promotion or legitimation of continuity, but specifically in the disengagement of law as a mode of change. They have, in common with each other, and with the concept of "framework," the taking for granted of what, otherwise, would come about. That is to say, they abstract from, and so obscure, the resolution of contin-

187

uity and change that will be brought about through the operation of the forces other than law, to the extent that law remains passive (thus promoting continuity, or acceptance of what otherwise transpires). The role, then, of these concepts—of noninterventionism, laissez faire, natural order, natural rights, and framework—is generally to promote an unchanging complex of legal participation. As representative of the classical theory of economic policy, they are incomplete in that they beg the question of the resolution of continuity and change through the other nonlegal and private forces, and are inaccurate so far as they fail to reflect the fact of legal activism, however limited, in the classical theory of economic policy. As Hayek points out, "Neither the much abused and much misunderstood phrase of 'laissez faire' nor the still older formula of 'the protection of life, liberty and property' are of much help. In fact, insofar as both tend to suggest that we can just leave things as they are, they may be worse than no answer; they certainly do not tell us what are and what are not desirable or necessary fields of government activity." [41] Nevertheless, noninterventionism does establish a presumption against law as a mode of change. In any theory of economic policy characterized by plural participation, that is, in which the legal process is, by the nature of the case, a limited part of the total decision-making process, and intentionally so, such a presumption has a place, however indiscriminate and ambiguous a prescription it may be.

Considerable evidence of such a presumptive approach is, of course, found in the classical literature. Reference has already been made to what Bentham laid down as the "general rule" governing *agenda:* ". . . nothing ought to be done or attempted by government for the purpose of causing an augmentation to take place in the national mass of wealth, with a view to encrease of the means of either subsistence or enjoyment, without some special reason. *Be quiet* ought on those

occasions to be the motto, or watch word, of government." [42]
That dictum is contained in the *Institute of Political Economy*; in the *Principles of the Civil Code* Bentham establishes
the same presumption through a different facet:

> . . . no restraint should be imposed, no power conferred, no
> coercive law sanctioned, without a specific and satisfactory
> reason. There is always one reason against every coercive law,
> and one reason which, were there no other, would be suffi-
> cient by itself: it is, that such a law is restrictive of liberty.
> Whoever proposes a coercive law, ought to be ready to prove,
> not only that there is a specific reason in favour of this law,
> but also that this reason is more weighty than the general
> reason against every law.[43]

So, also, with McCulloch:

> It cannot, however, be too strongly impressed upon those in
> authority, that non-interference should be the leading prin-
> ciple of their policy, and interference the exception only; that
> in all ordinary cases individuals should be left to shape their
> conduct according to their own judgment and discretion; and
> that no interference should ever be made on any speculative
> or doubtful grounds, but only when its necessity is apparent,
> or when it can be clearly made out that it will be productive
> of *public* advantage. The maxim *pas trop gouverner* should
> never be absent from the recollection of legislators and minis-
> ters. Whenever they set about regulating, they are treading a
> path encompassed with difficulties; and while they advance
> with caution, they should be ready to stop the moment they
> do not see the way clearly before them, and are not impelled
> by a strong sense of public duty, to go forward. But, so long
> as this is the case, they should never hesitate in their course.
> There are many instances in which government must, and
> many more in which it should interfere. And it is the duty
> of the legislature, having once fully satisfied itself, by a care-
> ful inquiry, of the expediency, all things considered, of any
> measure, resolutely to carry it into effect.[44]

Finally, there is the well-known proposition of John Stuart Mill: "*Laissez-faire*, in short, should be the general practice: every departure from it, unless required by some great good, is a certain evil." [45]

A presumption is thus established whose effect would be to limit the economic role of the state as an instrument of social change. But it should be clear that in each statement of this presumption formula, there is the appended *qualification:* with Bentham there is the caveat of "some special reason"; with McCulloch, of "necessity" or "*public* advantage"; with Stuart Mill, of "some great good." Thus, as has been seen in the case of Ricardo, there is the general rule "that no person ought to be controlled in his own arrangements, unless such control was rendered necessary by paramount political circumstances," [46] and although he could find no necessity for the merchant vessels apprenticeship bill,[47] he did deem it wise to alter the distribution of risk with regard to bills of lading.[48] It has also been seen that "To Smith the institutional variable is an important policy variable. Indeed, much of the burden of his argument in favor of free trade and *laissez faire* is designed to show how the institutional environment might best be altered in order to maximize the economy's rate of growth." [49] The import of this, however, is not merely negative, as was seen in Chapter Three; the state was vitally involved in the creation of the market system. Among other things, this involved the erection and maintenance of "those public institutions and those public works, which, though they may be in the highest degree advantageous to a great society, are, however, of such a nature, that the profit could never repay the expence to any individual or small number of individuals, and which it therefore cannot be expected that any individual or small number of individuals should erect or maintain." In the very next sentence, Smith points out that "The performance of this duty requires too very different degrees of expence in the different periods of society." [50] This latter point is very important, as will be seen in a moment.

The presumption, so far as it is reducible to a formal statement establishing the dual classification of (a) cases in which government should "interfere" and (b) cases in which government should not, is capable of being stated as a proposition emphasizing the imperativeness of government action in the former set of cases. Thus Bentham is able to write:

> I have not, I never had, nor ever shall have, any horror, sentimental or anarchical, of the hand of government. I leave it to Adam Smith, and the champions of the rights of man (for confusion of ideas will jumble together the best subjects and the worse citizens upon the same ground) to talk of invasions of natural liberty, and to give as a special argument against this or that law, an argument the effect of which would be to put a negative upon all laws. The interference of government, as often as in my humble view of the matter the smallest balance on the side of advantage is the result, is an event I witness with altogether as much satisfaction as I should its forbearance, and with much more than I should its negligence.[51]

And there is the positive statement by Senior:

> The only rational foundation of government, the only foundation of a right to govern and of a correlative duty to obey, is expediency—the general benefit of the community. It is the duty of a government to do whatever is conducive to the welfare of the governed. The only limit to this duty is its power. And as the supreme government of an independent state is necessarily absolute, the only limit to its power is physical or moral inability. And whatever it is its duty to do it must necessarily have a right to do.[52]

And again:

> I have already proved, I think satisfactorily, that it is the duty, and therefore the right, of a government to take any

191

measures, however they may interfere with the will of individuals, which are conducive to the general welfare of the community.[53]

It is thus instructive that Senior adopts a position with respect to change, i.e., intervention, similar to that of Smith, indicated or implied at the end of the preceding paragraph: the duty of providing certain public institutions and public works so far as it varies "in the different periods of society," must mean that government can introduce new institutions, i.e., bring about change. Senior declares in this respect "that the most fatal of all errors would be the general admission of the proposition that a government has no right to interfere for any purpose except for that of affording protection, for such an admission would prevent our profiting by experience, and even from acquiring it." [54] Much the same view was expressed by Ricardo in Parliament, when he "would not admit that conclusions hostile to the cause of reform could be drawn from the practices of past ages; because he denied that the present generation ought to be bound down by all that had been done by their ancestors. He thought the present generation possessed not only as much wisdom as any of those which had preceded it, but a great deal more." [55]

The more usual classical approach is in terms of the legal prevention of acts injurious to others, or injustices per se, generally specified in terms of injuries. Once again, however, whatever the ideological or propaganda usefulness of the usual formulation, the presumption is not substantively meaningful, for it formally establishes only a classification of categories. Moreover, when it is recalled that *all* law tends to establish who will injure whom (i.e., who the law will allow to injure whom), and that legal "intervention" means legal change of what existing law *pro tanto* enables or requires, it is clear that not only is there partial legal determination of what is injurious, but also that the real question is not whether

192

there will be legal change, but *when*—whether a specific injury claim will be treated in the category of (a) when government should "interfere," i.e., readjust the distribution of exposures, or (b) when government should not "interfere," not readjust the pattern of what reduces in part to cost distribution.

The injury qualification of the presumption formula is so important, and only in small degree because it is so usual, that extended examination is more than warranted. To begin with Smith, it is well known that in *The Wealth of Nations* he argues that "Every man, as long as he does not violate the laws of justice, is left perfectly free to pursue his own interest his own way . . ." in his "obvious and simple system of natural liberty," and that one of the duties of the sovereign is "the duty of protecting, as far as possible, every member of the society from the injustice or oppression of every other member of it, or the duty of establishing an exact administration of justice; . . ." [56] It is important to the understanding of this, and of what is involved, to point out that in the *Moral Sentiments* Smith distinguishes *beneficence* from *justice* in a very particular way. "Beneficence," says Smith, "is always free, it cannot be extorted by force, the mere want of it exposes to no punishment; because the mere want of beneficence tends to do no real positive evil." The want of beneficence "may disappoint of the good which might reasonably have been expected, and upon that account it may justly excite dislike and disapprobation: it cannot, however, provoke any resentment which mankind will go along with." This is because the want of beneficence "does no positive hurt to any body." Beneficence, then, has to do with those acts the omission of which, for example, incurs no injury. Justice, on the other hand, has to do with those acts the omission of which does engender injury, or of those acts the commission of which does incur injury.

> Justice is a virtue of which the observance is not left to the freedom of our own wills, which may be extorted by force,

and of which the violation exposes to resentment, and consequently to punishment. This virtue is justice: the violation of justice is injury: it does real and positive hurt to some particular persons, from motives which are naturally disapproved of. It is, therefore, the proper object of resentment, and of punishment, which is the natural consequence of resentment. As mankind go along with and approve of the violence employed to avenge the hurt which is done by injustice, so they much more go along with, and approve of that which is employed to prevent and beat off the injury, and to restrain the offender from hurting his neighbours. . . . We feel ourselves to be under a stricter obligation to act according to justice, than agreeably to friendship, charity, or generosity; that the practice of these last mentioned virtues seems to be left in some measure to our own choice, but that, somehow or other, we feel ourselves to be in a peculiar manner tied, bound, and obliged to the observation of justice. We feel, that is to say, that force may, with the utmost propriety, and with the approbation of all mankind, be made use of to constrain us to observe the rules of the one, but not to follow the precepts of the other.[57]

Once again, the problem is not one of whether the state is to act or not to act, but whether the particular act or omission in question is felt to be in the category of beneficence, and therefore presumably not subject to adjustment, redress, or correction by law, *or* whether the act or omission is in the category of justice, and therefore presumably subject to legal change. That Smith discusses and includes the protection "as far as possible, [of] every member of the society from the injustice or oppression of every other member of it," although it does not at all settle the question of when the state should adjust grievances or injury claims, none the less it encompasses both legal participation in the determination of the existing pattern of freedom, exposures and injuries, and legal participation in the alteration of such pattern. Needless to say, it has already been established that this is no infinitesimal task.

Government will no more adjust all injury claims in favor of the grieving party than it will provide all possible indiscriminate benefits, but government will participate in the process of injury determination and it will so adjust some, the only question being when. The invocation of the presumption formula does not, in and of itself, conclusively determine whether the weight is to be on the side of nonintervention or intervention, in the sense of legal adjustment or change. Preoccupation with the presumption formula, while of propaganda value, does not vitiate the fact that the formula establishes but a definitional system of classification, nor should it obscure the inevitable necessity for confrontation with the valuational choice of *when,* that is, in which category. This is no less true of Smith's system than it is in the common law, wherein legal rule is confronted with legal rule, and the exercise of judicial choice is inevitable, however conscious or unconscious the process. In both cases there is legal determination, legal choice, anl legal change.

This rendition of the presumption, coupled, as it were, with the injury qualification, either in terms of injury as such or in terms of justice, is found throughout the classical literature, and always with the same effect. So McCulloch, criticizing "An idea [which] seems, however, to have been recently gaining ground, that in so far as respects the production of wealth, the duty of government is almost entirely of an negative kind, and that it has merely to maintain the security of property and the freedom of industry," maintains ". . . but its duty is by no means so simple and easily defined as those who advocate this opinion would have us to believe. It is certainly, true, that its interference with the pursuits of individuals has been, in very many instances, carried to a ruinous excess." After laying it down, in this context, that freedom is a means and not an end, and that government is concerned with more than an oversimplified meaning of freedom, McCulloch contends, "In laying it down, for example, that individuals should be left at perfect liberty to engage in any business or profession they may think best for themselves, the condition that it is not injurious to others is always understood." [58] This passage is at the beginning of his chapter on the "Interference of Government," and it is at the end of this chapter that the lines quoted in the text at note 44 are given, to the effect that government must act when it must, that is, when there is a felt "necessity" or "*public* advantage."

The same is true of Bentham. In the *Principles of the Civil Code* (and it will be recalled that Lord Robbins identifies the Civil Code as one of the key aspects of the operation of law),[59] Bentham includes as *one* "of those cases in which the sacrifice of some portion of security, in respect of property, is necessary for the preservation of the greater mass . . . limitations of the rights of property, or of the use which each proprietor may make of his own goods, in order to prevent his injuring himself or others." In a note he further states that, "A general right of property in any thing, is possessed, when it may be used every way, with the exception of certain uses which are forbidden by special reasons. These reasons," he says, "may be referred to three heads:"

> 1. Private detriment—when a certain use of the thing would be injurious to a certain other individual, either in his fortune or otherwise. *Sic utere tuo ut alium non laedas. Sic utere tuo ut alienum non laedas.*
> 2. Public detriment—such as may result to the community in general. *Sic utere tuo ut rem publicam non laedas.*
> 3. Detriment to the individual himself: *Sic utere tuo ut semet ipsum non laedas.*

"An absolute and unlimited right over any object of property would be the right to commit nearly every crime." [60] Bentham, it has been seen, would no more deny that rights were relative to the limitations imposed by law than deny that these rights can be changed through law. The presumption does not, then, vitiate the conclusions of Chapter Four. Legal participation is not static; when certain rights formerly useful to society are now seen as "injurious," the presumption formula itself, through the injury-qualification appendage, enables such alteration.

In this way Adler takes notice that Bentham, among others, would impose limitations upon existing rights and liberties when injury or damage is felt to result otherwise.[61] He thus quotes Bentham's *Anarchical Fallacies*, in which Bentham, after arguing that the very liberty to which *The Declaration of Rights* refers "owes all the boundaries it has, all the extent it has, to the laws," [62] declares: "The liberty which the law *ought* to allow of, and leave in existence—leave uncoerced, unremoved—is the liberty which concerns those acts only, by which, if exercised, no damage would be done to the community upon the whole; that is, either no damage at all, or none but what promises to be compensated by at least equal benefit." [63]

So, also, with John Stuart Mill. Consider, for example, the essay "On Liberty," throughout which the great plea for individual autonomy is qualified repeatedly and formally by the injury consideration. Indeed, he declares:

> The object of this essay is to assert one very simple principle, as entitled to govern absolutely the dealings of society with the individual in the way of compulsion and control, whether the means used be physical force in the form of legal penalties, or the moral coercion of public opinion. That principle is, that the sole end for which mankind are warranted, individually or collectively, in interfering with the liberty of action of any of their number, is self-protection. That the only purpose for which power can be rightfully exercised over any member of a civilized community, against his will, is to prevent harm to others. . . . To justify that, the conduct from which it is desired to deter him must be calculated to produce evil to someone else.[64]

Freedom and, with it, variety, are the general rules, but "short of injury to others." [65] As with McCulloch and Senior, for example, the presumption can be reversed by the qualification, with the effective presumption, at least, establishing the possibility of legal alteration. "As soon as any part of a person's conduct affects prejudicially the interests of others, society has jurisdiction over it, and the question whether the general welfare will or will not be promoted by interfering with it, becomes open to discussion." [66] There are once again two categories, actions for which the individual is not accountable (which are not accountable because "these concern the interests of no person but himself"),[67] and actions for which the individual is accountable, ". . . for such actions as are prejudicial to the interests of others, the individual is accountable, and may be subjected either to social or to legal punishment, if society is of opinion that the one or the other is requisite for its protection." [68] (It is not irrelevant to point out that Mill proceeds to discuss "cases in which the reasons against interference do not turn upon the principle of liberty: the question is not about restraining the actions of individuals, but about helping them; . . ." [69] and the possibilities of governmental activism in this respect, which has been discussed in both Chapters Three and Four.)

What, then, of the classical presumption against law as a mode of change? The answer must be, that it is just that; it is a presumption against law as a mode of change, or against "intervention." But it is a presumption capable of being overcome by rebuttal, by a showing of a necessity for or the desirability of such change. As suggested previously, both aspects are to be expected in the context of the classical policy system, in which law is but one participant. Indeed, both aspects are derived from the underlying pluralism, and consequent limited activism, among participants. Stating the matter somewhat differently, but to the same effect, there is in the classical theory of economic policy no closed category of *mala in se* so far as the law is concerned, no *a priori* list of injuries against which the law once and for all can direct itself, and therefore there is no closed list of injuries (the scope of which concept, it will be recalled, following Smith, is broadly defined) against which the law may be directed. Determination is, with the classicists, essentially a question of experience or empirical results, and the determination is secured through the legal process, in interaction with the other forces in society. Intervention means change and, in the classical view, the state was not precluded from serving as a mode of change.

But what, then, is the classical theory of continuity and change? The author would suggest that clearly the classical theory is neither adequately nor accurately rendered by the laissez faire or nonintervention interpretation, not only because that interpretation sets forth inaccurately the classical view of the state as a mode of change, but also because the scope of that interpretation is limited to the role of the state. Fundamental is the fact that there is, in the classical literature, comprehension of both continuity and change, no matter how much statements made in consideration of particular issues seem to stress one over the other, a comprehension further distorted by the doctrinal approach to interpretation. As with freedom and control, the problem of continuity and change was not an either-or proposition, and the classical economists acknowledged both as part of a more complete policy system. Interpretation of the classical theory of economic policy is adequate and meaningful only so far as it correctly specifies the classicists' resolution of the problem as such.

The classical solution to the problem of continuity and change is manifest in the fundamental proposition that *change or reform should be incremental, thus gradual in character, and should take place under the constraint of maintaining a viable system of private participation or market forces.* There are two distinctive components to the classical theory: first, the basic valuational condition of the maintenance and strengthening of a viable pluralism so far as both the total decision-making process and the private market sector in particular, is concerned; and second, the element of incrementalism or gradualism, with respect to which it may be the case both (a) that the gradualism is derived from the incrementalism, and (b) that the incrementalism is derived, in turn, from the underlying pluralism. Above all, change must not prejudice the pluralist character of the total system nor, in particular, should it impede the continued and viable operation of private participation through private property and private enterprise.

Given the fundamental postulate of pluralism through private property and market forces, on the one hand, and the nonlegal and legal forces of social control, on the other, the reconciliation of continuity and change in the classical theory of economic policy is in terms of incrementalism and gradualism. Such incrementalism is both a condition and a consequence; in a pluralist system change would generally have to be incremental, otherwise the very pluralism of participation itself might tend to be compromised, and, in a system functioning with plural participation, any changes are more than likely going to be incremental. It is to be stressed, moreover, that incrementalism results from the primary classical reliance upon the nonlegal forces of social control and diffused private participation, so far as the great bulk of the stuff of life is concerned (or so far as the basic substance of the solutions to the basic economic problems is concerned). The resolution of continuity and change through the slow-moving nondeliberative forces and competitive, power-diffused private market forces meant, *pro tanto*, incremental, therefore gradual, change. Change resultant to the operation of the nondeliberative forces would necessarily tend to be gradual, and change through power-diffused private participation would also tend to be incremental and gradual.

But incrementalism and gradualism are also the consequence of the fact, in the classical policy system, that although the state is considered an active participant, its activism is limited, at least in the sense that it is not the only participant. Yet it also has been seen that the law itself was to be a conserving force, functioning to secure order and continuity as well as change, so that the operation of law as a mode of securing positive change would be cautious and incremental, and, again, within the constraint of maintaining a viable market system.

The classical theory of economic policy stands opposed, retrospectively, to the restrictionist or mercantilist system of meddling, to the Physiocratic system of "preference or of restraint," [70] and, prospectively, to complete state socialism, or the planned economy. Yet this does not preclude limited but active legal participation, gradual and incremental in character, that ultimately effectuates specific changes for specific purposes. Meaningful interpretation of the classical theory of economic policy must reflect this active but limited participation by law as a mode of effectuating change, just as it must reflect the primary reliance upon the nonlegal forces as well as the interplay of private market forces. It is the advantage of this interpretation of incremental change, within the constraint of a pluralist market regime, that it enables the incorporation of such factors.

In the preceding paragraph, the phrases "limited but active" and "active but limited" were both used to describe legal participation as a mode of change in the classical policy system. Inasmuch as one tends to emphasize the "active" and the other the "limited" element, both phrases are thereby incomplete and misleading. The point is that both elements are complementary, and derivative from the underlying pluralism.

To the extent, then, that the law is a participating mode of change, and *to the extent*, also, that law is, perforce, active and limited (or limited and active), it follows that, in the classical theory of economic policy, law as a mode of change has to do with "social engineering," and, thus, "with that part of the whole field which may be achieved by the ordering of human relations through the action of politically organized society." [71] "Law, according to this view, is a device for the improvement of the social and economic order by conscious, intelligent effort. It is an instrument of civilization. . . ." [72] It is possible, moreover, to interpret pluralism in such a way as to manifest "a continually increasing recognition of individual rights; but it would be quite as easy . . . to write it in terms of a continually wider recognition of social interests." [73] As the notes indicate, these quotations are from Roscoe Pound, and Edgar Bodenheimer's discussion of Pound's sociological positivism. It is remarkable how well the description fits the classical economists, *given* the recognition that law is but one participant, that it is but *one* device for social and economic improvement or change. Caution must be exercised, however, in discussing the classical view of freedom and control, and continuity and change, so that analysis will not seem to prejudice one factor to the detriment or neglect of the other, in either case. The law is only *pro tanto* an instrument of social engineering, for law is but one mode of change, and, in the classical system, continuity is reckoned with also. The same is true, incidentally, of Roscoe Pound as well. Therefore the concept of social engineering is applicable to the decision-making process as a whole, as well as to any and all participants therein, and so to the classical theory of economic policy; but the classical emphasis upon experience, and the needs of continuity and order, require that this usage, too, be tempered.

The author would suggest, then, that the interpretation of the classical theory of continuity and change, which correctly and adequately accounts for the materials examined in this study, is one which can do *no more than*, and do *no less than*, combine and emphasize these two elements: (a) the maintenance of a viable market sector and (b) incremental and gradual change. So far as continuity is specifically defined, as it were, in terms of a viable market sector (though in Smith's time, at least, it was something to be achieved), continuity may well be seen as the dominant factor. But change, including change through law—yes, once again, artifice—within that constraint is not precluded. Nor does the requirement of viability per se preclude legal change. With respect to legal artifice, alteration of the division of power among private, legal, and nonlegal forces, and alteration of the division of power within the private sector were both possible, though certainly neither necessary nor advisable in each and every plausible case, so long as, in Lord Robbins' terms once again, "the market and incentive system was not seriously affected." [74] "On the utilitarian view no institutions, no systems of rights, were sacrosanct. All were subject to the test of utility." But as Lord Robbins points out,

> It would be a mistake to interpret the principle of utility as implying no element of lasting value in institutions, no principles of morals involving more than a calculus of immediate pleasure and pain. It was perfectly consistent with this principle to attach, as indeed there was attached, the greatest value to stable institutions and general rules of conduct, . . . and, on the basis of this principle, the most powerful arguments could be deployed in favour of security of expectations and consistency in behaviour, which in turn afforded strong grounds for more or less settled codes of law and morals.

This is quite right, but some qualification must be made of the next proposition of Lord Robbins. His view of the classicists is that "on the utilitarian outlook, social arrangements were not provisional in the sense that they were liable to day-to-day change and upset; they were provisional only in the sense that they were all liable to the ultimate test of their ability to promote human happiness." [75] This is true of the classicists only with the further understanding that while "social arrangements were not provisional in the sense that they were liable to day-to-day change and upset," as a *group*, *individually* they were so provisional under the constraints of incremental, therefore gradual change, and the maintenance of both a viable general pluralism and a viable market sector. Just as "the most powerful arguments could be deployed in favour of security of expectations," i.e., continuity, so also could powerful arguments be made supporting particular changes. As with Lord Robbins' emphasis upon a static framework through reliance upon a conservative understanding of "rule of law," there is here, also, insufficient acknowledgment of legal activism in the classical theory of policy. Moreover, the provisional character of such individual changes also vitiates the Hayek-Robbins disclaimer of specific changes for specific purposes, and it is also further evidence of the presumption role of the (static) framework concept itself. A meaningful interpretation of the classical policy system must allow both for continuity and change, and for legal activism and the slowness, passivity, and therefore continuity wrought through reliance upon the nondeliberative forces—the activism and passivism are both limited.

It is submitted that this interpretation of change or reform, incremental and gradual in character, and consonant with a viable private market sector, is supported by, and correctly systematizes, the materials examined earlier in this study. The immediately distinctive facet being the element of incrementalism and gradualism, it may also be suggested that *in extenso* consideration of such subjects as Parliamentary Reform, the problem of adjusting security and equality, Poor Law reform, and the free trade issue (notably Corn Law reform), as presented in the classical literature as a whole, will further support the incrementalist interpretation. This is, for example, particularly evident in the exchange of letters between James Mill and Ricardo, in 1817, on the efficacy of change through legislation. Ricardo's considerations made him "determine to advance very cautiously," [76] a position not very different from that expressed by Trower in criticizing Ricardo's radicalism in the matter of Parliamentary Reform: "Limit the changes," wrote Trower, "to the *necessity*, and make these changes gradually." [77] Another case in point concerns Ricardo's understanding appraisal of popular discontent manifest in demonstrations and riots and in, for example, the Peterloo Massacre of August 16, 1819.[78] Still another case involves Ricardo's attitude toward interests vested under the system of commercial restrictions, and their status in the face of liberalizing legislation. With respect to the Merchants' of London Petition for Free Trade, Ricardo said:

> Another difficulty, and a greater, was, respecting the vested interests. Many persons vested their capital on the faith of the continuation of the restrictive system, and therefore, however injurious that system might be, nothing could be more unjust than, by the immediate abolition of that system, to occasion the absolute ruin of those who vested large capital on the faith of laws so long established as the restrictive laws. But from this no argument could be surely drawn to continue the system in future times. No argument appeared to him more mischievous—more calculated to promote commotion and rebellion, than this—that if they once did wrong they should never do right, but that they should go on in error and make every mischievous system perpetual.[79]

Transcending all discussion, of course, is the fact that there were marginal, and often more than marginal, differences between these men as to specifics. This question, however, will be discussed in the concluding major section. The interpretation of incrementalism and gradualism nevertheless may be underscored by reference to the view that Smith juxtaposed to that (already noted in Chapter Two) of the "man of system":

> The man whose public spirit is prompted altogether by humanity and benevolence will respect the established powers and privileges even of individuals, and still more those of the great orders and societies into which the state is divided. Though he should consider some of them as in some measure abusive, he will content himself with moderating what he often cannot annihilate without great violence. When he cannot conquer the rooted prejudices of the people by reason and persuasion, he will not attempt to subdue them by force, but will religiously observe what by Cicero is justly called the divine maxim of Plato, never to use violence to his country no more than to his parents. He will accommodate as well as he can his public arrangements to the confirmed habits and prejudices of the people, and will remedy as well as he can the inconveniences which may flow from the want of those regulations which the people are averse to submit to. When he cannot establish the right, he will not disdain to ameliorate the wrong; but, like Solon, when he cannot establish the best system of laws, he will try to establish the best that the people can bear.[80]

It has been noted before that the logic of naturalism is question-begging and incomplete in failing to specify the existence, nature, and genesis of that which is taken for granted by use of the concept. Be that as it may, and aside from the propaganda or legitimation roles thereof, *if* one specifically defines *natura* as the classicists' total decision-making process, then, with the doctrine of Marshall, *Natura non facit saltum.* But, switching to the point and language of Stuart Mill, society is variously in its *natural* state and its *transitional* state; and the increments, moreover, may be perceived as larger or smaller at any time by one man than another. The basic point is that the classical theory of economic policy involves the selective balancing of continuity and change in a pluralist regime, the participation of the state in that process of choice but consonant with a viable market sector, which, thereby, means extensive but not exclusive reliance upon the nondeliberative forces. Again, what this means with respect to law as an instrument of change, is that any particular proposal for legal change may be in either of two categories, one in which government should not intervene, and one in which government should intervene.

The Meaningfulness of the Classical Theory of Policy

Such, then, is the classical theory of economic policy. As a theory of economic policy, its substantive meaning derives from the fact that it is a theory of the economic decision-making process, and of such a process as a whole; from the fact that it is a theory concerning the way in which such a process should be organized and controlled; and from the fact that it is a theory inevitably intertwined with the subtleties involved in the solution of the dual basic social problems of freedom and control, and continuity and change. With respect to all of these facets, the classical theory of economic policy offered a distinctive resolution. The classical policy system was a theory of economic pluralism in the context of a general sociopolitical pluralism, effectuated in part through the institutions of private property and the free market; and it was a theory of gradual and incremental change wrought through the interaction of private, legal, and nonlegal participants, as identified previously.

"It is no exaggeration to say," as Lord Robbins emphasizes, "that it is impossible to understand the evolution and the meaning of Western liberal civilization without some understanding of Classical Political Economy," [81] and, particularly, the theory of economic policy of the English classical economists. Indeed, for those who live under Western liberal civilization, pluralism and incrementalism are the order of the day, so fundamental that they are taken for granted, and even scholars need to be reminded that such is the case.

It is remarkable that many of the ideas developed by the classical economists, examined in these chapters as part of their theory of economic policy, were later developed as institutional economics by John R. Commons. In Commons' writings there is to be found one of the most penetrating analyses of the underlying legal and nonlegal participation in nominally market-determined resource allocation and income distribution, an analysis, it is suggested, that is substantively parallel to the one found in the classical theory of economic policy. Commons' interactional and negotiational behaviorism, for example, clearly resembles that of the classicists. So, also, does his concern for the fundamentals of social control and social change mirror the classical economists. Particularly, the classicists' analysis of what reduces to a theory of relative rights and duties; freedom, coercion, and exposures; conflict resolution; and the role and development of legal and nonlegal working rules—all anticipate and may be interpreted in the light of Commons' more extensive and intensive inquiry. [82]

On the other hand, the interpretation suggested above does not enable the classical policy system to answer all the questions that contemporary discussion poses, and may not be very satisfying for that reason. This is especially true in the case of those who would invoke the classical theory of economic policy as the final and conclusive argument, or as, at least, an argument, against certain types of government intervention, or certain interventions. How convenient it is to be able to invoke the doctrine of laissez faire of *the* classical economists, or the classical presumption, in legitimation of a position! But the classical theory of economic policy is more than a propaganda; it is more than an incantation. It is an attempt to come to grips with certain fundamental problems, solutions to which are not easy, no matter how readily they submit to ideological sloganizing and exaggeration. Those who would invoke the classicists in support of a policy of governmental inaction or nonintervention in a particular case can really operate only on the level of propaganda and legitimation—a level by no means unimportant as part of the game of policy. Intervention, as has been seen, is generally alteration of the substance of what government is already involved in; and nonintervention would retain such extant substance of government participation, or allow change through nonlegal means. In addition, there is no complete disengagement of intervention, so understood, in the classical policy system; law is, however limited, an active mode of change. It is ultimately a question of the distribution of power in society, and in this distribution the classicists had government participate in no peripheral way. The invocation of the classical presumption is, to repeat, part of the game of policy, and is a stratagem in that game. But the question always persists, whether any particular proposal for legal change is to be in the category in which government should not intervene, or in the category in which government should intervene. This is precisely the issue, and the invocation of the classical presumption is itself directed at the solution of that question.

Yet if the laissez faire interpretation is clearly wrong, if the presumption formula and static framework approach are incomplete if not also misleading, and if the classical theory of policy as already interpreted fails to satisfy the felt needs of the role of propaganda, so, also, may this interpretation fail to yield a satisfying answer to those who conscientiously seek complete, final, and unerring guidance in the quest for solutions to problems of policy. This is the problem to which this section is addressed. What, then, is the meaningfulness of the classical theory of economic policy? What does it tell us? What does it stand for? What assistance does it provide in the solution of specific problems or issues of policy?

It should not be redundant—rather, it is quite important— to reiterate that the classical theory of economic policy is a theory of economic pluralism and incremental change, for as a theory of policy it is basically a theory of the decision-making process as a whole. It is therefore a *general* theory and, as a theory of constructive proposal, rather than a theory propounding an explanatory hypothesis, it is a theory of *general* principles, with an ultimate valuational stress upon meaningful individual participation as economic actors, these to be understood in terms of economic pluralism effectuated through private property as the means of private participation in the free market. It is a *general* theory of the pluralist or liberalist economic decision-making process.

It is not surprising, therefore, that Blaug and Knight are unable to comprehend a classical or Ricardian theory of policy, for both are seeking more *specifics* than the classical theory can provide. According to Blaug, "The banner of laissez faire did not furnish unambiguous answers to any of (the then-current, concrete) policy issues." [83] ". . . on many of the concrete policy issues under discussion in the period Ricardo offered no guidance whatever; on others, his proposals were either universally rejected or else outmoded by the course of events. In short, the Ricardian economist had no special position of his own on *any* question of economic policy." [84] (For example, the classicists were free traders, but their individual specific policy recommendations *in re* the Corn Laws were not identical, nor were they invariable.) So, also, with Knight: ". . . they never developed either a clear and defensible program of action or a 'theory' of economic policy," the "important point" being "that one cannot find any definite answers in what those writers 'said.' " [85]

The classical theory of economic policy is meaningful only as a general theory of the liberal economic regime, that is to say, as a general prescription that the economy should be organized and controlled along pluralist lines, in part through the institutionalization of private property and the free market. The classical theory of policy does not have the capacity to solve unequivocally by itself problems of the specific implementation of the system, or problems of the specific content of solutions to particular issues, nor can it indicate, or predict, what specific problems *will be* issues or problems of public policy. It contains neither the specific details with which to implement an evolving pluralism in the economic sphere, nor any precise calculus governing, or by which may be determined, the specific content of particular legal rights, or particular direct governmental participations, or particular legal changes, or, for that matter, the content of the substance and change of the nonlegal forces.

This was the understanding of the classicists themselves. Consider, for example, the dictum of John Stuart Mill in "On Liberty": "There is, in fact," he tells us, "no recognized principle by which the propriety or impropriety of government interference is customarily tested." [86] He echoes the proposition of Burke, quoted by McCulloch, concerning "one of the finest problems in legislation, namely to determine what the state ought to take upon itself to direct by the public wisdom, and what it ought to leave, with as little interference as possible, to individual exertion.[87] . . . [It] is one of the most difficult and complicated questions in the art of government. It is, in a great measure, a question of detail, in which many and various considerations must be kept in view, and no absolute rule can be laid down." [88]

This view is widely acknowledged and reflected in the interpretive literature. Just as Blaug concludes that "the Ricardian economist had no special position of his own on *any* question of economic policy," [89] so, also, does Lord Robbins emphasize that the felicific calculus involved no precise quantification, and was no ready calculus by which specific problems (or problems of specific content) could be solved unequivocally. The classicists' use of the felicific calculus was rather in the "rough judgments of the expediency of particular items of the penal law, in general estimates of the suitability of existing institutions or the desirability of other institutions to take their place." [90] As Bittermann points out, Smith's ethical and economic system "contained no implications of specific standards or policies;" these rather "had to be found in phenomena directly," [91] that is, from experience. No wonder, then, that Viner concludes that the classicists "all consequently acknowledged at one time or another that the issue as to desirable degree or kind of state intervention could not be satisfactorily resolved logically by abstract argument alone, based on the workings of a system of free competition in a society composed of 'economic men.' " [92] Viner therefore finds need to emphasize the dictum of Aquinas ("which impressed me," says Viner, "as having direct and weighty bearing on the intellectual history of laissez faire"): "When reason argues about particular cases, it needs not only universal but also particular principles," [93] which is the substantive equivalent of Holmes' dictum in his *Lochner* dissent that "general propositions do not decide concrete cases." [94]

The classical theory of economic policy, quite aside from its role as propaganda, is only a general theory of policy with general principles, not particular principles. For the purpose of resolving particular issues, or for providing specific content to social policy, a general theory of economic policy, such as that of the classical economists, is not enough, and it should not be expected to provide such answers. As Knight has put it, "There are grave problems, conflicts of values, including conditions of life prerequisite to the pursuit of all 'higher' value, which cannot be covered by any formula." [95] The classical theory of policy does not, and cannot, answer unequivocally all possible questions or problems of policy. It does not, and cannot, fully specify the details as to which interests the legal process is to reinforce through the creation of legal rights, and does not and cannot specify the substantive content of the categories of intervention and nonintervention, i.e., of legal activism and legal passivism. The classical theory of policy does have "a recognized emphasis, . . . in order that conscientious men may know which way to push," [96] but conscientious men may differ as to details: the classical theory of policy does not unequivocally indicate which manipulations are "unwise," which redistributions are "unjust," and which governmental participations or alterations are "excessive." [97] The details are a matter of judgment and are subjective in character, with the classical policy schema offering few, if any, intrinsic objective guidelines as to specifics. The conclusion is the same, whether the subject is examined in terms of specific policies, or the nature of freedom: "Freedom cannot afford an objective standard of policy, a way of escape from the subjectivity of moral judgments, when the feeling of freedom itself is derived from, or at best is another aspect of, moral approval." [98]

Inasmuch as the classical policy system is not fully specified as to details, to draw a parallel with contemporary methodological usage, the classical theory of economic policy is more a *model* than a *theory*. It serves only as a framework within which problems of content may be worked out; a framework for contextually relevant and determined solutions, not a prespecified set of policies or a detailed list of a priori solutions. What the classical economists have given the liberal tradition is a message, yes, but it is the message of pluralism; more immediately relevant, they have given their theory of economic policy as a framework, within which to arrive at and facilitate policy solutions and implementations, consonant with a pluralist regime, but not the solutions themselves.

There can, therefore, be varying programs and varying details as to specific content, all within the requirements of a viable pluralism and incremental change. Indeed, the inability of the classical policy system to yield unequivocal, or specific, or eternal answers to particular issues enables explanation of the significant diversity among classicists as to their position on specific issues. It also enables explanation of the transitions in the thinking of such men as Bentham, McCulloch, Stuart Mill, and Senior, which resulted in changing positions as to the relative weight explicitly assigned, say, to continuity vis-a-vis change, as well as to particular issues of policy such as the factory acts. Moreover, the substantial literature inquiring who is and who is not a classicist, and the appropriate credentials by which one may be called a classicist, is thrown in relief when it is realized that no particular position on any issue, or group of issues, of practical policy is sufficient. Probably there can be found discussions challenging the propriety of regarding almost every writer conventionally considered a classicist, and many of these challenges appear reasonable only when their particular views on specific issues are considered, or when assessments of their individual historical impact (e.g., responsibility for Marxian "scientific" socialism or the welfare state) are made. The interpretation already suggested, however, enables unequivocal identification of the writers examined as classicists with respect to policy, for they all, it is suggested, subscribed to, or may be interpreted in terms of, the economic pluralism and incremental change generic to the classical theory of economic policy. This adherence to the classical theory of economic policy, as interpreted herein, is what they have in common, and it is this that is important. Inasmuch as the classical theory of policy is a general theory—or model—there is no membership problem by that criterion. Variation between them as to specific details is quite as consistent with the character of a general model as are their changes in position as to individually preferred specific details.

A theory of economic policy, certainly the classical one, is not unlike what Lord Keynes called "the Theory of Economics." As is the case with the corpus of economic theory, a theory of economic policy does not furnish a body of settled conclusions immediately applicable to policy decisions, nor a specific program of particular policies. It is a framework or a model, rather than a complete theory, however much it is also a doctrine. It is a cosmological or valuational apparatus of the mind, which helps its possessor to draw conclusions related to the valuational or doctrinal premises of the particular model, but these conclusions are neither unilineal nor unequivocal, given the multiplicity of possible specifications of the problems of freedom and control, and continuity and change, within the given basic premises comprising the model. Although, it is not difficult, therefore, to carefully state the distinctive argument of a theory of economic policy, its implications for specific policy decisions are much less precise.[99]

This means that no complete and precise specification can be given to the substance of the concept of public interest,[100] in the classical theory of economic policy. On the level of the general model itself, the public interest is defined there in terms of pluralism, private property, the free market, incremental change, and the like. This is clear enough from the foregoing analysis. But, beyond this, it should be equally clear that the specific content of the public interest is not postulated as given, but is, rather, considered subject to continuing redefinition. This content is a continuing product of the interaction of all the participants, and their changing claims. That is to say, in the classical theory of economic policy, the specific content of the public interest is itself an open-ended product, the mode of determination of which is the economic decision-making process as a whole. In this respect, it might even be said that the provision of such implementation, or specification, was the crucial function of that decisional process. In any case, inasmuch as the classical theory of policy is a model of the decision-making process as a whole, it is not a schema specifying the substantive decisions which, it may be said, give content to the public interest concept—except so far as these substantive decisions may be affected by the structure and operation of that decisional process and, in turn, influence and react upon it.

The only further elements of specification that may be clearly identified in the classical theory of economic policy have already been established. These are the importance of material welfare, the cognate status of economic development, and the instrumental significance of capital accumulation, and the business class, as the strategic force in securing economic development. Yet, even in these matters, it was something of an open and continuing question as to *which* specific interests were the "legitimate interests" to which the ethical and legal system should give effect, as distinct from those which were not desirable and not permissible.[101] Just as important as these specifications, then, to the broad picture, is the fact that the classicists' pluralist decisional process was *explorative* and *emergent* with respect both to the structure of the decisional process itself, and the pattern and content of the decisions reached, and, therefore, with respect to all facets of the content of the public interest, the very details of which are the eternal subject of controversy, a controversy not precluded by invocation of the classical presumption.

To say this is to say that the establishment of the conditions and content of "harmony" *or* mutuality of interests, *or* of reconciliation of freedom and control, *or* of continuity and change, *or* of private interest and public or social interest, was a continuing effort, a quest truly both explorative and

216

emergent. What this means, once again, is that the classicists did not, and could not, have provided all the answers for liberal society. The classicists did not presume to have the knowledge of the world and of values with which to implement their system, unchanged, for all time. The classicists gave the liberal tradition a model of economic policy; the task of liberal society is to implement that model.

What the classicists do stress, however, is that economic policy should be carefully, if not cautiously, developed and administered; moreover, society's economic policy should be developed and administered on the basis of *knowledge*. Policy should devolve from settled knowledge. As Senior put it, "It is to be hoped that a further application of the division of labour, the principle upon which all government is founded, by providing an appropriate education for those who are to direct the affairs of the State, may protect us as effectually against suffering under ignorance or inexperience in our governors, as we are now protected against their injustice." [102] The classicists, though, went beyond the general proposition that policy should be based upon knowledge and, like the Physiocrats, emphasized that this knowledge, which was to serve as the benchmark of policy, would, to no small extent, be provided by economic science. Indeed, it is widely recognized that this motivation was highly instrumental in the development of the discipline. The point relevant here has been cogently expressed by Lord Robbins. Distinguishing the classicists from the "many reform movements and many schools of reformers" over the last three hundred years in England, Lord Robbins argues that "what distinguishes the Classical Theory of Economic Policy from most of these is that, rightly or wrongly, it professed to be based upon a systematic body of scientific knowledge—the newly emerging science of political economy." [103] If policy was to be a function of knowledge, knowledge was to be a proudct of economic science. It is the frequently invoked lesson ". . . that the most perfect knowledge of the science is required . . ." [104] in the conduct of economic policy—in tax policy no less than in respect to the corn laws, population, poor laws, or the supply of money, among the controversies of the era.

If policy is to be guided by economic knowledge, then the "economic laws" developed in the process of accumulating economic knowledge should operate as constraints upon the exercise of choice, which is the development of effective policy. Yet it must be clear from the previous chapters that these economic laws, as constraints upon policy, are themselves constrained, for these laws operate within the institutional system that is itself a function of policy. According to Senior (who hardly denigrated economics as a science),[105] with respect to problems of economic policy and particularly government policy,

> The principles supplied by Political Economy are indeed necessary elements in their solution, but they are not the only, or even the most important elements. The writer who pursues such investigations is in fact engaged on the great Science of legislation; a Science which requires a knowledge of the general principles supplied by Political Economy, but differs from it essentially in its subject, its premises, and its conclusions. The subject of legislation is not Wealth, but human welfare. . . . [The conclusions of the Political Economist], whatever be their generality and their truth, do not authorize him in adding a single syllable of advice. That privilege belongs to the writer or the statesman who has considered all the causes which may promote or impede the general welfare of those whom he addresses, not to the theorist who has considered only one, though among the most important, of those causes. The business of a Political Economist is neither to recommend nor to dissuade, but to state general principles, which it is fatal to neglect, but neither advisable, nor perhaps practicable, to use as the sole, or even the principal, guides in the

actual conduct of affairs. . . . To decide in each case how far those conclusions are to be acted upon, belongs to the art of government, an art to which Political Economy is only one of many subservient Sciences; which involves the consideration of motives, of which the desire for Wealth is only one among many, and aims at objects to which the possession of Wealth is only a subordinate means.[106]

Neither Senior himself nor the other classicists were so pure and reticent in the making of policy recommendations to which was cast the luster of their names and stature as political economists. But the main point, relevant here, is well put. Policy, in the classical model, was to be a function of knowledge, including the knowledge provided by the economist, but policy was also to be based on more than economic laws. The ends of economic policy were to be derived from sources additional to, if not outside of, economic science.[107]

The classical emphasis on knowledge as the basis of policy does reduce, however, to the idea of consciously *reasoned policy*. The Bentham that lamented that "even in the present state of civilization, it is almost a rare case, that by reason, looking to the end in view, matters of government are determined. . . ;" [108] then proposed that "the law-giver should be no more impassioned than the geometrician. They are both solving problems by sober calculation." [109] The emphasis is not on precision of calculation but, rather, on sober contemplation and consideration. The significance of the utilitarian calculus is not so much that it could serve as "an invitation to a continuous review of economic policy. . . ," [110] but that like the classical model of policy itself, it was to serve as a framework for policy analysis.

For the moral philosopher and the properly conditioned legislator, however, Bentham assigned more important roles to reason, first, that of moulding the passions of individuals so that they would contribute more to the augmentation of general happiness, and second, that of providing a technique for the comparison of passions of individuals with a view to making a socially oriented choice between them where choice had to be or could be made.[111]

The utilitarian calculus was an intellectual approach, emphasizing reason over emotion, and empirical considerations over a nondeliberative a priorism. As has been shown before, it would have no unimportant place for continuity (and the principle of the greatest happiness for the greatest number did not mean that the masses would be uncontrolled, or that government should be responsive to the undisciplined will of the masses). Its distinctive character lies rather in its emphasis upon results (or what Lord Robbins calls "the ultimate test of . . . ability to promote human happiness"),[112] in opposition to the manipulation of fictions, categories, and abstractions; in its emphasis upon empirical verification through resort to experience and objective confirmation, and especially in its emphasis upon direct confrontation with value choices.

Thus, as Harrison stresses, Bentham was an advocate of *rational* (in the sense of *reasoned*) policy ("that existing laws and institutions should be looked at critically, then renovated rationally . . ."); [113] of empiricism; [114] and of the avoidance of "begging ethical questions." [115] The science of law, with that of political economy, is to be "the foundation of the practice of the legal art," [116] or "the rational day-to-day use of the instrument of government." [117] In the *Constitutional Code*, Bentham presents a model of reasoned policy analysis not unlike that of Knight,[118] emphasizing policy as a function of reasoned consideration of "what ought to be," "what is," and the "means of bringing what is into accordance with what ought to be." [119]

This mandate, in the classical theory of policy, for reasoned policy is a manifestation of nineteenth-century methodological empiricism, philosophical relativism and politico-economic liberalism. It stands in contrast to the traditional rationalism which is the very opposite of deliberate consideration, relying rather on a belief in absolute and a priori universals.[120] The relative homogeneity between Smith and the later classicists, contrary to the view of Hayek, has already been discussed.

But such emphasis upon reasoned policy raises anew the problem of the relative status of the deliberative and non-deliberative forces, with respect both to control and the determination of knowledge. It should be clear, however, that to this mandate for reasoned policy is certainly added recognition of the operation of a nondeliberative Hayekian collective wisdom, and the forces of ignorance and indirection. There is, though, no more possibility of a precise quantitative specification of the division of power in society, in this respect, than there was in the others discussed before.

It would appear accurate, however, to conclude the following: (1) that the classicists envisioned, or had, the deliberative and nondeliberative forces coexisting and interacting; (2) that primary reliance was placed on the nondeliberative, in the sense that most of the stuff of life is, and must be, so governed, including to some extent the operation of the legal process itself; and (3) that at the margin of conflict between deliberative and nondeliberative, the classicists took a position in favor of the deliberative or reasoned policy approach, although this did not warrant or imply that legal change would necessarily ensue, as was seen before. Lord Robbins makes this quite clear, when he points out that the classicists did "believe in the conscious testing of all social institutions by the general principle of utility. . . . Moreover, these institutions are not natural in the sense that they arise inevitably. They can only be called natural if by that word is meant conformable to the principle of utility; and *while they may emerge without deliberate reflection on all their implications, their fitness to survive must be judged by rational criteria.*" [121]

It is instructive, in this connection, that Bentham's disdain for the mystery and indirection in the common law,[122] and preference for a science of legislation enabling direct confrontation with policy questions and choices, is not at variance with the position of Menger, an organic theorist comparable to Hayek.[123] Although Menger applauds "that suitability of common law, which is the unintended result of an 'organic process,' " [124] he nevertheless adopts what Schneider calls "his own rational outlook on social institutions," [125] at least at the margin, a position essentially the same as that attributed by Lord Robbins to the classicists. Wrote Menger:

> But never, and this is the essential point in the matter under review, may science dispense with testing for their suitability those institutions which have come about 'organically.' It must, when careful investigation so requires, change and better them according to the measure of scientific insight and the practical experience at hand. No era may renounce this 'calling.' [126]

In this matter, both Menger and the classicists manifested the spirit of their age. None of these writers adopted an exclusive or absolute anti-Cartesian position. It was a matter of balance, with reason over emotion at the margin.

The basic character of the classical theory of economic policy remains that of a multi-participant decision-making process, with individual autonomy and utility juxtaposed to authority, the latter in the form of the forces of social control, both deliberative and nondeliberative, with marginal conflicts between autonomy and control, between legal and nonlegal, between reason and emotion. Effective policy, in the classical policy schema, was a product of the interaction of all these forces, and the continuing resolution of these confrontations— a result of, or resulting in, the resolution of freedom and control in a pluralist regime, also balancing continuity and change in an incremental manner. The classical economists clearly confronted, and dealt with, the fundamentals of social life. It has been seen that their economic pluralism, and their theory of economic policy as a whole, is far more complex and sophisticated than the nonintervention interpretation and, to a much lesser degree, even the incomplete and static market-plus-framework approach allows. Finally, it is transcendental that the classical theory of economic policy is more appropriately considered a model; the burden of making continuous judgments for the implementation of it falls upon the decision-making process and decision makers in liberal society, for there remains the pervasive and eternal task of making effective choices, from which no theory or model of economic policy can afford escape.

NOTES: CHAPTER FIVE

1. Lionel Robbins, *Theory of Economic Policy* (London: Macmillan, 1953), pp. 23, 177.
2. On the propaganda or legitimation function, "apologetics," and the question of class bias, see, *inter alia*, Robbins, *ibid.*, pp. 20–22; Frank H. Knight, "Theory of Economic Policy and the History of Doctrine," *Ethics*, vol. 63 (1953), pp. 278, 279; S. G. Checkland, "The Propagation of Ricardian Economics in England," *Economica*, n.s., vol. 16 (1949), pp. 40–52, "The Prescriptions of the Classical Economists," *ibid.*, vol. 20 (1953), p. 65, and "Growth and Progress: The Nineteenth Century View in Britain," *Economic History Review*, II, vol. 12 (1959), pp. 49–62; Ronald L. Meek, "The Decline of Ricardian Economics in England," *Economica*, n.s., vol. 17 (1950), pp. 43–62; Sidney Webb, "The End of Laissez-Faire," *Economic Journal*, vol. 36 (1926), p. 436; Jacob Viner, "Bentham and J. S. Mill: The Utilitarian Background," *American Economic Review*, vol. 39 (1949), p. 361; T. W. Hutchison, "Robert Torrens and Classical Economists," *Economic History Review*, vol. 11 (1958), p. 321, and "Some Questions About Ricardo," *Economica*, n.s. vol. 19 (1952), p. 424; William Ashley, "A Retrospect of Free-Trade Doctrine," *Economic Journal*,

vol. 34 (1924), p. 509; C. C. North, "The Sociological Implications of Ricardo's Economics," *American Journal of Sociology*, vol. 20 (1915), pp. 774–76; L. Stephen, *The English Utilitarians* (New York: Peter Smith, 1950), vol. 2, pp. 51–53, 71; J. B. Brebner, "Laissez Faire and State Intervention in Nineteenth-Century Britain," *Journal of Economic History*, vol. 8, Supplement (1948), p. 65; B. A. Corry, *Money, Saving and Investment in English Economics, 1800–1850* (New York: St. Martin's Press, 1962), pp. 67–69; Henry Sidgwick, "Economic Method," *Fortnightly Review*, vol. 31 (1879), p. 307. See also Nassau W. Senior, *An Outline of the Science of Political Economy* (New York: Kelley, 1951), p. 3. According to Calvin B. Hoover, "Thus, the ability of the capitalistic system to maintain itself without the continued necessity for the use of force against revolutionary protests has depended heavily upon the development of a general feeling that the system was morally admirable and sanctioned by the Christian religion, that its replacement was unthinkable, that it was immortal. It was the development of this charism, quite as much as the demonstrable economic efficacy of the system, which enabled capitalism to survive for so long relatively unchanged." *The Economy, Liberty and the State* (Garden City, N. Y.: Doubleday, 1961), p. 17.

3. See, for example, Robbins, *op. cit.*, pp. 181 ff.; Ashley, *op. cit.*, pp. 502–3; O. H. Taylor, *The Classical Liberalism, Marxism, and the Twentieth Century* (Cambridge: Harvard University Press, 1960), e.g., pp. 7, 8; H. M. Robertson, *The Adam Smith Tradition* (London: Oxford University Press, 1950), pp. 13–14, 18; de Schweinitz, "Free Enterprise in a Growth World," *Southern Economic Journal*, vol. 29 (1962), pp. 103–4; and William Grampp, "Adam Smith and the Economic Man," *Journal of Political Economy*, vol. 56 (1948), pp. 333, 334.

4. Thus Adler considers Smith, Bentham, and Stuart Mill as adhering to what Adler calls the "circumstantial self-realization" concept of freedom, the circumstances in part depending upon the pattern of legal and nonlegal controls. *The Idea of Freedom* (Garden City, N. Y.: Doubleday, 1958), e.g., pp. 226–27, 234–35, 592–93; see also Nathan Rosenberg, "Some Institutional Aspects of the *Wealth of Nations*," *Journal of Political Economy*, vol. 68 (1960), p. 567; Grampp, "Adam Smith and the Economic Man," *op. cit.*, pp. 326, 332, 335, 336; and de Schweinitz, *op. cit.*

5. The material comprising the substance of these chapters is evidence of the classical recognition or premise of the social and situational character of man. In addition to the references cited in Chapter Two, note 5, see also Robertson, *op. cit.*, p. 12; William L. Davidson, *Political Thought in England* (New York: Holt, n.d.), pp. 65–67; Joseph Spengler, "Adam Smith's Theory of Economic Growth," Part

II, *Southern Economic Journal*, vol. 26 (1959), notes 1, 10, 14, 67; E. Burtt, ed., *The English Philosophers from Bacon to Mill* (New York: Modern Library, 1939), pp. 919, 920; John Stuart Mill, *Autobiography* (New York: Columbia University Press, 1924), p. 75; and Smith, *Wealth of Nations* (New York: Modern Library, 1937), p. 726.

6. See, e.g., H. J. Davenport and Glenn R. Morrow, "Discussion: The Ethics of the *Wealth of Nations*," *Philosophical Review*, vol. 34 (1925).

7. Robbins, *op. cit.*, pp. 187–88.

8. J. Bowring, ed., *The Works of Jeremy Bentham* (New York: Russell & Russell, 1962), vol. 9, pp. 18–19.

9. P. Wheelwright, ed., *Selected Writings of Jeremy Bentham, James Mill and John Stuart Mill* (Garden City, N. Y.: Doubleday, 1935), p. 215.

10. Bowring, *op. cit.*, vol. 3, p. 181. "There is not one of these rights which, in a system founded upon the principle of utility, ought not to have its limits." (P. 182.)

11. Bowring, *op. cit.*, vol. 2, p. 503. Cf. Stephen, *op. cit.*, vol. 1, pp. 292, 293.

12. Adler, *op. cit.*, p. 226. According to Smith, "To restrain private people, it may be said, . . . is a manifest violation of that natural liberty which it is the proper business of law, not to infringe, but to support. Such regulations may, no doubt, be considered as in some respect a violation of natural liberty. But those exertions of the natural liberty of a few individuals, which might endanger the security of the whole society, are, and ought to be, restrained by the laws of all governments; of the most free, as well as of the most despotical." *Wealth of Nations*, p. 308. Cf. Morrow, in *Adam Smith, 1776–1926* (Chicago: University of Chicago Press, 1928), p. 146.

13. W. Stark, *Jeremy Bentham's Economic Writings* (New York: Burt Franklin, 1954), vol. 3, p. 335. Cf. Bowring, *op. cit.*, vol. 2, p. 269.

14. Bowring, *op. cit.*, vol. 1, p. 301.

15. *Ibid.*, vol. 3, p. 185. "When a law is reproached as hurtful to liberty, the inconvenience is not a particular ground of complaint against that law—it is shared by all laws. . . . It is unfortunate that individual and political liberty have received the same name. By means of this double significance, a syllogism may be formed in favour of perpetual revolt. An established law is a restraint upon liberty: a restraint upon liberty is tyranny: tyranny is a legitimate reason for revolt." (P. 185.) Cf. Bentham, *The Limits of Jurisprudence Defined*, C. W. Everett, ed. (New York: Columbia University Press, 1945), pp. 50, 138 ff.

16. Bowring, *op. cit.*, vol. 1, p. 302.

17. *Ibid.*, vol. 2, p. 503.

18. Adler, *op. cit.*, pp. 226, 234.

19. Wheelwright, *op. cit.*, pp. 215, 221; cf. p. 224.

20. J. R. McCulloch, *The Principles of Political Economy* (Edinburgh: Tait, 1843), p. 88.

21. Wheelwright, *op. cit.*, pp. 188–89.

22. Bowring, *op. cit.*, vol. 9, p. 34. Smith also recognizes submission to superiors and "that fortunate violence which we are no longer capable of resisting; . . ." Smith, *Essays* (London: Ward, Lock, 1880, p. 225.

23. Adler, *op. cit.*, pp. 234–35.

24. Bowring, *op. cit.*, vol. 1, p. 301.

25. *Inter alia*, cf. Bowring, *op. cit.*, vol. 2, pp. 505–6; Adler, *op. cit.*, p. 235; and H. J. Bittermann, "Adam Smith's Empiricism and the Law of Nature," *Journal of Political Economy*, vol. 48 (1940), p. 732.

26. Adler, *op. cit.*, pp. 226–27; cf. Bowring, *op. cit.*, vol. 1, p. 302, and vol. 3, p. 185.

27. See Chapter Three, note 53.

28. W. D. Grampp, "On the Politics of the Classical Economists," *Quarterly Journal of Economics*, vol. 62 (1948), p. 741; cf. p. 742.

29. Bentham, *op. cit.*, p. 35. "But *grounded* expectation, the one important thing in possession, is really one aspect of security, the work of law." (P. 35.)

30. Robbins, *op. cit.*, p. 56.

31. *Ibid.*, p. 188.

32. *Ibid.*, p. 16. See also pp. 12, 182, 187. The emphasis upon the exercise of individual choice is a manifestation of the *desideratum* of meaningful individual participation which is to be effectuated through, and thus become a derivative of, pluralism. See also Chapter Two, text at note 9.

33. Checkland, "The Prescriptions of the Classical Economists," *Economica*, n.s. vol. 20 (1953), p. 72.

34. As early as A *Fragment on Government* (published in 1776) Bentham wrote: "In regard to a government that is *free*, and one that is *despotic*, wherein is it then that the difference consists? Is it that those persons in whose hands that power is lodged which is acknowledged to be supreme, have less power in the one than in the other, when it is from custom that they derive it? By no means. It is not that the power of one any more than of the other has any certain bounds to it. The distinction turns upon circumstances of a very different complexion:—on the *manner* in which that whole mass of power, which, taken together, is supreme, is, in a free state, *distributed* among the several ranks of persons that are sharers in it:—on the *source* from whence their titles to it are successively derived:—on the frequent and

easy *changes* of condition between governors and governed; whereby the interests of the one class are more or less indistinguishably blended with those of the other:—on the *responsibility* of the governors; or the right which a subject has of having the reasons publicly assigned and canvassed of every act of power that is exerted over him:—on the *liberty of the press*; or the security with which every man, be he of the one class or the other, may make known his complaints and remonstrances to the whole community:—on the *liberty of public association*; or the security with which malcontents may communicate their sentiments, concert their plans, and practise every mode of opposition short of actual revolt, before the executive power can be legally justified in disturbing them." *Op. cit.*, pp. 94–95; cf. pp. xxxii–xxxiii. Wrote Ricardo: "They spoke of the rights of kings, as if Government could be legitimately intended for any other purpose but the happiness of the people." P. Sraffa, ed., *The Works and Correspondence of David Ricardo* (Cambridge: Cambridge University Press, 1952), vol. 9, p. 213. *In re* the form of government see also: Robbins, *op. cit.*, pp. 194–205, and Grampp, "On the Politics of the Classical Economists," *op. cit.* The classical theory was unquestionably one of pluralism, or political democracy, but this is not to deny that their theory was a blend of what may be called realism and idealism: as Robbins points out, "The *Considerations on Representative Government* must be regarded as being as much a plea for adequate safeguards against the abuses of democracy as an argument for proceeding towards its realization." *Theory of Economic Policy*, p. 203. Yet it must be said that Stuart Mill's position tends to rest on the proposition that pluralism is its own best safeguard, given the type of circumstances against which he was directing his argument. John Stuart Mill, *Considerations on Representative Government* (2nd ed., London: Parker, Son, and Bourn, 1861). With respect to the paragraph in the text as a whole, see also John Stuart Mill, *Prefaces to Liberty*, Bernard Wishy, ed. (Boston: Beacon Press, 1959).

35. See John Stuart Mill, *The Subjection of Women*, of which there are several interesting editions: one with a foreword by Carrie Chapman Catt (New York: Stokes, 1911); another with an introductory analysis by Stanton Coit (New York: Longmans, Green, 1911); and a third coupled with Mary Wollstonecraft's *The Rights of Women*, with an introduction by G. E. G. Catlin (London: Dent, Everyman's Library, no. 825, 1929).

36. The same Smith who would utilize religion as an instrument of social control also argued that organized religion itself should be pluralistically structured: "The interested and active zeal of religious teachers can be dangerous and troublesome only where there is, either but one sect tolerated in the society, or where the whole of a large society

is divided into two or three great sects; the teachers of each acting by concert, and under a regular discipline and subordination. But that zeal must be altogether innocent where the society is divided into two or three hundred, or perhaps into as many thousand small sects, of which no one could be considerable enough to disturb the public tranquillity." *Wealth of Nations*, p. 745. Thus, as in the economic sphere, competition reducing to the division of power as a check upon power was the means to the attainment of a pluralistic conception of freedom.

Thus Ricardo, for example: "Blasphemy was an offence which it was quite impossible to define. Nobody, in committing it, was aware of what he was offending against. . . . [Prosecutions] ought never to be instituted for religious opinions. All religious opinions, however absurd and extravagant, might be conscientiously believed by some individuals. Why, then, was one man to set up his ideas on the subject as the criterion from which no other was to be allowed to differ with impunity? Why was one man to be considered infallible, and all his fellow men as frail and erring creatures? . . . A fair and free discussion ought to be allowed on all religious topics." Sraffa, *op. cit.*, vol. 5, pp. 278, 280. See also Cannan, "Ricardo in Parliament," *Economic Journal*, vol. 4 (1894), pp. 252 ff. In *re* Bentham, it is manifestly clear that in his overtly antireligious works, as discussed in Chapter Two, *supra*, the argument is directed among other things at the monism of existing religion, and that such religion as he would allow would have to operate under the conditions of pluralism. See also A *Fragment on Government* (Oxford: Blackwell, 1948), pp. 17 ff.

37. See William D. Grampp, "On the Politics of the Classical Economists," *Quarterly Journal of Economics*, vol. 62 (1948), pp. 717 ff.; Joseph Spengler and William Allen, eds., *Essays in Economic Thought* (Chicago: Rand McNally, 1960), pp. 9, 11, 16. See also Stuart Mill, *The Spirit of the Age, op. cit.*, e.g., pp. 25–27, 31, 35–36, 65; and McCulloch, *The Works of David Ricardo* (London: John Murray, 1881), pp. 553–54.

38. Sraffa, *op. cit.*, vol. 6, p. 180.

39. Smith, *Essays*, p. 205.

40. O. H. Taylor, A *History of Economic Thought* (New York: McGraw-Hill, 1960), pp. 138–39; W. Stark, *The Ideal Foundations of Economic Thought* (London: Kegan Paul, Trench, Trubner & Co., 1943), and "Liberty and Equality or: Jeremy Bentham as an Economist," *Economic Journal*, vol. 51 (1941), pp. 56–79. See also Bowring, *op. cit.*, vol. 1, pp. 301 ff. and 358 ff., vol. 2, pp. 269 ff., vol. 3, pp. 203, and vol. 9, pp. 11 ff.

41. Friedrich A. Hayek, *Individualism and Economic Order* (Chicago: University of Chicago Press, 1948), p. 17.

42. Stark, *op. cit.*, vol. 3, p. 333; cf. pp. 310, 337. See note 68.

43. Bowring, *op. cit.*, vol. 1, p. 301.

44. McCulloch, *Principles of Political Economy*, p. 294. In the *Treatise on the Succession to Property Vacant by Death*, McCulloch wrote: "The principle of *laissez faire* may be safely trusted to in some things, but in many more it is wholly inapplicable; and to appeal to it on all occassions, savours more of the policy of a parrot than of a statesman or a philosopher." *Op. cit.*, p. 156.

45. John Stuart Mill, *Principles of Political Economy* (New York: Kelley, 1961), p. 950; cf. pp. 792, 941 ff. Mill also wrote: "The jealousy which prevails in this country of any extension of the coercive and compulsory powers of the general government I conceive to be, though not always wisely directed, and often acting the most strongly in the wrong places, yet, on the whole, a most salutary sentiment, and one to which this country owes the chief points of superiority which its government possesses over those of the Continent." Abram L. Harris, "J. S. Mill on Monopoly and Socialism: A Note," *Journal of Political Economy*, vol. 67 (1959), p. 607. The issue in question relates in part to municipal *versus* central government activity. Statements to the same effect as to government per se may be found, e.g., in "On Liberty." Burtt, *op. cit.*, p. 955; and see also J. S. Mill, *Auguste Comte and Positivism* (Ann Arbor: University of Michigan Press, 1961), p. 78. See also Davidson, *op. cit.*, pp. 83, 197; Robbins, *op. cit.*, p. 40; Morrow, in *Adam Smith, 1776–1926*, pp. 140, 141, 144–45; Stephen, *op. cit.*, vol. 1, pp. 309–10, vol. 3, pp. 227, 267–70; and D. H. Macgregor, *Economic Thought and Policy* (London: Oxford University Press, 1955), p. 84.

46. Sraffa, *op. cit.*, vol. 5, p. 276.

47. See Chapter Three, note 27.

48. See Chapter Four, text at notes 42 and 43.

49. Irma Adelman, *Theories of Economic Growth and Development* (Stanford: Stanford University Press, 1961), p. 28.

50. Smith, *Wealth of Nations*, p. 681. See also K. W. Kapp, *The Social Costs of Private Enterprise* (Cambridge: Harvard University Press, 1950), p. 28; Morrow, in *Adam Smith, 1776–1926*, pp. 146–47; and Robbins, *op. cit.*, pp. 37–38, 59, 183, 188–89.

51. Stark, *op. cit.*, vol. 3, pp. 257–58; cf. Spengler and Allen, *op. cit.*, p. 340.

52. Nassau W. Senior, *Industrial Efficiency and Social Economy*, S. Leon Levy, ed. (New York: Holt, 1928) two volumes, vol. 2, p. 302. In this connection it will be well to recall a sentence from Hayek, already quoted: "Only indirectly, by depriving government of some means by which alone it might be able to attain certain ends, may this principle deprive government of the power to pursue those ends." *The Constitution of Liberty* (Chicago: University of Chicago Press, 1959), p. 221.

53. Senior, *op. cit.*, vol. 2, p. 307.

54. *Ibid.*, p. 302.

55. Sraffa, *op. cit.*, vol. 5, p. 283. The position taken by Senior and Ricardo in the quotations given in the text is essentially the same as that of Justice McKenna, dissenting, in *German Alliance Insurance Company v. Kansas*, 233 U.S. 389 (1914), to wit: "In other words, to say that government possessed at one time a greater power to recognize the public interest in a business and its regulation to promote the general welfare than government possesses to-day." (P. 411.) See note 66.

56. Smith, *The Wealth of Nations*, p. 651. See Adler, *op. cit.*, pp. 226–27; and Bittermann, *op. cit.*, pp. 518–19.

57. Smith, *Essays*, pp. 70–72, 73. See also Morrow, in *Adam Smith, 1776–1926*, pp. 144–45.

58. McCulloch, *Principles of Political Economy*, pp. 255, 256; cf. p. 528. Note, also, the following: "No authority should ever be granted to companies or individuals to undertake any work, however useful, by which the private property of others may be affected, without providing for their full indemnity. To act on any other principle would be to shake the security of property; it would be injuring one set of individuals for the benefit of some other set." (P. 289.) Although, parenthetically, the theory of competition allows competitors to "take" or "destroy" the property of others through competition, the law of torts and of unfair competition, even aside from the antitrust laws, govern the conditions of competition.

59. Robbins, *op. cit.*, p. 188.

60. Bowring, *op. cit.*, vol. 1, pp. 313–14.

61. Adler, *op. cit.*, pp. 234–35. See also Taylor, *The Classical Liberalism, Marxism, and the Twentieth Century*, p. 97.

62. "Till you know what the laws say to it, you do not know what there is of it, nor what account to give of it: and yet it existed, and that in full force and vigour, before there were any such things as laws; and so will continue to exist, and that for ever, in spite of anything which laws can do to it." Bowring, *op. cit.*, vol. 2, p. 505.

63. *Ibid.*, pp. 505–6. See the analysis of R. H. Coase, "The Problem of Social Cost," *Journal of Law and Economics*, vol. 3, (1960), pp. 1–44, as for example: "If factors of production are thought of as rights, it becomes easier to understand that the right to do something which has a harmful effect . . . is also a factor of production. . . . The cost of exercising a right (of using a factor of production) is always the loss which is suffered elsewhere in consequence of the exercise of that right. . . ." (P. 44.)

64. Burtt, *op. cit.*, pp. 955–56. The character of the analysis as a tautological system of classification is evident from the lines following those quoted in the text: "The only part of the conduct of anyone, for which he is amenable to society, is that which concerns others. In the

part which merely concerns himself, his independence is, of right, absolute. Over himself, over his own body and mind, the individual is sovereign." (P. 956.) See also J. S. Mill, *op. cit.*, pp. 141, 144, 145.

65. Burtt, *op. cit.*, p. 992.

66. *Ibid.*, p. 1008. Having quoted Justice McKenna in note 55, it is appropriate to acknowledge the well-known proposition of Justice Roberts in *Nebbia v. New York*, 291 U.S. 502 (1934): "It is clear that there is no closed class or category of businesses affected with a public interest. . . ." (P. 536.)

67. Burtt, *op. cit.*, p. 1023.

68. *Ibid.*, p. 1023. Stark considers the following sentence "as expressing in a nutshell Bentham's attitude to *laissez-faire*": "In the struggle for encreasing wealth, it will happen that one man shall give encrease to *his* wealth in such manner as shall occasion a more than equivalent decrease on the part of others: here then comes the demand for the interposition of the law." Stark, *op. cit.*, vol. 3, p. 522. It is to be recalled, of course, that the classical postulate is that of a created, not an automatic, harmony. For a more recent statement of this position *and* of its status: "In those cases where the welfare of the various members of the economy is partly dependent on each others' activity, it is possible that persons in pursuit of their own immediate interests will be led to act in a manner contrary to the interests of others. To the extent that such a situation is general, the members of the economy may find themselves busily engaged in the frustration of each others' desires. In these circumstances it may be to their mutual advantage to restrict their activity so as to prevent this happening. It may be that the disadvantage to each of them of such activity is so great and of such a sort that arrangements can be made on a purely voluntary basis whereby it can be avoided altogether. Where such arrangements cannot be relied on, it becomes advantageous to the members of the economy to have their activities restricted by coercive measures. This conclusion is pure tautology as it stands." William J. Baumol, *Welfare Economics and the Theory of the State* (Cambridge: Harvard University Press, 1952), p. 140; cf. pp. 11–18. See also Coase, *op. cit.*, and James M. Buchanan, "What Should Economists Do?", *Southern Economic Journal*, vol. 30 (1964), pp. 219–22.

69. Burtt, *op. cit.*, p. 1036.

70. Smith, *The Wealth of Nations*, p. 651.

71. Roscoe Pound, *Interpretations of Legal History* (New York: Macmillan, 1923), p. 152, quoted in Edgar Bodenheimer, *Jurisprudence* (New York: McGraw-Hill, 1940), p. 301.

72. Bodenheimer, *op. cit.*, pp. 301-2.

73. *Ibid.*, p. 302.

74. Robbins, *op. cit.*, p. 65.

75. *Ibid.*, pp. 178–79.

76. Sraffa, *op. cit.*, vol. 7, p. 205; see also pp. 198, 204, 211, 227–28, 228–29, 234–35.

77. *Ibid.*, vol. 9, p. 292. Cf. vol. 7, p. 266, and vol. 8, p. 197.

78. See, for example, Sraffa, *ibid.*, vol. 6, p. 180; vol. 7, p. 298; vol. 8, pp. 56–57, 80, 129–30, 133, 146–47; and vol. 9, pp. 42, 45. See also McCulloch, *The Works of David Ricardo*, pp. 551–52; Grampp, "On the Politics of the Classical Economists," *op. cit.*, p. 717; Viner, "Bentham and J. S. Mill: The Utilitarian Background," *op. cit.*, pp. 361-62.

79. Sraffa, *op. cit.*, vol. 5, pp. 43–44; see also vol. 8, p. 275.

80. Smith, *Essays*, p. 207. *In re* Bentham, opposing blind allegiance to custom, but supporting gentle reform, respect for established expectations, innovation through law with great caution, balancing the ideal and the practicable, and concern for the maintenance of the social order, see: Bowring, *op. cit.*, vol. 1, pp. 180–81, 302, 309, 311–12, 313, 320, 323, 326; vol. 2, pp. 459–60; vol. 3, p. 203; and vol. 5, p. 234.

81. Robbins, *op. cit.*, p. 4.

82. If the analysis in this book is correct, however, the classicists were not so myopic on the operation of the working rules (including both custom and common law) as Commons—among many others—thought. (See, for example, John R. Commons, *Legal Foundations of Capitalism* (Madison: University of Wisconsin Press, 1959), pp. 137, 241–42.) The classicists' analysis closely approximates what is to be found, more systematically presented, in Commons. Yet Commons is not the only subsequent analyst to whom the classicists were precursors. See also, for example, the works of Robert L. Hale, Frank H. Knight, and Roscoe Pound.

83. "Even the most zealous proponent of 'leaving things to their course' might accept state intervention in a specific case without derogation from the purity of his creed if the problem in question seemed incurable by means of the economic process 'working itself out.'" Blaug, *Ricardian Economics* (New Haven: Yale University Press, 1958), p. 193. See also O. H. Taylor, *Economics and Liberalism* (Cambridge: Harvard University Press, 1955), p. 99.

84. Blaug, *op. cit.*, p. 194.

85. Frank H. Knight, "Theory of Economic Policy and the History of Doctrine," *Ethics*, vol. 63 (1953), pp. 279, 282. In his essay, "Ethics and Economic Reform," Knight argued that "the social system of liberalism embodies a genuine ethical ideal" which could serve as the objective basis of policy, whereas "Christianity affords no concrete guidance for social action, beyond an urge to 'do good and avoid evil,'" a "moralism" which, "in the absence of careful economic and

politico-legal analysis, is virtually certain to have consequences utterly different from the intentions of the reformers, and predominantly evil." Knight, in part, is arguing against " 'moralistic' judgments of personal rights and duties. . . ." *Freedom and Reform* (New York: Harper, 1947), pp. 48, 124, 127.

86. Burtt, *op. cit.*, p. 955. "And it seems to me that in consequence of this absence of rule or principle, one side is at present as often wrong as the other: the interference of government is, with about equal frequency, improperly invoked and improperly condemned." (P. 955.)

87. McCulloch, *Principles of Political Economy*, p. 257.

88. Burtt, *op. cit.*, p. 1040; and see the following sentence, quoted in note 96. See also Malthus: "But it is to be recollected, in the first place, that there is a class of duties connected with these subjects, which, it is universally acknowledged, belongs to the Sovereign; and though the line appears to be drawn with tolerable precision, when it is considered generally; yet when we come to particulars, doubts may arise, and certainly in many instances have arisen, as to the subjects to be included in this classification." T. R. Malthus, *The Principles of Political Economy* (The London School of Economics and Political Science, series of Reprints of Scarce Works on Political Economy, no. 3; 1936), p. 14.

89. Blaug, *op. cit.*, p. 194. See also Blaug, "The Classical Economists and the Factory Acts—A Re-examination," *Quarterly Journal of Economics*, vol. 72 (1958), p. 212; and Ely, "The Past and the Present of Political Economy," Johns Hopkins University Studies in Historical and Political Science, vol. 2 (1884), pp. 17 ff.

90. Robbins, *op. cit.*, p. 181.

91. Bittermann, *op. cit.*, pp. 717–18.

92. Viner, "The Intellectual History of Laissez Faire," *Journal of Law and Economics*, vol. 3 (1960), p. 61.

93. *Ibid.*, p. 62; cf. p. 47.

94. *Lochner v. New York*, 198 U.S. 45 (1905), p. 74 (quoted in Carl A. Auerbach *et al*, eds., *The Legal Process* (San Francisco: Chandler, 1961), p. 374; see also pp. 371 ff.)

95. Frank H. Knight, "Virtue and Knowledge: The View of Professor Polanyi," *Ethics*, vol. 59 (1949), p. 284.

96. S. G. Checkland, "The Prescriptions of the Classical Economists," *Economica*, n.s., vol. 20 (1953), p. 71. As Stuart Mill pointed out (see text at note 88), the problem of the role of government "is, in a great measure, a question of detail, in which many and various considerations must be kept in view, and no absolute rule can be laid down. But," he goes on to say, "I believe that the practical principle in which safety resides, the ideal to be kept in view, the standard by which to test all arrangements intended for overcoming the difficulty,

may be conveyed in these words: the greatest dissemination of power consistent with efficiency; but the greatest possible centralization of information, and diffusion of it from the center." Burtt, *op. cit.*, p. 1040. The purpose of this quotation is not reiteration of the classical presumption but, rather, acknowledgment of the considered need for "the ideal to be kept in view. . . ."

97. Cf. Taylor, *The Classical Liberalism, Marxism, and the Twentieth Century*, p. 118.

98. Knight, *Freedom and Reform*, p. 11.

99. John Maynard Keynes, Introduction to D. H. Robertson, *Money* (New York: Harcourt, Brace and Co., 1929), p. v. The language in the text generally follows and to some extent paraphrases the language of Lord Keynes but departs from certain of his points.

100. The literature on the concept of the public interest is quite extensive, the analysis of which involves serious philosophical questions beyond the scope of the present work. The following, however, are, *inter alia*, relevant to this discussion. ". . . the concept of public interest has three specific functions in a democratic society (we are here concerned only with its application to government actions, even though actions of private citizens, companies, or groups may also be judged as to whether they are 'in the public interest'). First, it serves as a device by which individual citizens can judge government actions and communicate their judgments to one another. Second, since the concept implies that there is one common good for all members of society, transcending the good of any one member, appeals to the public interest can be used to coopt or to placate persons who are required by government policy to act against their own immediate interests. Third, the concept serves as a guide to and a check on public officials who are faced with decisions regarding public policy but have no unequivocal instructions from the electorate or their superiors regarding what action to take." Anthony Downs, "The Public Interest: Its Meaning in a Democracy," *Social Research*, vol. 29 (1962), p. 4.

". . . the public interest is the life hypothesis of a pluralistic society—enabling people with different religions, different philosophical convictions, or different subconscious value systems to have a common ground for promoting their various ultimate values. Without this common ground, representing more than an accidental coincidence of individual interests, a pluralistic democracy could not exist. In a theocratic or monolithic society, there can never in principle be controversy about ultimate objectives, only about means. In a pluralistic society, there can and will be controversy about ultimates, but the controversies will not become disruptive as long as there is some common ground with respect to the penultimate values, the public interest. There will never be unanimity about their exact definition; indeed, without some controversy about the changing meaning of the public interest, democ-racy would not be alive. But without some common ground concern-ing those changes in meaning, it could not survive." Gerhard Colm, "In Defense of the Public Interest," *Social Research*, vol. 27 (1960), pp. 300–301. It is instructive that Downs, for example, calls attention to the fact that "many decisions that affect society in general—and therefore lie within the realm of the public interest—concern choices among extremely detailed policy alternatives. . . ." (P. 7.) Moreover, what Colm refers to as "common ground," Downs identifies as the "minimal consensus," and Auerbach *et al* as "made up of the least common denominators that bind all the interest groups in our so-ciety." *The Legal Process*, p. 661.

101. Grampp, "On the Politics of the Classical Economists," *op. cit.*, pp. 741, 742.

102. Senior, *An Outline of the Science of Political Economy*, p. 76.

103. Robbins, *op. cit.*, p. 171.

104. Sraffa, *op. cit.*, vol. 8, p. 133. See also Carl S. Shoup, *Ricardo on Taxation* (New York: Columbia University Press, 1960), pp. 7–8. See also Sraffa, vol. 7, p. 366; vol. 8, p. 31; and vol. 9, p. 152.

105. Marian Bowley, *Nassau Senior and Classical Economics* (New York: Kelley, 1949), pp. 27–65; see also pp. 237–334.

106. Senior, *Outline*, pp. 2, 3. See Macgregor, *op. cit.*, pp. 84–85; and Scott Gordon, "The London *Economist* and the High Tide of Laissez Faire," *Journal of Political Economy*, vol. 63 (1955), pp. 476–77. See also Malthus: "In all cases of this kind there are higher con-siderations to be attended to than those which relate to mere wealth." *Op. cit.*, p. 380. According to Stuart Mill also, of course, questions of "general policy" transcend political economy. See Harris, *op. cit.*, p. 606. For a similar interpretation of Smith see, *inter alia*, J. A. R. Mar-riott, "Adam Smith and Some Problems of To-day," *Fortnightly Re-view*, vol. 82 (1902), pp. 976, 980–81.

107. Robbins, *op. cit.*, p. 177.

108. Bowring, *op. cit.*, vol. 2, p. 459.

109. Bentham, *Deontology*, quoted by A. J. Ayer in G. W. Keeton and G. Schwarzenberger, eds., *Jeremy Bentham and the Law: A Sym-posium* (London: Stevens, 1948), p. 245. On reasoned policy see also Bowring, *op. cit.*, vol. 1, pp. 301, 303, 304, 323–26; C. K. Ogden, *Bentham's Theory of Fictions* (London: Kegan Paul, 1932); Ricardo, *The Principles of Political Economy and Taxation* (New York: Dut-ton, 1911), p. 61; Malthus, *op. cit.*, pp. 13–14; Smith, *Lectures* (New York: Kelley & Millman, 1956), pp. 1 ff.; and J. S. Mill, "Chapters on Socialism," *Fortnightly Review*, vol. 31 (1879), pp. 217, 219, 220, 223, 529–30. The classical literature abounds with examples of the use of economic analysis in reasoned policy analysis. See, for example,

Ricardo, *op. cit.*, chap. 5 ("On Wages"); McCulloch, *The Works of David Ricardo*, pp. 391 ff. ("Proposals for an Economical and Secure Currency, with Observations on the Profits of the Bank of England" and "On Protection to Agriculture"); Bowring, *op. cit.*, vol. 8. pp. 359 ff., and 440 ff. ("Tracts on Poor Laws and Pauper Management" and "Observations on the Poor Bill"); Malthus, *The Measure of Value* (New York, Kelley & Millman, 1957); and Robert Torrens, *Letters on Commercial Policy* (London School of Economics and Political Science: Series of Reprints of Scarce Works on Political Economy, 1958).

110. Macgregor, *op. cit.*, p. 82. Cf. Keeton and Schwarzenberger, *op. cit.*, pp. 258–59; Robbins, *op. cit.*, p. 178–79; and text at note 75.

111. Viner, "Bentham and J. S. Mill: The Utilitarian Background," *op. cit.*, p. 367. With respect to Smith's empiricism and emphasis upon reasoned policy see Bittermann, *op. cit.*, and James F. Becker, "Adam Smith's Theory of Social Science," *Southern Economic Journal,*, vol. 38 (1961). See also J. S. Mill, *Auguste Comte and Positivism*, pp. 52, 80.

112. Robbins, *op. cit.*, p. 179. That is to say, that ". . . the expediency of any act of government must be judged solely by its consequences and not regarded as ruled out in advance by some metaphysical system of rights." (P. 41.)

113. Bentham, *A Fragment on Government*, p. xl.

114. *Ibid.*, p. xlvi.

115. *Ibid.*, p. xxxix; cf. p. xlv.

116. *Ibid.*, p. xxxix.

117. *Ibid.*, p. lvi.

118. Frank H. Knight, "Theory of Economic Policy and the History of Doctrine," *Ethics*, vol. 63 (1953), pp. 282 ff., and *Intelligence and Democratic Action* (Cambridge: Harvard University Press, 1960), p. 21.

119. Bowring, *op. cit.*, vol. 9, pp. 5–6.

120. The author is obligated to Alfred Chalk for underscoring the cosmological facet indicated in the text.

121. Robbins, *op. cit.*, p. 56; emphasis added.

122. See, for example, Bowring, *op. cit.*, vol. 7, pp. 310, 484.

123. On the relation of Menger to Hayek, see Louis Schneider, "The Role of the Category of Ignorance in Sociological Theory: An Exploratory Statement," *American Sociological Review*, vol. 27 (1962), p. 498, and the citation given.

124. Carl Menger, *Problems of Economics and Sociology*, ed., and with an introduction by, Louis Schneider; Francis J. Nock, trans. (Urbana: University of Illinois Press, 1963), p. 234.

125. *Ibid.*, p. 9.

126. *Ibid.*, p. 234.

Appendix

The Nature and Scope of Economic Policy*

The objective of this paper is to develop both the basic context in which the concept of policy in economics ultimately has meaning and the fundamental issues and problems of economic policy which comprise the substance of that meaning. In effect, then, the author will attempt an answer to this question: what are the basic problems of what has come to be called the "theory of economic policy?" That is to say, what is ultimately involved in a theory of economic policy?

In brief, the author is going to suggest that economic policy need be comprehended in the context of the economy seen as a process of making decisions toward the resolution of the basic economic problems; that the policy or decision-making process must be understood to include all the participants therein; and that any theory of economic policy ultimately has to confront the problem of structuring and restructuring the economic decision-making process itself. Inasmuch, then, as a theory of policy involves the distribution of power in society, it is involved with the problem of order—i.e., the continuing resolution of the dual basic problems of freedom and control, and continuity and change which impinge upon all aspects of life. It thus will be seen that the nature of policy encompasses choice, change, and control in a context of conflict; and that the scope of policy extends to include the exercise of choice governing the resolution of the basic economic problems as conventionally understood and the structuring of the decision-making process itself as well as the principles involved in the resolution of the problem of order and its elements. The latter will be considered, however, only insofar as they relate to economic policy.[1] The author will also suggest the consonance of various facets of the analysis herein developed with the major bodies of economic thought, arguing, as it were, that the present analysis of the nature and scope of economic policy actually underlies these bodies of thought.

I

Policy is an ubiquitous, if heterogeneous,[2] phenomenon, and all modern societies are preoccupied with it. " 'Policy,' " as the late Carl J. Friedrich remarked, "is one of the magic words of the contemporary world. . . . Today 'policy' has become central." [3] Indeed, modernity itself is in no small part a matter of policy-consciousness. This policy spirit of the age, of course, relates to the fact that modernity is what John Stuart Mill called an "age of transition." Even the concept of a "spirit of the age" is significant: "It is," wrote Mill, "an idea essentially belonging to an age of change." [4] So also with policy: both the concept of an age of change and of policy itself rest upon the fact of change. This policy consciousness, of what will be identified below as the exercise of choice over the control of change, is a facet of the empiricism, relativism, pragmatism, utilitarianism and evolutionism consequent to what John R. Commons called a "volitional psychology" [5] and Frank H. Knight, "the liberation of the mind." [6] This is manifest, for example, in operationalism and logical empiricism. As P. W. Bridgman foresaw, "The operational point of view involves

238

much more than a mere restriction of the sense in which we understand 'concept,' but means a far-reaching change in all our habits of thought. . . . Not only will operational thinking reform the social art of conversation, but all our social relations will be liable to reform." [7] Yet such relatively recent developments in epistemology are in this context the extension of an increasing policy consciousness, namely, the increasingly direct confrontation with matters of choice, control and change. It is but one manifestation of an age that has become "prepared to judge [its] standards by their consequences. . . ." [8] It is also true that the concept of policy maintained by participants in the policy process is an important facet of that process—anticipating, for the moment, some later discussion— but the fact of the aforementioned confrontation transcends all controversy over the relation of the fact of change and the idea of change.

Policy thus being ubiquitous, it is nonetheless true, however, that policy discussions are usually concerned with particular issues. Whether in learned studies or partisan pronouncements, preoccupation is generally with the issues of the day: tax cuts, bank mergers, steel strikes, balance-of-payments measures, Sherman Act violations, growth rates, structural unemployment, farm price supports, and the like. Contemporary policy-oriented existence is one of a series of immediate and particular issues and problems. It is thus one of the primary characteristics of the policy process that its participants are generally concerned with *implementational* details [9] and so with what has been called *intermediate* [10] concepts and goals.

The context of conventional policy discussions is thus one of specific problems and issues, and each is considered only incompletely. Yet this is quite appropriate, for the actual policy process in Western (and particularly American) society is *incremental* in character. [11] Incrementalism derives from the complexity of real-world policy issues, limitations of knowledge and ambition, and the general pluralism of the total social system. Decision making, as the concept is usually employed, is fragmented, and the consideration of policy issues is such that the issues themselves tend to be conceived (albeit variously) along relatively narrow and restricted dimensions. Incrementalism thus reinforces the tendency for attention to be focused on intermediate concepts and goals and on immediate problems and, further, tends to produce gradual alterations or changes. The practice, then, of economic policy has been one of pluralism, incrementalism, and gradualism, with policy discussions consequently tending to be limited and fragmented.

There are other important concomitants of the limited context of conventional policy discussion. Those to be considered here generally relate to the customary separation between economic *theory* and economic *policy*. The first is the differentiation between market and government, both as decision-making processes within themselves and as part of what may be conceived of as the total decision-making process. The second is that economic theory is generally conceived to be an analysis of the operation of the market (including both micro- and macro-economics.) The third is that, whereas the scope of theory is delimited to the market, that of policy is usually equated with *government* policy. Thus, as will be seen below, the concept of policy as well as the character of most policy dicussion ultimately reflect the market-plus-framework dichotomy (in which market forces are seen to operate within an institutional—usually legal—framework), which is the predominant approach to policy analysis, both sophisticated and unsophisticated.[12]

Several difficulties arise, however, with the particularized and fragmented context of most policy discussion. One problem that has been long commented upon is the mechanical character of orthodox economic theories and models; insofar as economic analysis is an approach to policy analysis and policy making (and the author has elsewhere argued that "formal economic analysis, considered as an approach to policy, has been the main contribution of the profession"),[13] the deficiencies of the former may be visited upon the latter.[14] The criticism of mechanism is neither beside the point nor wrong, but there is no necessary reason why open- and broad-minded and competent analysts cannot avoid or at least minimize such deficiencies as are usually alleged. Even more basic, in the view of the author, are two interrelated difficulties, namely, that the particularization and fragmentation of policy discussions and issues results in the neglect, first, of the larger context in which particular issues, arguments, and positions have ultimate significance, and, second, of what may be called the fundamental problems of any theory of economic policy. The author would suggest that the nature and scope of economic policy must be comprehended and defined in terms of what must ultimately be identified as the proper understanding of (a) the larger context in which policy issues are meaningful and (b) the fundamental problems of policy that transcend yet impinge upon all particular issues and arguments. Conventional discussions of policy (with significant exceptions) simply neglect both this larger context and the "fundamental questions" [15] or "fundamental problems of man in society" because of preoccupation with "the topical issues of the moment" [16] and incomplete conceptions of what is ultimately relevant in the sense of basic or transcendental problems.[17]

II

Traditional economic theory has been essentially the analysis of the operation of market forces consequent to the behavior of economic actors as buyers and sellers under competitive and noncompetitive conditions. Theory never has been unrelated to policy—policy questions have been the genesis of considerable theory, and theory always has had policy implications drawn from it—but economic theory has been primarily the study of catallactic forces operating in a market economy. Economic science has been largely the science of the market system.

In the context of the present paper, traditional economic theory may be considered to have provided (in addition to its analysis of the operation of the market) two basic lessons or conclusions of the utmost importance for any analysis of the nature and scope of economic policy. The first conclusion is that the economy may be functionally defined in terms of the basic economic problems toward the resolution of which all economies function and operate. The basic economic problems, commonly recognized as applicable to all economies regardless of type of system, are, of course, in summary form: resource allocation, income distribution, and aggregate-income determination. The second conclusion which traditional analysis of the market system has yielded is the insight that the economic process is one of making decisions involving the continuing exercise of choice between conflicting alternative possibilities. It is in this context, for example, that the concept of opportunity cost derives it significance.

The Economy as a Decision-Making Process: The conventional [18] view of the market is unquestionably one in which the market functions to allocate resources, distribute income, and determine the magnitude of the level of aggregate income. In this respect it is traditionally conceived as a system or process in which private economic actors participate as demanders and sellers in a multiplicity of subsidiary markets and, whether under competitive or noncompetitive conditions, so interact as to produce effective resolutions of the basic economic problems. If by the scope of policy, then, is at least meant the resolution of the basic economic problems, it is clear that the market system (and by inference any system of economic organization) is a decision-making or policy process. The individual economic actor is thus readily and conventionally seen as operating within the constraining framework of market forces. (In this respect, then, market forces serve as a form of social control—they are, indeed, the distinctive form of social control in the market economy. The control facet of policy is further discussed below.)

Indeed society (by which is meant the aggregate of individuals and their institutional and other relations) may also be conceived of as a decision-making process. It is a decisional process with and through which mankind comes to grip with and resolves in a continuing (and not always and unequivocally in a satisfying) manner what may be called the basic social problems, to wit: the social conditions of biological reproduction (e.g., the institutions of marriage and the family); coping with the elements and forces of the physical environment, or nature; the maintenance of life, with respect to the provsion of food, clothing and shelter; and the maintenance of social life, with respect to the constraints channeling behavior and enabling individuals to coexist with each other. Such a conception of society pervades modern social science. Reference may be made, for example, to social action theory in sociology and thereby to the analysis of the social system, and the economy as a subsystem, by such writers as Parsons and Smelser.[19] The economy thus may be conceived of as part of a larger system, interacting with other subsystems, and thereby participating in the production of social policy in terms of resolutions of the basic social problems enumerated above.[20] Similarly, it is possible to conceive of individual and small-group action as taking place within the framework of society.[21]

The economy *per se* also can be contemplated as a decision-making process functioning to continually resolve the basic economic problems. This is so of all economic systems regardless of how they are organized. The economy may be then almost literally defined, as traditional theory may be held to suggest, in terms of the basic economic problems toward the resolution of which the economy operates. It should be noted, however, that it is not necessary to conceive of the economy (or society) as simply a decision-making process: the economy is more than that—together with the larger society of which it is a part, it is the web of relations within which individuals lead their private lives; and neither economy nor society need be considered *a priori* as perfect and/or smooth decisional processes—for they need not be and evidently are not. But the economy is a process of coming to grips with the distinctly basic economic problems, and in that respect is a decision-making or policy process.

That such is the case is widely acknowledged, though it is not universally explicit that particular policy considerations derive their ultimate significance and meaning in a context of the economy and its various subprocesses as decision-making processes. It is thus the authors' suggestion that recent and contemporary developments in such fields as are generally described (with no small amount of overlap) as decision theory, organization theory, administrative science, management science, bargaining theory, systems analysis, behavioral political science, and policy science—all, in the context of this paper, inquire into and elucidate various aspects and segments of the economy and economic institutions in such a manner that the latter are ultimately reduced to decision-making processes.[22]

It may be also pointed out that the conception of the economy as a decision- or policy-making process is not only the crux by which traditional economic theory can be placed in perspective with respect to policy, but it is also suggestive of the

244

extent to which there has long been an existential element
in economic analysis. This is because emphasis on decision
making is a basic thrust of the existentialist view of the human
situation; for economic science to have emphasized the importance of making decisions concerning the basic economic problems is the equivalent of having emphasized the decision- or
policy-making facet of economy in an essentially existential
way, because it is *man* upon whom rests the burden of resolving the basic economic problems through his economic
decision-making process.

The author has suggested, then, that economic policy involves the conception of the economy as a decision-making or
policy-process functioning toward the continuing resolution of
the basic economic problems. The economy is a policy process,
and policy is at least coextensive in scope with the resolution
of the basic economic problems. But—and this is a major
theme of this paper—the economy considered as the market
(or the plan in a differently organized system) is not the
entirety of the economic decision-making process. If the scope
of economic policy is defined at least in terms of the resolution of the basic economic problems, it is necessary that the
scope of the economic policy process be understood to include
all of the participating forces involved in the resolution of
those problems.

The economic decision-making process is more than the
market. Yet, if policy making means participation in the process resolving the basic economic problems, then the conventional market-plus-framework approach to economic policy
has been deficient. First, while it has been the genius of that
approach to specify the operation of the institutional framework within which market activity takes place, it has obscured
the policy character of the operation of the market. Moreover,
the frequent taking for granted of the framework obscures

245

the dynamic interaction between market and framework (to continue the dichotomy) which interaction is an important part of the policy process.

In the paragraphs to follow, the author will not further criticize the market-plus-framework dichotomy as such. Rather he will attempt to examine the operation of framework institutions as vital parts of the policy process. It is the intent of the author to establish that the economy is a decision-making process involving private (or market), legal, and nonlegal participation, and thereby to elaborate further upon the scope of economic policy. The author thus would suggest that the proper scope of economic policy requires consideration of (a) the economy as a decisional process functioning to continually resolve the basic economic problems and (b) all of the participants in that decisional process.

The market-plus-framework approach to the theory of economic policy has indeed been the predominant conceptual schema which the profession has brought to policy problems. It has been, moreover, the approach of orthodoxy and heterodoxy alike; each has included both economic theory and theory of economic policy within the scope of what used to be called political economy. This is true of Henry Carter Adams, John R. Commons, and Edwin E. Witte; and is no less true of Thomas Nixon Carver, Frank H. Knight, and Friedrich A. Hayek.[23] While Commons' *Legal Foundations of Capitalism* (among his other works) is perhaps the classic study evidencing the market-plus-framework orientation and is indeed a masterful analysis of the operation of the framework, it is a classic in a crowded field. The writings of John M. Clark [24] and Robert L. Hale,[25] for example, manifest the approach and constitute analyses of the participation of framework institutions and forces in what ultimately reduces to the economic decision-making process. So also do such works as Boulding's *Principles of Economic Policy* [26] and Watson's

Economic Policy.[27] Spengler's essay on "The Problem of Order in Economic Affairs" [28] also develops the approach. As Robbins has shown, the approach is highly useful in interpreting the theory of economic policy of the English classical political economists.[29] Moreover, it is clear that the market-plus-framework approach is the view of Robbins himself.[30] Use, then, of the market-plus-framework schema in fact pervades the literature on economic policy.[31] (It has eclipsed, it may be noted in passing, the unsophisticated laissez-faire or laissez-faire-with-exceptions approach, which was more propaganda than analysis.)

In the view of some of those who have analyzed its functioning, the framework is composed of the institutions which "organize economic activity," [32] that is to say, of the "institutional constraints" [33] which enhance, implement, and control individual initiative and decision,[34] thus "patterning economic behavior." [35] It is within "the moral and legal framework in which economic life is lived," [36] and this framework of institutions operates, among other things, to "define the given conditions of market behavior, and also perform many essential functions. . . ." [37] In this respect, "society is a thing of institutions far more than of men." [38] Thus it is that the "general laws of economics" "work in an institutional setting, and upon institutional material; institutions supply much of their content and furnish the machinery by which they work themselves out, more or less quickly and completely, in different actual situations." [39]

The institutional framework, commonly juxtaposed to the market decisional process and even more commonly ignored, thus must be considered as part of the total decision-making process through which the basic economic problems are resolved. Given a decisional process comprised of private participation and framework institutions (without further disaggregating the latter), the practical resolution of the basic economic problems is, *pro tanto*, a function of those institutions. Both free market activity and the operaton of the framework are, truly, "two aspects of one and the same social process." [40] Resource allocation and income distribution are, again *pro tanto*, a function of the differential constraints and implementations provided by the institutional framework. This function of the framework, in terms ultimately reduceable to the operation of the legal system as part of the decision-making process, has been a major theme is the writings of Hale; [41] yet the concept of non-market decision making through the institutional framework is pervasive, as earlier references will allow. [42] As Knight has pointed out, any system of economic organization is characterized by "its manner of dealing with wants as they exist" and "its mechanism for comparing and equating and perhaps selecting among the various wants of the various persons and classes of persons which make up the society," such that "very different social value scales may be formed from the same set of individual wants by different methods of selection, equation, and combination." [43] It is precisely the institutional patterns (or differences between such patterns) operating as methods of selection which account for the forming of different social welfare functions or value scales. Income distribution is thus "a consequence of social institutions and law"; [44] the ability to earn income is "not solely the [result] of antecedent market processes," [45] it is a function of the law of property and other sociolegal institutions. C. E. Ayres thus has gone so far as to argue, with respect to "the conception of the market as the guiding mechanism of the economy or, more broadly, the conception of the economy as organized and guided by the market," that,

> It simply is not true that scarce resources are allocated among alternative uses by the market. The real determinant of whatever allocation occurs in any society is the organiza-

tional structure of that society—in short, its institutions. At most, the market only gives effect to prevailing institutions.[46]

The legal system (the state or government) is unquestionably part of the institutional framework as envisioned by the foregoing discussion. It was the genius, for example, of Commons to have developed the thesis that the foundations of capitalism are in fact at least partially legal in character and that polity and economy are inseparable—themes maintained by institutionalists in general. Yet Knight also points out that "the main function of government in the modern world is to provide and enforce a framework of rules for securing freedom, and the conditions necessary for effective freedom, in economic life." [47] The legal system thus operates as part of the total decision-making process and provides, or participates in the provision of, many of the institutional arrangements generally considered as constituting the fabric of the framework within which private market activity is undertaken. Moreover, the legal system is not simply part of the total economic decisional process but may itself be analyzed as a decision-making process. As such, government operates both as initiator of policies and as ratifier of effective decisions wrought elsewhere. That the law, including the system of the common law, is a process of making decisions, and in that capacity functions within the larger decisional system, has been stressed by the Sociological Jurisprudence of Pound and Stone; [48] by the Legal Realism of Holmes, Felix Cohen, and H. W. Jones, among others; [49] and by the behavioral political science and legal policy analysis of Lasswell and McDougal.[50] Moreover, not only is it widely stressed, of course, that politics is a vital part of the legal policy process,[51] but even the political process has been subjected to essentially traditional economic analysis [52] —and in such a way as not to obscure but rather to underscore its pervasive operation as a decision-making process.

But the institutional framework, as part of the total decision-making process, encompasses more than the legal system. The framework must be understood as also including the nonlegal institutions of (for instance) morals, religion, custom, and education. As the author has shown in the case of the classical economists, these nonlegal (the lawyer would refer to them as extralegal) institutions and processes are important parts of the decisional system whether seen as part of the framework or not.[53] With the legal system, the nonlegal institutions both inhibit and facilitate behavior as well as exert influence on the specific content of the nominal market resolution of the basic economic problems. Like their legal counterparts, the nonlegal forces function in a manner illustrative of Commons' definition of an institution, to wit: "collective action in control, liberation, and expansion of individual action,"[54] and in this and other respects participate in the economic decisional process.

The operation of the nonlegal facet of the framework part of the decision-making process is widely elaborated upon in the sociological and anthropological literature, especially perhaps with regard to custom and morality. It is, for example, evident in studies of the customary character of business behavior, viz, channeled by business convention and occupational morality.[55] Moreover, it was acknowledged by Commons, among other writers such as Knight, as correlative to the legal system. Finally, it is important to note that such writers as Morgenstern and Buchanan[56] have emphasized that welfare-economics considerations of Pareto optimality take place within the constraints of what the former calls the moral standard. That is to say, considerations of economic welfare are themselves predicated upon criteria embodied in the nonlegal (and legal, of course) framework. As Adam Smith put it, "The great secret of education is to direct vanity to proper objects."[57]

Appendix

The appropriate scope of economic policy must be the resolution of the basic economic problems through the economic decision-making process as a whole, and the appropriate scope of recognized policy-participation accordingly must be inclusive of nominally private participation and both legal and nonlegal institutions. Private market decision-making participation must be united with both types of institutionalized decision-making participation (abstracting, of course, from the fact that the market is an institution), at least with respect to analysis properly understood as a theory of economic policy.

Proceeding a step further, it should be clear that economic decision making is a mixture of both deliberative and non-deliberative elements. In no small (and perhaps an increasing) area of decision making, "policy" is conscious and deliberative (i.e., "rational"), and policy in that connection may be accordingly defined. Yet in other areas an Hayekian collective wisdom inhering, as it were, in received institutions pervades the decisional process.[58] Many "choices are instinctive, habitual, unconscious";[59] "much behavior and conduct is not freely chosen, but socially conditioned."[60] The economy, no less than society as a whole, is not a simple, "coherent unity, deliberately moving toward goals self-consciously perceived." Its shaping forces are "rarely the products of deliberate decisions."[61] It is widely recognized, thus, that the nonlegal institutions are largely nondeliberative in character; and it is also recognized that the legal system has nondeliberative characteristics. Moreover, both types of institutions manifest the principles of ignorance and indirection: the practice of delusion and pretense is not characteristic of religion alone.[62] These principles pervade the decisional process, noncognitively except in regard to manifest function.

If the economic policy process be understood as the making of decisions on the basis of knowledge and values, there are, then, several types of decision-making rationality and thus

251

several modes of bringing knowledge and values to bear on decision making. Diesing, for example, has identified five types of decision-making rationality in society: the technical, economic, social, legal, and political. Society as a decision-making process is constituted by these types of rationality.[63] This is, however, but one of many relevant studies, both analytical and exhortative, of the types of reason in society.[64] Suffice it to say here that the scope of economic policy must include all sub-processes of decision making, including all those through which man translates knowledge and values into effective decisions. Yet this is only the equivalent to suggesting that the concept "theory of economic policy" include all participants in the economic decision-making process, both market and nonmarket and both deliberative and nondeliberative.

With respect to the economic decision-making process as a whole, composed of the three general components of nominally private, legal and nonlegal participants, there are two major characteristics that may be briefly acknowledged at this point. The first is that the framework is a function of the market just as the market is a function of the framework.[65] Put differently, the decisional process encompasses three major forces *interacting* upon each other such that each is both determined and determining with respect to the others. This of course is a derivative of the underlying pluralism. The second is that the decision-making process is one of *conflict*: the great causes and episodes in the history of economic policy have been predominantly confrontations between these three participants or, more commonly, certain of their subgroups. The conflict between market and government determination,[66] or between legal and nonlegal social control,[67] are general types of cases in point. The resolution of the basic economic problems is a continuing product, then, of the interaction between conflicting participants which conflict is continually resolved, one way or another, through that interaction. This discussion, however, raises both the question of the character of policy as it is made in such process and the problem of structuring the decisional process itself. The former is discussed in the next subsection; and the latter, in the following major section.

The Choice Nature of Policy: The author has suggested that economic policy is meaningful in a context in which the economy is viewed as a multiparticipant decision-making process continually involved with the resolution of the basic economic problems. It is suggested, to this point, that policy is ultimately such resolution of the basic economic problems and that the scope of policy participation must be seen as all the participants in the decisional process.

Given this context of meaningfulness of economic policy, the inference is inescapable that one basic characteristic of policy is *choice*. The economy, operating as a decision-making process, is vitally involved in the making of choices between alternative patterns of resolution of the basic economic problems. Indeed, the choice character of policy is widely acknowledged in the literature.[68] According to von Mises, for example, economic science and perforce economic policy are central parts of a general science of human action, or praxeology, and this general science is fundamentally a science of choice.[69] It is a science derived from the proposition that "man chooses between alternative modes of conduct." [70] Policy is ultimately, then, choice between alternatives: "Decisions are decisions between alternatives," and "Decision-making . . . is always choosing between alternative courses of action." [71] As Lord Robbins expressed it, "behaviour necessarily assumes the form of choice." [72]

In a work on metaphysics, Douglas Browning has developed the theme that man is not only a sentient but a choosing being. Men's acts are ultimately acts of choice. Assessment and valuation (i.e., approbation or disapprobation) are not of behavior but of the choice effectively underlying behavior, for it is choice itself which is the moral act.[73] Although Browning excludes the nondeliberative components of the choosing (or decision-making) process,[74] his analysis is highly suggestive and elaborative of the existential character of choice which pervades the decisional process. The human situation is manifestly one of policy, by which is meant choice; in Browning's view, man acts and thereby chooses and functions as an agent of choice.[75]

The choice character of policy is so fundamental that positivist policy analysis must proceed upon the understanding of the inevitability and ubiquity of choice. This organizing conception is an important facet of the approach to policy developed in this paper. It does not, however, challenge (in terms of value-status) those who would obscure the choice character of the economy in order to preclude revision of past choices (i.e., change); rather it attempts to interpret and understand such advocacy as part of the game of policy, i.e., serving to promote continuity. The inevitability and pervasiveness of policy, and therefore of choice, is fundamental to policy analysis, both when it is not explicit and when it is denied. It was, for example, a constitution that the Supreme Court was making even when its members denied that they were in fact making it.[76] The making of decisions involving the exercise of choice or discretion between alternative courses of action is a "ubiquitous aspect of human life." [77] "choice and decision are inevitable in the life of the law," [78] but not only the law; choice is inescapable throughout all of life including economy and is perforce a fundamental characteristic or dimension of economic policy.[79] There is a place for obscurantism and obfuscation but the analysis of the theory of economic policy, if it is to avoid sterility, must put that place in functional perspective.[80]

254

It should be made clear, to proceed, that although particular choices on the micro-economic level (as, for example, with respect to the choices underlying utility functions and the operation of the equimarginal principle—and the consumption function on the macro-economic level)are an important facet of the total decision-making process (as are votes of Congressional subcommittees, or court decisions), the concept of choice in the context of this paper is on a different and more abstract level. The author would have it understood that by choice is meant *effective* choice, namely, the ultimate choices between alternative resolutions of the basic economic problems to which a particular individual's choices are but incrementally contributory.[81] Individual decisions are thus to be differentiated from the effective social choices and decisions emerging from the interplay of individual choices. The operation of the total economic decision process produces such effective decisions and is perforce the most encompassing form of what Commons called collective action.

What this means, of course, is that "the price system is a mechanism for social decisions, not individual decisions"; [82] it is rather "a machinery for making social choices from individual tastes"; [83] and it is in this context that Schumpeter's proposition that prices are coefficients of economic choice has meaning.[84] Prices are not the important thing, for they are means; what is important rather are the resolutions of the basic economic problems, and it is—in this context—the market (through relative prices) which is "the institutional mechanism for directing production and distribution in accord with individual wants." [85] "In the apportioning and proportioning decisions of a modern economy the ordinary individual plays a quite limited and indirect role. To a much greater extent, they are made by enterprises (individual entrepreneurs or firms), but in the main they result from the interaction of choices in a complicated network of markets." [86] The market is part of the total decisional process and is characteristic of the larger process as a collective or collaborative and choosing phenomenon,[87] "a process of reaching collective decisions." [88]

But this is characteristic not only of the market but of the entire decision-making process. Both deliberative and non-deliberative decision-making contribute to the resolution of the basic economic problems, and decisions with respect to the latter are effective whatever the mode of choice. Many of the particular decisions are a matter of deliberate choice, but others are impulsive and still others are habitual and non-cognitive. As Benham wrote:

> Nevertheless all such acts of choosing, whether deliberate or impulsive or the result of habit, can be treated as "decisions", for we are trying to explain how the economic system works and are therefore interested in the results of these acts of choosing, and the results are the same however much or little deliberation took place before they were made.[89]

Most important, this is no less valid on the aggregate or social level than on the individual. As Sir Frederick Pollock in effect suggested, policy is policy even if no one is conscious of it or of the choices made:

> If . . . all the Utopians [i.e., members of a utopian community] did agree, they would live under a custom that would be no less their rule of life because a blessed unanimity would make it needless for them so much as to think of enforcing it.[90]

Or, the author would add, to think of having adopted it as policy. Just as "policy" tends to be anathema to the opponent of change, so also is it unknown to and unsensed by those who live blissfully under a custom all the more ubiquitous as policy because it is unanimously adhered to or at least—thanks to the operation of the forces of discipline in society—unquestioned.

256

The concept of "intermediates" is thus applicable to the operation of the entire decision-making process and not just the primarily nondeliberative modes of decision—of which it is, of course, vitally characteristic. The basic economic problems are resolved largely through individual and subgroup decision making, which decisions are incrementally contributory to the emergent effective decision. The total decisional process is pervaded with attention directed to immediate aims, issues, problems, techniques, arguments, and the like—all of which contribute to the ultimate effective policy choices though such latter are no part (or at most a small part) of the original intention or field of interest of the micro-level decision maker. (This is a function, of course, of both knowledge and concentration of power.) Thus, attention to intermediate principles [91] (as in the case of principles of the common law and constitutional law) is instrumental to the making of effective decisions and suggestive of the extent of the practice of ignorance and indirection.

A brief word should be directed to the existence of constraints upon choice and their meaningfulness in the context of this discussion. There can be no question that there are constraints upon choice pervading the entire decision-making process, applicable both to segments of that process and to the process as a whole. The author would make the following comments, however, emphasizing that the subject calls for more systematic analysis than is possible here. (1) Such limitations as are imposed by technology are of major significance. Yet it is the long-run effect of man's efforts to escape from, for example, diminishing returns, thus circumscribing such constraint. This is the conventional view. (2) There are also many types of institutional limitations. As Harry G. Johnson has pointed out, "Policy is not made in a vacuum, but is worked out in a social and political environment which imposes definite limitations on both the aims and means of policy." [92] Care, however, must be taken to avoid the fallacy of composition; short-term limitations found in a part of the decisional process may or may not apply to the process as a whole and thus may or may not be subject to long term alteration or elimination (through, for example, restructuring the decision-making process). This will be discussed further below. There are, in other words, levels on which constraints have meaning: from within, a limitation seems inescapable; yet from without the limitation is observed as quite functional and artificial as well as transitory. (3) One traditionally recognized limitation is lack of knowledge—but this is also subject to the fallacy of composition; the market and indeed the decision-making process as a whole are processes of marshaling knowledge both of reality and of values. "Fragmentation would seem to substitute politics for brains in problems of co-ordination that run beyond human intellectual capacity." [93] (4) There is also the widely acknowledged tendency to accept a determinism consequent to an identification of what is customary as natural. As Commons pointed out, what people have tended to mistake "for the order of nature or divine providence was merely the common law silently growing up around them in the decisions of judges who were quietly selecting and standardizing the good customs of the neighborhood and rejecting the bad practices that did not conform to the accepted rules of reason. Legislatures and monarchs are dramatic, arbitrary and artificial; courts are commonplace and natural." [94] (Perhaps nowhere is this phenomenon more important than in the development of the Law Merchant.) (5) However, it is important to recognize that institutional constraints are in fact manifestations of social control (with no presumption, of course, of consensus, either original or produced) and the identification as natural of what is relatively transient in comparison is part of the legitimation of the *status quo* and the indirect securing of continuity as opposed to change. (6) It should be acknowledged not only that constraints are generally relative to the level on which they are considered (and of course to time and place)—and this essay is on a rather abstract level—but also that choice is often if not generally over the efficient causes manipulating ultimate causal sequences. (7) These comments notwithstanding, the existence of constraints upon choice *is* significant, but, and this is a major point, the existence of such constraints (and on whatever level analyzed) does not negate the choice character of policy. To the contrary, it may be noted that one of the inherent thrusts of decision makers is to extricate themselves from the limitations imposed by accumulated constraints.

III

In the preceding section the author has suggested that the proper context of meaningfulness of economic policy is one in which the economy is seen as a mode of making social decisions, i.e., of translating the desired choices of participating forces—noble and ignoble—into social choices; and that, as consequences, the proper scope of economic policy includes the resolution of the basic economic problems, and the proper scope of policy participation extends to include all the forces participating in the decisional process. These forces are more than market forces; and "policy" is more extensive than government policy. The economy is a policy process.

In such a context, however, the basic economic problems as conventionally understood are *not* the most fundamental problems of economic policy. The resolution of the basic economic problems are a function of the policy process and the ultimate problem of economic policy is the *structuring of the decision-making process itself*. This means that the perennial task of economic policy is not merely to resolve the basic economic problems but also to structure the decision-making process; this is the *structural* problem of policy. The scope of economic policy thus must be considered to include the exercise of effective choice governing the structure of the economic decision-making process.[95]

The transcendental problem of policy, then, is the distribution of *power*, by which the author intends to connote the distribution of participation in the economic decision-making process. As Knight took pains to point out, "The central issue of economic policy *is* the distribution of power between individuals (families and other actual units or organizations) and between them and the 'community', ultimately the sovereign state." [96] Thus C. A. Auerbach writes that, "The problem of ordering social life may be viewed as the problem of allocating the making of decisions concerning the conduct of individual and group life between 'private' agencies (the individual himself, family, church, other voluntary associations, etc.) and 'public-legal' agencies (the law making institutions)." [97] This view, as Auerbach acknowledges, reflects that of J. W. Hurst, to wit: "By balance of power, I mean the allocation of decision making in the society: who has The Say." [98] The same concept, to the effect of the importance of the distribution of power, i.e., the structure of the decisional process, is manifest throughout the work of Commons, who wrote, for example, of the problem of "the proper proportioning of relative degrees of power" and the proportioning of the "behavior of citizens." [99] Compare further the views of Harrod and Hawtrey. According to Harrod, "The distribution of income," and presumably the other basic economic problems, "is intimately connected with the balance of social and political forces," but, he goes on to say, "the study of which is outside the economist's province." [100] It is hard to see, however, how a theory of economic policy can dispense with such considerations, however necessary and/or appropriate it may be for economic theory. Hawtrey, on the other hand, argued that economic science "has not taken sufficient account of *power* as a continuing and dominating object of economic policy." [101]

Two examples should suffice to suggest the scope of import of the basic concept, though the matter is developed throughout the works of such writers as Commons, Hale, and Knight. The first is that of R. M. Lemos, who acknowledges that "the ultimate actual source of the constitution of a state, and thus of the possession of sovereignty and of the law of the state, is the distribution of power among the various groups in the state." [102] The second is that of E. W. Kemmerer:

> It is difficult to tell just where to draw the line in apportioning power between the banking community on one hand and the public at large on the other. Any plan which is to be enacted into law will require the support of the public at large and also of the banking interests. It is a case of steering a safe course between Scylla and Charybdis.[103]

The problem thus being that of the distribution of power or participation in the decisional process, the author would have it recognized that such problem is not simply one of the distribution of power between "private" and "public" spheres, though that is of course a part. The problem is one of the division of power within and between *all* participating forces in the decisional process, which forces are only artificially categorized or classified in private/public, market/framework, or market/nonmarket dichotomies. Thus the structure of the market is itself part of the problem of the distribution of "private" power. Structuring is a continuing process, resulting (at least in part) from the interaction of all participants, such that structure is related to process, and the outcomes in terms of basic-economic-problem resolutions contribute to an enhanced or weakened relative position of participants as they continue to interact. (For example, relative power influences or governs constitution making, and the latter in turn influences or governs the relative distribution of power in the future.)

The problem of structuring the economic decision-making process may be interpreted not only as the problem of the distribution of power in society but also as that of how the economy is to be "organized and controlled." (Commons' works, for example, manifest both specifications of the general problem, which are largely perfect substitutes.) This was apparently the continuing view of Sumner Slichter, who focused many of his basic discussions of economic policy on this thematic concept; [104] and also of J. M. Clark, whose seminal *Social Control of Business* was a brilliant exposition of the theme of organization and control.[105] This view is also manifest, for example, throughout Dahl and Lindblom's *Politics, Economics and Welfare*; [106] Knight's "Social Economic Organization;" [107] and in the treatment of the economic management function by Chamberlain [108] and Copeland.[109]

It should be apparent that the fundamental structural problem of economic policy is *the* problem, as it were, of the field of comparative economic systems. This field is, after all, the study of alternative modes of organizing and controlling economic activity (as well as of the implementations thereof)— i.e., of alternative decision-making systems, such that the several variants of plan and market, including the mixed economy itself, appear as so many decision-coordinating processes. (See for example, the recent changes in Soviet organization and control of the planning process.) [110] Such fundamental concern is reflected in many of the basic works in the field.[111]

For this reason, the author has elsewhere suggested that the comparativist has much to contribute to economic-policy analysis.[112]

The problem is also recognized in the field of economic development. Its importance is increasingly urged through recognition of the necessity to organize the decisional system in such a way as to facilitate industrialization. The parallel emphasis upon the necessity of some group in society with an interest in and the power to seek economic development is also equivalent to emphasis upon a proper structuring of the decision-making process.[113] The structural problem must be central to any theory of economic development policy.

Economic policy with respect to structuring the economic decision-making process is important not only because it gives rise to the social economic system characterizing any particular regime, but also because specific details of the resolution of the basic economic problems are derived from the decisional structure. In the view of the participants in the economic policy process, structure is important largely because particular decisions are (*pro tanto*) derived therefrom; different decisional structures produce different decisions, and changes in structure (as well as in tastes, values, *et cetera*) produce changed decisions—with impact on social status and the like. Given the earlier discussion of the differential decisions contingent upon differences in framework institutions, attention may be focused at this point on recognition of the general principle. As Walton H. Hamilton expressed it, the principle is that

> Economic organization . . . comprehends all the usages and arrangements, formal and informal, consciously contrived or adventitious, which present so much of an institutional answer as we have to such questions as what is to be produced, who is to share in the productive process, how the resulting goods are

263

to be consumed, where power and discretion in industrial matters are to lie and how fully and to what good ends the human and material resources of society are to be employed.[114]

As Knight already has been seen to urge, different *methods* of selection, equation, and combination—which here must be taken to mean different decisional structures—form "very different social value scales . . . from the same set of individual wants. . . ." Moreover, "the form of organization also goes far to determine what is to be wanted, and to mould the attitudes of persons toward their work and toward each other." [115] "It is," as Kirschen puts it, "the structural context which determines the primary selection between the preferences of the different policy makers according to their respective weights." [116] The principle is derived from and expressed in a variety of contexts. In one, it is concluded that "the size and completeness of the compensations for both costs inflicted and gains bestowed depend upon bargaining strengths and circumstances. . . ." (The writer also recognizes, therefore, "that many questionable policies or choices are inherent in the institutional framework. . . .") [117] In another, it is written that "decisions about the forms of government have an impact on which policies get adopted and whose values are represented." [118] No wonder that debate over voting rights and reapportionment is so emotional: the issues are strategic in structuring the decisional process and in governing the outcome of the political process. Decisions, then, are a function of structure, and they are thereby a function of power play and therefore of interacting strategies, both in the context of society and social policy as a whole and in the market (or "business") as a subsidiary thereof.

Emphasis must be placed on the proposition that the scope of economic policy extends to the structuring of the decision-making process itself. This is part of the burden, as it were, of existential man, though, as developed above, such structuring is generally approached only indirectly and incrementally. That such structuring is subject to (or may be usefully treated as if subject to) the exercise of choice is widely developed in the literature.[119] The ultimate createdness or artifact character is acknowledged and/or stressed by many writers.

> But a mark of the progress . . . has been the emergence of the concept of good or bad political economy out of mythical entities such as nature's harmony, natural law, natural order, natural rights, divine providence, oversoul, invisible hand, social will, social-labor power, social value, tendency towards equilibrium of forces, and the like, into its proper place as the good or bad, right or wrong, wise or unwise proportioning by man himself of those human faculties and natural resources which are limited in supply and complementary to each other.[120]   —John R. Commons

> Culture exists or operates in human beings, who, by their patterned conduct and way of life, create whatever social order there is.
> Social order arises, therefore, not from some mysterious cosmic mechanism but from the patterning of human behavior into the conduct approved by the group traditions.[121]
>   —Lawrence K. Frank

> What determines the choice of an economic system? As in the case of all things subject to choice, it is in the first place a matter of taste and temperament.[122]   —Leopold Kohr

> Neither God nor a mystical "Natural Force" created society; it was created by mankind.[123]   —Ludwig von Mises

> Systems of government, property relationships, and the like, can be conceived as the result of choice.[124]   —Lionel Robbins

The view here adopted . . . treats social institutions as a product of social choice based on social knowledge of patterns between which choice is made, and has meaning only in so far as such social choice may be real.[125]   —Frank Knight

The future itself is a product created by the will of man meeting the issues of his day. The economy, consequently, is what men in science, technology, business and government make it.[126]   —Walter A. Morton

Thus the institutions comprising the structure are portrayed by Loucks as being "created, destroyed, replaced, molded and remolded, time without end, by people acting as legislators, workers, consumers, citizens, investors, judges, enterprisers, government administrators, and so on." [127]

Finally, it need be noted that structural policy involves *principles* of structuring, i.e., organizing principles governing the organization and control which is the structuring of the decision-making process. This is the ultimate significance of treating private property, competition, contract, and the price system itself as principles; and the same is true of monetary and banking standards, such as the gold or gold-exchange standards. With respect to private property, for example, its organizing function is clearly evident in such statements as:

It should be understood that our property system is really an essential part if not the major part of the modern political constitution, in its aspect of economic control. It is one method of selecting, motivating, and remunerating the functionaries who actually direct a social-economic organization, and is to be compared with other types of machinery for effecting the same result.[128]

Private property is more than claims to the income from assets; it is also a system of rules concerning the use of the assets. And on these rules is built a system of cues and incentives ... [and] the coordinating function of private property.[129]

Whatever the verbal obfuscations that special pleaders may on occasion employ, one ... comes back finally, therefore, to the central problem of property as the problem of how the people of a community can best use their resources for the fullest achievement of their values.[130]

The basic problem of property law in general is nothing more or less than determining the relation of individual to community with regard to use and exploitation of resources. . . .[131]

Property regulations, in defining the relation between persons and scarce values, necessarily also define social relations.[132]

Similarly, contract has been considered as "a principle of order"; [133] and competition not only as a principle by which to structure (or hope to structure) the market sector but also as a mode and principle of order and social peace.[134] Clearly, the scope of economic policy includes the choice of such principles, as well as the intermediate principles referred to above.

IV

The major thrust of the preceding section has been to suggest that the proper meaning of the scope of economic policy includes not only the resolution of the conventional basic economic problems but also, and more fundamentally, the resolution of the structuring problem. Policy is comprised of the total resolution of all these problems. In the remainder of this paper the analysis will be developed, however, largely in terms of the transcendental problem of structuring the decision-making process. The analysis nonetheless also applies, *mutatis mutandis*, to the basic economic problems since their resolution (through the interaction of all participants) is properly within the scope of policy.

The structuring problem is one of control, and control is perforce a fundamental dimension of policy and exhibits a status heightened by recognition that the resolution of the basic economic problems is contingent upon the exercise of power or control. Yet, in another context it is only that part of the total resolution of the structuring problem that comes into dispute and is critical at any time which is obtrusively a matter of policy. This is to say that in addition to the *choice* and *control* characteristics of policy there is a third—namely, *change*. The great issues of policy (directly or indirectly reflected in the immediate issues with which discussion is preoccupied) involve control over the choice of change (or, if one prefers, effective choice over the control of change), which ultimately reduces to the *restructuring* of the decision-making process.

But *change* has as its correlative *continuity*, and to say that change is a characteristic of policy is really to say that the balancing or discriminating between continuity and change is a characteristic of policy. Policy is both continuity and change, both structure and restructuring. It is policy to continue the *status quo* power structure just as it is to change it. Both continuity and change are *desiderata*, albeit each in its own way and differently to different people and at different times. Both may be and must be balanced, the result at any time having been worked out through the interaction of all the forces and strategies in the decisional process: ultimately, power play. Most if not all intermediate issues and arguments function (latently and/or manifestly) to promote either continuity or change or what reduces to some compromise. Moreover, what was initially a mode of securing one may turn into a force for the other. Finally, it is important to note that policy is as much a response to change as the initiation thereof, though, of course, the precise import of this will vary with the level of analysis.

That policy involves the exercise of choice between continuity and change—not as mutually exclusive categories but as subject to incremental adjustments along narrower or wider margins—is widely acknowledged in the relevant literature and in a variety of contexts. In *Freedom and Reform*, Knight writes of "the social problem as such, i.e., the problem of law making, which always means law changing, and in general means *legally* changing an existing law." [135] Friedrich writes of policy making as "shaping social change"; [136] and Lasswell's activist policy approach is epitomized, as it were, "man is taking evolution in his own hands." [137] In altogether different contexts, Boulding, Tinbergen, and Vining consider policy as comprised of change or variation of means or variables under control. Although these latter, at least, explicitly write only in terms of *deliberate* change, it is instructive that change is considered a definitional basis of policy. Witness Boulding: " 'Policy' is the deliberate distortion of the ecosystem in favor of the objectives of the policymaker," and "It is these volitional changes of ideal states that best deserve the name of 'policy.' " [138] Similarly, Grampp and Weiler reach the same conclusion as to the change character of policy: "The manner in which the rules change, as well as the substance of the change, is a part of economic policy." [139] (Change in the working rules is discussed below.)

But the change or continuity that is fundamental relates to the *status quo* power structure. Pervading all particular and immediate policy issues is the jockeying for position that reduces to challenge to and defense of the existing distribution of power in whole or in part. Restructuring—i.e., changing—the decision-making process is the highest and most subtle level of policy, and is generally achieved incrementally and indirectly, though sophisticated participants treat the matter on the level of manifest function.[140] The problem of restructuring may be contemplated in highly abstract and aggregate terms—power play between participants in the total decisional process; in terms of market structure *per se*; in terms of changing the "framework"; or in terms of particular power struggles—between particular protagonists, between classes, or between institutions (church versus state, private sector versus public sector, labor versus management). But the ultimate issue is always that of changing the distribution of power and thus restructuring the decision-making process.

It is probable, however, that the restructuring problem is most frequently and directly raised in terms of changing the framework—a view quite appropriate when it is considered that much change comes through the institutions which appear as the framework within which individual or private activity is undertaken. (Some of such change is ratification of the results of nominally private power play, and other change the result of private forces endeavoring to capture framework forces, e.g., the state, to effectuate their own ends.) To Commons, since structuring the decisional process appeared as "proportioning" participation, restructuring was "the reproportioning of inducements, opportunities, and disabilities." [141] Institutionalists in general have recognized that "economic systems are only bundles of institutions, and like institutions, subject to change." [142] As Edwin Witte put it, "Institutions cannot be taken for granted, as they are man-made and changeable." [143] This is particularly so, because "the masses [have] desired changes, not merely in surface phenomena, but in the very foundations of the social order" [144]—a phenomenon which has been a concomitant of capitalism, though it is still equivocal as to whether (and if so, how) the system has fundamentally changed. Similarly, from another point of view but to the same end, Knight has been seen to comprehend the social problem as one of law making, which he correctly holds to mean "law changing." In Knight's view, "The social problem is a matter, first, of attitude toward the law or the rules of the social game as they stand at any place and time, and second, of attitude toward higher general cultural and human values as a basis for changing such an existing set-up. It is the second which is the social problem in the strict sense." [145] (The former has to do with continuity; and the latter, with change.) A "basic problem," then, to Knight, is "determining or 'molding' the society of the future and its 'culture.' In this . . . field lie the crucial value problems of our society and civilization, primarily those of social relations and institutions." [146] It is Knight's view, of course, that "the essence of the crisis of modern civilization is evidently the loss in the public mind of faith in the fundamental equity of the values and terms of relationship established in the open market." [147] But Knight also recognizes both that "the social economic problem is to create an institutional and moral order in which those characteristics of the economic individual—actually for the most part the family—which are necessarily taken as given conditions by the economic analyst, will be what they 'ought' to be," and that "economic analysis . . . makes it only too clear that no such result is to be expected through the exclusive play of market transactions, even if social action and moral sentiment were to succeed in enforcing the 'ideal conditions' of economic theory in the most extreme interpretation." [148] Restructuring what has been called here the decision-making process *is* thus the crucial problem (though of course not the only one: the substance of what structural change is to effectuate is also important, reducing ultimately to changed resolutions of the basic economic problems). In this context, as Bonn pointed out, "Economic policy is largely directed toward the creation or destruction of institutions. . . . The totality of such efforts might be called institutional policy. . . . It is the most important branch of economic policy whenever the final stage of transition from one social system to another . . . is necessary." [149] (But to Bonn, economic policy is only government policy; and certainly his "institutional policy" is no less basic when the changes are less extensive than the final transition between social systems.) *Structural policy* (i.e., policy involving change in framework organization) thus involves what Buchanan calls "constructive institutionalism," [150] which is to say, a change in the allocation of resources through a change in the transmutation mechanisms inherent in the *status quo* framework. As Morgenstern has pointed out, "Thus it is not enough only to study variations in the quantities of goods and services in order to determine where the Pareto optimum lies. There may also be possible and profitable variations in their 'allocations' which are non-permissible under the existing moral code." [151] It should be clear, however, that whether or not expressed in terms of changing the framework, the restructuring problem always involves the conflict of continuity and change (of the decisional structure), and the proper scope of policy always extends to include whatever total resolution of that problem is made on a continuing basis.

The problem (or should it be the possibility?) of restructuring the decisional process gives rise to a variety of conflicts not the least of which is that between the deliberative and nondeliberative forces of social control. Accordingly it is possible to define freedom in terms of gradual change or change effectuated only through the nondeliberative forces, a position generally maintained by Leoni as well as Knight; [152] but it is also possible "to regard the state as an instrument for creating freedom, and the restrictions which it imposes . . . as means to that end." [153] Needless to reiterate, the author is here not concerned with the truth value (or value status, or propaganda value) of these views but with their instrumental functioning to sanction or disengage, for example, state activity, i.e., to promote continuity or change. Moreover, two points are of the utmost significance. First, as Hale has developed *in extenso* throughout many writings, nonintervention does not mean the absence of the state, for the accumulated action of the state is, albeit unobtrusively, an integral part of the *status quo* division of power, both within the market and between the market and other institutions.[154] Second, intervention does generally mean participation (consciously or otherwise) directed to secure results different from what would otherwise be the case. Intervention, indeed policy itself then, involves "the desire to promote what [is] considered to be social improvement," [155] and "usually emerges as a consequence of tensions between the actual state of the economy and some desired state. . . ." [156] "Man acts because he is dissatisfied with the state of affairs as it prevails in the absence of his intervention." [157] Change, particularly through the restructuring of the decisional process, is truly a fundamental characteristic of policy; it is of the ultimate nature of policy for it to be involved with the juxtaposition of continuity and change. Thus nonintervention (e.g., on the part of the state) means either continuity *per se* or, more generally, the disengagement of the state as a means of change and the presumed approval of such change as comes about through other channels (e.g., through market forces).

V

From the vantage point of fundamental questions and issues, the commonplace takes on deeper meaning. Private property, whatever else it may also be or seem, is a system of economic organization, a system of institutionalized decision making, a system of social control.[158] So also with business. As Walton Hamilton commented, "business is the most conspicuous of the agencies of control in the modern economic system." [159] There is, as John M. Clark made clear for all time, the "social control of business," but business itself is an interacting part of the total system of control. Control is thus a fundamental characteristic of policy.

Moreover, a central question of control and thus of policy is *responsibility*. Although it is beyond the scope of this paper to examine at length, it should be pointed out that responsibility is more than a pluralistic division of power. It involves, *inter alia*, institutionalizing "due process"—this itself is an intermediate concept—throughout society. It is indeed a concept about which it is easy to write dissimulating and platitudinous propositions. Suffice it to say that "how to enforce responsibility to his fellow men is the largest question in the whole field of social control." [160]

But policy is more than *control*: it is also *choice* and *change*. This trinity of fundamental characteristics is revealed, necessarily, in basic discussions of economic policy.[161] And, of course, there is a fourth—*conflict*—that pervades all discussions of the other three.

What this means is that, at bottom, the nature and scope of economic policy—and any theory of economic policy—is necessarily involved with the *problem of order*. Order has to do with the conditions of social interaction; and is a concept whose variety of definitions reflects different interpretations, anxieties, expectations, and desires as to its substantive resolution. As Spengler has incisively developed, it is the dual problem of reconciling freedom (or autonomy) and control, and continuity and change. It involves the making of ostensible incompatibles compatible.[162] It may be seen as conflict resolution producing an integrated, "orderly and sensible pattern of choices." [163] It is a recurrent phenomenon; [164] it is continuing, something to be achieved.[165] And it is paradoxical that order may be achieved out of division; as Smith and Durkheim [166] saw, order derived from the cohesion generated through the division of labor, though conflict was seen as a by-product also.

Order *is* important. To Knight, "'the' *supreme* value is *order*." [167] But—viewed from the continuity and change dimension—it is capable of being weighed either way; indeed it is difficult not to overstress one at the expense of the other. Knight has written that:

> Growth, or any tendency toward cumulative change, is a fundamentally disruptive force, and a conscious effort toward progress further intensifies the problems of order and efficiency almost beyond comparison.[168]

He says also:

> The moral problem of free society is to criticize, change, and improve custom and law—with a "practical minimum" of disorder and of injustice to individuals. . . . Traditionalism means a fixed order, and the distinctive modern problem is to have freedom (enough and of the right kind) for change and progress, without having so much (or the wrong kind) as to bring chaos or to destroy itself.[169]

It is not enough to say that we must balance continuity and change, and autonomy and freedom; but that is what, at bottom, is involved in both the problem of order and any theory of economic policy.

The matter is, of course, even more complicated. Considering both continuity and change, and freedom and control, and necessarily having to oversimplify, the problem of the "conservative" tends to be—in our pluralistic society—that he is in favor of the *status quo*, but that the *status quo* is one in which power is concentrated, Whereas the problem of the "liberal" is that he is in favor of the wide diffusion of power, as well as changing the *status quo*, the latter requires the concentration of power in order to effectuate change. (The same is true of the "conservative" who would like to change the *status quo* along the lines of what he considers to be some earlier "golden age.") And the problem of order is that of making these ostensibly incompatible positions—each with their own incompatibilities—compatible.

It should be evident that the transcendental problem of economic policy, that of structuring and restructuring the economic decision-making process, is one phase of the delicate yet crucial problem of reworking the accumulated and received resolution of the problem of order—i.e., reworking the existing balance of freedom and control, and continuity and change. In any theory of economic policy there is nothing more fundamental than this.

What the problem of order, insofar as it bears on the nature and scope of economic policy, involves (and insofar as it is possible and necessary to discuss here) is the development of what Commons called the "working rules" [170] or the intermediate principles through which argument, energy, and strategy is directed in the powerplay which is the game of policy. The working rules, in all their forms, are the material of which the decision-making structure is built. Order emerges out of the juxtaposition, confrontation, and rearrangement of these working rules in ever new situations, and part of this order is the economic decision-making process. This is to say, in part, that the working rules are the intermediate principles functioning through indirection (though not necessarily always through ignorance—viz., the manifest function concept) to resolve the problem of structure and restructuring. And it is also to say that both conflict and growth (change) take place through the modification of rules. "Economic policy is the set of rules which govern the ordinary business of making a living," and, as has been already seen, "The manner in which the rules change, as well as the substance of the change, is a part of economic policy." [171] It is a question of changing the parallelogram of interests to which the rules give effect; "It is a question of *changing the rules*." [172]

This process of changing the rules, and thereby resolving the substance of the problem of order—i.e., restructuring the economic decision-making process—is complex and, because the rules are both legal and moral and more, its analysis requires a total social science (or interdisciplinary) approach. But, in the view of the author, important lessons are to be found in the following statements excerpted from Edward H. Levi's *An Introduction to Legal Reasoning*:

> It is important that the mechanism of legal reasoning should not be concealed by its pretense. The pretense is that the law is a system of known rules applied by a judge; the pretense has long been under attack. In an important sense legal rules are never clear, and, if a rule had to be clear before it could be imposed, society would be impossible. The mechanism accepts the differences of view and ambiguities of words. It provides for the participation of the community in resolving the ambiguity by providing a forum for the discussion of policy in the gap of ambiguity. On serious controversial questions, it makes it possible to take the first step in the direction of what otherwise would be forbidden ends. The mechanism is indispensable to peace in a community.
>
> Yet this change in the rules is the indispensable dynamic quality of law. It occurs because the scope of a rule of law, and therefore its meaning, depends upon a determination of what facts will be considered similar to those present when the rule was first announced. The finding of similarity or difference is the key step in the legal process.
>
> The kind of reasoning involved in the legal process is one

in which the classification changes as the classification is made. The rules change as the rules are applied. More important, the rules arise out of a process which, while comparing fact situations, creates the rules and then applies them. . . . Not only do new situations arise, but in addition peoples' wants change.[173]

There is much worthy of comment and elaboration in these suggestive statements, but the author must limit himself to the objective of merely having presented a glance into the subtleties of the problem of order which is at the heart of any theory of economic policy. The problem of structuring the economic decision-making process is that of arranging and rearranging the working rules, which continuing restructuring is part of the resolution of the larger problem of order.

Finally, it should be pointed out that in any social economic system there is the problem of *authority* comprising part of the problem of order. Under this rubric there is included: the institutionalization of (a) principle(s) of authority, the legitimation of both the principle(s) and the institutionalization, and the absolutist formulation that is generally characteristic of or given to that legitimation even in a pluralistic society. With respect to the first, there is need for some mode(s) of conflict resolution between otherwise authoritative institutions, a set of benchmarks to govern the decisions of formal authorities and thus discipline and integrate them into society as well as function similarly toward the mass of men in society. These high-level working rules serve to constrain discretion. They comprise an institutionalized fount of authority.

But if there is need for a fount of authority in society, there is need also for the legitimation of that fount and thereby of all that the fount itself stands for. Indeed, the fount itself must have unquestioned status. In every society there are thus at work forces, intellectual and others, which render to the minds of all participants in the decisional process the sanctity of authority. Authority is not authority without the sanctity of legitimation, without that which renders it above all controversy. There is thus need for a "propaganda for economic freedom." [174] To discuss the substance of legitimation is to many true believers to open it to question and thence to doubt, which is to render it, like other matters, no longer sanctified and thus open to change.[175]

Yet just as authority is not authoritative unless it is legitimized, so also legitimation is not sanctified unless it is absolutely formulated. In a pluralistic society, absolutes are hard to come by; the problem of order, and of authority, is much more difficult to resolve in such a society. But the existing set of authorities, each of which is authoritative only in conjunction with the others with whom each interplays, nonetheless tends to become legitimized through the absolutist expression of the accepted rationales of their existence. In law this is true of both common law, statute law, and constitutional law, i.e., of inferior courts and legislature and supreme court. Thus the history of popular and intellectual thought on the institution of judicial review over our national history (and particularly over the last three-quarters of a century) has been caught up in the conflict of various absolute formulations of the legitimation of supreme court power, which conflict with the absolutist formulations legitimizing other founts of authority. That this is the case is not always appreciated by those who participate in or play the game of power, though manifest function is relevant here also.

This is to say, of course, that economic policy has within its domain strands not only of the general problem of order but also of authority, legitimation, and absolute formulation. This means, moreover, that economic policy is no sophomoric subject; it is involved with some of the most subtle and intricate processes of social organization.

Law, for example, may be a mode of effectuating change or

a mode of preserving continuity; legal briefs may seek either change or continuity of precedent.[176] Theory, like argument, may serve to cast luster on either continuity or change.[177]

Since participation in the decision-making process is meaningful only in the context of the total pattern of freedom and control, change in that pattern means change in the balance of power. This is not harmony, either providential or automatic. Though this may be good theology or propaganda, it is poor social science. As the author has suggested elsewhere, "The crucial question for policy analysis is of course 'harmony of interests' by what criteria, on what terms, and in the context of what system of social control (or decision making process). Moreover, the ideas of an invisible hand or a pre-existent and pre-eminent order or of harmony itself, were epistemologically either mere asertion or hypothesis. The history of subsequent economic thought may be viewed as efforts aiming at the specification of the conditions of mutuality or harmony of interests." [178]

Harmony, like order itself, is a problem and not a datum.[179] Its solution, in terms of means and ends, is produced through the decision-making process.[180] The harmony, such as it is, that exists is a created and contingent harmony between interests.[181] It is a contrived harmony,[182] subject to revision. The assumption of an automatic harmony may be considered as utopianism,[183] a *deus ex machina*.[184] Interests are, after all, both substitutes for and complements to one another.[185] Reconciliation, as in the existentialist view, is produced by man himself, though not entirely deliberatively; with no calculus to yield precise solutions, it is rather worked out than solved. In praise of Commons, Harold Groves appropriately has written that, "the institutionalists were resigned to much conflict held within some bounds by a balance of power, compromise agreements, and working rules some of which were

280

sanctioned in the last instance by the Supreme Court." [186] Policy analysis, if it is to be meaningful and deal with fundamentals, can take no other view. In this context the task of policy analysis is to concern itself with the institutionalized transmutation mechanisms or rules which create harmony between private interests and between these and whatever content is given to the social interest. (The author would suggest a qualified realist view of the concept, "public interest.") [187] As the author has suggested, the institutionalists, no more than the classicists, were preoccupied with institution building, which institutions may be seen as embodying forces to promote their respective views of the public weal.[188]

VI

The nature of economic policy centers on choice, in a context of control, change, and conflict. The economy, in that context, is a process of making choices, i.e., a decision-making or policy process. The scope of economic policy encompasses both the resolution of the basic economic problems *and* the structuring of the economic decision-making process itself, the consequences of the former interacting with the consequences of the latter. The scope of policy participation includes interacting market, legal, and nonlegal forces.

The economic policy process may be seen, then, as one of mutual and reciprocal participation between the various classes of participants and the subgroups of each, down to the individual buyer, seller, legislator, and moralist. As Commons would put it, the policy process is one of mutual liberties and exposures to the liberties of others. The same point may be made in terms of coercion: the economic policy process may be seen as a system of mutual coercion, with coercion connoting the impact of the participation of others, ultimately the capacity to withhold.[189]

The author would suggest that there are a number of elemental questions of policy which pervade the entire policy process and enter even if unobtrusively upon every particular issue of policy. While these questions are normally resolved (really, worked out) incrementally and indirectly, one of the tasks of policy analysis must be to identify and comprehend them. This section is an attempt to state these questions, simply and without much elaboration. It is beyond the author's expectations to be conclusive in their listing or substance; nor does space and purpose allow for further analysis. Given the foregoing discussion, however, on which they are founded, these questions are self-evident and rather suggestive.

(1) *Whose Interests?* Participants in the economic decision-making process—individuals and collectives—have what they consider to be their "interests," or their "wants." An elementary problem, then, of the economic policy process is to decide somehow whose interests,[190] whose values,[191] whose welfare,[192] whose ends,[193] or whose wants—which is to say, which wants [194] —are to be gratified and to what extent in each case. Put variously: How much should one social goal be sacrificed for another,[195] i.e., whose social goals; whose interests is the law to protect and whose to leave open to competition and the liberties of others; [196] whose ends does any particular rule serve; [197] But particularly incisive are: "Who shall be sacrificed for whom" [198] and "what kind of opportunity, and opportunity for whom"? [199]

(2) *Whose Freedom?* The second elementary question inquires into the distribution of freedom, for which word one can here substitute "power" or "participation." If freedom means participation in the economic decision-making process, and if freedom is freedom within the pattern of freedom or participation, who is free (or who participates) and on what

terms? Who is free to do what, and free from whom and from what? What is the distribution of freedoms and of exposures to the freedoms of others? The working rules which apportion liberty both create and destroy liberty concomitantly. As Bentham put it: "It is impossible to create rights, to impose obligations, to protect the person, life, reputation, subsistence, or liberty itself, but at the expense of liberty." [200] "To say that a law is contrary to natural liberty, is simply to say that it is a law: for every law is established at the expense of liberty— the liberty of Peter at the expense of the liberty of Paul." [201] To resolve the problem of structural policy is to determine the loci, limits, and conditions of participation in the decision-making process, and to do that is to determine "whose freedom?" (The problem is particularly but not exclusively acute in underdeveloped nations where both elites and masses contemplate the meaning of freedom in terms of the pattern of the *ancien régime,* or *status quo* power structure and *its desiderata,* whereas economic development may require both a change in the power structure and in the goals of life.)

(3) *Whose Capacity to Coerce?* Whether it be through the control exercised through market price,[202] i.e., the coercion of "rationing through the purse," [203] or through the coercive potential residing in private property and, indeed, in all loci of participation in the decisional process, coercion through the impact of the participation of others is pervasive. This is as true on a generalized level—the coercion of moral rules, for example—as it is on a particularized level—the demands of one's union, employer, or customer.[204] Since each participant is endeavoring to impose or exercise his will (or defend against other wills) through the decisional process, each in turn is exposed to the efforts of the others. The question that is elemental, then, is which coercive power will prevail, or who will have what capacity to coerce. Effective decision is necessarily forthcoming governing the pattern of capacities to coerce and

immunities from coercion. The law may reinforce (or be used to reinforce) the existing coercive capacity of one participant in the market or it may countervail (or be used to countervail) such capacity.[205] That one is exposed to the freedom of another(s) is to say that one may be coerced, and the question is, who may coerce whom?

(4) *Who May Injure Whom?* From still another facet, but to the equivalent effect, the decision-making process governs not only the distribution of participation—in terms either of freedom or coercive capacity—but also the distribution of benefits and deprivations. This is perhaps most apparent in terms of income (and wealth) distribution, but such is but one example of a general phenomenon which may be referred to as the distribution or incidence of injury. When will an act, imposing economic loss, deprivation, or injury on another, yet not *mala in se*, be justified as an exertion of freedom and (say) an inevitable consequence of market forces, and when will it be held (say) tortious because undesirable or against public policy? Welfare economics, for example, has been preoccupied with the conditions of optimization and the trading of costs and benefits; and the problem of injury has been a difficult one—it is a question of valuing injuries (or disutilities).[206] In other contexts, the question takes the form, who bears the risk of change,[207] and "who bears the cost of economic development"?[208] But in all cases, "The real question that has to be decided is: should A be allowed to harm B or should B be allowed to harm A?"[209] In economic terms, it is directly the question of who will have the capacity to impose costs on others.[210] Thus the common law of torts (*inter alia*) has operated, in its own way—using its own intermediate principles—to assess and attribute liability and thereby *pro tanto* govern the distribution of risk and of business or economic costs.[211] As von Mises and Coase, among others, have pointed out, it is always an open-ended matter whether "reform of the

laws concerning liability for damages" [212] will serve to improve welfare.

(5) *Whose Rights?* Arguments over freedom, power, coercion, and injury—that is, arguments over interests and wants—frequently if not generally take the form of disputes over "rights." The parallelogram of mutual and reciprocal (as well as situational and historical) participation which is the economic decision-making process is identifiable as the pattern of rights into which the developing decisional structure tends to be crystallized and in terms of which it is discussed and argued.[213] In this context, the elemental question of policy is, "whose rights," for choice necessarily must be exercised between competing rights' claimants.[214] This is so whether discussion is about *de facto* or *de jure* rights, for the decisional process is comprised of both. The question of the choice of the right of Alpha over the right of Beta is also, it should be clear, the question of Alpha's freedom, his capacity to coerce and to impose injury with respect to Beta, and *vice versa*.

(6) *When is a Rose a Rose?* Throughout all of the foregoing elemental questions there runs the thread of another, the question of *specific content*. Discussions of legal and economic policy issues generally involve categories or classifications, and conclusions to particular questions or problems of policy are usually expressed in terms of these taxonomic creations, often quite artificial if not fictional. But underlying any conclusion is the question, which pigeon-hole? The following are taken from a wide variety of situations which have this elemental question in common: When is a taking of property a taking under eminent domain; [215] when is a (property) right a right; [216] when is a particular benefit to be in the category of discriminate and when of indiscriminate benefits; [217] when are appropriate institutional arrangements appropriate; [218] when is a company poorly managed; [219] when is a theft a theft, and when is it competition; [220] and when does the liberty

285

of the factory-owner work out to the oppression of the laborers? [221]The scope of economic policy must perforce include the particular choices effectively made governing these specific determinations. To write or speak of property as a legally protected interest (or otherwise) and of tort as an actionable wrong, *et cetera*, is to "assume the answers to the question which is in issue whenever they are relevant." [222] There is a difference between the institution of private property and particular property rights. *When* is an interest to be made into property, and when is an injury to be recognized as a tort? This is as specific and as elemental a question of policy as can be posed.

(7) *Who Decides?* The resolution of—or answers to, as it were—the foregoing questions is worked out through the power play of the economic decision-making process. But the correlative question remains, *who decides?* Who decides which freedom, which coercive power, which injury, whose rights, and whose interests and wants? As suggested earlier, the solution of this problem is the province of structural policy, for the effective decisions governing the structure of the decisional process itself is the transcendental subject of policy analysis. The question "Who . . . prescribes what rules, with respect to what values, for whom, and by what procedures?" [223] is ultimately the questions who regulates,[224] who controls,[225] and who decides,[226] or who makes the decisions? [227] But it is also the questions, who can create enforceable interests; [228] who educates society; [229] and, above all, what *order*; [230] or, what decision-making structure?

VII

In this paper the author has attempted to explore and identify the nature and scope of economic policy in terms of funda-

286

mental questions. In his view the problems herein identified and correlated are properly understood to rest at the foundation of any theory of economic policy.

That is not to say, however, that all policy discussions do or should involve conscious consideration of such fundamental problems: they do not, as a matter of fact. Moreover, the author has attempted to be descriptive and not exhortative with respect to the question of the "proper" balance between deliberate and nondeliberate forces (itself a fundamental question of policy)—though he has made his position clear with respect to the professional discussion of such questions.

It has not been the purpose of the author to construct a closed system: although he has endeavored to analyze systematically the nature and scope of economic policy, the result is a model comprised of the fundamental problems with which any theory of economic policy ultimately must come to grips and not a set of solutions to those problems. The author's approach has been essentially a formal one, and he has abstracted from questions of immediate and intermediate aims and means of economic policy, though he has tried to place several of them in functional perspective. There is no question but that the scope of economic policy, and of policy analysis, includes areas beyond those discussed here. It is to be remembered also that economic policy involves a constant flow of many interacting forces or participants. Similarly, policy analysis appropriately encompasses many interacting subject-fields and approaches. Also important is the fact that the economic decision-making process should not be overintellectualized, for its core is a process of power play. This caution is warranted notwithstanding the fact that the analysis of power and its incidents can be made too systematic and formal; though a system of power play, the process involves more than power for the sake of power, and it includes the irrational and the noneconomic forces of sociocultural life.

In brief, the author would suggest that economic policy is ultimately characterized by choice and its involvement with the problem of order and, perforce, by control, continuity-change, and conflict. The scope of policy is the making of the effective choices which constitute the resolution of the basic economic problems as well as govern the structuring and re-structuring of the decisional process itself. The scope of policy participation appropriately then includes all the interacting participants in the decision-making process, to which the author has referred as nominal private (or market), legal, and nonlegal participation. Finally, the elemental questions posed in Section VI are self-evident, with the culminating and trans-cendental question always being, who decides? Yet they are only questions; insofar as any theory of economic policy concerns basic problems for which resolutions must be worked out, it is the task—and at times the burden—of man to work out those resolutions.

NOTES

* The preparation of this article (of which a summary was pre-sented at the Southern Economic Association meeting, in November 1965) was facilitated by a University of Miami Grant for Support of Research in the Humanities and by the School of Business Admin-istration Research Fund, the latter from a contribution by Southern Bell Telephone and Telegraph Company, for both of which the author is gratefully indebted. Acknowledgment is due the personnel of the Richter Library of the University of Miami for both coopera-tion and patience; to James C. Nicholas for research assistance, and to Ogden O. Allsbrook, Edward J. Fox, Ignacio Martinez, Jr., Vergil A. Shipley, Theo Suranyi-Unger, and particularly Grover A. J. Noetzel for their comments and suggestions.

1. A parallel summary and suggested application is presented by

the author in W. J. Samuels, "History of Economic Thought: Discussion," *American Economic Review, Papers and Proceedings*, vol. 55 (1965), pp. 146–47.

2. There are a multiplicity of (a) what may be called "approaches" to or models of policy analysis and of policy; (b) differentiations between types or elements of policy; and, *inter alia*, (c) types of statements on policy, classified in terms of criteria of meaningfulness. Analysis of even the most important of these would require a lengthy analysis of an extensive literature. Such an analysis is beyond the scope of this paper, as, indeed, are many subjects necessarily touched upon later in the paper. The analysis and view presented is sufficiently abstract as not to require such examination. It should be pointed out that the analysis reflects essentially Anglo-American literature and treatment, and regrettably not the extensive Continental literature on the subject, though the influence of Max Weber, for example, will be apparent.

3. C. J. Friedrich, *Man and His Government* (New York: McGraw-Hill, 1963), p. 79; and "Policy—A Science?" in C. J. Friedrich and J. K. Galbraith, eds., *Public Policy* (Cambridge: Harvard University Press, 1953), vol. 4, p. 269.

4. John Stuart Mill, *The Spirit of the Age*, with Introductory Essay by F. A. Hayek (Chicago: University of Chicago Press, 1942), p. 1.

5. John R. Commons, *Legal Foundations of Capitalism* (Madison: University of Wisconsin Press, 1959), and *Institutional Economics* (Madison: University of Wisconsin Press, 1959) two volumes.

6. Frank H. Knight, *Intelligence and Democratic Action* (Cambridge: Harvard University Press, 1960).

7. P. W. Bridgman, *The Logic of Modern Physics* (New York: Macmillan, 1961), pp. 31–32. See also John Dewey: "*Objects* are finalities; they are complete, finished. . . . But data signify 'material to serve;' they are indications, evidence, signs, clues to and of something still to be reached; they are intermediate, not ultimate; means, not finalities. . . . Greek and medieval science formed an art of accepting things as they are enjoyed and suffered. Modern experimental science is an art of control." *The Quest for Certainty* (New York: Minton, Balch & Co., 1929), pp. 99–100; cf. pp. 312–13.

8. Lionel Robbins, *Politics and Economics* (London: Macmillan, 1963), p. 22. See also, for example, Harold Koontz and Richard W. Gable, *Public Control of Economic Enterprise* (New York: McGraw-Hill, 1956), p. 819.

9. The concept of *implementational* policy is to be differentiated from that of *structural* policy, discussed below.

10. The concept of *intermediate* goals relates to the principles and practice of ignorance and indirection characteristic of the nondeliberative forces of social control, as developed, for example, in Louis Schneider, "The Role of the Category of Ignorance in Sociological Theory: An Exploratory Statement," *American Sociological Review*, vol. 27 (1962), and used by the present author in "The Classical Theory of Economic Policy: Non-Legal Social Control," *Southern Economic Journal*, vol. 31 (1964), e.g., p. 11, and *passim*. See below.

11. See C. E. Lindblom, "Policy Analysis," *American Economic Review*, vol. 48 (1958), pp. 298–312; and "Tinbergen on Policy-Making," *Journal of Political Economy*, vol. 66 (1958), pp. 531–38.

12. The concepts of policy and theory identified in the text have played a role in shaping the mentality of all participants in the decisional process. (Thus, for example, the complementary notions that the market is spontaneous and natural whereas government is artificial and forced have served to disengage government from what it might otherwise have been envisioned and called upon to effectuate.) These concepts have thus had—to use R. K. Merton's terminology (*Social Theory and Social Structure* [Glencoe, Ill.: Free Press, 1949], chap. 1)—the latent function of influencing (*inter alia*) what people understand as and expect from "policy," from the economy, and from government; and have been subject to the role of manifest function insofar as the promulgation of an appropriate concept has been the conscious preoccupation of some. Moreover, it should be apparent that the analysis and approach taken in this article are themselves "subject" to the analysis which is to follow, which is indicative of the proposition that *discussions of* the policy process ultimately must be considered as *part of* that process and thus a fit subject for analysis themselves. Nothing is more basic than the approach to and concept of policy; and insofar as this paper on the nature and scope of policy involves an approach to policy, it logically may be treated as it treats other approaches. It should also be obvious that the author is not concerned in this paper with the truth-value (or value status) of propositions usually entering into debates over policies, but rather with the consequences for analysis, and largely in terms of functional roles.

13. Samuels, "History of Economic Thought: Discussion," *op. cit.*, p. 145.

14. See, for example, the works of Commons cited above; K. H. Parsons, "Institutional Economics: Discussion," *American Economic Review, Papers and Proceedings*, vol. 47 (1957), pp. 25–26; and H. G. Vatter, "Another Look at the Theory of 'Consumer Choice,'" *Challenge*, vol. 13 (February 1965), p. 39.

15. David Braybrooke, "The Relevance of Norms to Political

Description," *American Political Science Review*, vol. 52 (1958), p. 992.

16. Daniel Lerner and Harold D. Lasswell, eds., *The Policy Sciences* (Stanford: Stanford University Press, 1951), p. 8. Cf. Friedrich, "Policy—A Science?" *op. cit.*, p. 270.

17. For example, the issues in welfare economics discussed by S. K. Nath, "Are Formal Welfare Criteria Required?" *Economic Journal*, vol. 74 (1964), pp. 549–50.

18. *Per contra*, see James M. Buchanan, "What Should Economists Do?" *Southern Economic Journal*, vol. 30 (1964), p. 219. Compare, however, Israel M. Kirzner, "What Economists Do," *Southern Economic Journal*, vol. 31 (1965), pp. 257–61.

19. Talcott Parsons, *The Structure of Social Action* (New York: McGraw-Hill, 1937); Talcott Parsons and Neil J. Smelser, *Economy and Society* (Glencoe, Ill.: Free Press, 1956); and Neil J. Smelser, *The Sociology of Economic Life* (Englewood Cliffs, N.J.: Prentice-Hall, 1963). See also Alfred Kuhn, *The Study of Society* (Homewood, Ill.: Irwin, 1963), especially but not only chaps. 14–16; and Robert A. Dahl and Charles E. Lindblom, *Politics, Economics and Welfare* (New York: Harper, 1953).

20. See Joseph J. Spengler, "The Problem of Order in Economic Affairs," *Southern Economic Journal*, vol. 15 (1948), p. 1 ff., reprinted in Joseph J. Spengler and William R. Allen, eds., *Essays in Economic Thought* (Chicago: Rand McNally, 1960), p. 6 ff.

21. Ludwig von Mises, *Human Action* (New Haven: Yale University Press, 1949), p. 143 ff.

22. The organizing concept of the economy as a decision-making process is also evident in such writings as Polanyi's essay on "The Economy as Instituted Process" in Karl Polanyi *et al*, eds., *Trade and Market in the Early Empires* (Glencoe, Ill.: Free Press, 1957), pp. 243–69; Knight's essay on "Social Economic Organization"—in Frank H. Knight, *The Economic Organization* (New York: Kelley, 1951), pp. 3–30; and, for example, in writings by Neil W. Chamberlain and Edward E. LeClair, Jr. The concept of the economy (and its suborganizations) as a decisional process pervades Chamberlain's major works and is especially evident in his *Private and Public Planning* (New York: McGraw-Hill, 1965), particularly chaps. 1 and 8, in which the economy is explicitly examined as a decision-making system or process. In LeClair's article on "Economic Theory and Anthropology," *American Anthropologist*, vol. 64 (1962), pp. 1179–203, the economy is considered a social process and system functioning to resolve "economizing problems" as a decisional process (p. 1190). In this connection, attention should be directed also to George Dalton,

"Economic Theory and Primitive Society," *American Anthropologist,* vol. 63 (1961), pp. 1–25.

23. On Hayek, for example, see C .W. Guillebaud, Book Review, *Economica,* n.s. vol. 11 (1944), p. 215.

24. *Social Control of Business* (2nd ed., New York: McGraw-Hill, 1939), chap. 5; and *Economic Institutions and Human Welfare* (New York: Knopf, 1957).

25. Robert L. Hale, *Freedom Through Law* (New York: Columbia University Press, 1952).

26. Kenneth E. Boulding, *Principles of Economic Policy* (Englewood Cliffs, N.J.: Prentice-Hall, 1958), p. 172, and *passim.*

27. Donald S. Watson, *Economic Policy* (Boston: Houghton Mifflin, 1960), p. 17, and *passim.*

28. Spengler, *op. cit.*

29. Lionel Robbins, *The Theory of Economic Policy in English Classical Political Economy* (London: Macmillan, 1953). See also Samuels, "The Classical Theory of Economic Policy: Non-Legal Social Control," *op. cit.,* pp. 1–2.

30. Lionel Robbins, *An Essay on the Nature and Significance of Economic Science* (London: Macmillan, 1952), pp. 75–77, 134, 144; and *Politics and Economics,* pp. 8, 9, 34–35, 50, 135, and *passim.*

31. See, for example, Vatter, "Another Look at the Theory of 'Consumer Choice,' " *op. cit.;* James C. Bonbright, *Principles of Public Utility Rates* (New York: Columbia University Press, 1961), p. 23; M. J. Bonn, "Economic Policy," *Encyclopaedia of the Social Sciences* (New York: Macmillan, 1931), vol. 5, p. 335; Wilbert E. Moore, *Industrial Relations and the Social Order* (rev. ed., New York: Macmillan, 1951), p. 597; Frederic Benham and Francis M. Boddy, *Principles of Economics* (New York: Pitman, 1947), p. 6; and George L. Bach, *Economics* (4th ed., Englewood Cliffs, N.J.: Prentice-Hall, 1963), p. 448.

32. Morris A. Copeland, *Our Free Enterprise Economy* (New York: Macmillan, 1965), p. v.

33. Rutledge Vining, *Economics in the United States of America* (Paris: UNESCO, 1956), p. 12; cf. p. 14.

34. Leverett S. Lyon, "The Private-Enterprise System Confronts Emergency," *Journal of Business,* vol. 14 (1941), p. 261.

35. William C. Bagley, Jr., "The Task of Institutionalism," in Robert A. Solo, ed., *Economics and the Public Interest* (New Brunswick, N.J.: Rutgers University Press, 1955), p. 21.

36. Frank H. Knight, *The Ethics of Competition* (New York: Kelley, 1951), p. 337.

37. Frank H. Knight, "Economics, Political Science, and Educa-

tion," *American Economic Review, Papers and Proceedings,* vol. 34 (1944), p. 72; cf. Knight, "The Meaning of Freedom," *Ethics,* vol. 52 (1941), p. 107.

38. Frank H. Knight, *Freedom and Reform* (New York: Harper, 1947), p. 122.

39. Knight, *The Ethics of Competition,* p. 137.

40. Robbins, *The Theory of Economic Policy,* p. 191.

41. Hale, *op. cit.;* "Coercion and Distribution in a Supposedly Non-Coercive State," *Political Science Quarterly,* vol. 38 (1923), p. 470 ff.; and "Force and the State: A Comparison of 'Political' and 'Economic' Compulsion," *Columbia Law Review,* vol. 35 (1935), p. 149 ff.

42. See also E. Ronald Walker, *From Economic Theory to Policy* (Chicago: University of Chicago Press, 1943), p. 100 ff.; and see the perceptive review thereof by Henry W. Spiegel, "Economic Theory and Economic Policy," *Journal of Business,* vol. 18 (1945), pp. 56–59.

43. Knight, *The Ethics of Competition,* p. 45.

44. Knight, *Freedom and Reform,* p. 152.

45. Robbins, *Politics and Economics,* p. 18; cf. p. 16.

46. Clarence E. Ayres, "Institutional Economics—Discussion," *American Economic Review, Papers and Proceedings,* vol. 47 (1957), p. 26.

47. Knight, *Freedom and Reform,* p. 205. "Whatever proportion of the actual organization of life is left to individualistic market dealings, it is the political framework which is 'fundamental,' since the latter must make and enforce the rules according to which a market economy operates. Consequently, the market economy, in whatever form and degree it exists, must be regarded as the creature of the sovereign state, and an expression of its policy. This is no less true if the state acts permissively rather than positively. This reasoning also holds for all voluntary associations, the plural-sovereignty theorists notwithstanding, and in full view of the fact that associations possess and exercise political power." Knight, *The Ethics of Competition,* p. 318.

48. Roscoe Pound, *The Spirit of the Common Law* (Boston: Marshall Jones, 1921); *Social Control Through Law* (New Haven: Yale University Press, 1942); "Common Law and Legislation," *Harvard Law Review,* vol. 21 (1908), pp. 383–407; "Liberty of Contract," *Yale Law Journal,* vol. 18 (1909); and, *inter alia,* "The Call for a Realist Jurisprudence," *Harvard Law Review,* vol. 44 (1931), pp. 697–711. By Julius Stone, see "The Province of Jurisprudence Redetermined," *Modern Law Review,* vol. 7 (1944), pp. 97–112, 177–92; and "The Myths of Planning and Laissez Faire: A Reorientation," *George Washington Law Review,* vol. 18 (1949), pp. 1–49.

49. See, for example, Felix S. Cohen, *The Legal Conscience* (New

Haven: Yale University Press, 1960); Harry W. Jones, "Law and Morality in the Perspective of Legal Realism," *Columbia Law Review*, vol. 61 (1961), pp. 799–809; and Wolfgang Friedmann, "Legal Philosophy and Judicial Lawmaking," *Columbia Law Review*, vol. 61 (1961), pp. 821–45.

50. Lerner and Lasswell, *op. cit.*; Harold D. Lasswell and Abraham Kaplan, *Power and Society* (New Haven: Yale University Press, 1950); Lasswell, "The Interplay of Economic, Political and Social Criteria in Legal Policy," *Vanderbilt Law Review*, vol. 14 (1961), pp. 451–71; Lasswell and M. S. McDougal, "Legal Education and Public Policy: Professional Training in the Public Interest," *Yale Law Journal*, vol. 52 (1943), p. 203 ff.; M. S. McDougal, "Law as a Process of Decision: A Policy-Oriented Approach to Legal Study," *Natural Law Forum*, vol. 1 (1956), p. 53 ff.

51. E.g., Watson, *op. cit.*, p. xii; E. S. Kirschen *et al*, *Economic Policy in Our Time* (Chicago: Rand McNally, 1964), vol. 1, p. 153 ff.; and Lindblom, "Tinbergen on Policy-Making," *op. cit.*

52. James M. Buchanan and Gordon Tullock, *The Calculus of Consent* (Ann Arbor, Mich.: University of Michigan Press, 1962); Anthony Downs, *An Economic Theory of Democracy* (New York: Wiley, 1957); and Roland N. McKean, "The Unseen Hand in Government," *American Economic Review*, vol. 55 (1965), pp. 496–506. See also Friedrich, *Man and His Government*; and Nelson W. Polsby *et al*, *Politics and Social Life* (Boston: Houghton Mifflin, 1963), particularly Section 4.

53. Samuels, "The Classical Theory of Economic Policy: Non-Legal Social Control," *op. cit.*

54. John R. Commons, *The Economics of Collective Action* (New York: Macmillan, 1950), p. 21.

55. Stewart Macaulay, "Non-contractual Relations in Business: A Preliminary Study," *American Sociological Review*, vol. 28 (1963), pp. 55–67, and William M. Evan, "Comment," *American Sociological Review*, vol. 28 (1963), pp. 67–69.

56. James M. Buchanan, "The Relevance of Pareto Optimality," *Journal of Conflict Resolution*, vol. 6 (1962), pp. 341–54; and Oskar Morgenstern, "Pareto Optimum and Economic Organization," in Norbert Kloten *et al*, eds., *Systeme und Methoden in den Wirtschafts- und Sozialwissenschaften* (Tubingen: Mohr [Siebeck], 1964), pp. 573–86.

57. Adam Smith, *Essays Philosophical and Literary* (London: Ward, Lock & Co., 1880), p. 230.

58. Friedrich A. Hayek, *Individualism and Economic Order* (Chicago: University of Chicago Press, 1948), particularly chaps. 1–4. See also Ludwig von Mises, *Socialism* (New Haven: Yale University Press, 1951), pp. 112–13.

294

59. "But its crucial choices are conscious, perhaps deliberative." Commons, *Legal Foundations of Capitalism*, p. 72. And see Knight: "Our behavior is largely of the type variously designated as social habit, custom, tradition, usage, or institutions. Such behavior forms are perpetuated by processes which sociologists call imitation and suggestion, acculturation and the like. . . ." *Freedom and Reform*, p. 211. See Note 47, *supra*.

60. Friedrich, *Man and His Government*, p. 74.

61. Oscar and Mary Handlin, "The Dimensions of Liberty," *Harvard Today* (Spring 1962), p. 4. See also Arthur Schlesinger: "I think the historian tends in retrospect to make the processes of decision far more tidy and rational than they are: to assume that people have fixed positions and represent fixed interests and to impose a pattern on what is actually a swirl if not a chaos. I think the historian doesn't realize the opaqueness of the process." Henry Brandon, "Schlesinger at the White House," *Harper's* (July 1964), p. 56.

62. Karl N. Llewellyn, *The Bramble Bush* (New York: Oceana, 1951); and Jerome Frank, *Law and the Modern Mind* (New York: Coward-McCann, 1949). Also see text at Note 173, *infra*.

63. Paul Diesing, *Reason in Society* (Urbana, Ill.: University of Illinois Press, 1962).

64. See, for example, Graham Wallas, *Human Nature in Politics* (London: Constable, 1910); Sidney Hook, *Reason, Social Myths and Democracy* (New York: Humanities Press, 1940); Michael Oakeshott, *Rationalism in Politics* (New York: Basic Books, 1962); Morris Ginsberg, *Reason and Unreason in Society* (Cambridge: Harvard University Press, 1948); Kenneth J. Arrow, *Social Choice and Individual Values* (2nd ed., New York: Wiley, 1963); and, *inter alia*, Elizabeth E. Hoyt, "Choice as an Interdisciplinary Area," *Quarterly Journal of Economics*, vol. 79 (1965), pp. 106–12. Lindblom's work is also relevant: see his recent *The Intelligence of Democracy: Decision Making Through Mutual Adjustment* (New York: Free Press, 1965). See also the articles in *The Distrust of Reason* (Middletown, Conn.: Wesleyan University Press, 1959).

65. Cf. S. G. Checkland, "The Prescriptions of the Classical Economists," *Economica*, n.s., vol. 20 (1953), pp. 68–72; and, e.g., William S. Hopkins, "The Framework for the Use of Labor," *Annals*, vol. 206 (November 1939), p. 42.

66. Cf. Helmut Schoeck and James W. Wiggins, eds., *The New Argument in Economics* (Princeton: Van Nostrand, 1963).

67. In general, see the works by Hayek and Knight, already cited; and Bruno Leoni, *Freedom and the Law* (Princeton: Van Nostrand, 1961).

68. See, for example, William D. Grampp and Emanuel T. Weiler,

eds., *Economic Policy* (1st ed., Homewood, Ill.: Irwin, 1953), p. 4, and rev. ed. (1956), p. 7; Vining, *op. cit.*, p. 9 ff.; Lerner and Lasswell, *op. cit.*, p. 5; and David Braybrooke and Charles E. Lindblom, *A Strategy of Decision* (New York: Free Press, 1963). See also Henry Margenau, *Open Vistas* (New Haven: Yale University Press, 1961), pp. 202, 213.

69. Cf. K. William Kapp, "Economics and the Behavioral Sciences," *Kyklos*, vol. 7 (1954), p. 205; Kirzner, "What Economists Do," *op. cit.*, p. 258, and *Market Theory and the Price System* (Princeton: Van Nostrand, 1963), p. 5.

70. Ludwig von Mises, *Theory and History* (New Haven: Yale University Press, 1957), p. 77. See also his *The Ultimate Foundation of Economic Science* (Princeton: Van Nostrand, 1962), pp. 4–5.

71. Friedrich, *Man and His Government*, pp. 77, 74. Cf. H. Theill, *Economic Forecasts and Policy* (Amsterdam: North-Holland, 1958), p. 381.

72. Robbins, *The Nature and Significance of Economic Science*, p. 14.

73. Douglas Browning, *Act and Agent* (Coral Gables, Fla.: University of Miami Press, 1964), pp. 2, 3, 9, 35, 36, 39 ff.

74. *Ibid.*, e.g., pp. 19, 20.

75. As Lord Robbins put it, "Economics brings into full view that conflict of choice which is one of the permanent characteristics of human existence." *The Nature and Significance of Economic Science*, p. 30. Again, compare Buchanan, "What Should Economists Do?" *op. cit.*, pp. 212–17.

Transcending all discussion of choice, of course, are several of the antinomies of metaphysics and philosophy, particularly those of free will and determinism, absolutism and relativism, and realism and idealism. It is patently beyond the scope of this paper, however, to discuss them *in extenso*. It may be remarked, nonetheless, that policy analysis, as with social and natural science in general, has not been recently detoured by these antinomies—though there is substance to the charge that social and physical scientists have neglected them. One can summarize, e.g., the tentative working hypothesis with respect to free will and determinism, as an "as if" assumption of the efficacy of choice. (The subject of limitations upon choice is discussed below in the text.) For discussions both characteristic and suggestive, see G. L. S. Shackle, *Decision, Order and Time in Human Affairs* (London: Cambridge University Press, 1961), p. 271; A. W. Macmahon, "Conflict, Consensus, Confirmed Trends, and Open Choices," *American Political Science Review*, vol. 42 (1948), p. 1 ff.; Gordon W. Allport, *Becoming* (New Haven: Yale University Press, 1955), pp. 83–85;

Ladis K. D. Kristof, "The Origins and Evolution of Geopolitics," *Journal of Conflict Resolution*, vol. 4 (1960), e.g., p. 45; Wilhelm Keilhau, *Principles of Private and Public Planning* (London: Allen and Unwin, 1951), pp. 22, 25; Clarence Philbrook, " 'Realism' in Policy Espousal," *American Economic Review*, vol. 43 (1953), pp. 846–59; and Warren C. Scoville, "History of Economic Thought—Discussion," *American Economic Review, Papers and Proceedings*, vol. 55 (1965), pp. 147–48.

76. Robert G. McCloskey, ed., *Essays in Constitutional Law* (New York: Knopf, 1957), pp. 3–19. And see Jones, "Law and Morality in the Perspective of Legal Realism," *op. cit.*, p. 806: "Lawyers, more than any other group in our society, are the architects and engineers of our economic system. The structures of American economic development have had their origin, times without number, in major law offices."

77. Friedrich, *Man and His Government*, p. 73.

78. Jones, "Law and Morality in the Perspective of Legal Realism," *op. cit.*, p. 802.

79. Cf. Grampp and Weiler, *op. cit.*, 1st ed., p. 13; and Jack W. Peltason and James M. Burns, *Functions and Policies of American Government* (Englewood Cliffs, N.J.: Prentice-Hall, 1958), pp. 429–31.

80. There is, of course, the serious question of the precise scope for and limitations upon "public" discussion of fundamental questions, which is part of the general problem of order discussed below. The case for taciturnity has been baldly expressed in Knight's review of Slichter's *Modern Economic Society*:

> Education, like other fields of social activity, has this interesting feature, that there are many things about it which are obviously "true," and it may be entirely proper to mention them in friendly conversations, in either a reverent or irreverent tone, yet to "say" them publicly and officially would simply sink the ship. . . . The point is that the "principles" by which a society or a group lives in tolerable harmony are essentially religious. The essential nature of a religious principle is that not merely is it immoral to oppose it, but to ask what it is, is morally identical with denial and attack.

"The Newer Economics and the Control of Economic Activity," *Journal of Political Economy*, vol. 40 (1932), pp. 441, 448; see also the exchange between Knight and Slichter, "Modern Economic Society—Further Considered," *ibid*, pp. 814–27. Although Knight has long been concerned with the problems raised by the liberation of the mind, i.e., with the dangers from policy consciousness, his position is not as absolute, by any means, as the excerpts quoted above may suggest: see, for example, his "Natural Law: Last Refuge of the Bigot," *Ethics*, vol. 59 (1949), pp. 127–35, and below. As Browning, *op. cit.*, p. 65, puts it: "A standard loses its character as a standard when it is considered as an object of worldly interest."

It is obviously beyond the scope of this paper to analyze this matter *in extenso*, but the position of the author should be clear. As E. A. Ross [*Social Control* (New York: Macmillan, 1926), pp. 395–442; cf. R. C. and G. J. Hinkle—*The Development of Modern Sociology* (New York: Random House, 1954), p. 14] and others have stressed, order does require some limitations; the real question *is* that of scope and limits, particularly with respect to details. The modern mind— particularly that of the university scholar—rebels at what was, for example, the "church" view of the needs of order in eighteenth and nineteenth century conservative religious circles in England, and, appropriately, in the view of the author, challenges restrictions upon and threats to the use of the intellect. But the question is always one of reasonableness and responsibility (or situational propriety). There probably will always be a need and place for dissimulation, but there is an even greater need for free inquiry into and discussion of fundamentals. The author would thus *defend* the discussion of fundamentals. With Lord Robbins he would contend that

It may be argued that such an admission is dangerous, that once it is conceded . . . we have opened the floodgates to any sort of folly, and . . . interventionist opportunism. I admit the danger. But I cannot accept the implication that we should deny the facts of life and pretend that such circumstances are inconceivable. (*Politics and Economics*, p. 50.)

Indeed:

And thus in the last analysis Economics does depend, if not for its existence, at least for its significance, on an ultimate valuation— the affirmation that rationality and ability to choose with knowledge is desirable. . . . The revolt against reason is essentially a revolt against life itself. (*The Nature and Significance of Economic Science*, p. 157.)

The aspects of the matter of precise scope and limits most relevant here may be expressed: what questions, and (particularly) by whom? As Knight recently put it:

There can be no truth which is not open to question; but

discretion must be used—very great discretion—as to what questions are raised and discussed; . . . Furthermore, discussion is necessarily limited to those persons who are to some degree capable of it. (*Intelligence and Democratic Action,* p. 133.)

The writings of Knight himself stand as a magnificent example of an academician discussing fundamentals. It is anxiety of an extreme variety to see intrusion into forbidden ideas in every discussion of fundamentals. There is manifestly considerable difference between scholarly works, on the one hand, and the revolutionary cell, on the other. Yet even here, while one can support even a limited social control of public discussion of fundamental questions (particularly through noninstitutionalized moral rules and custom), the regime that is strong enough to practice safely and openly such control, as well as the control of revolution itself, might not be a very desirable regime indeed, in which case the option to challenge fundamentals of the *status quo*—and the option to revolt itself—may appear quite attractive.

As John Stuart Mill recognized, "It is, therefore, one of the necessary conditions of humanity, that the majority must either have wrong opinions, or no fixed opinions, or must place the degree of reliance warranted by reason, in the authority of those who have made moral and social philosophy their peculiar study." Still, "It is right that every man should attempt to understand his interest and his duty. It is right that he should follow his reason as far as his reason will carry him, and cultivate the faculty as highly as possible. *The Spirit of the Age,* p. 31. There is a great difference between the operation of the *principle* of ignorance and a *policy* based on "a belief that what was socially dangerous could not possibly be true." Ronald L. Meek, "The Decline of Ricardian Economics in England," *Economica,* n.s. vol. 17 (1950), p. 61. See Samuels, "The Classical Theory of Economic Policy: Non-Legal Social Control," *op. cit., passim.*

81. See, for example, Lindblom, "Tinbergen on Policy-Making," *op. cit.,* p. 536.

82. W. Allen Wallis, "Invited Lecture—Discussion," *American Economic Review, Papers and Proceedings,* vol. 52 (1962), p. 17.

83. Arrow, *op. cit.,* p. 7.

84. J. A. Schumpeter, "The Nature and Necessity of a Price System," in Richard V. Clemence, ed., *Readings in Economic Analysis* (Cambridge: Addison-Wesley, 1950), vol. 2, p. 2.

85. Frank H. Knight, Book Review, *Virginia Law Review,* vol. 39 (1953), p. 872.

86. Frank H. Knight, "Institutionalism and Empiricism in Eco-

nomics," *American Economic Review, Papers and Proceedings*, vol. 42 (1952), p. 47. See also Knight, *On the History and Method of Economics* (Chicago: University of Chicago Press, 1956), pp. 133, 174; but compare Knight, "Is Group Choice a Part of Economics?—Comment," *Quarterly Journal of Economics*, vol. 67 (1953), pp. 605–609.

87. Cf. Boulding, *op. cit.*, p. 19; Myres S. McDougal and David Haber, *Property, Wealth, Land: Allocation, Planning and Development* (Charlottesville, Va.: Michie Casebook Corp., 1948), p. 9; Chamberlain, *op. cit.*, p. 193; and, generally, the works of Commons.

88. Knight, *Intelligence and Democratic Action*, p. 70.

89. Frederic Benham, with Friedrich A. Lutz, *Economics* (New York: Pitman, 1941), p. 8.

90. Sir Frederick Pollock, *The Genius of the Common Law* (New York: Columbia University Press, 1912), p. 53. See also Thomas Nixon Carver, *Essays in Social Justice* (Cambridge: Harvard University Press, 1915), p. 47.

91. Cf., for instance, Braybrooke and Lindblom, *op. cit.*, pp. 9, 10, 15, 25.

92. Harry G. Johnson, "The Taxonomic Approach to Economic Policy," *Economic Journal*, vol. 61 (1951), p. 828.

93. Lindblom, "Tinbergen on Policy-Making," *op. cit.*, p. 537; also cf. McKean, "The Unseen Hand in Government," *op. cit.*, pp. 500–501.

94. Commons, *Legal Foundations of Capitalism*, pp. 241–42; cf. pp. 2, 300.

95. This is recognized, for example, throughout the works of Commons and Knight, as well as of Hale; see also, *inter alia*, Chamberlain, *op. cit.*, chaps. 8, 9; Vining, *op. cit.*, pp. 11–14; von Mises, *Socialism*, p. 24 and *passim*; and Robbins, *Politics and Economics*, p. 13.

96. Frank H. Knight, "Theory of Economic Policy and the History of Doctrine," *Ethics*, vol. 63 (1953), p. 282; cf. *The Ethics of Competition*, p. 102, and "Professor R. B. Perry on Value," *Journal of Political Economy*, vol. 63 (1955), p. 168.

97. Carl A. Auerbach, "Law and Social Change in the United States," *UCLA Law Review*, vol. 6 (1959), p. 517; reprinted in Auerbach *et al*, *The Legal Process* (San Francisco: Chandler, 1961), p. 646.

98. James Willard Hurst, "Law and the Balance of Power in the Community," *Oklahoma Bar Association Journal*, vol. 22 (1951), p. 1224; cf. p. 1225.

99. Commons, *Legal Foundations of Capitalism*, pp. 73, 123.

100. R. F. Harrod, "Scope and Method of Economics," in Clemence, *op. cit.*, vol. 1, p. 15.

101. R. G. Hawtrey, *Economic Destiny* (London: Longmans, Green,

1944), p. 2. Cf. Shackle, *op. cit.*, p. 273; and F. Zeuthen, *Economic Theory and Method* (Cambridge: Harvard University Press, 1955), pp. 331–32.

102. R. M. Lemos, "Power, Authority, and Sovereignty," *Methodos*, vol. 14 (1962), p. 124. See also the work of the political pluralists in political theory.

103. E. W. Kemmerer, "Banking Reform in the United States—Discussion," *American Economic Review, Papers and Proceedings*, vol. 3 (1913), p. 88. Also see Spengler and Allen, *op. cit.*, p. 9; Robbins, *Politics and Economics*, pp. 8, 16, 18; and Carl J. Friedrich, ed., *The Philosophy of Hegel* (New York: Modern Library, 1953), p. 541.

104. Sumner H. Slichter, "The Organization and Control of Economic Activity," in R. G. Tugwell, ed., *The Trend of Economics* (New York: Knopf, 1924), pp. 303–55; *Modern Economic Society* (New York: Holt, 1928), p. 35 ff.; and *What's Ahead for American Business* (Boston: Little, Brown, 1951), p. 181.

105. J. M. Clark, *Social Control of Business*, especially chaps. 1, 2, 4, 5.

106. Dahl and Lindblom, *op. cit.*, p. 512, and *passim*.

107. Knight, *The Economic Organization*, p. 3 ff.

108. Chamberlain, *op. cit.*, chap. 1, and *passim*, e.g., p. 11.

109. Copeland, *op. cit.*, chap. 2, and *passim*. It is also recognized and developed in Edwin Cannan, *Wealth* (3rd ed., New York: Staples, 1928), p. 63 ff.; Walton H. Hamilton, "Economic Organization," *Encyclopaedia of the Social Sciences* (New York: Macmillan, 1933), vol. 11, p. 484 ff.; Benham and Lutz, *op. cit.*, p. 10; W. A. Mackintosh, "Government Economic Policy: Scope and Principles," *Canadian Journal of Economics and Political Science*, vol. 16 (1950), p. 314; D. H. Robertson, *The Control of Industry* (London: Nisbet, 1947), p. 3; Boulding, *op. cit.*, p. 1, and *passim*; and Leverett S. Lyon, "Government and American Economic Life," *Journal of Business*, vol. 22 (1949), pp. 84–85.

110. Yevsei Liberman, "Profits and Socialism," *New World Review*, vol. 33 (1965), pp. 10–18.

111. William N. Loucks, *Comparative Economic Systems* (7th ed., New York: Harper, 1965); George N. Halm, *Economic Systems* (Rev. ed., New York: Holt, Rinehart and Winston, 1960); Carl Landauer, *Contemporary Economic Systems* (Philadelphia: Lippincott, 1964); Nicolas Spulber, *The Soviet Economy* (New York: Norton, 1962); Theo Suranyi-Unger, *Comparative Economic Systems* (New York: McGraw-Hill, 1952); Leopold Kohr, "Economic Systems and Social Size," in Solo, *Economics and the Public Interest*, (New Brunswick, N. J.: Rutgers University Press, 1955), p. 197 ff.; and Trygve Haavelmo,

"The Notion of Involuntary Economic Decisions," *Econometrica*, vol. 18 (1950), pp. 1–8.

112. Samuels, "History of Economic Thought—Discussion," *op. cit.*, p. 146.

113. *In re* the political element, see G. A. Almond and J. S. Coleman, *The Politics of Developing Areas* (Princeton: Princeton University Press, 1960); and S. N. Eisenstadt, *The Political Systems of Empires* (New York: Free Press, 1963). *In re* the question of rationality, cf, the works of Max Weber; also, K. William Kapp, "Economic Development in a New Perspective: Existential Minima and Substantive Rationality," *Land Economics*, vol. 18 (1965), pp. 49–77; and H. D. Lasswell, "The Policy Sciences of Development," *World Politics*, vol. 17 (1965), pp. 286, 309. *In re* economic development analysis *per se*, see: A. A. Pepelasis, "The Legal System and Economic Development of Greece," *Journal of Economic History*, vol. 19 (1959), pp. 173–98; C. E. Black, "The Politics of Economic Growth," *World Politics*, vol. 13 (1961), pp. 622–32; Bert F. Hoselitz, *Sociological Aspects of Economic Life* (Glencoe, Ill.: Free Press, 1960); John H. Adler, "Some Policy Problems in Economic Development," *Economic Development and Cultural Change*, vol. 9 (1961), pp. 111–19; Clark Kerr *et al*, *Industrialism and Industrial Man* (Cambridge: Harvard University Press, 1960); E. E. Hagen, *On the Theory of Social Change* (Homewood, Ill.: Dorsey Press, 1962); Karl de Schweinitz, Jr., *Industrialization and Democracy—Economic Necessities and Political Possibilities* (New York: Free Press, 1964); R. Braibanti and J. J. Spengler, eds., *Tradition, Values, and Socio-Economic Development* (Durham, N. C.: Duke University Press, 1961); and David C. McClelland, *The Achieving Society* (Princeton: Van Nostrand, 1961). In addition, there is a brief but singularly lucid discussion of legal alteration of framework institutions to promote development in Peter T. Bauer and Basil S. Yamey, *The Economics of Under-developed Countries* (Chicago: University of Chicago Press, 1957), pp. 171–74, and *passim*.

114. Hamilton, "Economic Organization," *op. cit.*, p. 484.

115. Knight, *The Ethics of Competition*, pp. 45, 102.

116. Kirschen, *op. cit.*, vol. 1, p. 236. See also Joseph J. Spengler, "Power Blocs and the Formation and Content of Economic Decision," in Industrial Relations Research Association, *Proceedings*, vol. 2 (1949), pp. 174–91.

117. McKean, "The Unseen Hand in Government," *op. cit.*, pp. 498–99, 504–505.

118. Peltason and Burns, *op. cit.*, p. 10; cf, Friedrich, *Man and His Government*, chap. 3; Boulding, *op. cit.*, p. 13; Lindblom, "Tinbergen

on Policy-Making," *op. cit.*, pp. 536, 538; and Carl Latham, *The Group Basis of Politics* (Ithaca, N. Y.: Cornell University Press, 1952).

119. *Per contra*, cf. Checkland, *op. cit.*

120. Commons, *Legal Foundations of Capitalism*, p. 2.

121. Lawrence K. Frank, "What is Social Order," in J. G. Manis and S. I. Clark, eds., *Man and Society* (New York: Macmillan, 1960), pp. 550, 551.

122. Kohr, in Solo, *op. cit.*, p. 197.

123. Von Mises, *Socialism*, p. 515; cf. p. 13.

124. Robbins, *The Nature and Significance of Economic Science*, p. 134; and see p. 155: "Without economic analysis it is not possible rationally to choose between alternative *systems* of society." Also: "Moreover, these institutions are not natural in the sense that they arise inevitably. They can only be called natural if by that word is meant conformable to the principle of utility; and while they may emerge without deliberate reflection on all their implications, their fitness to survive must be judged by rational criteria." Robbins, *The Theory of Economic Policy*, p. 56.

125. Knight, *The Ethics of Competition*, p. 285. Cf. *The Economic Organization*, pp. 23–24; and *Freedom and Reform*, pp. 39, 114, 185, 214.

126. Walter A. Morton, "Creative Regulation," *Land Economics*, vol. 39 (1963), p. 368.

127. Loucks, *op. cit.*, p. 6. "Although the operation of basic economic principles transcends all types of economic organization, the specific forms that their operation takes on and the specific social consequences which flow from their operation differ widely from one type of economy to another. . . . [Yet] whereas the people of each given nation may choose the particular set of economic institutions through which they will turn productive resources into consumable goods and services, their choices must be adapted to the limitations imposed by economic principles" (pp. 11, 13). See also Halm, *op. cit.*, p. v; Grampp and Weiler, *op. cit.*, 3rd ed., 1961, p. 415; and Emmette S. Redford, *American Government and the Economy* (New York: Macmillan, 1965), p. 88.

128. Knight, *The Ethics of Competition*, p. 311. This is the equivalent of Maitland's statement that "our whole constitutional law seems at times to be an appendix to the law of real property." Quoted in McDougal and Haber, *op. cit.*, p. 14. See also Milovan Djilas, *The New Class* (New York: Praeger, 1957), pp. 35, 44, 65, 66, and *passim*.

129. Dahl and Lindblom, *op. cit.*, pp. 512–13.

130. McDougal and Haber, *op. cit.*, p. 43.

131. Robert S. Hunt, in McDougal and Haber, *op. cit.*, p. 71. See

also Ludwig Erhard, "Problems of Economic Order and Cooperation," *German Economic Review*, vol. 1 (1963), p. 371.

132. Moore, *op. cit.*, p. 602, and *Economy and Society* (New York: Random House, 1955), p. 12.

133. Friedrich Kessler and Malcolm P. Sharp, *Contracts* (New York: Prentice-Hall, 1953), p. 1. Cf. H. C. Havighurst, *The Nature of Private Contract* (Evanston, Ill.: Northwestern University Press, 1961).

134. Jacob Viner, " 'Possessive Individualism' as Original Sin," *Canadian Journal of Economics and Political Science*, vol. 29 (1963), pp. 552–53.

135. Knight, *Freedom and Reform*, p. 114; cf. p. 63. Also, Knight, *The Ethics of Competition*, p. 347 ff.

136. Friedrich, "Policy—A Science" *op. cit.*, p. 274.

137. Harold D. Lasswell, "The Shape of the Future," *The American Behavioral Scientist*, vol. 8 (1965), p. 3.

138. Boulding, *op. cit.*, pp. 17, 167. Cf. Vining, *op. cit.*, p. 39; and J. Tinbergen, *Centralization and Decentralization in Economic Policy* (Amsterdam: North-Holland, 1954), p. 45; *On the Theory of Economic Policy* (2nd ed., Amsterdam: North-Holland, 1955), p. 2; and *Economic Policy: Principles and Design* (Amsterdam: North-Holland, 1956), pp. xi. 6, 7.

139. Grampp and Weiler, *op. cit.*, 1st ed., p. 4.

140. Cf., for example, F. A. Hayek, *The Constitution of Liberty* (Chicago: University of Chicago Press, 1960), p. 221; and Richard M. Weaver, "Relativism and the Use of Language," in Helmut Schoeck and James W. Wiggins, *Relativism and the Study of Man* (Princeton: Van Nostrand, 1961), p. 236.

141. Kenneth H. Parsons, "Institutional Economics: Discussion," *op. cit.*, p. 26. Cf. Karl Brunner, "Institutions, Policy, and Monetary Analysis," *Journal of Political Economy*, vol. 73 (1965), p. 216.

142. John S. Gambs and Sidney Wertimer, Jr., *Economics and Man* (Homewood, Ill.: Irwin, 1959), p. 172.

143. Edwin E. Witte, "Institutional Economics as Seen by an Institutional Economist," *Southern Economic Journal* vol. 21 (1954), p. 134.

144. Richard T. Ely, *Ground Under Our Feet* (New York: Macmillan, 1938), p. 66.

145. Knight, *Freedom and Reform*, pp. 114, 110. Cf. Homer Hoyt: "The whole system of jurisprudence is made to grow by mingling into the substance of the law the viewpoints of each successive age." Quoted in Walton Hale Hamilton, ed., *Current Economic Problems* (Chicago: University of Chicago Press, 1915), p. 658. See also Benjamin N. Cardozo, *The Growth of the Law* (New Haven: Yale University Press,

1924), and *The Paradoxes of Legal Science* (New York: Columbia University Press, 1928), particularly chap. 1.

146. Knight, "Value Theory for Economists," *American Economic Review*, vol. 46 (1956), p. 149.

147. Knight, "Lippman's *The Good Society*," *Journal of Political Economy*, vol. 46 (1938), p. 871.

148. Knight, "The Meaning of Freedom," *op. cit.*, p. 107.

149. Bonn, "Economic Policy," *op. cit.*, p. 337.

150. Buchanan, "The Relevance of Pareto Optimality," *op. cit.*, p. 354. See also Buchanan, "An Economic Theory of Clubs," *Economica*, n.s., vol. 32 (1965), e.g., pp. 13–14. But compare the critical reference to "social engineering" in "What Should Economists Do?" *op. cit.*, p. 221. Cf. R. H. Coase, "The Problem of Social Cost," *The Journal of Law and Economics*, vol. 3 (1960), pp. 1–44.

151. Morgenstern, "Pareto Optimum and Economic Organization," *op. cit.*, p. 583.

152. Leoni, *op. cit.*, and Knight, e.g., *Freedom and Reform* and *Intelligence and Democratic Action*.

153. Slichter, *Modern Economic Society*, p. 57.

154. Hale, *op. cit.* See also Knight, *Intelligence and Democratic Action*, p. 155.

155. Arthur Smithies, "Economic Welfare and Policy," *Economics and Public Policy* (Washington, D.C.: Brookings, 1955), p. 1.

156. Tinbergen, *Economic Policy: Principles and Design*, p. 10.

157. Von Mises, *The Ultimate Foundation of Economic Science*, pp. 2–3.

158. Cf. Djilas, *loc cit.*

159. Hamilton, "Economic Organization," *op. cit.*, p. 487.

160. Thomas Nixon Carver, "The Possibilities of Price Fixing in Time of Peace," *American Economic Review, Papers and Proceedings*, vol. 9 (1919), p. 248.

161. See, for example, Grampp and Weiler, *op. cit.*, 1st ed., pp. 3, 4, 11, 13; Lerner and Lasswell, *op. cit.*, pp. vii–viii, ix, 5, 12, 100, 102, and *passim*; and Boulding, *op. cit.*, pp. 9, 17–20, 167, and *passim*.

162. Spengler and Allen, *op. cit.*, p. 9.

163. McKean, "The Unseen Hand in Government," *op. cit.*, p. 500.

164. Friedrich, *Man and His Government*, p. 349.

165. Robbins, *Politics and Economics*, p. 27 ff. Cf. e.g., Heinrich Niehaus, "Problems of Order of Economic and Agricultural Policy," *Journal of Farm Economics*, vol. 37 (1955), pp. 25–37.

166. Emile Durkheim, *The Division of Labor in Society* (Glencoe, Ill.: Free Press, 1947).

167. Knight, *Intelligence and Democratic Action*, p. 16. "For man

is a romantic animal; and until a people is prepared to make changes by intelligent agreement, supernatural sanctions are required to make them accept what is established and not criticize or try to change it. . . . Since order is the absolute requisite of civilized life, we must stick to the order that is, until there is a reasonable agreement on changes that will be on balance beneficial. . . . As T. H. Huxley said, the ways of the cosmos are not our ways. Rather it is man's work to remake the world, as far and as fast as he can, according to his sentiments and ideas about which the Cosmos gives no evidence of the least concern—and to be careful not to defeat the whole project by trying to go too far or too fast with it." Knight, "The Role of Principles in Economics and Politics," *American Economic Review*, vol. 41 (1951), pp. 24, 25, 27.

168. Knight, *The Ethics of Competition*, p. 310.

169. Knight, "Professor Heimann on Religion and Economics," *Journal of Political Economy*, vol. 56 (1948), pp. 493, 495.

170. Commons, *Legal Foundations of Capitalism*, pp. 134–42, 313–59, and *passim*; and *Institutional Economics*, *passim*.

171. Grampp and Weiler, *op. cit.*, 1st ed., pp. 1, 3.

172. Knight, "Virtue and Knowledge: The View of Professor Polanyi," *Ethics*, vol. 59 (1949), p. 280. "The essential ethical problem, from the standpoint of power relations, is that of formulating ideals for guidance in *changing* the law, taking the law in its broadest sense, to include good manners, and public and constitutional and administrative law as well as law in the narrower sense of statute and recorded decision." Knight, "Bertrand Russell on Power," *Ethics*, vol. 49 (1939), pp. 282–83.

173. Edward H. Levi, *An Introduction to Legal Reasoning* (Chicago: University of Chicago Press, 1961), pp. 1, 2, 3–4; cf. pp. 7–8. See also the works of Cardozo, cited *supra.*; and Knight, *Intelligence and Democratic Action*, pp. 105–106, and *passim*.

174. Knight, "Theory of Economic Policy and the History of Doctrine," *op. cit.*, p. 279.

175. See Note 80, *supra*.

176. Herman Oliphant, "A Return to Stare Decisis," *American Bar Association Journal*, vol. 14 (1928), pp. 71–72 ff.

177. Cf. Robbins, *Politics and Economics*, p. 3; and Paul A. Samuelson, "Problems of Methodology—Dicussion," *American Economic Review, Papers and Proceedings*, vol. 53 (1963), p. 233.

178. Samuels, "The Classical Theory of Economic Policy: Non-Legal Social Control," *op. cit.*, p. 2.

179. John F. A. Taylor, "Is the Corporation Above the Law?" *Harvard Business Review* (March/April 1965), p. 121.

Appendix

180. Cf. Knight, *Freedom and Reform*, p. 401.

181. Robbins, *Politics and Economics*, pp. 8, 9, 135; and cf. Samuels, "The Classical Theory of Economic Policy: Non-Legal Social Control," *op. cit.*, pp. 2–3. "It was the aim of the liberal plan to create a framework within which private plans might be harmonized." Robbins, *Economic Planning and International Order* (London: Macmillan, 1937), p. 7.

182. Reinhold Niebuhr, *Christian Realism and Political Problems* (New York: Scribner's, 1953), p. 51.

183. Lerner and Lasswell, *op. cit.*, p. 264. "Yet such is the blindness of a certain form of libertarian outlook that in just such circumstances as these, security is expected to arise from a universal perception of harmony of interests; and restrictions on sovereignty are denounced as restrictions upon liberty." Robbins, *Politics and Economics*, p. 36.

184. Ely, *op. cit.*, p. 125.

185. Vatter, "Another Look at the Theory of 'Consumer Choice,'" *op. cit.*, p. 38.

186. Harold M. Groves, "Institutional Economics and Public Finance," *Land Economics*, vol. 40 (1964), p. 244.

187. See Glendon A. Schubert, *The Public Interest* (Glencoe, Ill.: Free Press, 1960); and Anthony Downs, "The Public Interest and Its Meaning in a Democracy," *Social Research*, vol. 29 (1962), pp. 1–36.

188. Samuels, "The Classical Theory of Economic Policy: Non-Legal Social Control," *op. cit.*, p. 100.

189. Hale, *op. cit.*; Robbins, *Politics and Economics*, p. 16; McDougal and Haber, *op. cit.*, p. 37; Henry M. Oliver, Jr., "Ordo and Coercion: A Logical Critique," *Southern Economic Journal*, vol. 27 (1960), pp. 81–91; Carver, *Essays in Social Justice*, p. 35; Clark, *Social Control of Business*, p. 111 ff.; and Shackle, *op. cit.*, p. 273.

190. Henry M. Oliver, Jr., "Established Expectations and American Economic Policies," *Ethics*, vol. 51 (1940), p. 106, and *passim*; and the references to Pound, *supra*.

191. William Orton, "Prices and Valuation in the Soviet System—Discussion," *American Economic Review, Papers and Proceedings*, vol. 26 (1936), p. 287.

192. Boulding, *op. cit.*, pp. 11, 18.

193. Buchanan, "What Should Economists Do?" *op. cit.*, p. 214.

194. Knight, *The Economic Organization*, pp. 8–9; and *The Ethics of Competition*, p. 45.

195. Grampp and Weiler, *op. cit.*, 1st ed., p. 393.

196. Slichter, *Modern Economic Society*, pp. 49–50; and Niebuhr, *op. cit.*, p. 90.

197. Braybrooke and Lindblom, *op. cit.*, p. 15.

198. L. K. Frank, "What is Social Order," in Manis and Clark, *op. cit.*, p. 553. Cf. Moore, *Industrial Relations and the Social Order*, pp. 598, 630; Knight, *The Economic Organization*, p. 13; and Ely, *op. cit.*, p. 271 ff.

199. Moore, *Industrial Relations and the Social Order*, p. 609.

200. John Bowring, ed., *The Works of Jeremy Bentham* (New York: Russell & Russell, 1962), vol. 1, p. 301.

201. *Ibid.*, vol. 3, p. 185. See also Boulding, *op. cit.*, p. 147; and Niebuhr, *op. cit.*, p. 91.

202. Carver, *Essays in Social Justice*, p. 35.

203. Robbins, *Politics and Economics*, p. 16.

204. Wrote Slichter: "Industry produces men as well as goods and the kind of men which a democratic community needs may not be produced in shops which are small oriental despotisms." Quoted in Edwin E. Witte, "Role of the Unions in Contemporary Society," *Industrial and Labor Relations Review*, vol. 4 (1950), p. 14.

205. Cf. Hale, *op. cit.*; Clark, *Social Control of Business*, p. 111 ff.; Zeuthen, *op. cit.*, p. 286 ff.; Shackle, *op. cit.*, p. 273; and Walter Nelles, "Commonwealth v. Hunt," *Columbia Law Review*, vol. 32 (1932), pp. 1128–69; and "The First American Labor Case," *Yale Law Journal*, vol. 32 (1931), pp. 165–200.

206. Philip H. Wicksteed, *The Common Sense of Political Economy* (London: Routledge & Kegan Paul, 1933), vol. 2, p. 680; Harrod, "Scope and Method of Economics," in Clemence, *op. cit.*, vol. 1, pp. 14–15; Nath, "Are Formal Welfare Criteria Required?" *op. cit.*, pp. 549 ff.; Groves, "Institutional Economics and Public Finance," *op. cit.*, pp. 241, 242; and McKean, "The Unseen Hand in Government," *op. cit.*, p. 498.

207. Robbins, *Politics and Economics*, p. 21.

208. Robert J. Alexander, in Robert A. Solo, ed., *Economics and the Public Interest*, (New Brunswick, N.J.: Rutgers University Press, 1955), p. 283.

209. Coase, "The Problem of Social Cost," *op. cit.*, p. 2. "If factors of production are thought of as rights, it becomes easier to understand that the right to do something which has a harmful effect . . . is also a factor of production. . . . The cost of exercising a right (of using a factor of production) is always the loss which is suffered elsewhere in consequence of the exercise of that right. . . ." (*Ibid.*, p. 44.)

210. James M. Buchanan, "Politics, Policy, and the Pigovian Margins," *Economica*, n.s., vol. 29 (1962), p. 27; and Coase, "The Problem of Social Cost," *op. cit.*, *passim*.

211. Cf. Levi, *op. cit.*, p. 9 ff.; McDougal and Haber, *op. cit.*, p. 227 ff.; Roscoe Pound, *An Introduction to the Philosophy of Law*

(New Haven: Yale University Press, 1922), chap. 4; William H. Spencer, *A Textbook on Law and Business* (Chicago: University of Chicago Press, 1929), p. 812 ff.; G. Calabresi, "Some Thoughts on Risk Distribution and the Law of Torts," *Yale Law Journal*, vol. 70 (1961), p. 499 ff.; E. W. Patterson, "The Apportionment of Business Risks Through Legal Devices," *Columbia Law Review*, vol. 24 (1924), p. 335 ff.; and J. H. Beale, "Social Justice and Business Costs—A Study in the Legal History of Today," *Harvard Law Review*, vol. 49 (1936), p. 593 ff.

212. Von Mises, *Human Action*, p. 653; Coase, "The Problem of Social Cost," *op. cit.*, p. 44; and see Commons, *Legal Foundations of Capitalism*, chaps. 6, 8.

213. Samuels, "The Classical Theory of Economic Policy: Non-Legal Social Control," *op. cit.*, p. 5.

214. McDougal and Haber, *op. cit.*, p. 11; and Cohen, *op. cit.*, p. 33 ff.

215. See, e.g., *United States v. Causby*, 328 U.S. 256 (1946).

216. McDougal and Haber, *op. cit.*, pp. 33 ff.; and Cohen, *op. cit.*, *passim*.

217. Robbins, *Politics and Economics*, p. 17; and *The Theory of Economic Policy*, pp. 188–89.

218. McKean, "The Unseen Hand in Government," *op. cit.*, pp. 496, 500.

219. Bonbright, *op. cit.*, p. 153.

220. Boulding, *op. cit.*, p. 123; and Carver, *Essays in Social Justice*, p. 376, and cf. p. 46.

221. Edwin Borchard, "The Supreme Court and Private Rights," *Yale Law Journal*, vol. 47 (1938), p. 1053.

222. McDougal, "Law as a Process of Decision: A Policy-Oriented Approach to Legal Study," *op. cit.*, p. 61.

223. *Ibid.*, p. 55.

224. J. C. Palamountain, Jr., *The Politics of Distribution* (Cambridge: Harvard University Press, 1955), p. 154.

225. Walter Adams, *The Structure of American Industry* (3rd ed., New York: Macmillan, 1961), p. 547

226. Bertrand de Jouvenel, *Sovereignty* (Chicago: University of Chicago Press, 1957), p. 3 ff.

227. Slichter, *What's Ahead for American Business*, p. 189; and McDougal and Haber, *op. cit.*, pp. 2–3.

228. McDougal and Haber, *op. cit.*, p. 72.

229. Knight, *Freedom and Reform*, p. 39.

230. Knight, *Intelligence and Democratic Action*, p. 16.

Bibliography

WORKS QUOTED AND CITED

BOOKS

ADAMS, WALTER. *The Structure of American Industry*. 3rd edition. New York: Macmillan, 1961.

ADELMAN, IRMA. *Theories of Economic Growth and Development*. Stanford: Stanford University Press, 1961.

ADLER, MORTIMER J. *The Idea of Freedom*. Garden City, N.Y.: Doubleday, 1958.

ALEXANDER, ROBERT J. in SOLO, ROBERT A. (ed.). *Economics and the Public Interest*. New Brunswick, N.J.: Rutgers University Press, 1955.

ALLPORT, GORDON W. *Becoming*. New Haven: Yale University Press, 1955.

ALMOND, G. A., and COLEMAN, J. S. *The Politics of Developing Areas*. Princeton: Princeton University Press, 1960.

ARROW, KENNETH J. *Social Choice and Individual Values*. 2nd edition. New York: Wiley, 1963.

ASHTON, T. S. *The Industrial Revolution, 1760–1830*. London: Oxford University Press, 1948.

AUERBACH, CARL, *et al. The Legal Process*. San Francisco: Chandler, 1961.

BACH, GEORGE L. *Economics*. 4th edition. Englewood Cliffs, N.J.: Prentice-Hall, 1963.

BAGLEY, WILLIAM C., JR. "The Task of Institutionalism," in SOLO, ROBERT A. (ed.). *Economics and the Public Interest*. New Brunswick, N.J.: Rutgers University Press, 1955.

BAIN, ALEXANDER. *John Stuart Mill: A Criticism*. London: Longmans, Green, and Co., 1882.

311

The Classical Theory of Economic Policy

BAUER, PETER T., and YAMEY, BASIL S. *The Economics of Underdeveloped Countries*. Chicago: University of Chicago Press, 1957.

BAUMOL, WILLIAM J. *Welfare Economics and the Theory of the State*. Cambridge: Harvard University Press, 1952.

BENHAM, FREDERIC (with FRIEDRICH A. LUTZ). *Economics*. New York: Pitman, 1941.

―――― and BODDY, FRANCIS M. *Principles of Economics*. New York: Pitman, 1947.

BENTHAM, JEREMY. (BEAUCHAMP, PHILIP,) *Analysis of the Influence of Natural Religion on the Temporal Happiness of Mankind*. London: Carlile, 1822.

――――. *Church-of-Englandism and Its Catechism Examined*. London: Wilson, 1818.

――――. *A Fragment on Government and an Introduction to the Principles of Moral and Legislation*. WILFRID HARRISON. (ed.). Oxford: Blackwell, 1948.

――――. *An Introduction to the Principles of Morals and Legislation*. London: Oxford University Press, 1907.

――――. *The Limits of Jurisprudence Defined*. C. W. EVERETT. (ed.). New York: Columbia University Press, 1945.

――――. (SMITH, GAMALIEL,) *Not Paul, But Jesus*. London: Hunt, 1823.

――――. *Plan of Parliamentary Reform*. London: 1817.

BLAUG, MARK. *Economic Theory in Retrospect*. Homewood, Ill.: Irwin, 1962.

――――. *Ricardian Economics*. New Haven: Yale University Press, 1958.

BODENHEIMER, EDGAR. *Jurisprudence*. New York: McGraw-Hill, 1940.

BONAR, JAMES. *Malthus and His Work*. New York: Harper, 1885.

――――. *Philosophy and Political Economy*. New York: Macmillan, 1893.

―――― and HOLLANDER, J. H. (eds.). *Letters of David Ricardo to Hutches Trower*. Oxford: University Press, 1899.

BONBRIGHT, JAMES C. *Principles of Public Utility Rates*. New York: Columbia University Press, 1961.

BONN, M. J. *Encyclopaedia of the Social Sciences*. "Economic Policy." Vol. 5. New York: Macmillan, 1931.

BOULDING, KENNETH E. *Principles of Economic Policy*. Englewood Cliffs, N.J.: Prentice-Hall, 1958.

BOWLEY, MARIAN. *Nassau Senior and Classical Economics*. New York: Kelley, 1949.

BOWRING, JOHN. (ed.). *The Works of Jeremy Bentham*. New York: Russell & Russell, 1962.

Bibliography

BRAIBANTI, R., and SPENGLER, J. J. (eds.). *Tradition, Values, and Socio-Economic Development*. Durham, N.C.: Duke University Press, 1961.

BRAYBROOKE, DAVID, and LINDBLOM, CHARLES E. *A Strategy of Decision*. New York: Free Press, 1963.

BRIDGMAN, P. W. *The Logic of Modern Physics*. New York: Macmillan, 1961.

BROWNING, DOUGLAS. *Act and Agent*. Coral Gables, Fla.: University of Miami Press, 1964.

BUCHANAN, JAMES M., and TULLOCK, GORDON. *The Calculus of Consent*. Ann Arbor, Mich.: University of Michigan Press, 1962.

BURTT, EDWIN A. (ed.). *The English Philosophers from Bacon to Mill*. New York: Modern Library, 1939.

CANNAN, EDWIN. *A Review of Economic Theory*. London: King, 1929.

———. *Wealth*. 3rd edition. New York: Staples, 1928.

CARDOZO, BENJAMIN N. *The Growth of the Law*. New Haven: Yale University Press, 1924.

———. *The Paradoxes of Legal Science*. New York: Columbia University Press, 1928.

CARVER, THOMAS NIXON. *Essays In Social Justice*. Cambridge: Harvard University Press, 1915.

CHAMBERLAIN, NEIL W. *Private and Public Planning*. New York: McGraw-Hill, 1965.

CLARK, JOHN M. *Economic Institutions and Human Welfare*. New York: Knopf, 1957.

———. *Social Control of Business*. 2nd edition. New York: McGraw-Hill, 1939.

CLEMENCE, RICHARD V. (ed.). *Readings in Economic Analysis*. 2 vols. Cambridge: Addison-Wesley, 1950.

COHEN, FELIX S. *The Legal Conscience*. New Haven: Yale University Press, 1960.

COMMONS, JOHN R. *The Economics of Collective Action*. New York: Macmillan, 1950.

———. *Institutional Economics*. 2 vols. Madison, Wis.: University of Wisconsin Press, 1959.

———. *Legal Foundations of Capitalism*. Madison, Wis.: University of Wisconsin Press, 1959.

COPELAND, MORRIS A. *Our Free Enterprise Economy*. New York: Macmillan, 1965.

CORRY, B. A. *Money, Saving and Investment in English Economics, 1800–1850*. New York: St. Martin's Press, 1962.

DAHL, ROBERT A. and LINDBLOM, CHARLES E., *Politics, Economics and Welfare*. New York: Harper, 1953.

313

DAVIDSON, WILLIAM L. *Political Thought in England.* New York: Holt, n.d.

DE JOUVENEL, BERTRAND. *Sovereignty.* Chicago: University of Chicago Press, 1957.

DE QUINCEY, THOMAS. *Theological Essays.* Boston: Ticknor, Reed, and Fields, 1854.

DE SCHWEINITZ, KARL, JR. *Industrialization and Democracy—Economic Necessities and Political Possibilities.* New York: Free Press, 1964.

DE TOCQUEVILLE, ALEXIS. *Democracy in America.* 2 vols. New York: Vintage Books, 1954.

DEWEY, JOHN. *The Quest for Certainty.* New York: Minton, Balch & Co., 1929.

DIESING, PAUL. *Reason in Society.* Urbana, Ill.: University of Illinois Press, 1962.

DJILAS, MILOVAN. *The New Class.* New York: Praeger, 1957.

DOWNS, ANTHONY. *An Economic Theory of Democracy.* New York: Wiley, 1957.

DURKHEIM, EMILE. *The Division of Labor in Society.* Glencoe, Ill.: Free Press, 1947.

EISENSTADT, S. N. *The Political Systems of Empires.* New York: Free Press, 1963.

ELLIOT, HUGH S. R. (ed.). *The Letters of John Stuart Mill.* London: Longmans, Green and Co., 1910.

ELY, RICHARD T. *Ground Under Our Feet.* New York: Macmillan, 1938.

———. "The Past and the Present of Political Economy." Vol. 2 (1884). *Johns Hopkins University Studies in Historical and Political Science.*

FAY, C. R. *The World of Adam Smith.* Cambridge: Heffer, 1960.

FRANK, JEROME. *Law and the Modern Mind.* New York: Coward-McCann, 1949.

FRANK, LAWRENCE K. "What is Social Order," in MANIS, J. G. and CLARK, S. I. (eds.). *Man and Society.* New York: Macmillan, 1960.

FRIEDRICH, C. J. *Man and His Government.* New York: McGraw-Hill, 1963.

——— (ed.). *The Philosophy of Hegel.* New York: Modern Library, 1953.

——— and GALBRAITH, J. K. (eds.). "Policy—A Science?" *Public Policy.* Vol. 4. Cambridge: Harvard University Press, 1953.

GAMBS, JOHN S. and WERTIMER, SIDNEY, JR. *Economics and Man.* Homewood, Ill.: Irwin, 1959.

GINSBERG, MORRIS. *Reason and Unreason in Society.* Cambridge: Harvard University Press, 1948.

GRAMPP, WILLIAM D. and WEILER, EMANUEL T. (eds.). *Economic Policy*. 1st edition (1953), rev. edition (1956), and 3rd edition (1961). Homewood, Ill.: Irwin.

GRAY, ALEXANDER. *Adam Smith*. London: The Historical Association, 1948.

HAGEN, EVERETT E. *On the Theory of Social Change*. Homewood, Ill.: Dorsey Press, 1962.

HALE, ROBERT L. *Freedom Through Law*. New York: Columbia University Press, 1952.

HALEVY, ELIE. *The Growth of Philosophic Radicalism*. Boston: Beacon Press, 1955.

HALM, GEORGE N. *Economic Systems*. rev. edition. New York: Holt, Rinehart and Winston, 1960.

HAMILTON, WALTON H. *Encyclopaedia of the Social Sciences*. "Economic Organization. Vol. 11. New York: Macmillan, 1933.

———— (ed.). *Current Economic Problems*. Chicago: University of Chicago Press, 1915.

———— and ADAIR, DOUGLASS. *The Power to Govern*. New York: Norton, 1937.

HARROD, R. F. "Scope and Method of Economics," in CLEMENCE, RICHARD V. (ed.). *Readings in Economic Analysis*. Vol. 1 Cambridge: Addison-Wesley, 1950.

HAVIGHURST, HAROLD C. *The Nature of Private Contract*. Evanston, Ill.: Northwestern University Press, 1961.

HAWTREY, R. G. *Economic Destiny*. London: Longmans, Green, 1944.

HAYEK, FRIEDRICH A. *The Constitution of Liberty*. Chicago: University of Chicago Press, 1960.

————. *Individualism and Economic Order*. Chicago: University of Chicago Press, 1948.

HINKLE, R. C. and G. J. *The Development of Modern Sociology*. New York: Random House, 1954.

HOOK, SIDNEY. *Reason, Social Myths and Democracy*. New York: Humanities Press, 1940.

HOOVER, CALVIN B. *The Economy, Liberty and the State*. Garden City, N.Y.: Doubleday, 1961.

HOSELITZ, BERT F. *Sociological Aspects of Economic Life*. Glencoe, Ill.: Free Press, 1960.

HURST, JAMES W. *Law and the Conditions of Freedom in the Nineteenth Century United States*. Madison, Wis.: University of Wisconsin Press, 1956.

HUTT, W. H. *Economists and the Public*. London: Cape, 1936.

KAPP, K. W. *The Social Costs of Private Enterprise*. Cambridge: Harvard University Press, 1950.

315

KAYSER, ELMER LOUIS. *The Grand Social Enterprise.* New York: Columbia University Press, 1932.

KEETON, G. W. and SCHWARZENBERGER, G. (eds.). *Jeremy Bentham and the Law: A Symposium.* London: Stevens, 1948.

KEILHAU, WILHELM. *Principles of Private and Public Planning.* London: Allen and Unwin, 1951.

KERR, CLARK, et al. *Industrialism and Industrial Man.* Cambridge: Harvard University Press, 1960.

KESSLER, FRIEDRICH, and SHARP, MALCOLM P. *Contracts.* New York: Prentice-Hall, 1953.

KEYNES, JOHN MAYNARD. Introduction to ROBERTSON, D. H. *Money.* New York: Harcourt, Brace and Co., 1929.

KEYNES, JOHN NEVILLE. *The Scope and Method of Political Economy.* 4th edition, New York: Kelley & Millman, 1955.

KIRSCHEN, E. S., et al. *Economic Policy in our Time.* Chicago: Rand McNally, 1964.

KIRZNER, I. M. *Market Theory and the Price System.* Princeton: Van Nostrand, 1963.

KNIGHT, FRANK H. *The Economic Organization.* New York: Kelley, 1951.

———. *The Ethics of Competition.* New York: Kelley, 1951.

———. *Freedom and Reform.* New York: Harper, 1947.

———. *Intelligence and Democratic Action.* Cambridge: Harvard University Press, 1960.

———. *On the History and Method of Economics.* Chicago: University of Chicago Press, 1956.

KOHR, LEOPOLD. "Economic Systems and Social Size," in SOLO, ROBERT A. (ed.). *Economics and the Public Interest.* New Brunswick, N.J.: Rutgers University Press, 1955.

KOONTZ, HAROLD, and GABLE, RICHARD W. *Public Control of Economic Enterprise.* New York: McGraw-Hill, 1956.

KUHN, ALFRED. *The Study of Society.* Homewood, Ill.: Irwin, 1963.

LANDAUER, CARL. *Contemporary Economic Systems.* Philadelphia: Lippincott, 1964.

LANSDOWNE, MARQUIS OF (ed.). *The Petty Papers.* 2 vols. London: Constable, 1927.

LARRABEE, HAROLD A. (ed.). *Bentham's "Handbook of Political Fallacies."* Baltimore: Johns Hopkins Press, 1952.

LASSWELL, HAROLD D. and KAPLAN, ABRAHAM. *Power and Society.* New Haven: Yale University Press, 1950.

LATHAM, CARL. *The Group Basis of Politics.* Ithaca, N.Y.: Cornell University Press, 1952.

LEONI, BRUNO. *Freedom and the Law.* Princeton: Van Nostrand, 1961.

Bibliography

LERNER, DANIEL, and LASSWELL, HAROLD D. (eds.). *The Policy Sciences.* Stanford: Stanford University Press, 1951.

LEVI, EDWARD H. *An Introduction to Legal Reasoning.* Chicago: University of Chicago Press, 1961.

LINDBLOM, C. E. *The Intelligence of Democracy: Decision Making Through Mutual Adjustment.* New York: Free Press, 1965.

LINK, ROBERT G. *English Theories of Economic Fluctuations, 1815–1848.* New York: Columbia University Press, 1959.

LLEWELLYN, KARL N. *The Bramble Bush.* New York: Oceana, 1951.

LOCKE, LOUIS G. *Tillotson.* Anglistica, Vol. IV. Copenhagen: Rosenkilde and Bagger, 1954.

LOUCKS, WILLIAM N. *Comparative Economic Systems.* 7th edition. New York: Harper, 1965.

McCLOSKEY, ROBERT G. (ed.). *Essays in Constitutional Law.* New York: Knopf, 1957.

McCULLOCH, J. R. *The Principles of Political Economy.* Edinburgh: Tait, 1843.

———. *A Treatise on the Succession to Property Vacant by Death.* London: Longman, Brown, Green, and Longmans, 1848.

——— (ed). *The Works of David Ricardo.* London: John Murray, 1881.

McDOUGAL, MYRES S. and HABER, DAVID. *Property, Wealth, Land: Allocation, Planning and Development.* Charlottesville, Va.: Michie Casebook Corp., 1948.

MACGREGOR, D. H. *Economic Thought and Policy.* London: Oxford University Press, 1949.

MALTHUS, T. R. *The Measure of Value.* New York: Kelley & Millman, 1957.

———. *The Principles of Political Economy.* The London School of Economics and Political Science, Series of Reprints of Scarce Works on Political Economy, No. 3; 1936.

MANIS, J. G., and CLARK, S. I. (eds.). *Man and Society.* New York: Macmillan, 1960.

MARGENAU, HENRY. *Open Vistas.* New Haven: Yale University Press, 1961.

MARSHALL, ALFRED. *Principles of Economics.* 8th ed. New York: Macmillan, 1920.

MARX, KARL. *Theories of Surplus Value.* New York: International Publishers, 1952.

MENGER, CARL. *Problems of Economics and Sociology.* ed. and with an introduction by LOUIS SCHNEIDER. Translated by FRANCIS J. NOCK. Urbana, Ill: University of Illinois Press, 1963.

MERTON, R. K. *Social Theory and Social Structure*. Glencoe, Ill.: Free Press, 1949.

MILL, JOHN STUART. *Auguste Comte and Positivism*. Ann Arbor, Mich.: University of Michigan Press, 1961.

———. *Autobiography*. New York: Columbia University Press, 1924.

———. "The Claims of Labor," *Dissertations and Discussions*. Vol. 2, New York: Holt, 1882.

———. *Considerations on Representative Government*. 2nd edition. London: Parker, Son, and Bourn, 1861.

———. *Prefaces to Liberty*. WISHY, BERNARD. (ed.). Boston: Beacon Press, 1959.

———. *Principles of Political Economy*. New York: Kelley, 1961.

———. *The Spirit of the Age*. With Introductory Essay by HAYEK, F. A. Chicago: University of Chicago Press, 1942.

———. *The Subjection of Women*. New York: Longmans, Green, 1911.

———. *The Subjection of Women*. New York: Stokes, 1911.

———. *The Subjection of Women* and WOLLSTONECRAFT, MARY. *The Rights of Women*. London: Dent, Everyman's Library, No. 825, 1929.

———. *A System of Logic*. London: Longmans, Green, and Co., 1879.

———. *Three Essays on Religion*. 3rd edition. London: Longmans, Green & Co., 1885.

MISES, LUDWIG VON. *Human Action*. New Haven: Yale University Press, 1949.

———. *Socialism*. New Haven: Yale University Press, 1951.

———. *Theory and History*. New Haven: Yale University Press, 1957.

———. *The Ultimate Foundation of Economic Science*. Princeton: Van Nostrand, 1962.

MITCHELL, WESLEY C. *The Backward Art of Spending Money*. New York: Kelley, 1950.

MOORE, WILBERT E. *Economy and Society*. New York: Random House, 1955.

———. *Industrial Relations and the Social Order*. rev. edition. New York: Macmillan, 1951.

MORGENSTERN, OSKAR. "Pareto Optimum and Economic Organization," in KLOTEN, NORBERT, *et al.* (eds.). *Systeme und Methoden in den Wirtschafts- und Sozialwissenschaften*. Tubingen: Mohr (Siebeck) 1964.

———. *The Ethical and Economic Theories of Adam Smith*. New York: Cornell University Studies in Philosophy; Longmans, Green & Co., 1923.

Bibliography

NIEBUHR, REINHOLD. *Christian Realism and Political Problems.* New York: Scribner's, 1953.

OAKESHOTT, MICHAEL. *Rationalism in Politics.* New York: Basic Books, 1962.

OGDEN, C. K. *Bentham's Theory of Fictions.* London: Kegan Paul, 1932.

PAGLIN, MORTON. *Malthus & Lauderdale, the Anti-Ricardian Tradition.* New York: Kelley, 1961.

PALAMOUNTAIN, J. C., JR. *The Politics of Distribution.* Cambridge: Harvard University Press, 1955.

PALGRAVE, R. H. INGLIS. *Dictionary of Political Economy.* 3 vols. London: Macmillan, 1894–1899.

PARSONS, TALCOTT. *The Structure of Social Action.* New York: McGraw-Hill, 1937.

————, and SMELSER, NEIL J. *Economy and Society.* Glencoe, Ill.: Free Press, 1956.

PELTASON, JACK W., and BURNS, JAMES M. *Functions and Policies of American Government.* Englewood Cliffs, N. J.: Prentice-Hall, 1958.

PETTY, SIR WILLIAM. *Essays on Mankind and Political Arithmetic.* London: Cassell, 1888.

POLANYI, KARL, et al. (eds.). *Trade and Market in the Early Empires.* Glencoe, Ill.: Free Press, 1957.

POLLOCK, SIR FREDERICK. *The Genius of the Common Law.* New York: Columbia University Press, 1912.

POLSBY, NELSON W. et al. *Politics and Social Life.* Boston: Houghton Mifflin, 1963.

POUND, ROSCOE. *Interpretations of Legal History.* New York: Macmillan, 1923.

————. *An Introduction to the Philosophy of Law.* New Haven: Yale University Press, 1922.

————. *Jurisprudence.* 5 vols. St. Paul, Minn.: West Publishing Co., 1959.

————. *Social Control Through Law.* New Haven: Yale University Press, 1942.

————. *The Spirit of the Common Law.* Boston: Marshall Jones, 1921.

Rae, John. *Contemporary Socialism.* 2nd edition. New York: Scribner's, 1891.

REDFORD, EMMETTE S., *American Government and the Economy.* New York: Macmillan, 1965.

RICARDO, DAVID. *The Principles of Political Economy and Taxation.* New York: Dutton, 1911.

The Classical Theory of Economic Policy

ROBBINS, LIONEL. *Economic Planning and International Order*. London: Macmillan, 1937.

———. *An Essay on the Nature and Significance of Economic Science*. London: Macmillan, 1952.

———. *Politics and Economics*. London: Macmillan, 1963.

———. *Robert Torrens and the Evolution of Classical Economics*. London: Macmillan, 1958.

———. *The Theory of Economic Policy in English Classical Political Economy*. London: Macmillan, 1953.

ROBERTSON, D. H. *The Control of Industry*. London: Nisbet, 1947.

ROBERTSON, H. M. *The Adam Smith Tradition*. London: Oxford University Press, 1950.

ROEPKE, WILHELM. *A Humane Economy: The Social Framework of the Free Market*. Chicago: Regnery Co., 1960.

ROSS, E. A. *Social Control*. New York: Macmillan, 1926.

SCHOECK, HELMUT, and WIGGINS, JAMES W. (eds.). *The New Argument in Economics*. Princeton: Van Nostrand, 1961.

SCHUBERT, GLENDON A. *The Public Interest*. Glencoe, Ill.: Free Press, 1960.

SCHUMPETER, J. A. "The Nature and Necessity of a Price System," in CLEMENCE, RICHARD V. (ed.). *Readings in Economic Analysis*. Vol. 2. Cambridge: Addison-Wesley, 1950.

SENIOR, NASSAU WILLIAM. *Industrial Efficiency and Social Economy*. LEVY, S. LEON (ed.). 2 vols. New York: Holt, 1928.

———. *An Outline of the Science of Political Economy*. New York: Kelley, 1951.

SHACKLE, G. L. S. *Decision, Order and Time in Human Affairs*. Cambridge University Press, 1961.

SHOUP, CARL S. *Ricardo on Taxation*. New York: Columbia University Press, 1960.

SLICHTER, SUMNER H. *Modern Economic Society*. New York: Holt, 1928. "The Organization and Control of Economic Activity," in TUGWELL, R. G. (ed.). *The Trend of Economics*. New York: Knopf, 1924.

———. *What's Ahead for American Business*. Boston: Little, Brown, 1951.

SMELSER, NEIL J. *The Sociology of Economic Life*. Englewood Cliffs, N.J.: Prentice-Hall, 1963.

SMITH, ADAM. *Essays Philosophical and Literary*. London: Ward, Lock, & Co., 1880.

———. *An Inquiry into the Nature and Causes of the Wealth of Nations*. New York: Modern Library, 1937.

———. *Lectures on Justice, Police, Revenue and Arms*. New York: Kelley & Millman, 1956.

320

Bibliography

SMITHIES, ARTHUR. "Economic Welfare and Policy," in *Economics and Public Policy*. Washington, D.C.: Brookings, 1955.

SOLO, ROBERT A. (ed.). *Economics and the Public Interest*. New Brunswick, N.J.: Rutgers University Press, 1955.

SPENCER, WILLIAM H. *A Textbook on Law and Business*. Chicago: University of Chicago Press, 1929.

SPENGLER, JOSEPH J., and ALLEN, WILLIAM R. (eds.). *Essays in Economic Thought*. Chicago: Rand McNally, 1960.

SPULBER, NICOLAS. *The Soviet Economy*. New York: Norton, 1962.

SRAFFA, PIERO. (ed.). *The Works and Correspondence of David Ricardo*. Cambridge: Cambridge University Press, 1952.

STARK, W. *The Ideal Foundations of Economic Thought*. London: Kegan Paul, Trench, Trubner & Co., 1943.

———. *Jeremy Bentham's Economic Writings*. 3 vols. New York: Burt Franklin, 1954.

STEPHEN, LESLIE. *The English Utilitarians*. New York: Peter Smith, 1950.

STIGLER, GEORGE J. *Five Lectures on Economic Problems*. London: Longmans, Green and Co., 1949.

STONE, JULIUS. *The Province and Function of Law*. Cambridge: Harvard University Press, 1950.

SURANYI-UNGER, THEO. *Comparative Economic Systems*. New York: McGraw-Hill, 1952.

TAYLOR, OVERTON H. *The Classical Liberalism, Marxism, and the Twentieth Century*. Cambridge: Harvard University Press, 1960.

———. *Economics and Liberalism*. Cambridge: Harvard University Press, 1955.

———. *A History of Economic Thought*. New York: McGraw-Hill, 1960.

THEILL, H. *Economic Forecasts and Policy*. Amsterdam: North-Holland, 1958.

TINBERGEN, J. *Centralization and Decentralization in Economic Policy*. Amsterdam: North-Holland, 1954.

———. *Economic Policy: Principles and Design*. Amsterdam: North-Holland, 1956.

———. *On the Theory of Economic Policy*. 2nd edition. Amsterdam: North-Holland, 1955.

TORRENS, ROBERT. *Letters on Commercial Policy*. London School of Economics and Political Science: Series of Reprints of Scarce Works on Political Economy, 1958.

USHER, A. P. *Explorations in Economics: Notes and Essays Contributed in Honor of F. W. Taussig*. New York: McGraw-Hill, 1936.

VINING, RUTLEDGE. *Economics in the United States of America*. Paris: UNESCO, 1956.

WALKER, E. RONALD. *From Economic Theory to Policy*. Chicago: University of Chicago Press, 1943.

WALLAS, GRAHAM. *Human Nature in Politics*. London: Constable, 1910.

WATSON, DONALD S. *Economic Policy*. Boston: Houghton Mifflin, 1960.

WEAVER, RICHARD M. "Relativism and the Use of Language," in SCHOECK, HELMUT, and WIGGINS, JAMES W. *Relativism and the Study of Man*. Princeton: Van Nostrand, 1961.

WHEELWRIGHT, PHILIP. (ed.). *Selected Writings of Jeremy Bentham, James Mill and John Stuart Mill*. Garden City, N.Y.: Doubleday, Doran & Co., 1935.

WHITTAKER, EDMUND. *Schools and Streams of Economic Thought*. Chicago: Rand McNally, 1960.

WICKSTEED, PHILIP H. *The Common Sense of Political Economy*. London: Routledge & Kegan Paul, 1933.

ZEUTHEN, F. *Economic Theory and Method*. Cambridge: Harvard University Press, 1955.

Adam Smith, 1776–1926, Chicago: Chicago University Press, 1928.

The Distrust of Reason, Middletown, Conn.: Wesleyan University Press, 1959.

ARTICLES

ADLER, JOHN H. "Some Policy Problems in Economic Development," *Economic Development and Cultural Change*, Vol. 9 (1961).

ANONYMOUS. Book Review, *Edinburgh Review*, Vol. 52 (1831).

ASHLEY, WILLIAM. "A Retrospect of Free-Trade Doctrine," *Economic Journal*, Vol. 34 (1924).

AUERBACH, CARL A. "Law and Social Change in the United States," *UCLA Law Review*, Vol. 6 (1959).

AYRES, CLARENCE E. "Institutional Economics—Discussion," *American Economic Review, Papers and Proceedings*, Vol. 47 (1957).

BASTABLE, C. F. "Adam Smith's Lectures on 'Jurisprudence'," *Hermathena*, Vol. 10 (1889).

BEALE, J. H. "Social Justice and Business Costs—A Study in the Legal History of Today," *Harvard Law Review*, Vol. 49 (1936).

BECKER, JAMES F. "Adam Smith's Theory of Social Science," *Southern Economic Journal*, Vol. 38 (1961).

BITTERMANN, HENRY J. "Adam Smith's Empiricism and the Law of Nature," *Journal of Political Economy*, Vol. 48 (1940).

Bibliography

BLACK, C. E. "The Politics of Economic Growth," *World Politics,* Vol. 13 (1961).

BLACK, R. D. COLLISON. "The Classical Economists and the Irish Problem," *Oxford Economic Papers,* Vol. 5 (1953).

BLAUG, MARK. "The Classical Economists and the Factory Acts—A Re-examination," *Quarterly Journal of Economics,* Vol. 72 (1958).

BONAR, JAMES. " 'The Theory of Moral Sentiments,' by Adam Smith, 1759," *Journal of Philosophical Studies* (now *Philosophy*), Vol. 1 (1926).

————. "Where Ricardo Succeeded and Where He Failed," *American Economic Association Bulletin,* Fourth Series, Vol. 1 (1911), Supplement.

BORCHARD, EDWIN. "The Supreme Court and Private Rights," *Yale Law Journal,* Vol. 47 (1938).

BRANDON, HENRY. "Schlesinger at the White House," *Harper's* (July, 1964).

BRAYBROOKE, DAVID. "The Relevance of Norms to Political Description," *American Political Science Review,* Vol. 52 (1958).

BREBNER, J. BARTLET. "Laissez Faire and State Intervention in Nineteenth-Century Britain," *Journal of Economic History,* Vol. 8, Supplement (1948).

BRUNNER, KARL. "Institutions, Policy, and Monetary Analysis," *Journal of Political Economy,* Vol. 73 (1965).

BUCHANAN, JAMES M. "An Economic Theory of Clubs," *Economica,* n.s., Vol. 32 (1965).

————. "Politics, Policy, and the Pigovian Margins," *Economica,* n.s., Vol. 29 (1962).

————. "The Relevance of Pareto Optimality," *Journal of Conflict Resolution,* Vol. 6 (1962).

————. "What Should Economists Do?" *Southern Economic Journal,* Vol. 30 (1964).

CALABRESI, G. "Some Thoughts on Risk Distribution and the Law of Torts," *Yale Law Journal,* Vol. 70 (1961).

CANNAN, EDWIN. "Adam Smith as an Economist," *Economica,* Vol. 6 (1926).

————. "Ricardo in Parliament," *Economic Journal,* Vol. 4 (1894).

CARVER, THOMAS N. "The Possibilities of Price Fixing in Time of Peace," *American Economic Review, Papers and Proceedings,* Vol. 9 (1919).

CHALK, ALFRED F. "Natural Law and the Rise of Economic Individualism in England," *Journal of Political Economy,* Vol. 59 (1951).

CHECKLAND, S. G. "Growth and Progress: The Nineteenth Century View in Britain," *Economic History Review,* II, Vol. 12 (1959).

———. "The Prescriptions of the Classical Economists," *Economica*, n.s., Vol. 20 (1953).

———. "The Propagation of Ricardian Economics in England," *Economica*, n.s., Vol. 16 (1949).

COASE, R. H. "The Problem of Social Cost," *The Journal of Law and Economics*, Vol. 3 (1960).

COLM, GERHARD. "In Defense of the Public Interest," *Social Research*, Vol. 27 (1960).

COOKE, C. A. "Adam Smith and Jurisprudence," *Law Quarterly Review*, Vol. 51 (1935).

DALTON, GEORGE. "Economic Theory and Primitive Society," *American Anthropologist*, Vol. 63 (1961).

DAVENPORT, H. J. and MORROW, GLENN R. "Discussion: *The Ethics of the Wealth of Nations*," *Philosophical Review*, Vol. 34 (1925).

DILLARD, DUDLEY. "Ricardo in Retrospect," *Journal of Economic History*, Vol. 13 (1953).

DOWNS, ANTHONY. "The Public Interest: Its Meaning in a Democracy," *Social Research*, Vol. 29 (1962).

DUNBAR, CHARLES F. "The Reaction in Political Economy," *Quarterly Journal of Economics*, Vol. 1 (1886).

DUNN, WILLIAM CLYDE. "Adam Smith and Edmund Burke: Complementary Contemporaries," *Southern Economic Journal*, Vol. 7 (1941).

ERHARD, LUDWIG. "Problems of Economic Order and Cooperation," *German Economic Review*, Vol. 1 (1963).

FAY, C. R. "Adam Smith and the Dynamic State," *Economic Journal*, Vol. 40 (1930).

FRIEDMANN, WOLFGANG. "Legal Philosophy and Judicial Lawmaking," *Columbia Law Review*, Vol. 61 (1961).

GORDON, SCOTT. "The London *Economist* and the High Tide of Laissez Faire," *Journal of Political Economy*, Vol. 63 (1955).

GRAMPP, WILLIAM D. "Adam Smith and the Economic Man," *Journal of Political Economy*, Vol. 56 (1948).

———. "On the Politics of the Classical Economists," *Quarterly Journal of Economics*, Vol. 62 (1948).

———. Book Review, *American Economic Review*, Vol. 52 (1962).

GROVES, HAROLD M. "Institutional Economics and Public Finance," *Land Economics*, Vol. 40 (1964).

GUILLEBAUD, C. W. Book Review, *Economica*, n.s., Vol. 11 (1911).

HAAVELMO, TRYGVE. "The Notion of Involuntary Economic Decisions, *Econometrica*, Vol. 18 (1950).

HALE, ROBERT L. "Coercion and Distribution in a Supposedly Noncoercive State," *Political Science Quarterly*, Vol. 38 (1923).

Bibliography

———. "Force and the State: A Comparison of 'Political' and 'Economic' Compulsion," *Columbia Law Review*, Vol. 35 (1935).

HANDLIN, OSCAR and MARY. "The Dimensions of Liberty," *Harvard Today* (Spring, 1962).

HANEY, L. M. "The Ricardo Centenary—Discussion," *American Economic Association Bulletin*, Fourth Series, Vol. 1 (1911), Suppl.

HARRIS, ABRAM L. "J. S. Mill on Monopoly and Socialism: A Note," *Journal of Political Economy*, Vol. 67 (1959).

HOLLANDER, JACOB H. "The Work and Influence of Ricardo," *American Economic Association Bulletin*, Fourth Series, Vol. 1 (1911), Supplement.

HOPKINS, WILLIAM S. "The Framework for the Use of Labor," *Annals*, Vol. 206 (November, 1939).

HOYT, ELIZABETH E. "Choice as an Interdisciplinary Area," *Quarterly Journal of Economics*, Vol. 79 (1965).

HURST, JAMES WILLARD. "Law and the Balance of Power in the Community," *Oklahoma Bar Association Journal*, Vol. 22 (1951).

HUTCHISON, T. W. "Bentham as an Economist," *Economic Journal*, Vol. 66 (1956).

———. "Robert Torrens and Classical Economics," *Economic History Review*, Vol. 11 (1958).

———. "Some Questions About Ricardo," *Economica*, n.s. Vol. 19 (1952).

JOHNSON, HARRY G. "The Taxonomic Approach to Economic Policy," *Economic Journal*, Vol. 61 (1951).

JONES, HARRY W. "Law and Morality in the Perspective of Legal Realism," *Columbia Law Review*, Vol. 61 (1961).

KAPP, K. WILLIAM. "Economic Development in a New Perspective: Existential Minima and Substantive Rationality," *Land Economics*, Vol. 18 (1965).

———. "Economics and the Behavioral Sciences," *Kyklos*, Vol. 7 (1954).

KEMMERER, E. W. "Banking Reform in the United States—Discussion," *American Economic Review, Papers and Proceedings*, Vol. 3 (1913).

KIRZNER, ISRAEL M., "What Economists Do," *Southern Economic Journal*, Vol. 31 (1965).

KNIGHT, FRANK H., "Bertrand Russell on Power," *Ethics*, Vol. 49 (1939).

———. "Economics, Political Science and Education," *American Economic Review, Papers and Proceedings*, Vol. 34 (1944).

———. "Institutionalism and Empiricism in Economics," *American Economic Review, Papers and Proceedings*, Vol. 42 (1952).

———. "Is Group Choice a Part of Economics?—Comment," *Quarterly Journal of Economics*, Vol. 67 (1953).

———. "Lippman's *The Good Society*," *Journal of Political Economy*, Vol. 46 (1938).

———. "The Meaning of Freedom," *Ethics*, Vol. 52 (1941).

———. "Natural Law: Last Refuge of the Bigot," *Ethics*, Vol. 59 (1949).

———. "The Newer Economics and the Control of Economic Activity," *Journal of Political Economy*, Vol. 40 (1932).

———. "Professor Heimann on Religion and Economics," *Journal of Political Economy*, Vol. 56 (1948).

———. "Professor R. B. Perry on Value," *Journal of Political Economy*, Vol. 63 (1955).

———. "The Role of Principles in Economics and Politics," *American Economic Review*, Vol. 41 (1951).

———. "Theory of Economic Policy and the History of Doctrine," *Ethics*, Vol. 63 (1953).

———. "Value Theory for Economists," *American Economic Review*, Vol. 46 (1956).

———. "Virtue and Knowledge: The View of Professor Polanyi," *Ethics*, Vol. 59 (1949).

———. Book Review, *Virginia Law Review*, Vol. 39 (1953).

KRISTOF, LADIS K. D., "The Origins and Evolution of Geopolitics," *Journal of Conflict Resolution*, Vol. 4 (1960).

LASSWELL, HAROLD D. "The Interplay of Economic, Political and Social Criteria in Legal Policy," *Vanderbilt Law Review*, Vol. 14 (1961).

———. "The Policy Sciences of Development," *World Politics*, Vol. 17 (1965).

———. "The Shape of the Future," *The American Behavioral Scientist*, Vol. 8 (1965).

———, and McDOUGAL, MYRES S. "Legal Education and Public Policy: Professional Training in the Public Interest," *Yale Law Journal*, Vol. 52 (1943).

LeCLAIR, EDWARD E. "Economic Theory and Anthropology" *American Anthropologist*, Vol. 64 (1962).

LEMOS, R. M. "Power, Authority, and Sovereignty," *Methodos*, Vol. 14 (1962).

LIBERMAN, YEVSEI. "Profits and Socialism," *New World Review*, Vol. 33 (1965).

LINDBLOM, C. E. "Policy Analysis," *American Economic Review*, Vol. 48 (1958).

———. "Tinbergen on Policy-Making," *Journal of Political Economy*, Vol. 66 (1958).

Bibliography

LINNENBERG, CLEM, JR. "The Laissez-Faire State in Relation to the National Economy," *Southwestern Social Science Quarterly*, Vol. 24 (1943).

LYON, LEVERETT S. "Government and American Economic Life," *Journal of Business*, Vol. 22 (1949).

————. "The Private-Enterprise System Confronts Emergency," *Journal of Business*, Vol. 14 (1941).

MACAULAY, STEWART. "Non-contractual Relations in Business: A Preliminary Study," *American Sociological Review*, Vol. 28 (1963).

MACFIE, A. L. "Adam Smith's *Moral Sentiments* as Foundation for his Wealth of Nations," *Oxford Economic Papers*, n.s., Vol. 11 (1959).

————. "Adam Smith's Theory of Moral Sentiments," *Scottish Journal of Political Economy*, Vol. 8 (1961).

MACKINTOSH, W. A. "Government Economic Policy: Scope and Principles," *Canadian Journal of Economics and Political Science*, Vol. 16 (1950).

MACMAHON, A. W. "Conflict, Consensus, Confirmed Trends, and Open Choices," *American Political Science Review*, Vol. 42 (1948).

MARRIOTT, J. A. R. "Adam Smith and Some Problems of To-day," *Fortnightly Review*, Vol. 82 (1902).

McDOUGAL, MYRES S. "Law as a Process of Decision: A Policy-Oriented Approach to Legal Study," *Natural Law Forum*, Vol. 1 (1956).

McKEAN, ROLAND N. "The Unseen Hand in Government," *American Economic Review*, Vol. 55 (1965).

MEEK, RONALD L. "The Decline of Ricardian Economics in England," *Economica*, n.s., Vol. 17 (1950).

MEENAI, S. A. "Robert Torrens—1780–1864," *Economica*, n.s., Vol. 23 (1956).

MORROW, GLENN R. "The Significance of the Doctrine of Sympathy in Hume and Adam Smith," *Philosophical Review*, Vol. 32 (1923).

MORTON, WALTER A. "Creative Regulation," *Land Economics*, Vol. 39 (1963).

NATH, S. K. "Are Formal Welfare Criteria Required?" *Economic Journal*, Vol. 74 (1964).

NELLES, WALTER. "Commonwealth v. Hunt," *Columbia Law Review*, Vol. 32 (1932).

————. "The First American Labor Case," *Yale Law Journal*, Vol. 32 (1931).

NIEHAUS, HEINRICH. "Problems of Order of Economic and Agricultural Policy," *Journal of Farm Economics*, Vol. 37 (1955).

NORTH, CECIL CLARE. "The Sociological Implications of Ricardo's Economics," *American Journal of Sociology*, Vol. 20 (1915).

The Classical Theory of Economic Policy

OLIPHANT, HERMAN. "A Return to Stare Decisis," *American Bar Association Journal*, Vol. 14 (1928).

OLIVER, HENRY M., JR. "Established Expectations and American Economic Policies," *Ethics*, Vol. 51 (1940).

———. "Ordo and Coercion: A Logical Critique," *Southern Economic Journal*, Vol. 27 (1960).

ORTON, WILLIAM. "Prices and Valuation in the Soviet System—Discussion," *American Economic Review, Papers and Proceedings*, Vol. 26 (1936).

PARRY, D. HUGHES. "Economic Theories in English Case Law," *Law Quarterly Review*, Vol. 47 (1931).

PARSONS, K. H. "Institutional Economics: Discussion," *American Economic Review, Papers and Proceedings*, Vol. 47 (1957).

PATTERSON, E. W. "The Apportionment of Business Risks Through Legal Devices," *Columbia Law Review*, Vol. 24 (1924).

PEPELASIS, A. A. "The Legal System and Economic Development of Greece," *Journal of Economic History*, Vol. 19 (1959).

PHILBROOK, CLARENCE. "'Realism' in Policy Espousal," *American Economic Review*, Vol. 43 (1953).

POUND, ROSCOE. "The Call for a Realist Jurisprudence," *Harvard Law Review*, Vol. 44 (1931).

———. "Common Law and Legislation," *Harvard Law Review*, Vol. 21 (1908).

———. "Liberty of Contract," *Yale Law Journal*, Vol. 18 (1909).

ROBERTS, R. O. "Ricardo's Theory of Public Debts," *Economica*, n.s., Vol. 9 (1942).

ROSENBERG, NATHAN. "Some Institutional Aspects of the *Wealth of Nations*," *Journal of Political Economy*, Vol. 68 (1960).

SALOMON, ALBERT. "Adam Smith as Sociologist," *Social Research*, Vol. 12 (1945).

SAMUELS, WARREN J. "The Classical Theory of Economic Policy: Non-Legal Social Control," *Southern Economic Journal*, Vol. 48 (1958).

———. "History of Economic Thought: Discussion," *American Economic Review, Papers and Proceedings*, Vol. 55 (1965).

———. "The Physiocratic Theory of Economic Policy," *Quarterly Journal of Economics*, Vol. 76 (1962).

SAMUELSON, PAUL A. "Problems of Methodology—Discussion," *American Economic Review, Papers and Proceedings*, Vol. 53 (1963).

SAYERS, R. S. "Ricardo's Views on Monetary Questions," *Quarterly Journal of Economics*, Vol. 67 (1953).

SCHNEIDER, LOUIS. "The Role of the Category of Ignorance in Sociological Theory: An Exploratory Statement," *American Sociological Review*, Vol. 27 (1962).

Bibliography

SCHWEINITZ, KARL DE. "Free Enterprise in a Growth World," *Southern Economic Journal*, Vol. 29 (1962).

SCOVILLE, WARREN C. "History of Economic Thought—Discussion," *American Economic Review, Papers and Proceedings*, Vol. 55 (1965).

SENIOR, NASSAU WILLIAM. Book Review, *Edinburgh Review*, Vol. 88 (1848).

SIDGWICK, HENRY. "Economic Method," *Fortnightly Review*, Vol. 31 (1879).

SINGER, KURT. Book Review, *The Economic Record*, Vol. 29 (1953).

SINGH, V. B. "Adam Smith's Theory of Economic Development," *Science and Society*, Vol. 23 (1959).

SORENSON, LLOYD R. "Some Classical Economists, Laissez Faire, and the Factory Acts," *Journal of Economic History*, Vol. 12 (1952).

SPENGLER, JOSEPH J. "Adam Smith's Theory of Economic Growth," *Southern Economic Journal*, Vol. 26 (1959).

———. "Malthus the Malthusian vs. Malthus the Economist," *Southern Economic Journal*, Vol. 24 (1957).

———. "Power Blocs and the Formation and Content of Economic Decision," Industrial Relations Research Association, *Proceedings*, Vol. 2 (1949).

———. "The Problem of Order in Economic Affairs," *Southern Economic Journal*, Vol. 15 (1948).

SPIEGEL, HENRY WILLIAM. "Economic Theory and Economic Policy," *Journal of Business*, Vol. 18 (1945).

———. Book Review, *American Economic Review*, Vol. 43 (1953).

STARK, W. "Liberty and Equality or: Jeremy Bentham as an Economist," *Economic Journal*, Vol. 51 (1941).

STONE, JULIUS. "The Myths of Planning and Laissez Faire: A Reorientation," *George Washington Law Review*, Vol. 18 (1949).

———. "The Province of Jurisprudence Redetermined," *Modern Law Review*, Vol. 7 (1944).

TAYLOR, H. C. "The Ricardo Centenary—Discussion," *American Economic Association Bulletin*, Fourth Series, Vol. 1 (1911), Supplement.

TAYLOR, JOHN F. A. "Is the Corporation above the Law?" *Harvard Business Review* (March/April, 1965).

VATTER, H. G. "Another Look at the Theory of 'Consumer Choice,'" *Challenge*, Vol. 13 (February, 1965).

VINER, JACOB. "Adam Smith and Laissez Faire," *Journal of Political Economy*, Vol. 35 (1927).

———. "Bentham and J. S. Mill: The Utilitarian Background," *American Economic Review*, Vol. 39 (1949).

————. "The Intellectual History of Laissez Faire," *Journal of Law and Economics*, Vol. 3 (1960).

————. " 'Possessive Individualism' as Original Sin," *Canadian Journal of Economics and Political Science*, Vol. 29 (1963).

WALKER, FRANCIS A. "Recent Progress of Political Economy in the United States," American Economic Association, *Publications*, First Series, Vol. 4 (1889).

WALKER, KENNETH O. "The Classical Economists and the Factory Acts," *Journal of Economic History*, Vol. 1 (1941).

WALLIS, W. ALLEN. "Invited Lecture—Discussion," *American Economic Review, Papers and Proceedings*, Vol. 52 (1962).

WAND, BERNARD. "Hume's Non-utilitarianism," *Ethics*, Vol. 72 (1962).

WEBB, SIDNEY. "The End of Laissez-Faire," *Economic Journal*, Vol. 36 (1926).

WITTE, EDWIN E. "Institutional Economics as Seen by an Institutional Economist," *Southern Economic Journal*, Vol. 21 (1954).

————. "Role of the Unions in Contemporary Society," *Industrial and Labor Relations Review*, Vol. 4 (1950).

CASES

German Alliance Insurance Company v. Kansas, 233 U. S. 389 (1914)
Lochner v. New York, 198 U. S. 45 (1905)
Nebbia v. New York, 291 U. S. 502 (1934)
United States v. Causby, 328 U. S. 256 (1946)

Index

INDEX OF NAMES

Index

Index

Index

Index

INDEX OF SUBJECTS AND CASES

Index

Index

341